WERTHEIM FELLOWSHIP PUBLICATIONS

Availability for Work

A Study in Unemployment Compensation

BY

RALPH ALTMAN

CAMBRIDGE · MASSACHUSETTS

HARVARD UNIVERSITY PRESS

1950

LONDON · GEOFFREY CUMBERLEGE · OXFORD UNIVERSITY PRESS

TO THE MEMORY OF MY FATHER

ABRAM ALTMAN

1874–1947

A cedar fell in Lebanon

WERTHEIM FELLOWSHIP PUBLICATIONS

In 1923 the family of the late Jacob Wertheim established the Jacob Wertheim Research Fellowship for ". . . the support of original research in the field of industrial coöperation . . ." The Fellowship was intended to enable men and women ". . . who already have expert knowledge of this subject, to pursue research that may be of general benefit in solving the problems in this field . . ." Fellowships are awarded annually by the President and Fellows of Harvard College on the recommendation of the Wertheim Committee.

The Committee undertakes to provide general supervision to the program of research of the Wertheim Fellow. When that research yields findings and results which are significant and of general interest, the Committee is authorized by the terms of the grant to Harvard University to recommend publication. The Jacob Wertheim Research Fellow alone has responsibility for the facts, analysis, and opinions expressed in this volume.

JOHN D. BLACK, *Chairman*
SUMNER H. SLICHTER
B. M. SELEKMAN
SAMUEL A. STOUFFER
JOHN T. DUNLOP, *Secretary*

WERTHEIM FELLOWSHIP PUBLICATIONS

Ralph Altman, *Availability for Work: A Study in Unemployment Compensation,* 1950

Dorothea de Schweinitz, *Labor and Management in a Common Enterprise,* 1949

Walter Galenson, *Labor in Norway,* 1949

Leo C. Brown, S.J., *Union Policies in the Leather Industry,* 1947

Paul H. Norgren, *The Swedish Collective Bargaining System,* 1941

Johnson O'Connor, *Psychometrics,* 1934

William Haber, *Industrial Relations in the Building Industry,* 1930

Wertheim Lectures on Industrial Relations, 1929

J. D. Houser, *What the Employer Thinks,* 1927

FOREWORD

IN ORDER to draw unemployment compensation, among other qualifications, a worker must be able to work and be available for work.
These simple phrases have no ready counterpart in the complexities
of the labor market. Mr. Altman has explored the full range of
problems involved in determining "availability for work." This
study has the merit that it cuts across a variety of disciplines and
fields of interest. The book will be helpful alike to labor economists,
to union and management representatives confronted with practical
questions under unemployment compensation statutes, to vocational
counselors and social workers considering the problems of the many
millions of our population who are sometimes in and at other times
outside the labor force and who are frequently near the borderline,
to referees making decisions on appeal cases for benefits, to lawyers
and courts concerned with the litigation of precedent-making cases,
to federal and state officials and their staffs charged with policy
making in the administration of all social insurance programs, and
to thoughtful persons interested in the perplexing problems of
giving meaning to "full employment."

In the haste to outline programs to achieve or to guarantee
"high-level" or "full" employment, economists have generally overlooked many ambiguities in the objective. What wages may a man
reject and be counted as unemployed rather than entirely outside
the labor force? What shifts in occupation or job are required of
a worker to remain within the labor force? What hours may a
housewife refuse to work and still be counted in the labor market?
Mr. Altman's study of the administration of unemployment compensation has the merit of compelling attention to these thorny
questions. While the discussion is in the context of the unemployment compensation system, analogous questions are relevant to
the measurement of the labor force.

The mobility of labor has been a neglected phase of the labor
market. Particularly under conditions of high-level employment,
the administration of the "availability for work" provisions of
unemployment compensation is apt to have a significant effect upon

the patterns of movement not alone within the labor market but also on shifts between the labor force and outside the job market. This study has well surveyed the administrative standards for availability which are presumed to affect mobility. It is not altogether clear, however, what the net effect of the unemployment compensation system has been upon short term and long term mobility of the labor force. Herein lies an area of further research.

Mr. Altman is keenly aware of both the difficulties of administering the "availability for work" provisions and the possibilities of misuse of the unemployment compensation system by seasonal employees and those who have really left the labor force.

As the unemployment compensation system is extended in coverage and as benefits are increased, the problems of "availability" are certain to receive increasing attention. Mr. Altman's comprehensive survey of the field should be widely used.

JOHN T. DUNLOP

CONTENTS

AUTHOR'S PREFACE xiii

I. INTRODUCTION I

II. THE LABOR MARKET 20

III. THE LABOR FORCE 36

IV. ORGANIZING THE SEARCH FOR WORK 55

V. STATUTORY PROVISIONS 74

VI. GENERAL PRINCIPLES 96

VII. GENERAL PRINCIPLES (CONTINUED) 122

VIII. ABILITY TO WORK 139

IX. WAGES AND WORK 158

X. HOURS AND OTHER TIME LIMITATIONS 180

XI. RESIDENCE AND WORK LOCATION 198

XII. WOMEN WORKERS 215

XIII. SELF-EMPLOYMENT 238

XIV. CONCLUDING OBSERVATIONS 250

APPENDIX 263

NOTES 291

INDEX 347

TABLES

1. Ratios of Denials of Unemployment Benefits on Issue of "Able and Available" to Insured Claimants   5

2. Percentages of the Population and Labor Force by Regions, 1940   42

APPENDIX

A. Availability Provisions: Total Benefit Disqualifications: State Unemployment Compensation Laws, July 31, 1948   264

B. Factors Considered in Determining Suitable Work: State Unemployment Compensation Laws, July 31, 1948   283

C. Specific Periods of Inability to Work for Pregnant Women in State Unemployment Compensation and Labor Laws . .   286

AUTHOR'S PREFACE

THE UNITED STATES has now had an unemployment compensation system for a dozen years. Fifty-one American jurisdictions — the forty-eight states, Alaska, the District of Columbia, and Hawaii — each have their own unemployment compensation laws. Every one of these laws stipulates that unemployed workers may not draw benefits unless they are able to work and available for work. The meaning of that statutory provision is the subject of this book.

On its face, availability for work may appear to be an obvious concept which requires little or no explanation. Actual operations, however, have revealed to state unemployment compensation agencies how difficult it is to apply the availability requirement. In fact, the availability provisions of the American unemployment benefit laws have already given rise to almost four hundred thousand appeals to referees, boards of review, and the courts, each of these appeals raising the question: Is the claimant available for work? In about a third of the appeals, the appellate tribunals have reversed or substantially modified the previous decision and reached a different conclusion as to the claimant's availability.

Despite the numerous administrative decisions on the subject and a growing body of judicial opinion, the literature on the availability for work requirement is scant. A handful of articles have appeared, in law journals and in the *Social Security Bulletin,* dealing mostly with specific subdivisions of the total subject. Although referees and other workers in unemployment compensation have often expressed the need for a full-scale study of availability for work, no such study has previously appeared. This book has been prepared in order to help fill that gap.

Primarily, this volume is intended for the use of students and workers in the social insurance field. Because they are constantly confronted with actual cases in which a knowledge of previous trends of decision is important, attorneys, referees, and others who deal with the interpretation of unemployment compensation laws have a need for citations of cases in point. This thought has prompted me to include extensive notes to Chapters VI–XIII which refer such users to appropriate decisions. Aside from the needs of this group, I have also attempted to take broader considerations of labor-force measurement and social policy into account in my presentation.

While not hesitating to suggest modifications and changes in the laws and their administration, throughout the book I have assumed that the present basic structure of the American unemployment compensation system will continue. Among the principal characteristics of that system are the following: (1) A pay-roll tax is the principal source of the unemployment benefit fund. (2) Benefit eligibility is confined to those unemployed workers who have, within a specified past period, worked in employment that is subject to the unemployment compensation tax. (3) The weekly benefit amount depends upon previous earnings. (4) The number of weeks of unemployment during a benefit year for which benefits will be paid is limited. (5) Unemployed workers are required to be capable of working and available for work as a condition of benefit eligibility.

Arguments against the desirability of retaining some or all of these features may readily be advanced. It may be contended that unemployment benefits should come out of general revenues or that the general treasury should be an additional contributor to the benefit fund. Sentiment is strong, among unemployment compensation personnel, to divide the tax between workers and employers. Making previous employment a condition of benefit eligibility obviously bars new labor-market entrants from benefits. Gearing the weekly benefit amount to prior earnings has been attacked as socially illogical. The movement to include additional benefit allowances based upon the number of the claimant's dependents takes that argument into account. Limited duration of benefit status has been criticized as limited protection. The push has been constant to increase the maximum weeks of benefits allowable in the benefit year — from sixteen weeks in most states in 1937 to twenty or more in most states in 1949. Conceivably an unemployment compensation system could be devised that would dispense with the availability requirement for some or all claimants. The effect might be similar to a dismissal wage plan. Despite such objections and substitute proposals, the basic features I have outlined seem relatively stable. Consequently I have sought to keep my suggestions for change within the framework of our existing system.

I am glad to have the opportunity to acknowledge here the many debts I have contracted in writing this book. It would be impossible to list all the referees and members of unemployment compensation boards of review and commissions. Their decisions constitute the base upon which this book rests. Their pioneer work in developing the meaning of the unemployment compensation laws, case by case, without benefit of guide or precedent, deserves the thanks of the entire nation. My colleagues in the Bureau of Employment Security have given generously of their time and thought. Abraham Abramowitz, Joseph H. Barker, Hermon E. Eisler, Olga S. Halsey, Stuart Morrison, and Helen Tippy — all members of the bureau staff — have each read part or all of the manuscript and made helpful suggestions. Professors John T. Dunlop and Sumner H. Slichter, both of the Harvard faculty, aided immeasurably with careful, searching criticism. I am indebted to John and Harriet Armstrong of the Industrial Relations Library in the Littauer Center of Public Administration for many kindnesses.

Some of the typing was done by Sylvia Hecht and Kate Krupen, but most of that burden was assumed by my wife, Jeanne, who meanwhile continued, with great patience and fortitude, to perform a second miracle of bearing with me.

I wish to thank the Wertheim Committee of Harvard University for the grant which made it financially possible for me to devote myself, for an extended period, to this work. My thanks are due also to the Bureau of Employment Security for permitting me to take a prolonged leave of absence in order to work on this book.

Although I am a member of the staff of the Bureau of Employment Security, the opinions and conclusions expressed in this book are my own and do not necessarily represent the views of the Bureau of Employment Security.

RALPH ALTMAN

CHAPTER I

INTRODUCTION

DOES A UNION MAN, living in a nonunion town, leave the labor force when he refuses to consider nonunion work? Does a pregnant factory worker remain in the labor force if she gives up her job as too heavy and will accept "lighter" work only? How about the pregnant receptionist who leaves her job because of "modesty" and says she will work only where she will not meet the public? How do we decide the labor-force attachment of a college student who will work afternoons, evenings, and week ends only? How about the seventy-year-old longshoreman who is no longer able to work in the hold? When the bride who left work to make a home finds that her earnings are needed to finance the home, is she back in the labor force? Automatically? Or must she demonstrate it in some way? What way?

The subject of availability for work is concerned with specific problems like these. Solving them is no mere itemized application of preconceived theories. The labor-force concept, like the labor-market concept, is an exercise in imagination and generalization. Close examination has an atomizing effect upon it. Under scrutiny, the labor force resolves itself into a gigantic cluster of individual situations. Most of them are clearly within any boundaries we might reasonably draw. When we begin to draw those boundaries, however, we are confronted with numerous questionable and tantalizing cases. Thus defining availability for work and circumscribing the labor force quickly simmer down to the practical problems of the borderline cases. True, this is inherent in any task of definition. In considering availability for work, however, it is especially necessary to be aware of the peculiar importance of borderline cases both because of their range and their intangible character.

In solving availability cases there are two major tools. One is the total picture of the labor force and the labor market which we get from the facts of our economic life. The other is the detailed consideration of the facts of the individual cases and their relationship to that total picture. Neither the total picture nor the details can be seen with understanding, however, without the perspective of purpose. Unless we understand fully why we seek a concept of availability for work and the drives behind the concepts we shall consider, it will be impossible to formulate any usable approach to this subject.

SIGNIFICANCE OF AVAILABILITY FOR WORK

Importance in Unemployment Compensation

Most immediately and practically, the importance of availability for work lies in unemployment compensation. Drawing upon its roots in the Poor Laws which spoke of "sturdy beggars" and "able-bodied laborers," compulsory unemployment compensation everywhere requires a current labor-force attachment of its claimants. The requirement has taken somewhat different forms in different places. In this country, however, the typical statutory requirement has been that, in order to be eligible for benefits, the unemployed worker must, among other things, be "able to work and available for work." What this has meant has, of course, varied with time and place, with statutory structure, and with the nature and quality of administration.

The availability requirement in unemployment compensation is universal as an inevitable result of a program which compensates for wage loss. There must be a reasonable assurance that the beneficiaries are ordinarily wage earners, individuals who would, but for their inability to secure suitable work, be working and earning their living. The worker's past practice is tested by a requirement that he shall have earned a specified amount of wages during a designated period or been employed for a specified portion of that period. Similarly his present continued status as a worker but without work is the concern of the availability provision.

The Wage and Employment Qualification and Availability

Comparison of the two requirements, of past and present labor-force attachment, emphasizes the peculiarities of the availability requirement. Past labor-force attachment is — comparatively — easy to measure. Setting the standard for such attachment may be difficult and is bound to be arbitrary. Once it is determined, however, applying the standard is relatively simple. All that is necessary is to obtain the worker's wage or employment record and determine from it whether or not he meets the test of dollars earned or weeks worked. That this may be expensive, complicated, and a cumbersome clerical task is obvious; employers and administrators bemoan it and business machine companies profit handsomely from it. But the factor being measured is tangible and clear devices exist for applying it. There can be little doubt that the method used has complied with the standard in admitting some persons to eligibility for benefits and excluding others.

Lexicography

Worlds apart from the sphere of wage and employment "objectivity" is the test of present labor-force membership. What do we mean when we ask an unemployed worker if he has been "able and available" during the past week? Obviously, if he has been flat on his back all that time he has not been able to work. Once we move away from that simple situation the answer is no longer clear cut.

The dictionary definition of "available" offers such phrases as "usable," "at disposal," "accessible," "attainable." "Usable for work?" "Accessible for work?" Clearly these seem to miss our point of inquiry, that is, to discover if the individual has ordinarily been a worker and would be one now if he could find a suitable job. Even the common parlance translation of "available" into "ready, willing and able" is only a little less indefinite.

To translate further into dictionary words "ready to work" may mean "prepared for work," "equipped or supplied with what is needed for work," "prepared for immediate work," "being in such a state as to be likely to work," "immediately at hand for work," or, finally, "available for work." We have made the circuit! "Willing to work" may mean "inclined or favorably disposed in mind to work," "desirous of work," or "ready to work." There we are again! "Able to work" may mean "having sufficient power, skill or resources to work," "competent to work," "qualified to work," "capable of working," or "having intellectual qualifications for working."

All in all, it is easy to see how vague and indefinite are the words, "available for work." Experience has shown, however, that it is not so much the statutory language as the statutory concept that needs clarifying. That clarification can be reached only by proper analysis of the subject and general agreement upon fundamental principles and procedures. The very vagueness of so basic a portion of the unemployment compensation system makes its study and understanding of key importance to the satisfactory operation of the whole program.

Appeals and Benefit Denials

This indefiniteness makes the availability provision of the unemployment compensation laws, particularly in recent years, a constant source of dispute. More appeals are taken from administrative determinations on availability than from any other type of determination made under state unemployment compensation laws.[1] Part of the explanation for the high proportion of appeals on availability may be found in the large number — both absolutely and relatively — of ineligibility determinations made on that issue. During the years 1945, 1946, and 1947 more claimants under state unemployment compensation laws were held ineligible on the ground of being either unable to work or unavailable for work than were disqualified for all other reasons combined (voluntary leaving without good cause, refusing suitable work, being involved in a labor dispute, being discharged for industrial misconduct, and the other miscellaneous disqualifications).[2]

It is questionable, however, whether this can be said to gainsay the indefiniteness of the availability requirement and its ballooning effects upon appeals. Instead, the continued high percentage of unavailability rulings after ten years of benefit administration points to the very indefiniteness we have been discussing. During the same period denial ratios for such other ineligibilities as insufficient wage credits and failures to register for work have steadily declined. In ten years claimants have generally learned the broad difference between covered and noncovered employment. They have learned that when they file a claim for unemployment benefits they must register for work with the employment service. They have yet to understand the difference between being available for work and being unavailable for work. Furthermore the unemployment compensation agencies have yet to make up their minds as to what, in practice, not theory, availability for work means. Consider Table 1, which gives the record of five states during the first four calendar quarters of the postwar period.

Disparities within and among States

Making due allowance for the turbulence of the period chosen, it is nonetheless difficult to understand the disparities shown in Table 1 except in terms of inadequately understood or inadequately applied definitions of availability. The differences within a state are insubstantial when compared with the differences among states. Of the fifty-one states and territories operating unemployment compensation systems under the aegis of the Social Security Act, two denied no claims on the issue of "able and available" during 1946. Twenty others denied claims on that issue to 4.9 per cent or less of their insured claimants (new claims with sufficient wage credits and additional claims); fifteen made such denials to between 5 per cent and 9.9 per cent of their insured claimants. Nine denied benefits on the "able and available" issue to between 10 and

TABLE 1

RATIOS OF DENIALS OF UNEMPLOYMENT BENEFITS ON ISSUE OF "ABLE AND AVAILABLE" TO INSURED CLAIMANTS (NEW CLAIMS WITH SUFFICIENT WAGE CREDITS AND ADDITIONAL CLAIMS), BY CALENDAR QUARTER, JULY 1945–JUNE 1946 FOR FIVE SELECTED STATES

	July–Sept. 1945	Oct.–Dec. 1945	Jan.–Mar. 1946	Apr.–June 1946
National average........	3.6	6.6	4.8	6.4
Alabama..............	5.3	9.5	10.1	12.1
Connecticut...........	3.5	17.2	14.1	25.4
Ohio.................	6.3	19.6	14.2	9.0
Pennsylvania..........	.6	.6	.4	4.4
Texas................	9.2	15.8	13.3	31.1

Source: *Employment Security Activities*, Vol. 2, Nos. 8–10.

19.9 per cent of insured claimants. Five states denied benefits to 20 per cent or more of the insured claimants.[3]

These are manifestations of the haze that surrounds the availability requirement. As we move along in this study we shall examine that haze more closely, as it shows itself in conflicting decisions. At this point there is, however, evident in the availability concept a vagueness which makes further study important.

Size of Operation

Availability stands out as an important issue in unemployment compensation because of the size of the operation involved. In state-administered unemployment compensation, in the first half of 1945, there were over 78,000 claim denials for unavailability. This almost tripled during the second half of 1945 when almost

220,000 were denied benefits for this reason. In 1946 the increase continued as the denials came close to the 590,000 mark.

Cases on the availability issue disposed of by lower administrative appeals authorities were almost 9,000 in the first half of 1945, over 16,000 in the second half of 1945, and over 72,000 each year in 1946 and 1947. How much all this costs in time and money is at present impossible to ascertain since the time and cost recording system of state unemployment compensation agencies is not constructed upon a statutory issue basis. It appears that the availability requirement accounts for 10 per cent of the staff time of an American unemployment compensation agency, and that the total annual dollar cost of administering the availability requirement may be six or seven million dollars.

Public Interest and Opinion

Few aspects of unemployment compensation compare, in public interest, with availability for work. This is to be expected since availability deals directly with one of the great worries of social insurance: Are we paying people for loafing? Are we making loafers out of good workers? Furthermore, availability problems are "human interest" problems, often deceptively simple in appearance. Who can understand the technicians' wrangles over experience rating schemes or benefit formulas? To the ordinary citizen they are mere "squabbles over figures." But tell him that little Susie Jones, fresh out of a dollar-and-a-half an hour war job, got her benefits even though she refused to go back to her fifty-cent an hour work at the five and ten notion counter, or tell him that Joe Miller, fifty years old and a union man all his working life, was denied benefits because he wouldn't take a "scab" job and you will witness a rapid rise in interest and temperature in the ordinary citizen. We should not be surprised, then, when we find that "availability" and the benefit amount form the basis for newspaper campaigns on unemployment compensation and for Congressional inquiries at committee hearings.

Listen to Congressman Knutson, erstwhile Chairman of the House Ways and Means Committee:

While I was home in northern Minnesota a short time ago, I met a man at a small inland store who was up in our section for a vacation. He had his family in the car, as I recall, even a small dog. We got to talking and, as he said, he had been at war work for three years and was taking a vacation with pay. I was rather surprised to find he was going to have twenty weeks' vacation at $20 a week. Perhaps his wife was also a war worker — I did not inquire; I should have. If so, that would make $40 a week for twenty weeks. At least, that is what he told me — that he was going to take a good, long vacation because he was tired. Of course, we are all tired and, when we are paid for being tired, we are even more so.[4]

This was but a reflection of the ever increasing vocal concern that was being expressed about the availability of benefit claimants. The end of World War II created considerable labor-market activity. War jobs ended and servicemen were rapidly demobilized. While these potential workers milled about in the labor market, employers with a plethora of job holes produced by reconversion to civilian production, soon saw that not enough worker-pegs were dropping into those holes. Then came cries that unemployment compensation was feeding the labor shortage. Some said benefits were too high, but most charged that not enough was being done to make unemployment compensation claimants available for work.

Series of newspaper articles began to appear. The Baltimore *Sun* ran eighteen articles by Howard M. Norton on unemployment compensation in Maryland. They charged that administration was lax and not enough was being done to check on the actual availability of claimants for work. These articles were circulated throughout the country. Unemployment compensation officials in every state soon felt their effects. Local business people and civic organizations made similar inquiries and charges. Local newspapers ran similar articles and article series.[5]

Investigations were called for by the Oakland (California) *Tribune* (July 16, 1946), Jamestown (New York) *Post-Journal* (August 6, 1946), and the New York Citizens Public Expenditure Survey, a taxpayers group.[6] But the Providence *Journal-Bulletin* hired John J. Corson, one-time director of the federal Bureau of Employment Security and the United States Employment Service, to investigate the Rhode Island administration. Corson found that "almost half of the men and women listed in the files of the employment offices as applicants for jobs currently refuse to come in to discuss jobs when notified by employment office officials." He concluded that a minority of benefit recipients "have drawn benefits because the governmental agencies responsible for determining who should receive benefits have been unable to single out those not willing to work."[7]

The Alabama Department of Industrial Relations instituted an administrative requirement that claimants make an independent search for work in proof of their availability. And both the Atlanta *Constitution* (September 13, 1946) and the Jackson (Mississippi) *Clarion-Ledger* (September 13, 1946) applauded and inquired why the Alabama rule wouldn't be just what their states needed. The *Christian Science Monitor* (August 15, 1946) appealed for an "awakening moral sense" but was willing to settle for "more restrictive legislation and more stringent administration."

Ray Poor pointed the finger to the availability issue in a series of articles in the Oklahoma City *Oklahoman* (September 15–20, 1946): "Officials struggling to administer the fund in a period of boom employment are faced with one question for which no answer has been found: How you gonna tell when a man is willing and available for work?" As the year came to an end the Omaha *World-Herald* (December 27, 1946) wailed: "Some means ought to be found to see to it that a man who is quite capable of driving a truck, but insists that he is trained only to polish the underside of widgets, is made to take a job driving a truck and not loaf on money provided by those who do work."[8]

Such attacks are to be expected in any period of heavy labor demand. The American tradition of work and disdain for shirkers exerts a continuing challenge to the effectiveness of unemployment compensation. Now that the right of workers to an unemployment compensation system has been generally conceded the point of controversy inevitably becomes the administration of that system. And the anti-loafer tradition substitutes for "rugged individualism" in the new battle of words. The storm center, as we have seen, is the meaning of availability for work.

Availability Policy as an Influence upon Claimant Behavior

Constant public interest, inquiry, and attack are bound to be concentrated upon the availability provisions of unemployment compensation because they are an effective means to influence the behavior of benefit recipients. True, this effectiveness is not measurable and it is limited. The salesgirl who marries and moves to the "miles from nowhere" sheep ranch is unlikely to leave her husband and move into town merely because the unemployment compensation agency decides that she has made herself unavailable for work. But unemployment compensation and employment service people everywhere will testify to the frequency with which claimants change their minds and remove self-imposed work limitations when it is explained to them that loss of benefits may result.

This is particularly true when the explanation is accompanied by referral to a specific opportunity for suitable work. Workers who begin by saying they will take no less than a dollar an hour usually settle for ninety cents when it is explained to them that ninety cents is the going wage, that a dollar demand is unreasonable and may indicate unavailability, and that at ninety cents several specific job referrals can be given to them. Certainly the beneficiary who is reluctant to take work that involves commuting to another town is confirmed in that reluctance if he knows that the local policy is to consider refusal of such work no breach of the availability requirement.

Labor-Force Measurement

The study of availability for work has a part to play in labor-force measurement. In measuring the labor force, we ask, "Who are the unemployed?" and we soon find the question to be synonymous, in many ways, with the inquiry into the meaning of availability for work. During the nineteen-thirties economists and statisticians wrangled over the enumeration of the unemployed. A recapitulation of that controversy is unnecessary here. Today the Census Bureau includes among the unemployed those individuals who were not at work but were "seeking work" during the week of the enumeration. It is this census category that the study of availability can help clarify. As generally accepted rules and policies on availability are reached it will become easier to formulate, in instructions to enumerators, the boundaries of this category.

In the 1940 Census of Population, enumerators were instructed to count as "seeking work" individuals who were making an active effort to secure a job or a business or professional opening. Individuals without work and making no active effort to secure work were counted as "seeking work" in such cases as: (1) if the community had but a few dominant industries (or only one industry) and the worker was not actively seeking work because those industries were shut down, (2) if the individual would have been actively seeking work but for a temporary illness such as a cold, (3) if he would have been actively seeking work except for the fact that there was no work to be had, or no work to be had in his occupation.[9] Such instructions are really little more than a direction to consider an unemployed worker in the labor force if he thinks he is.

It is obvious that the census-taking process cannot be so refined an instrument for weighing and measuring availability as the unemployment compensation-employment service machinery. The study of availability for work in unemployment compensation will, however, have some application here and furnish both additional devices and positive checks for the census method. For example, the census takes little account of the amount of work an unemployed worker will take as a criterion of his "seeking work." As Clarence Long said, "many theoretical definitions and all statistical definitions give the impression that willingness to work is what mother love ought to be — independent of the character and mood of the subject and of the attractiveness of the object." [10] Consideration of individual case histories in availability shows the inflationary effect such an approach must have upon measurement of the unemployed labor force.

Full Employment Policy

One of the results of the recent war was that the nations of the world became actively interested in achieving "full employment" through government leadership. The 1944 British White Paper on Employment Policy stated clearly, "The Government accept as one of their primary aims and responsibilities the maintenance of a high and stable level of employment after the war." The Canadian, Australian, and Swedish governments made similar commitments. In our own country, the Employment Act of 1946 declared it the policy and responsibility of the federal government to use all practicable means to create and maintain "conditions under which there will be afforded useful employment opportunities, including self-employment, for those able, willing and seeking to work."

The pursuit of full employment is closely tied to availability for work. Full employment may be variously defined as a rough balance between vacant jobs and jobless workers, or as an excess of unfilled jobs over unemployed people.[11] However defined, "full employment" is meaningful only if conceived within the social and institutional pattern which determines the size of the labor force and customary hours of work. The concept presupposes a normal labor force working at a customary and prevailing work week.[12] Again, regardless of the precise definition used, all concepts of full employment assume a common agreement upon the meaning of labor-force attachment. In trying to reach full employment we are trying to secure a continuing high level both of actual employment and of work opportunity for available workers. To plan for this we must know who are the available workers.

In addition, the availability policies pursued in unemployment compensation are vital to implement a full employment program. Even with full employment, there must always be unfilled jobs and people not working. Old businesses and industries die and new ones are born. Workers leave their jobs, for many reasons, and seek other work. Population centers change and employment changes with them. With the best planning, substantial seasonal unemployment is unavoidable. To maintain optimum employment, with these inevitables, optimum labor mobility is a necessity. Beveridge lists the "controlled mobility of labor" as one of the three conditions of success in the attack on unemployment.[13] To maintain full employment it is necessary that unemployed workers be ready, when conditions require it, to change their usual places of employment, occupations, industries, or even residences. The mobility of the unemployed worker may be impeded if the unemployment compensation authorities hold him available for work and pay him benefits while he is clinging, vainly, to the old work or the old community. This has concerned students of full employment.[14]

In some cases unemployment compensation policies on availability which go along with the worker's choice of action will be in direct accord with a full employment program. The worker who is laid off by or leaves a declining industry and refuses to go back but, instead, seeks new opportunities, is in line with that program. Holding him unavailable for work for refusing work in the old industry may be inconsistent with maximizing employment. The worker who moves to a new area where work opportunities are opening or are about to open is evidencing the labor mobility necessary to keep "everyone working who can and wants to work." If he is paid benefits that mobility is supported. If he is found unavailable for work the incentive to move when and where necessary is weakened.

Full Employment and Availability Administration

What effects upon "availability" administration may we expect from a full employment program?

Employment Service. Students are agreed that no full employment program can operate unless there is an employment service system that can find the best job for the worker and the best worker for the job wherever the two may be. This involves efficient handling by the employment service of a substantial portion of the existing job openings, if not the bulk of such vacancies. It involves highly qualitative placement work by that service rather than a mere quantity job. To service more employers, more employers must be satisfied that they are getting service, that the workers referred to them are qualified. Workers must be sent, not to blind openings, but to jobs that fit their training and experience.

With a full employment program that achieves such results availability interpretations in unemployment compensation are bound to change. The registration for work with the employment service would truly become the claimants' way to a job. In such circumstances there could seldom be any justification for requiring claimants to make an independent search for work as evidence of their availability.

A Sellers' Labor Market. Full employment tends to make the labor market a sellers' market. During the war the government had to intervene to stop "pirating" of labor. War powers had to be invoked to stabilize wages and to keep war workers from job-shopping. Full employment under conditions of peace may be expected to produce similar results. When jobs are plenty and men are rare unemployed workers will tend to limit themselves as to the kind of work, pay, hours, locality, and other working conditions they will accept. This is natural and may be desirable. Under common availability interpretations, however, such workers are now often denied benefits. In a full employment, high wage economy, without the compulsion of a war, it would seem anomalous to continue these interpretations.[15]

Labor-Force Expansion. A sellers' labor market may be expected to attract the "marginal" workers, members of the labor-supply reserve. The war period, when the elderly and the women, the children, and the physically handicapped sought and found work, is a good case in point. Peacetime full employment would, of course, not furnish the same incentives to such industrial reservists. Particularly, if real wages were high there would be a tendency to keep children in school for longer periods and for the married women and old folks to stay at home.[16] Admittedly in our current postwar economy, there are few signs that this tendency has so far had any considerable effect.

Certainly the opportunities of a peacetime full employment economy will be hardly less attractive to the physically handicapped workers.

If we achieve a "full employment" economy, the relative scarcity of labor thereby created will force our society to tackle more vigorously the problem of training and educating some portion of the "so-called" unemployables, making them sufficiently efficient to be added to the employable labor force. This we have never done in the past because there has typically been available a reservoir of unemployed to draw upon. A full employment society, continuously maintained, will discover that it is quite possible through education and training to reduce very substantially the proportion of the population which has in the past been regarded as unemployable.[17]

This has real meaning for the application of the availability test. If industry must, for example, adapt its hours, equipment, location, and other working conditions so as to fit the special requirements of the additional workers it needs — women, older workers, students, the physically handicapped — it is bound to have a broadening effect upon concepts of ability to work and availability for work.

CONDITIONING FACTORS IN DEFINING AVAILABILITY FOR WORK

Some of the difficulties of achieving a satisfactory definition of availability for work have been suggested. Others will appear as we discuss specific problem situations. Certain basic factors which condition availability interpretations in unemployment compensation may be indicated before attempting any detailed analysis. The precise content of the availability requirement is constantly changing. This change is a response, both conscious and unconscious, to the changes in a number of controlling elements that are closely tied together. First and most potent is the general level of employment.

General Employment Level

During a period of job shortage, workers' job demands are modest. Self-imposed, substantial limitations by claimants upon their availability for work are infrequent. It is then that availability policies tend to be "liberal." Not only do few questionable cases arise, but also few cases are questioned. In such circumstances little reason exists to inquire into a claimant's statement that he would take an offered, suitable job. Many are unemployed and why should it be supposed that he is different from the others in his genuine interest in work? Furthermore few or no jobs exist to which he may be referred in test of his availability. As a result, in 1938, for example, only 1.8 per cent of the cases reviewed by state lower-level appeal bodies dealt with the availability for work issue.[18]

Public Opinion

During low-level employment periods public opinion stands behind the "easy" rule on availability and is offended by stringent policies of inquiry into the availability for work of the unemployed. Thus, in 1930, during a depression, the British law was stripped of the "genuinely seeking work" requirement that had been part of the unemployment insurance scheme since 1924. As business improves and unemployment recedes, the availability policy changes. Claimants are "choosier" and unemployment compensation authorities are more careful. They challenge and test the availability of more and more applicants for benefit — now they have the tools to do it. The "able and available" issue takes the lead as a source of claim denials and benefit appeals. And public opinion applauds this. As we have seen, it may even complain that there are not enough teeth in the law or the administration. Legislators react to this. During 1947–49's full employment sixteen American legislatures added "seeking work" provisions to their unemployment compensation laws.

National Employment Policy

Another important conditioner of availability administration is the national employment policy. Since the advent of compulsory unemployment compensation in the United States we have witnessed two main phases of that policy. The "prewar effort" stage, the period before 1940, was characterized by government work-aid programs for the unemployed. These programs provided, in many communities, the bulk of employment "opportunities." Two classes of labor market resulted, a first-class labor market where the principal demand for labor was from private employers and a second-class labor market where the purchasers of labor were "emergency" government agencies.

The unemployment compensation claimant came from the first-class market. The public employment office, to which he had to report, operated in both markets. Because it was popularly associated with relief programs and the second-class labor market, the employment service was stigmatized and employers were reluctant to use it. This is one of the reasons why the employment services of the time were far from effective in placing benefit claimants even though they were among the best-qualified registrants. The futility of the employment services during this period partially explains the then lenient availability policy in unemployment compensation.

The war effort brought a new national policy for employment. War industries became the chief buyers of unemployed labor. The employment services were nationalized and war contractors were required to use them. The employment offices practically stopped giving service to "nonessential" employers. Ultimately administrative brakes were put on war workers who sought to move from one industry or employer to another. At the same time the employment service vigorously recruited workers to go into war work and to move to areas of acute labor shortage. During this period unemployment dropped to phenomenally low figures and the average weekly number of unemployment compensation beneficiaries hovered around the 100,000 mark. Nonetheless, unemployment compensation administrators drove hard on availability and the percentage of benefit denials on that score rose sharply. Claimants who refused war work were held ineligible for benefits. Unemployed workers who lacked War Manpower Commission statements of availability were, in many instances, considered unavailable for work because their access to the labor market had been restricted.[19]

"Normal" Industrial Conduct

The content of the availability test inevitably varies with changes in the norm of industrial conduct. In applying the availability requirement we are in constant pursuit of "normal" conduct.

Whether or not the limitations on the worker's availability destroy his labor-force attachment depends upon what we conceive to be the normal practice in industry. The factory worker who would work no more than forty hours a week during the war was often held unavailable for work. Today, with the forty-hour week the national average in industry, the result is usually different. Not that the national norm will always govern. On the contrary, we are more concerned in availability for work with local and industry norms. Thus, even today, the worker who holds himself available for work in a creamery or a flour mill only, where the work week hovers around the forty-eight-hour mark, may not satisfy the requirement with a forty-hour specification.

Political Concepts

Somewhat less prominent and more indirect than the factors we have been considering is the effect upon availability interpretations of some of our basic political concepts. As we have already seen, the subject of availability for work touches many aspects of the worker's life, such as the place where he lives and the work he chooses. Traditional American policy has always been that the individual is and should be generally free of legal restraints in choosing and changing his way of making a living. We have always thought that generally he should be free to move or refuse to move from place to place, subject to no legal compulsions. True, like all our liberties, these individual rights have been subject to some governmental regulation. Their exercise has also been controlled by economic and social institutions and circumstances. Such qualifications, however, do not destroy the basic tenets that Americans share of freedom of choice in occupation and residence.

The availability requirement brings the American state into the sphere of these rights. To administer the availability provisions requires examining the worker's employment prospects in his chosen occupation and community. If those prospects are bad, readiness to abandon a choice of occupation or residence may be the price of benefits. What then becomes of the claimant's freedom? It may be argued that this leaves him no worse off than he would have been without an unemployment compensation system; and therefore his freedom has been in no way impaired.

Such arguments assume an impossibility: that, with an unemployment compensation system in existence, workers should act as though it did not exist. They further fail to distinguish between simple economic pressure on the worker and economic pressure upon him through the direct agency of the state. In the first case the effect is comparatively gradual. The worker, although realizing he acts involuntarily, has a chance to feel that he is adjusting in his own way and at his own pace. When the pressure is applied by the unemployment compensation authorities, the worker is apt to be adjusted on a schedule that he has no part in making. In such situations there can be little doubt that the personal freedom of the claimant has been modified.

There are yet other freedoms which availability problems may involve. The right to marry and raise a family is basic in our society. Does that right go unimpaired if we discriminate between the married and the unmarried in our availability interpretation? What is the real difference between the woman who leaves a job to take care of a sick mother and the one who leaves to take care of a sick husband? Yet, in some states, to be eligible for benefits, the good daughter need but show that the mother is again well. The good wife, however, must first find a job and be employed for a specified period or earn a specified amount before she can again draw benefits.

Freedom of conscience may also play a part in availability cases. Usually quiescent, this became an issue during the war. Claimants who had been factory workers but were also conscientious objecttors or Jehovah's Witnesses refused to accept jobs in war work. Perennially, there are the Seventh Day Adventists and the Orthodox Jews who will not work on Saturdays. The answer in all such cases depends upon the weight we are willing to give the right of freedom of conscience.

Purposes of Unemployment Compensation

Finally, the purpose of unemployment compensation must be considered as a determinant of availability policy. It has already been suggested that unemployment compensation is intended to pay benefits to the individual who has ordinarily been a worker and would be a worker now but for his inability to find a suitable job. The basic purpose has always been to provide an orderly way, free from the stigma of charity, to relieve the distress of unemployed workers. This is done by compensating them for their wage loss without inquiring as to their individual need. Although relief from the distress of unemployment is the main purpose of the system other purposes have also been attached to it, such as maintaining purchasing power, stabilizing employment, and preserving labor standards.

All American unemployment compensation laws provide that

workers shall not be denied benefits for refusing new work if the wages, hours, or other conditions of work are substantially less favorable than those prevailing for similar work in the locality. This has been our formal answer to the question: Is unemployment compensation intended to preserve the claimant's status, improve it or let it seek its "natural" level? That it is not the entire answer was evident from the controversy that followed World War II. The question was how fast should claimants be sent down the hill of declining earnings. Should a worker whose $1.50 an hour war job had just ended be considered available for work if he now insisted on a comparable wage rate? How soon must he adjust his wage sights downward? How fast? Underlying these questions is the basic query: Should unemployment compensation be a floor or a counterweight?

It can hardly be said that it was ever intended that unemployment compensation administrators should take it upon themselves to determine what the wage rate should be for any worker. During the war wage-fixing was a governmental function. Fixing of minimum wages has been put in the hands of other governmental agencies. Otherwise our policy has, in general, been to leave wage rate determination to nongovernmental institutions. But it is clear that unemployment compensation authorities are expected to follow the labor market closely and make their rulings as the changes in that market may indicate. In so doing they must balance temporary and short-run market changes against permanent, long-time trends. For example, when a temporary shortage of building materials cuts off the work for a carpenter during a housing shortage that cannot be filled for years, there is no reason that the unemployed carpenter must take work in another trade or be considered ineligible.

Is it the function of unemployment compensation (that is, the state) to help, guide, or force an unemployed worker toward a job? Polanyi, arguing against any kind of compulsion, suggests that unemployment benefits should be fixed low enough to permit the lawful choice of idleness to those who prefer it. He contends further that compulsion makes sense in the case of the traffic policeman who can see both streets while the motorist can see only one, but, normally, in the choice of occupation or residence the state is in no better position than the individual to judge the latter's personal interests.[20]

To most of us, however, although compulsion is distasteful, complete laissez-faire policy is also undesirable. It seems preposterous to bend all national efforts to reduce unemployment to a minimum and then stop short when unemployed workers refuse to leave dying industries or localities. We seek a middle ground of incentives and education. We are well aware the price of social security is not, as Gertrude Williams said, that it weakens the incentive to find paid employment.[21] The price of social security is continual watchfulness that it shall not be permitted to weaken that incentive. Part of that watchfulness must be in the form of civic education that teaches the citizen's duty to coöperate in making a productive society.

There are two alternatives. Either some new incentives must be found to replace the old one of personal gain and the emphasis laid on the right of the citizen vis-a-vis the State must be balanced by an equal insistence on his duty to contribute to the community; or else freedom of choice of occupation must be abandoned as an anachronistic survival in a world which has given up the principle of individual responsibility.[22]

Through vocational guidance in the community we may help channel new entrants into the labor force. An employment service which concentrates on the problems of young workers and works closely with schools, churches and civic organizations can contribute much here. To the experienced but unemployed worker we can offer vocational training with higher and extended unemployment benefit if he will accept that training when requested to do so, with perhaps lower or no benefits after extended unemployment has indicated how poor his prospects of employment are within his own conditions. We have yet to provide subsidies or financial aids to unemployed workers to move to places where there is employment. By methods such as these we may meet the challenge of finding a middle way.

CHAPTER II

THE LABOR MARKET

LABOR–MARKET CHARACTERISTICS

UNDERSTANDING THE LABOR MARKET is fundamental in studying availability for work. Availability problems are determined and colored by the nature of the labor-market process. How workers are hired and jobs are found, when and why we have labor turnover, what influences a worker to take or leave a job or induces an employer to hire or to fire, how the price of labor is established — all help to determine what kind of cases shall arise on the question of availability.

We have referred to the labor market as a *process*. Labor market may also mean a place or area. In both senses, it may have different connotations depending on whether it is used to refer to wage-setting or to job-finding (or hiring). In the individual's case, wage-setting and hiring are often rolled into a single transaction. But there are differences between the two, in terms of place and process, when we attempt to generalize for many cases. The first major section of this chapter deals with characteristics of the labor market as process. The second treats of labor-market areas.

Nonstandardized Character of the Labor Transaction

The market for labor is a personalized market. Although he is concerned with price, the seller of labor is more concerned with other factors. The wage is important in the worker's job decisions and attitudes, but it is not the most important factor. He is more concerned with social recognition in the job, security of tenure, opportunity for advancement and training, congeniality of his fellow workmen, and the like.[1] To decide on a job offer, the worker wants to know just what use will be made of his services. Will he be able to cope with the job? Or will it be markedly below — or above — his capacities? Is the employer "reliable"? Will the job be steady? How will he get along with others — workers and supervisors — on the job? How will the job affect his standing in the community? Since he ordinarily can sell his labor to but one employer at a time, these are crucial considerations for the job-seeking worker. It follows that, so far as he can, the unemployed worker will want to be highly selective in picking customers for the labor he is selling.

This personalized view of labor-market transactions is not limited to workers. It is shared by the buyers of labor. Employers are ever aware of the individual differences among their workers. Differences in intelligence, physical ability, aptitudes, training, and countless other factors make for great disparity in the quality and quantity of individual work. Using identical work layouts and equipment, a group of experienced workers doing identical jobs may vary in individual output by more than 150 per cent.[2] Even where workmen agree on a standard of daily output individual differences persist. And these often are not explainable in terms of innate differences in capacity. Thus, in the Western Electric Company experiments, where this was the case, the lowest producer in the Bank Wiring Observation Room ranked first in intelligence and third in dexterity and the highest producer in the room ranked seventh in dexterity and lowest in intelligence.[3]

The hour of labor is far from being a standardized unit. It varies with the worker and the capacity, skill, and training he brings to the job. It also varies with the time of day, the quality of supervision, the worker's home circumstances, his social relations on the job, and other elements. Absenteeism and voluntary quitting will vary from worker to worker, depending on a complex set of circumstances. Age, sex, marital status, skill, personal habits — all factors over which the employer has little control — help determine the reliability of his workers. As a natural consequence, employers have always dealt in the labor market in much different fashion than in the market for goods.

Efforts have been made to standardize labor. Time studies, designed to find "normal" times to perform work operations, and motion studies, designed to ascertain the most efficient way of performing a given work operation, both look toward more uniform patterns of work activity. Piece-rate plans basically are attempts to get standardization by a uniform wage measurement plan, the pay being based, not upon hours of work, which admittedly differ from worker to worker in resultant production, but upon supposedly similar units of production. That these methods are not entirely successful has often been demonstrated.

Even with rigid inspection systems, noteworthy differences exist among workers in the quality of the work done. In addition, the effort expended is a matter of considerable individual variation that is not readily measurable.[4] These differences, regardless of the wage plan used, will, if overhead costs and capital investment are to be uniformly apportioned per worker, produce substantial variations, from worker to worker, in the labor cost of each unit produced. Furthermore relative differences persist among workers and are not wiped out by training.[5]

The nonstandardization of the labor market has a narrowing effect on worker availability. Unemployed workers tend to restrict themselves to jobs and establishments where they "know," from their own experience or that of friends, that they will be satisfied. Employers, on the other hand, are influenced to rely on "personal" hiring — of workers whom they know or have employed before, or who are recommended by present employees. This limits the effectiveness of the employment service and, in consequence, the operation of the availability requirement.

Labor Immobility

One of the outstanding characteristics of the labor market is the relative immobility of workers. Adam Smith's description is classic.

The prices of bread and butcher's meat are generally the same or very nearly the same throughout the greater part of the united kingdom . . . But the wages of labour in a great town and its neighborhood are frequently a fourth or a fifth part, twenty or five-and-twenty per cent. higher than at a few miles distance . . . Such a difference in prices, which it seems is not always sufficient to transport a man from one parish to another, would necessarily occasion so great a transportation of the most bulky commodities, not only from one parish to another, but from one end of the kingdom, almost from one end of the world to the other, as would soon reduce them more nearly to level. After all that has been said of the levity and inconstancy of human nature, it appears evidently from experience that a man is of all sorts of luggage the most difficult to be transported.[6]

That similar differences exist today in the United States and similarly indicate labor immobility few will dispute. Some examples will illustrate this. A recent survey showed the average hourly earnings of production workers in the slaughtering and meat-packing industry to be somewhat over $1.06 in the northern states and over $.87 in the southern states.[7] In July 1945 the average hourly earnings of plant workers in the electric light and power systems of the Southeastern states were $.87; in the Pacific states they were $1.13.[8] Full-fashioned hosiery plant workers earned, on the average, $1.08 an hour in the Middle Atlantic states in January, 1946; in the Southeastern states the average hourly earnings figure was $.88.[9]

Only a small proportion of the population is mobile. The 1940 census showed that 12.0 per cent of the people of the United States were, at the time of enumeration, residing in a county different from their 1935 county of residence. A March 1945 census survey revealed a similar percentage (12.2 per cent) of the civilian population living in a county different from the county of residence on December 7, 1941, the day of the Pearl Harbor attack. The percentage of migrants in the civilian labor force shown by this survey was but slightly higher (12.8 per cent).

The immobility of labor is occupational as well as geographic. Although occupational immobility is a matter of common observation, demonstrating it is not as easy as supplying evidence of geographic stability. In both instances workers can and do move. Few workers go through life in a single job or occupation. Some of this occupational change is forced by business deaths, seasonal layoffs, discharges, and so on. In any one year, it seems, from 20 to 40 per cent of the labor force works for more than one employer.[10] But how much of this represents occupational change is unknown. That labor's occupational mobility is not sufficient to get the most desirable response to industrial change is agreed upon by most writers on economics.

Dougherty says that labor's immobility keeps "most workers in the same locality and industry most of their lives, thus maintaining an oversupply of labor and a low wage level in old places and failing to make adjustments to new work opportunities elsewhere." [11] Professor Yoder and Messrs. Millis and Montgomery point out that the marginal productivity analysis of wages assumes a degree of labor mobility that is nonexistent. Workers are not sufficiently adaptable or versatile to shift jobs at will, and artificial barriers to occupational mobility are prominent. This occupational immobility accounts in part for the volume of unemployment and helps to reduce labor's bargaining power.[12]

Occupational and geographic immobility account as well for

many of the availability cases in unemployment compensation. The unemployed worker who clings to the community or occupation of declining work opportunity prompts the administrator to question his continued attachment to the labor force. At the same time worker immobility constitutes a frame of reference against which the individual claimant's conservatism of place or occupation must be viewed.

A whole series of availability problems arise from a different type of worker "mobility" — movement in and out of the labor force. We will discuss this again, more specifically, in connection with women workers in Chapter XII. Women workers, aged workers, labor-market entrants, to name three of the most obvious groups, shuttle between membership and nonmembership in the labor force. Home, health, school, family needs are important considerations for these individuals in their choice. Their work or nonwork status will often fluctuate with the changes in these factors. The extent of movement of people in and out of the labor force is unknown. It happens often enough, however, to present a significant number of problem cases in availability to unemployment compensation authorities. Theirs is the problem of determining whether the individual who has been alternating between labor-force and non-labor-force status is, at the time he is seeking benefits, in or out of the labor force.

The Labor Supply and Wage Change

For the worker the labor bargain can never be a mere economic transaction. He has too much at stake. In return for a wage, he not only offers his strength, skill, energy, and training, he risks his physical and mental health and his social standing. The job is the most important thing in the wage earner's life. Working, going to, and coming from work, plus the additional necessary time spent on the employer's premises take most of his waking hours. The job helps determine his friends and his social activities. In countless ways, other than merely economic, it determines what he will or may do on his "own time." Is he too tired to go out in the evening? Does he quarrel with his wife? These may be results of his labor bargain.

Mainly because of the noneconomic factors involved in the labor bargain, the labor-supply effects of wage changes are far from predictable. In any one establishment, industry, or occupation it may be expected that higher earnings will attract more workers.

It is not clear, however, that an increase in the earnings level for all industry will similarly increase the total supply of labor. Increased earnings permit workers' children to stay in school longer, reduce the need of married women to work and help provide support for workers of retirement age.

Professor Douglas's studies tend to show that a 1 per cent increase in real hourly wages causes a decrease of one-quarter to one-third per cent in the amount of labor supplied. But these are short-run conclusions. Over a long period the labor supply is governed by the population changes in the country. Here again, however, a long run increase in real wages may be associated, at least in the history of the West, with a decreasing birth rate and a higher standard of living. In such circumstances the labor supply has increased, but not so fast as the real wage.[13]

Not all occupations or industries respond in the same way, in rate or degree, to wage changes. Increased earnings for tool-and-die makers, whose apprenticeship is normally a long one, manifestly could not effect a drastic and immediate increase in the supply of such workers. Increased earnings for office boys may produce a quick response. We may note that the power of wage increases to attract workers to a given occupation depends upon a combination of circumstances.

The increase must be considered not only in relation to the general-earnings level, but also in relation to the earnings level of that segment of the population on which the occupation may be expected to draw. Increased wages for tabulation card key punch operators may draw other clerical workers but have little effect on labelers in food canneries. Increased wages for personnel technicians in government service may attract schoolteachers but mean little to coal miners. Here we encounter such intangible and nonmeasurable realities as the standing of an occupation in the social scale and the relative unpleasantness of an occupation.

If the flow of labor in the direction of higher wages were immediate, perfect, and automatic, wages, from place to place, would vary but little and not long. For higher earnings to attract more workers to a single employer, as suggested above, there must be workers elsewhere — in other occupations, industries, establishments, or not employed — who can come to work with the high-paying employer. If the workers are immobile or the employer is inaccessible, the employer's wage increase may even decrease his labor supply. Thus the large employer in the remote small town is often in a far different position than the employer in the crowded industrial area. The former, by raising his workers' wage, has in many instances little to expect in the way of an increased labor supply; by reducing the wages he may even increase that labor force. The latter, with many other competitors for workers around him, may have to outbid them on wages in order to increase his labor force. If the wages he offers drop significantly below those offered by competing employers, his labor supply is apt to slip away.

Again we need to emphasize the nonmonetary aspects of workers' reactions to wage changes. The employer who raises his wages above his competitors' may nevertheless fail to attract to himself many new workers. If the differential is not great and wages elsewhere are adequate, workers may shy away from such an offer because "it's not a good place to work." Production methods or the quality of supervision may repel them. Or the potential new workers may be satisfied where they are.

This is pertinent background when we consider the occupational and wage restrictions upon claimants' availability. Some workers, when unemployed, not only limit themselves to a single industry or occupation. They restrict themselves as well to a single employer. Often claimants are unwilling to consider work outside their usual occupations even when such work may ultimately be more remunerative. Often they will not change their residence or commute, even for higher-paying work.

Nonstandardized Price of Labor

Such considerations lead directly to another characteristic of the labor market — the nonstandardized price of labor. Not only do wages for the same work vary from region to region, as we have seen, but from one local area to its neighbor, and from one local plant to another. A survey of 83 metal manufacturing plants in the Philadelphia area in 1927 showed 1456 men in seven standard occupations: drill-press, milling-machine, turret-lathe, screw-machine, engine-lathe, planer, and boring-mill operating. In each of these occupations there was a considerable range in average hourly earnings, from 38.2 cents to 65.4 cents separating the highest from the lowest. A resurvey in 1929 showed similar figures.[14] In the spring and summer of 1943, the average hourly entrance rate of the common laborer in the building trades was 95.4 cents in the Yonkers–New York City area; across the river in the Newark–

Elizabeth–Jersey City–Paterson area it was $1.043. In Boston it was 95.9 cents but in Providence, only 45 miles away, it was 82 cents.[15]

There are yet other bases for wage variations. Size of establishment is a consideration. Wage studies often show bigger plants paying higher wages. Another element is the size of the community. Generally, the larger the community the higher the wage. (But this is no more than a generalization as the New York–New Jersey common laborer wage cited above will show.) Unionization is important, but its effect is not always clear. In the seamless hosiery industry in January 1946, union workers although only about a sixth of all workers studied, earned, on the average, 6 per cent an hour more than nonunion workers. Unionized full-fashioned hosiery workers in the Middle Atlantic region, comprising 62 per cent of the workers studied in their industry, earned, in the case of men, but 1 per cent and, in the case of women, 2 per cent higher than nonunion workers.[16]

The precise effect of unionization on wage levels, and particularly on real wages, is a matter of considerable dispute. In the absence of virtually complete unionization it seems reasonable to assume that, on the whole, unionized workers will get better pay than the nonunionized. Cases such as those of the hosiery workers indicate that the disparity in wage rates between union and nonunion establishments may tend to narrow with increasing unionization.

Unionization is but one side of the picture. Employer organization also has its effect upon the price of labor. Adam Smith recognized it when he wrote: "Masters are always and everywhere in a sort of tacit, but constant and uniform combination, not to raise the wages of labour above their actual rate." Employer's organizations are not always formal, but in the past they have been effective in controlling wages and in resisting the demands of unions.

Nor must we neglect the profound effects of custom and politics upon wages. The unequal wage treatment of Negroes and women clearly falls in this category. Here, too, we have the special protections of minimum wage and maximum hour laws which lean heavily in favor of women and young workers. Such wage controls reveal that the labor market is far different from the ordinary trading process. Minimum wage laws, for example, indicate the state's concern that, regardless of what prices an uncontrolled labor market would bring, the price of labor, or a specified kind of labor, should not be permitted to fall below a set figure. This is formal recognition that the labor market inherently tends to be a buyers' market.

The foregoing is a brief sketch of some of the factors that impinge upon the determination of prevailing wages. As we noted in Chapter I, American unemployment compensation laws protect claimants from benefit denials if the work refused offers wages that are substantially less favorable than those prevailing, in the locality, for similar work. If the worker's availability limitation comes within this protection he may not be denied benefits. Both from the wording of the statutory provisions and the factors involved it will be seen that this resolves itself into a local question. This does not necessarily make it a simple one.

Bargaining Strength of Workers and Employers

The relative numbers of buyers and sellers have often been cited as evidence that inherently our labor markets are tipped in the buyers' favor. In 1939 there were roughly 3.3 million nonagricultural enterprises in this country. Of these about 1.5 million had no employees. The remaining 1.8 million establishments employed roughly 27 million persons. About 6 million unemployed workers might well be added to these 27 million employees to get the total number of sellers of labor in the 1939 nonagricultural labor mart. It would appear then that there were some 15 to 18 sellers of labor to each buyer.

Actually this ratio varied considerably, by industry and by locality. In the retail trades slightly over one-fourth of the employees worked for firms employing one hundred or more. In manufacturing, well over three-fourths worked for employers of one hundred or more. In many a moderate-sized community an individual enterprise may be the employer of more than half the local working force. For the entire nation, in 1939, outside of agriculture, forestry, and the professions, less than five thousand enterprises employed 40 per cent of the gainfully employed.

Because of these employer-worker ratios it has often been noted that the employer, even without organization, has far greater economic strength than his workers, as individuals and even when they are combined. We have already noted as well the "coöperation," both formal and informal, that exists among employers in setting wages. Again and again this has been confirmed by investigation.

One of the key ways in which the labor market is often biased in the employer's favor is the employer's superior wage information. The individual worker can seldom discover the "going" rate in his own occupation. By informal contacts with workers in other plants he may get some information. His union may be able to give him more and so may the employment service. The sum of these sources, however, will usually not be sufficient to tell the worker where to go to get the best wage. Employers, however, particularly large employers, are much better off. They can use trade associations, contacts with other employers, and governmental wage information. What is equally important, they can hire technicians to explain the wage data to them. A 1936 survey of some sixty large employers showed that most of them gathered information on wages and working conditions in other establishments, but did not report to their employees the information they obtained in labor-market surveys.[17]

Judicial approvals of labor unions and their activities, and the legal protections that have been given them rest largely upon a similar view of the labor market. In upholding the constitutionality of the Wagner Act, Mr. Chief Justice Hughes wrote:

Long ago we stated the reason for labor organizations. We said that they were organized out of the necessities of the situation; that a single employee was helpless in dealing with an employer; that he was dependent ordinarily on his daily wage for the maintenance of himself and family; that, if the employer refused to pay him the wages that he thought fair, he was nevertheless unable to leave the employ and resist arbitrary and unfair treatment; that union was essential to give laborers opportunity to deal on an equality with their employer.[18]

Although union policies have gone far beyond simple bargaining considerations and have made such matters as industry and market stabilization key items on the program of organized labor, the union's basic function still remains the improvement of the worker's position in the labor market. No quantitative devices exist to measure what effect the growth of unionism has had upon that position. The last century and a half has witnessed two great economic phenomena in the United States — the passing of the western frontier and rise of unionism. The conjunction of these two events in an era of industrial growth has blurred their separate effects. Had there been no frontier, had our industrialization been relatively stabilized, the effect of unionization might be more readily measured. The rough instruments which are available, such as comparing the position of workers in union and nonunion establishments of the same industry, or comparing the strength of the workers in a unionized industry with their position before unionization do, however, indicate that workers have gained in market power from organization.[19]

Not all students of the labor market will agree that the labor market is inherently a buyers' market. Some will contend that the gradual but steady net rise of wages throughout our history reveals the basic superior bargaining power of workers. Others believe that unionization has given the workers control of the labor market. The Labor-Management Relations Act of 1947 (Taft-Hartley Act) showed how widespread was the view in many influential circles that "the unions are running the country."

These propositions are hardly susceptible of exact proof either way. It cannot be insisted that wages and hours alone tell the whole story of the balance of power in the labor market. These are results that may spring from causes other than worker strength in direct bargaining. (Consider the case of the telephone operators and the installation of the dial system.) As to the effect of unions, the experience of the past two decades tends to show that the general level of employment is a more potent determinant of the workers' bargaining strength and that unionization rises and falls in somewhat similar fashion as the employment level. That same experience tends to show the dependence of unions, for their growth, and workers for their bargaining strength upon a governmental atmosphere of beneficence. In some occupations and industries, particularly those characterized by small employers, strong unions have apparently had the effect of balancing, if not upsetting, the employer's bargaining strength. The New York dress manufacturing industry is one such instance.

The perspective of the relative bargaining position of workers and employers puts a different light upon many limitations on claimant availability for work. So viewed, many of these limitations, as to wage, place of employment, kind of work, hours, and the like, become part of the bargaining process. Often, it will be seen, these are not firm restrictions at all, instead they are bargaining devices. Restrictions based upon union membership may also be understood as part of a pattern of activity designed to protect and strengthen the worker's bargaining power. Cognate with this, we may note, is the entire unemployment compensation system which is intended to give the unemployed worker a floor of protection. This in itself has bargaining-position overtones.

Restriction of Entrance to the Labor Market

One basic feature of the labor market is the existence of definite barriers to those who seek to enter it. These barriers are of every type that human ingenuity can evolve. Some are governmental; licensing provisions, child labor laws, prohibitions on the employment of women and minors come under this category. Some are rooted in custom and tradition: women are seldom hired as firemen, policemen, law school professors, or veterinarians; men seldom appear as telephone operators, typists, dressmakers, or nurses. Some restrictions on labor market entrance are the result of employer practices; some employers will not hire married women, relatives of employees, Negroes, Jews, or girls who use red nail polish.

The "blacklist," a hiring restriction based on union membership or activity, has not yet disappeared. Many employers will not hire another firm's workers. Myers and Maclaurin quote the personnel manager of a furniture firm: "I always phone the personnel man at the firm an applicant says he's last worked for. If he wants the man, we don't hire him." [20] During the summer of 1946 the writer listened to nonunion workers of a Connecticut ball-bearing plant complaining that when they were laid off, as the result of a materials shortage caused by a national labor dispute, no other firm would hire them for fear of offending their last employer.

Some restrictions on labor-market entrance stem from union practices. The first and most obvious of these, at least before the Taft-Hartley Act, was the closed shop agreement which requires the employer to hire none but members of the contracting union. To a lesser extent the union shop agreement which requires, as a condition of continued employment, that new employees join the union within a specified period, also acts as a labor-market bar to antiunion workers. In 1945 about 13.8 million workers in the United States were covered by collective-bargaining agreements. Some 30 per cent of these workers, a little over 4 million, worked under closed shop contracts. An additional 15 per cent, somewhat over 2 million workers, were employed under union shop agreements.[21]

Apprenticeship limitations imposed by unions are an additional method of restricting trade entrance. Particularly in the skilled occupations this has been an effective bar to would-be workers. In some instances local unions have closed their membership books and refused to accept new members. This is unusual but in some instances it has tied up trade in an entire local market.[22] High initiation fees and various devices to exclude aliens, women, or Negroes from membership have been used by some unions in an effort to control labor-market access. Although the unions which create such bars to the free exercise of the right to work are but a small minority, the fact that such unions are among our oldest and strongest makes these restrictions especially significant.[23]

The barriers to labor-market entrance continually raise problems of availability administration. It is a commonplace saying in unemployment compensation that the availability requirement refers to the claimant's availability *for* work and not to the availability *of* work for the claimant. Nonetheless, what is to be done in the case of the woman claimant who restricts herself to work as a policeman? To take a more common instance, what of the availability of the CIO carpenter in the A.F. of L. town?

LABOR–MARKET BOUNDARIES

Wage-Setting Areas

It is a truism that the labor market is primarily a congeries of local market areas. Both in its wage-setting and labor-hiring aspects the labor market works on a local rather than a national basis. Wage-setting localities, however, are usually far broader in area than hiring markets. In good part, this is the result of the growth of both employer and worker organization. Multiple unit enterprises — grocery store chains, utility "empires," steel companies, railroads, and many other firms that do business in several localities — have grown rapidly in the United States since the end of the Civil War. These multi-unit, inter-area concerns vary considerably in their wage policies. The Ford Motor Company, for example, tends to follow the same wage policy both in the North and the South. Often, it is true, a geographic wage differential is consciously and deliberately adopted.[24] Even when this is done, however, the wage policy followed stems from a company policy that is only partially based upon local considerations.

At the same time, the rise of unionism has led to a similar broadening of worker wage policies. Thus there has been a growing tendency, in recent years, to industry-wide bargaining. Among coal miners, longshoremen, glass, steel, and garment workers, and many other groups, industry-wide bargaining on a regional or seminational scale has become the order of the day. Although industry-wide bargaining has not wiped out inter-area wage differentials and industry agreements have often been careful to preserve them, it is clear that such a practice does broaden the bargaining area. The trend to industry-wide bargaining antedates World War II.[25] The war and its aftermath have advanced this trend. There seems little reason to believe that it will soon be reversed.

Aside from its bargaining aspects, the labor market as a wage-setting area is subject to controls that transcend the boundaries of the city or county where a plant is located. The wages an employer pays depend a good deal upon his other costs and upon the selling price he can command. In a thoroughly competitive market his selling price will be beyond his control. So may some of his costs, such as materials and goods transportation. Even though they may be many miles away, his competitors who get their labor at low wages may force him to keep his own workers' wages low or even reduce them. In such instances it is obvious that the local character of the wage-fixing area is apt to be illusory.

Job-finding Areas

The hiring or job-finding area is primarily local. It is this area that the United States Employment Service has in mind when it refers to a "labor-market area." Unlike the wage-setting area, the hiring area can be described quite specifically in terms of the space it covers. The United States Employment Service defines it roughly and for working purposes as an area within which workers can and do commute regularly from their homes to jobs without having to change their residence. When we think of the job-finding area for a particular point we may think of the surrounding territory within a radius that seldom exceeds fifty miles. Thus the job-finding area for a Harlan County coal miner is considerably smaller than the area within which his wage is set.

It is important to realize that the labor-market area, so understood, may be a composite of two or more smaller areas. A metropolitan city may contain within itself several distinct areas in each of which workers live, and seek and find employment, seldom venturing in their search for a job to one of the neighboring areas within the city. In New York City, for example, the Brooklynite

will seldom seek work in the Bronx; Manhattan is about as far as
he will venture from the Gowanus. Or the component areas may
be adjacent communities. Myers and Maclaurin, from their study
of the records of nearly 16,000 factory workers in two contiguous
New England cities, state:

Despite the fact that over a period of years workers living in one of
the two adjacent cities comprising this labor market had frequently
been employed in the other, nearly 90 per cent of the moves made
among the 37 firms in the 1937–39 period were between companies
located in the same city.[26]

The concept of the job-finding area emphasizes the effects of commuting. Commuting, in its present breadth and scope, is a comparatively new factor in our social and economic life. The private
automobile and the fast commuter trains and busses are distinctly
twentieth century developments. They have helped to produce
population and industrial shifts whose end is not yet in sight. Suburbanization is one of the major products of these transportation
changes. The 1940 census was the first to show a decline in the
percentage of Americans living in cities of 100,000 or more, but
with no change in the decades-old trend toward an ever increasing
proportion of urban dwellers. The war and its immediate aftermath
may have slowed down the decline of the large cities, but only
temporarily. The increase in suburban living and commuting to
work would seem to spell out a long period of spatial expansion
for individual labor-market areas.

It should be noted that labor-market areas are economic and
social areas, not political entities. It is obvious that they are not circumscribed by municipal or county boundary lines. What is often
not realized is that they are not limited by state boundaries. The
point is made here for its particular bearing upon the administrative
problems in unemployment compensation which is state-operated.
Workers in New York City live in New Jersey or Connecticut.
Indiana residents find employment in Chicago, and some Ken-
tuckians need but walk across a bridge to their jobs in Cincinnati.
All in all, it has been estimated, there are seventy such interstate
but local labor-market areas.

In addition we must recognize that the boundaries of a labor-
market area will vary, depending upon such factors as the occupation or industry involved and the level of employment or wages

offered. Skilled occupations tend, both because of the higher wages paid and the relative scarcity of jobs, to have larger labor-market areas. In some occupations, among sandhogs, for example, the entire country may be said to constitute a single labor market. Thus we may find that because of occupational and industrial differences a single area may be one market for some occupations and two or three separate markets for others. In New York State, for example, the three cities of Albany, Troy, and Schenectady are usually considered a single labor-market area. Although this is generally true for factory labor, it is generally not true in such occupations as waitresses or salesclerks.

A new industry brought into a labor-market area may, by virtue of the additional employment opportunities and, perhaps, the higher pay it offers, have the effect of "expanding" the area. The war furnished many illustrations not only of this but also of the expansive effects of high wages and plentiful jobs. The commuting area around any war manufacturing center, despite wartime travel difficulties, stretched miraculously. Workers in New York City were known to travel to work ninety miles each day to Bridgeport and then back again at night. Every war boom town had similar commuters.

To speak of the expansive possibilities of the labor-market area is but one way of saying there are no fences around it. Inter-area migration provides another. Although these two factors involve geographic mobility which has important effects, as we have noted, upon the wage-setting labor market, they are crucial to the successful organization of the labor market as a worker-hiring and job-finding mechanism.

The boundaries of labor markets as hiring areas and the factors that control those boundaries are deeply involved in availability administration. As we shall see, in later chapters, the very heart of availability determination is the need to find that the claimant is available for a sufficient amount of work. What is sufficient must depend upon the conditions in the local labor-market area. This, in turn, involves definition of that area.

Again, defining the labor-market area is essential in all cases where the claimant has restricted his work-commuting radius. In such cases industrial and occupational differences in labor-market boundaries have a significant effect upon the result entailed in the availability restriction.

CHAPTER III

THE LABOR FORCE

THE NATURE AND CHARACTERISTICS of the labor force are basic to availability studies. This chapter is intended to sketch the rough outlines of the labor-force picture. Later chapters will furnish more details on specific labor-force groups as they are involved in particular problems of availability.

DIMENSIONS AND DISTRIBUTION

Size

In December 1946, 58.4 million Americans were in the labor force, an increase of some 5.6 millions over the number shown by the 1940 census figures.[1] Both the 1940 and the December 1946 figures reveal substantially the same proportion of the total population in the labor force — roughly two-fifths. This ratio is the product of a complex of factors — productivity, birth and death rates, living standards and costs, income distribution, schooling, law, custom, and so on. Censuses and countries vary too much to permit accurate comparisons with ratios in other nations. It is interesting to note that in recent times the gainfully occupied as percentages of national population have been as low as 31.2 (Brazil, 1940) and as high as 67.6 (Lithuania, 1923). Among the great European industrial countries, the last reported percentages were: Great Britain, 47.0 (1931), France, 52.4 (1931), Germany, 51.0 (1939), the Soviet Union, 57.5 (1926).[2]

Age and Sex Composition

There has been little change since the beginning of this century in the ratio of the total labor force to the total population of the United States. In 1900, 38.3 per cent of our total population were gainful workers. The 1940 figures (which are not precisely comparable with those of any previous census) showed 40.1 per cent of the people in the labor force. The stability of these ratios conceals a good deal of change in the composition of the labor force and the population. The change may be summed up in these words: ageing and feminization. Both are long-run trends that antedate 1900 and may be expected to continue throughout the twentieth century.

A hundred years ago the American people were literally young — over half of them were under twenty. By the beginning of this century, well over half the population was past twenty. In 1940 almost two-thirds of the people were over twenty. Before the century is out it is expected that three-quarters of the population, at any one time, will be in the twenty-or-older group. Since the years between twenty and sixty-four are the most productive, the next generation may be expected to see a steady increase in our potential working force — at least until substantial segments of that group enter the 65-or-older category. In 1900 over half the population (51.5 per cent) was in the twenty- to sixty-four-year-old bracket; in 1940 it was close to three-fifths (58.7 per cent). By 1970 it is expected that about 63 per cent of the population will be in this "working" age bracket. An increase in the labor-force ratio would seem in order.

The similarity between the 1900 and the 1940 labor-force ratios may seem contradictory, but only apparently so. We have been reducing the labor-force participation of our young people, those under 20, and increasing it in the 20- to 64-year-old group. The 1900 census, like other pre-1940 censuses, checked on the work status of all persons 10 years old and over. By 1940, the 10 to 13 year olds were so insignificant in the work force that the census began to omit them and considered in the labor force count only those persons 14 years and older. But even the 14- to 19-year-old workers have dwindled since 1900. More schooling, child labor laws, less immigration, the depression of the thirties, and decline as a population group all had their effect. For every 1000 of population, 1900 had 121 of the 14 to 19 year olds, of whom 54 were gainful workers; 1940 had but 112, of whom only 30 were in the labor force.

At the same time the 20 to 64 year olds have increased, both in the population and in the labor force. In 1900 there were 516 people between the ages of 20 and 64 for every 1000 of total population; these included 302 gainful workers of the age group. In 1940 there were 586 of the 20–64 year olds per 1000 people and 355 of them in the labor force. From furnishing 71 per cent of the gainful workers in 1900 the 20–64 year olds advanced to 88.5 per cent of the 1940 labor force. Two subsidiary groups of workers account for this change — the women workers between the ages of 25 and 44 and the men workers between the ages of 45 and 64.

The increase in the 45- to 64-year-old male work force followed the population trend. In 1900 there were 72 men aged 45 to 64 for every 1000 of total population, in 1940 there were 101 such men. Their ratio to the total population had increased by 40 per cent. In 1900, for every 1000 people there were 68 men workers aged 45–64; in 1940 this group numbered 90 such men for 1000 people, an increase of 32.3 per cent in their ratio to the population. This increase of 45- to 64-year-old men workers accounted for almost 43 per cent of the increase that took place over the forty years in the ratio of the entire 20- to 64-year-old work force to the population.

The increase of the 25- to 44-year-old women workers also accounted for almost 43 per cent of the labor-force ratio increase among the 20 to 64 year olds. This age group of women numbered 135 and 151 per 1000 population in 1900 and 1940, respectively. Between these two census years they increased 11.1 per cent as a portion of the total population. In 1900, however, there were 24 gainful women workers, per 1000 population, within the 25 to 44 year age group; in 1940 there were 46 of them. Their work force ratio had increased by 91.7 per cent. In other words, this age group of women workers grew more than eight times as fast as a segment of the population than the total population of women in the 25- to 44-year-old age bracket.

The increased ratio of 25- to 44-year-old women workers reflects the increasing employment of married women. The years between 25 and 44 are years of marriage and family responsibility. In 1940 2 of every 5 women workers in the 25 to 44 bracket were married and living with their husbands. The 1940 figures, it should be noted, showed increases in the labor-force ratios of every age segment of the female population. In 1900 the women workers were 7 per cent of the population and 18.3 per cent of all gainfully occupied. In 1940 the women in the labor force were 9.8 per cent of the total population and 24.3 per cent of the total labor force. In December 1946, the women were 28.1 per cent of the civilian labor force.

Dr. Alba M. Edwards's words are significant:

This movement of women into gainful occupations cannot be viewed as a mere makeshift to bridge over temporary economic conditions, nor as the result of a transient feminine whim. It is a basic movement, to which society must adjust itself and with the social and economic effects of which society must reckon. It will continue, and women will form a larger and larger proportion of the Nation's labor force.[3]

These basic movements of our labor force toward increasing feminization and ageing have their effect upon the meaning of availability. An ageing work force will be constantly more and more concerned with job security. We may expect more emphasis on seniority plans and a greater tendency for workers to cling to a regular employer during periods of unemployment. This will run head on against some of our accepted availability doctrines. The increasing feminization of the labor force is bound to create more situations where women claimants' home responsibilities conflict with working hours in offered jobs. In addition, unless sound health or sickness insurance plans provide an orderly way out, both these trends may be expected to bring a steady increase in cases of questionable physical ability to work — pregnancies, nervousness, and the various ailments that are the peculiar lot of women and older workers.

The slow and steady increase in the ratio of the labor force to the total population, coupled with the expected increases in productivity, make shorter hours of work a real possibility. At the moment, the forty-hour week appears to be a sort of national standard. With peacetime conditions, a thirty-hour week may not be far off. This would narrow the gap between part-time and full-time work considerably. The amount of work — in terms of total weekly hours — for which a worker must be available to qualify for benefits would be more difficult to determine.

These are but some of the availability problems that are implied in the basic trends of our labor-force growth. None of these problems is new. Already they are with us. But the foreseeable labor-force changes of the future will bring them to us with greater acuteness and in greater volume.

Industrial and Occupational Distribution

Originally our country was agricultural, but after 1840 there was rapid change as transportation and industry developed. By 1900 the proportion of workers on farms was half that of 1840.

Half of those released from the farms went into manufacturing, the rest mainly into distribution and trade. In 1820 out of every twenty workers, seventeen were engaged in physical production and two in personal service. In 1940 out of every twenty workers only ten were in physical production, five in transportation, distribution, and administration, three in professional or public service, two in personal service.

Looking at the work force changes by socio-economic groups, we find these changes in the thirty years that elapsed between 1910 and 1940: Of every 1000 workers: in 1910, 310 were farmers (owners, tenants, or laborers); in 1940, 182 were in this class. Wholesale and retail dealers numbered 33 in 1910, were 39 in 1940. Other proprietors, managers, and officials numbered 32 in 1910 and 37 in 1940. There were 44 professional persons in 1910 and 65 in 1940. Clerks and kindred workers grew in number from 102 in 1910 to 172 in 1940. Skilled workers and foremen, after having risen to 135 in 1920, dropped to 129 in 1930, and in 1940 returned to their 1910 number, 117. Semiskilled workers, however, grew steadily in numbers from 147 in 1910 to 210 in 1940, the largest single increase of all. Unskilled nonfarm laborers dropped from 147 in 1910 to 107 in 1940. The servant classes rose in number from 68 in 1910 to 80 in 1940 (although in 1930 they had numbered but 69).

Several salient facts stand out here — the rise of the clerks and the semiskilled, the growth of the trade and service occupations, the increase in the professional groups. These trends, we may expect, will continue. Continued mechanization robs the skilled worker of the opportunity to use his craft and the unskilled laborer of the chance to use his brawn. Both are increasingly sucked into the middle group of the semiskilled — the machine tenders, the deliverymen, and the like. As our economy becomes ever more complex, clerical occupations continue to grow. More careful office planning and the increasing use of office machines may slow down that growth, but the forces that increased the 7 women stenographers of 1870 to the 1.1 million women stenographers, typists, and secretaries of 1940 are still at work.

The outstanding occupational change of our time is the shift to the tertiary occupations. As we have seen, we began our economy with almost complete concentration upon primary production, mainly agriculture. In the nineteenth century we moved over to processing as primary production receded from its command of the work force. The twentieth century is the century of distribution and services. In 1870 there were a little over three producers for every person engaged in services and distribution. In 1940 there was a shade less than one person in production for each person engaged in services and distribution. With increasing productivity and diversity of production, a constant growth of demands for government services, and an ever growing awareness of the need for broader markets, foreign and domestic, for our goods, there seems no reason to expect any reversal of this trend.

These occupational and industrial trends, on the whole, dovetail with the patterns we have noted in the age and sex composition of the labor force. There we saw the growing importance of older and women workers. These are workers who fit easily into an economy that emphasizes clerical work, in offices and stores for example. Older workers may suffer from the decline of skilled occupations. Many of them, however, and most women workers will gain in work opportunities as semiskilled occupations replace the unskilled jobs with their demands upon physical strength. Here again we may note that availability doctrines will be affected. As sedentary occupations become more prevalent we are, for example, bound to develop more catholic concepts of physical ability to work. As skilled occupations decline we may also expect greater interoccupational mobility which would tend to loosen up some of the problems availability administration has encountered.

Geographic Distribution

Important differences appear when the labor force is examined by states or regions. In 1940 the New England, Middle Atlantic, Eastern North Central, and Pacific regions were the only ones which contained a greater percentage of the national labor force than they had of the total population. These regions combined furnished 54.9 per cent of the population and 57.5 per cent of the labor force. The West North Central, South Atlantic, East South Central, West South Central, and Mountain states had 45.1 per cent of the population but only 42.5 per cent of the labor force. Table 2 shows these population and labor-force differences by regions.

Although, as Table 2 shows, the regional distributions of the population and of the labor force differ somewhat, population change by natural increase and migration remain the key to labor-force distribution. Natural increase varies from region to region.

By and large the suppliers of labor have been the agricultural regions, particularly the South. The surplus of births over deaths in the United States in the 1930–1940 decade was responsible for a 6.6 per cent increase in the total population. In the New England, Middle Atlantic, East North Central, and Pacific regions the natural increase during this period was substantially below the average for the nation. The West North Central region's rate of natural increase was just a shade better than the national rate, but in the East South Central region the percentage of natural increase between 1930 and 1940 was 10.1. This was followed by the South

TABLE 2

PERCENTAGES OF THE POPULATION AND LABOR FORCE BY REGIONS, 1940

Region	Population	Labor Force
Total..	100.0	100.0
New England................................	6.4	6.9
Middle Atlantic.............................	20.9	22.4
East North Central.........................	20.2	20.5
West North Central.........................	10.3	9.9
South Atlantic..............................	13.5	13.2
East South Central.........................	8.2	7.4
West South Central.........................	9.6	9.3
Mountain...................................	3.2	2.9
Pacific....................................	7.4	7.8

Source: United States Census Bureau.

Atlantic region, 10.0 per cent, the Mountain states, 9.7 per cent, and the West South Central region, 9.4 per cent.

Interstate migration, which has been heaviest to the Pacific Coast since World War I, redistributes some of the uneven natural increase. Since 1920 the Pacific Coast states, Nevada, Arizona, Indiana, Connecticut, Maryland, the District of Columbia, and Florida have continuously gained population from migration. Nineteen states have continuously lost through migration. By region, these have been: New England — Maine, Vermont; Middle Atlantic — Pennsylvania; East North Central — Wisconsin; West North Central — Iowa, Missouri, North Dakota, South Dakota, Nebraska, Kansas; South Atlantic — West Virginia, North Carolina, South Carolina, Georgia; East South Central — Kentucky,

Alabama, Mississippi; West South Central — Arkansas, Oklahoma; Mountain — Montana.

In the states of Massachusetts, Rhode Island, New Jersey, Michigan, Ohio, and Illinois there was a favorable migration balance both during World War II and the 1920–1930 decade, although the depression years of the 1930–1940 period had produced a migration loss. New Hampshire, Tennessee, Louisiana, Minnesota, Wyoming, Idaho, Colorado, and New Mexico lost population through migration both during the twenties and during World War II. They gained in 1930–1940. New York, which gained from migration during the two decades 1920–1940, lost during the war. Texas which gained during the twenties as a result of the oil boom had a minor gain in the thirties and a slight loss during the war. Virginia lost during the twenties but has been gaining since then as the metropolitan area has grown around Washington. Delaware followed a similar pattern in migration gains and losses and Utah, which had been losing by migration in 1920–1940, gained during the war from the construction of war plants.[4]

It should be noted that these effects of migration are the result of a two-way flow of population. The gains and losses mentioned are net gains and net losses.

In general, it would appear that the trend of the labor force is westward to the Pacific Coast. It has been estimated, for example, that the labor force of the North, which was 32.6 millions in 1940, will in 1950 be between 35.4 and 35.7 millions. The labor force of the South, 16.3 millions in 1940, will be between 18.6 and 19.7 millions. The greatest relative increase, almost wholly the result of migration, is expected in the West, from 5.8 millions in 1940 to 7.2 to 8.0 millions in 1950.[5]

An equally important aspect of our internal migration is the relationship between our rural and urban areas. Our farms grow more than food for our cities. They grow workers. Our economy's movement from agricultural to industrial predominance has been accompanied by a continuous trek of workers from the farms to the cities. This was slowed down somewhat by the depression years of the thirties. World War II, however, lifted it to new heights and the aftermath of that war will probably see even further acceleration of this trend. In stressing the favorable balance the cities have had in this migration, it should not be overlooked that it is a two-way movement. During the twenties over 13 million people moved to rural areas, during the thirties close to 11 millions, and in 1940–

1942 almost two millions. But such has been the volume of the city-ward movement, that the nonfarm areas gained in the migration balance a net of 6.3 millions during the twenties, 3.7 millions during the thirties, and 3.3 millions in the first three years of this decade.[6]

Our internal migration has visible effects upon availability administration. States that are losing population have a natural tendency to try to retain their citizens. This has sometimes affected unemployment compensation. In a few states benefits have been denied to individuals who left their work, went to another state and would not return to accept an offered job. One state went so far as to require that claimants, in order to be eligible, must register and report to that state's employment service. One result of population loss by migration is to change the age and sex composition of the losing state's population. Since, most frequently, it is the younger men who migrate, they leave behind them an older and more female labor force. This changes the character of that state's availability problems.

By the same token, the labor force of the gaining state is changed in its age and sex make-up. The young men it is acquiring, because they are young and without roots, tend to be unstable elements. They increase turnover. Their attachment to the labor force will often tend to be marginal.

Both the cities and the gaining states also have to deal with the immigrants who work a while and then go back home. Often they return to areas that are sparsely settled and remote from any work opportunities. These individuals present difficult administrative problems in the field of availability.

LABOR MOBILITY

Successful operation of an industrial economy is conditioned upon a mobile labor force. Ours is the first economic system to rely upon free labor for its entire work force. Using free labor gives greater assurance that workers will be mobile. It does, however, involve the risk that workers will stay or move where and when they are needed. In a free society we have had to rely upon economic rather than legal pressures and inducements to get workers to the jobs where they were wanted. How well this has worked may be learned by comparing the modern labor force with the work force of preindustrial society, where workers were often under a legal obligation to work.

Before the industrial revolution even craftsmen were comparatively rooted. Agricultural workers were, of course, almost completely immobile. Workers were "frozen" not only in terms of geographic movement but in terms of occupational shifts as well. One entered a craft through a long and carefully regulated apprenticeship in its "mysteries." Transfer to another craft was almost an impossibility. Compare that with the present situation.

Modern industrial operations are so mechanized and standardized that a relatively small proportion of workers need to have a highly developed skill. There is, therefore, little occasion for persistent labor immobility attributable directly to the decline of certain industries or occupations.[7]

The functions of a dynamic labor force in a society such as ours have been well and simply stated by Myers and Maclaurin:

In a country where workers are free to change jobs and to seek work of their own choice, the movement of labor should fulfill several important functions. First, it should tend to equalize wage rates and other conditions of work for comparable jobs. Second, it should serve to distribute labor where the need is greatest, geographically and industrially. Third, it should give workers an opportunity to utilize their capacities and abilities most effectively. To the extent that there is insufficient movement, these functions will be imperfectly fulfilled. On the other hand, if many workers move without these results being realized in some degree, movement is wasteful and uneconomic. Waste is also incurred if more movement takes place than is necessary to fulfill these functions.[8]

Characteristics of Migrants

How does our labor force measure up to these criteria? We have seen that its movement is cityward and westward. But who does the moving? As we might expect, the findings are that it is mostly the younger workers who move. The 1940 census showed 15.7 million persons who had changed their county of residence between 1935 and 1940. Well over half this group (54.7 per cent) were persons between the ages of twenty and forty-four, although that age group comprised less than half (48.9 per cent) of the total population. The division of migrants by sex followed closely the sex composition of the population, with but a slightly higher percentage of men migrants than women.

Comparable figures for internal labor-force migration, rather than population migration, would show substantially higher migration of men workers than women workers.[9] However, a Bureau of Labor Statistics survey in 1945–46 of what happened to some two thousand workers in various war industries when reconversion took place states:

Age appeared to be closely associated with the tendency to move; the differences among the age groups were surprisingly uniform as between men and women. Among those under 20 years of age, about two-fifths of each sex had moved since the spring of 1945. Somewhat over a quarter of both men and women from 20 to 45 were no longer living where they were first surveyed. Among the older workers, almost a fifth each of the men and of the women had left their wartime homes.[10]

Workers who migrate tend, on the whole, to earn more than nonmigrant workers. Such is the evidence found in a review of the 1938–1943 earnings of a 1 per cent sample of all workers with taxable wages under the old Age and Survivors Insurance program. In 1938, for example, the medium annual taxable wage for the migrants in this sample was $735 as compared with $660 for the nonmigrants.

When a comparison was made of migrants and non-migrants with similar employment experience in terms of numbers of quarters of employment and number of employers, the migrants proved to be higher paid. That is to say, the average quarterly wages of the migrants were higher, as a rule, than those of the non-migrants with the same number of employers and the same number of quarters of employment . . .[11]

Costs of Moving

The money costs of moving act to restrain worker mobility. In over a fifth of the cases where costs of moving were reported by workers in a Saint Paul propeller plant, the cost was $100 or more. Moving expenses ran highest among family heads but even among the single workers there were moving costs of over $75.

Outlays for moving were not in all cases offset by immediate increases in income. In 89 cases the workers earned more on the first job obtained after the move than they had earned before, three migrations resulted in no change in earnings, and 35 migrations were followed by decreases in weekly earnings.[12]

This is partly because workers who earn more can better afford to move. When Camp Blanding was built in Florida in late 1940, it was found that almost 67 per cent of the skilled production workers seeking jobs came more than one hundred miles to the project. Only 39.9 per cent of the unskilled production workers came from outside the hundred-mile radius.[13]

The social costs to the worker of changing communities are equally important but not so readily assessable. Moving to another place may mean leaving friends and family, all the familiar social ties. The worker may be going from a town where he has a definite social status to a community where he is a "nobody." His children may have to change schools, his wife may have to reorient herself, make new friends. He may have to search for a new church, a new club, a new union. He may have to build a new credit standing in a new locality. If he is a homeowner in the old locality there is an added financial risk or cost. If there are other wage earners who help support the family there may be a problem of separation. If the worker is one of the subsidiary supports of the family, moving to a new locality where separate maintenance is necessary may make it more difficult for him to give his family the supplementary aid they need.

Although both the financial and social costs of moving may often be formidable, the fact remains that most American worker migration is induced by prospect of greater gains. The young worker leaves the small town, because the big city offers more. The gains that induce workers to migrate are not always financial, however. Some move for reasons of health, their own or that of a family member. Others move to be near — or to get away from — their relatives or to be near schools, churches, or recreational facilities. Unemployment compensation must deal with both kinds of situations — unemployed workers who cling to declining communities because of the cost of moving and workers who move to new localities because they expect to profit thereby, either financially or otherwise. Both groups may present serious questions as to availability for work.

Occupational Mobility

How about occupational mobility? How do American workers respond to the times in choosing and adhering to an occupation? Our information on this subject is very slim. Most of the studies that have been made deal with inter-industrial, rather than interoccupational mobility. In 1927 Sorokin suggested the following general rules:

1. Within the same occupation, the more qualified and better paid groups shift less intensively than the less qualified and more poorly paid groups.

2. Members of disappearing occupations shift more intensively than members of developing and prospering occupations.

3. Unskilled labor is more mobile than skilled labor.

4. Business and professional groups (at the higher levels) are likely to be more stable than unskilled labor groups.

5. In each concrete case, intensiveness of shifting depends considerably upon the age of the people engaged in an occupation. Other conditions being equal, shifting is likely to be greater among young people (who are just engaged in finding a suitable occupation) and among people forty years old and over (who are retiring, voluntarily or involuntarily, or moving to easier work for age or health reasons).

By way of example, Sorokin presented figures on occupational change among two groups of Minneapolis businessmen and their sons. In one group there had been no occupational change for over 57 per cent of the fathers and over 43 per cent of the sons. In the other group almost 69 per cent of the fathers and over 64 per cent of the sons had no occupational change. In one group 28.3 per cent of the sons had two or more occupational changes, but the other group of sons had only 5.8 per cent in this category. Their fathers were represented in this category by 10.2 and 6.3 per cent, respectively.[14]

As he himself points out, there are many exceptions to Sorokin's general rules on occupational mobility. The decline of an industry is not always accompanied by greater occupational mobility. A 1941 study among weavers exemplified the immobility of workers in an occupation of declining work opportunity. Workers were studied in three textile centers over a ten-year period. Although those weavers who moved directly from or to jobs in other industries, or in and out of textiles at some time during the period reported least employment for the whole ten years, such mobile weavers constituted less than a third of the entire group. The average number of years spent in weaving in these three centers ranged from seventeen to twenty-one.[15]

Again, skilled craftsmen are not always the least mobile of all occupational groups. The Wharton School's Industrial Research

Department found in a study of Philadelphia toolmakers that these expert workmen made many job changes. Interviews with them revealed a widespread belief that such changes were essential to develop the highest degree of skill.[16]

There seems nonetheless little doubt that mobility is higher among younger than among older workers, among unskilled than skilled workers. A study of two adjacent New England communities states: "The workers who moved voluntarily were mostly young, short-service workers, frequently women, whose earnings were relatively low in the job they quit. These workers had less to lose by moving than did the older longer-service workers who held the better paying jobs." [17] But more than a third of these voluntary moves resulted in lower earnings.

An investigation, in twenty-seven different New England companies, of cotton textile workers who stayed with the industry during the war showed that 70 per cent of the men and 50 per cent of the women were at least forty-five years old. Over one-fifth had not changed jobs in twenty years; nearly three-quarters had been in the same occupation in the same mill for at least five years.[18]

This body of cotton textile workers presents almost all the bars to occupational mobility. They were narrow specialists in their work. Over four-fifths of them had learned their occupation on the job, without benefit of apprenticeship or trade or vocational schools. They were tied to their jobs by a seniority system which gave them rights they sought to protect. Hiring, promotion, and layoffs all depended on length of service in a single occupation, although consideration was given to skill and efficiency. Even if a transfer was accepted to another unit within the same mill, these workers lost, after a year, all their seniority in the occupation they had vacated. Quitting the mill meant forfeiting all seniority rights.

There were strong social and cultural reasons for not leaving the industry. For many of the workers, to work in the mill was part of a family tradition, which often extended back to their grandfathers and great-grandfathers. Community life, to a large extent, centered on mill employment. In part this was sponsored by the employers' recreation and welfare programs. In large measure, however, it was but a natural result of the friendships formed over the years of working together. The job was a primary social contact and a source of conversation, entertainment, and mutual interest.

Leaving the mill divorced the worker from that contact and

separated him from his friends. The separation entailed more than mere physical separation during working hours. It extended beyond the working hours, for the worker who left the mill for employment elsewhere no longer had the same basis for social intimacy with his former fellow workers. He was out of the group. Similarly, leaving the mill would mean leaving the activities of the union. In mill towns unions are usually more than mere bargaining agents. They serve as the centers for much of the workers' social life. To the union member, the regular union meeting is apt to be more of an opportunity for the sociable rather than the political aspects of economic democracy. Leaving the union means leaving his club.

Fear of unemployment, even during the job-plenty years of the war, deterred many New England cotton textile workers who thought of leaving the industry. As the age distribution mentioned above reveals, the workers who stayed with the mills during the war were usually old enough to have been materially affected by the depression of the thirties. That depression was particularly severe in the New England textile centers. For example, in New Bedford, one of the centers covered by the study, in May 1939, almost thirty in every hundred workers were unemployed. Almost two-thirds of all the then unemployed cotton textile workers in New Bedford had been out of work one year or more. In one out of every four New Bedford families in May 1939 there was no one working. Two-thirds of all the unemployed families had no member working for one year or more; more than one out of every four unemployed families had no member working for five years or more.[19] With such recent memories as these, there is little wonder that mature cotton textile workers in New Bedford were hesitant to take the plunge and look for other work.

Occupational Versatility

Our knowledge of the occupational versatility of the labor force is limited. Americans are traditionally handy men, jacks-of-all-trades. The extent of their trade versatility, however, has seldom been measured. Neither do we know whether that versatility is increasing or is on the wane. A Cincinnati study, made during the late thirties, of 95,000 workers registered at the local employment center showed an average of 6 occupational skills each. One applicant preferred a job as a short-order cook but, according to his work record, he could also operate a sock-knitting machine, a shirt-folder and finisher, a body press, or qualify as a dishwasher or tray waiter. Another, a 22-year-old medical student seeking summer work, had been self-supporting since the eighth grade. He wrote "clerical" as his first choice and "anything" as his second. His work record showed 27 different skills, including masoning, bookbinding, steel mill work, lumber mill work, statistician, lecturer.[20] The Florida Industrial Commission's Department of Research and Statistics concluded that the Camp Blanding construction project could have been largely staffed from within a fairly close geographic area if the "invisible" but unknown skills of the local workers had been tapped.[21]

Although these instances, and the entire war experience, indicate that our workers are often capable of handling many different jobs, there are long-range factors that work against this versatility. Union and management policies conspire to keep the worker attached, not only to a single industry, but usually to a single occupation and employer. Technological advance tends to increase the narrowness of specialization. It is true that this very factor puts more jobs in the semiskilled class where no great training is involved. But it also makes skilled jobs so highly technical that even workers in related skills cannot master them without prolonged training. Speaking of the printing trades, Loft says:

Characteristic of the entire period following 1900 are composing room employees unable to run a press and pressmen knowing nothing of composition. Even within the field of presswork, the great number of innovations and different model presses created a situation in which, for example, a "black and white" pressman could operate a color press only with much difficulty, or a pressman versed in relief printing presswork could qualify for offset presswork only after intensive schooling.[22]

LABOR–SUPPLY UTILIZATION

Utterly aside from the voluntary or imposed preferences of workers that may impede optimum mobility is a complete set of institutional inhibitions that prevent full utilization of our labor supply. We discriminate against the young and old. An investigation by the National Association of Manufacturers of 2485 firms employing over 2¼ million workers revealed 38 per cent who admitted a hiring preference for workers under 40.[23] The 1940 census showed 9.6 per cent of the total labor force unemployed and seeking work. At the same time, however, 17.1 per cent of the labor force that was less than 25 years old was jobless and seeking work.

We discriminate against women and Negroes. The discriminations against women are, in part, the results of legal protections. Mostly, however, they are the result of traditional male attitudes which seek to exclude women from higher-skilled, better-paying jobs. Similar discriminations exist against Negroes but in even greater degree. The customary treatment we accord them often excludes them, not only from skilled jobs but from any jobs as well. Traditionally the last hired and the first fired, Negroes suffered the greatest unemployment of any American racial group in the thirties. In 1940, for example, 12.6 per cent of the white labor force in the northeastern states was unemployed, 20.5 per cent of the Negro labor force.

We discriminate against convicts in the labor force. Goods produced in federal prisons may not be sold to the public. Goods produced by other prison labor may not be shipped in interstate commerce. All but ten states in 1940 prohibited the sale of prison-made goods. In every state there is at least one occupation that is barred by the law to the noncitizen.

Job-classification schemes, with detailed job requirements, may be and often are effective in securing an under-utilization of our labor supply. By setting physical ability, skill, or experience requirements too high they reduce the number of applicants who may be considered for hiring. The employment services are familiar, through long experience, with the penchant of employers for placing job orders for workers who are absolutely physically fit. This often holds true when the job makes limited physical demands on the worker and can just as well be done by one who is physically handicapped.

Our governmental policy toward the labor supply has been a patchwork of varying means and objectives. A recent survey of national labor policy says:

To accomplish diverse objectives, the government has done a number of things that have influenced the labor supply. But during both periods of employment and unemployment the same policies have been pursued, and inconsistent policies have been applied to meet a given problem.[24]

Some national policies have tended to increase the number of trained workers available — vocational education, vocational rehabilitation, encouragement of apprentice training. The author of the above quotation states that these programs have been carried on both during periods of job plenty and job shortages. But it should be noted that these programs have been intensified during periods of labor shortage, such as the recent war.

Other governmental policies and programs reduce the supply of labor. We have mentioned the laws against the sale of prison-made goods. The Fair Labor Standards Act prohibits the employment of children under fourteen years in interstate commerce or in producing goods for such commerce and persons under sixteen in mining and manufacturing. Although under its provisions learners, apprentices, and handicapped workers may be hired at less than the minimum wage rates, a finding by the administrator is required that such hiring is necessary in order to prevent curtailment of opportunities for employment. In the opinion of one observer, this has had a restrictive effect upon the employment of learners.[25]

Under the Walsh-Healy Public Contracts Act, which applies to all federal government contracts over $10,000, industrial homework is prohibited. The Wage-Hour Administrator's regulations, under the Fair Labor Standards Act, require each subject employer of homeworkers to apply for and procure a handbook from the Wage and Hour Division for each homeworker. The detailed reporting required by the administrator has tended to discourage homework.

The bars this country has put up against immigration are another way in which our governmental policy has restricted our labor supply. In the first ten years of this century we admitted over eight million immigrants. In the years ending with 1944 the number of immigrants admitted was less than half a million.

Although, of course, there are good and sufficient other reasons for most of these restrictive governmental policies, they do have the effect of reducing the number of workers available to do the nation's job. Although these and other similar policies were in instances somewhat lightened during the war, they have, on the whole, been equally enforced both when jobs and when men were hard to find.

Finally, we may consider unemployment compensation as an expression of government labor policy. There is little reason to believe that unemployment compensation has any substantial effect upon the number of people in the labor force. Unlike wage and hour laws, it sets no minimum wage standards that destroy the demand for unproductive labor. It does not prohibit access to our labor markets, like the immigration laws. It does not train workers, like the apprenticeship programs, or retrain the disabled, like the vocational rehabilitation agencies. Indirectly, however, unemployment compensation can and often does participate in many of these activities.

Availability interpretations are especially important to such participation. The weekly benefit amount often serves as a wage floor. Claimants are reluctant to consider work paying less than that amount. In California the law specifies that work is not suitable unless the wage offered is equal to the benefit amount. In Connecticut it must exceed the weekly benefit amount.

By their availability interpretations, unemployment compensation agencies may either encourage or deter the retraining of unemployed workers.[26] During World War II unemployed workers engaged in vocational training for war work were helped considerably by the benefits they received from the unemployment compensation agencies which ruled that they were available for work while in training.

Unemployment compensation agencies who pay benefits to unemployed workers on a short layoff without requiring them to be available for other work aid in preserving an employer's labor supply.[27] Although this can have little effect upon the total labor supply it does tend to keep workers where they are needed.

Particularly as the result of experience rating plans, which often make an employer's tax depend upon the unemployment benefits drawn by his former workers, unemployment compensation does have some effect upon the demand for labor. Since even workers who quit without good cause may, in many states, draw benefits against the employer's account after serving out a disqualification period, unemployment compensation furnishes one more reason for employers to try to secure "stable" workers. The primary justification for experience rating has been that it would induce employers to plan their operations so as to stabilize employment. The intervention of the war period prevented any real test of this contention. To the extent that the tax incentives of experience rating do stimulate regularization of employment, the unemployment compensation system does have a direct effect upon the demand for labor and, in turn, upon the supply.

CHAPTER IV

ORGANIZING THE SEARCH FOR WORK

How the availability requirement is administered depends in large measure upon what facilities exist to help workers to find jobs and employers to find workers. These facilities will determine what activity is reasonably to be expected of a claimant in search of work. One significant question, in recent years, has been: What search for work ought to be required of a claimant in fulfillment of the availability provision? More fundamentally, the existing placement machinery will control and condition the practical meaning of the availability requirement. Only if facilities exist to assure that claimants will be regularly and frequently exposed to suitable work opportunities can there be any real meaning in the test of availability for work. Such exposure is the best test of availability for work.

THE NEED FOR LABOR-MARKET ORGANIZATION

The need to systematize our placement and hiring facilities has a broader basis than unemployment compensation. That need has its roots in the complexities of our economic life and addresses itself to such questions as minimizing unemployment, reducing job turnover, and attaining more successful job relationships. The recurring phenomenon of groups of unemployed workers and unfilled jobs existing side by side is often a result of inadequacies in our placement system. Again, truly matching workers and jobs is, for the most part, a goal we have yet to achieve.

Employer Needs

In peacetime the need for placement organization is more likely to be felt by workers, than by employers. Employers, however, have a continuing need for the aid of an employment service, both in peace and in war. Small employers can seldom afford an adequate personnel department. Attracting applicants is often expensive. In sparsely settled areas, employers sometimes need more workers than the locality can supply. When this is true, as in the case of construction contractors, lumber camps, and the like, methods must be found to tap the resources of a state, a region, sometimes of the nation.

Needless to say, in times of worker shortage the employer must often use "outside" help to get employees. Even during a depression, a hiring employer may find pre-selection and referral by a competent, outside agency helpful. It assists him to do his necessary hiring without the undesirable and time-consuming work of interviewing and rejecting countless job seekers. A service that can select, for consideration in hiring, the best qualified of the available workers, aids an employer to develop an efficient work force and to reduce labor turnover. The 1947 manufacturing quit rate of 40.7 per cent indicates the seriousness of this turnover.[1]

Worker Needs

Usually it is the worker who is most in need of the benefits of labor-market organization. Where to find a job? Throughout his working life, the ordinary worker is periodically bedeviled by this question. From his first entry into the labor market, finding a job is a problem for him. As he grows older he can expect to hunt for work again and again. Always it is bewildering to him. Even in "good times" there are so many places to look, so many methods to try, that the search for work is apt to be far more tedious and burdensome than work itself.[2]

With the growth of the public employment services, some of the confusion has been dissipated for the experienced, unemployed worker. But only some of it. The experienced worker knows that the public employment office is not yet the sole, or even the major channel of job opportunities. Numerous other ways remain to find work and the unemployed worker in need of a job may find the hunt for work almost as confusing and taxing as it was before the present national network of employment services. The "hawking of labor" from door to door which Beveridge decried forty years ago continues as the principal method of obtaining employment.

For some workers and in some occupations almost the only practical means of making an intelligent search for work is through some central agency. The unemployed stranger in a new city, without such assistance, can hardly be expected to find his way to a job except through luck. The specialized worker whose work opportunities are scattered over a wide area with never more than a few in any one place usually finds a personal canvass an impossibility. School teachers are usually in this class. So are many heavy construction workers. In some occupations job opportunities may be physically scattered over an entire city — watchmen, elevator men, domestics, stenographers. A personal search for a job may, in such cases, be almost as wasteful as in the case of a rural school teacher trying to find a new job. Some individuals are good workers, but poor job hunters. This is often true of older workers who have had few spells of joblessness.

In addition, from the earliest studies of unemployment to the present, it has been clear that employment service aid is important to workers suffering from some disability — whether it be women because of their sex, the physically handicapped because of their infirmity, or the merely inefficient because of their unproductivity. It is upon these workers that the onus of unemployment falls most frequently. (When this is said, it must in fairness be noted that their unemployment is mainly the result of some factor in the business of their employer, rather than their own special disability. Their disability may do no more than prompt their employer to impose upon them, rather than other workers, the layoffs he feels required to make. Often their lack of job seniority exposes them to layoffs. Frequently this is causally connected with their disability.)

When job-seeking morale has been destroyed by prolonged or repeated unemployment, the counteracting influence of an outside placement agency can be most helpful to catalogue the worker's strengths and weaknesses and help him find employment where he can capitalize upon his qualifications. It is futile to expect the long unemployed worker to be able to do this by himself.[3]

JOB-FINDING METHODS

How does the unemployed worker find a job? A 1932 survey of over four thousand Philadelphia hosiery workers showed that more than half found work through friends or relatives; over a fifth got jobs by applying at the plant. No other single method accounted for as much as 4 per cent of the successful job hunts. Only two of the entire group got their jobs through the State Employment Service, twenty-four through the Board of Public Education's Junior Placement Service.[4]

A study of two hundred unemployed workers in New Haven in 1933 found that the three most used methods were direct application at the employer's place of business (used by 77 per cent), registration at employment bureaus (used by 38 per cent), and aid from friends and relatives (used by 38 per cent). The effect of unemployment compensation upon the use of the employment service was shown in New Haven when a 1938 survey revealed the number of unemployed almost equal with those registered with the State Employment Service.[5]

The Myers and Maclaurin study of workers in two New England communities (1937–1940) showed results generally similar to those reported in Philadelphia and New Haven. They interviewed 233 workers and secured reports covering the method used in getting 694 different jobs. The aid of friends or relatives ranked first and accounted for almost 2 out of every 5 successful job contacts. A third of the jobs were acquired through direct application at the plant and over a fifth were call-backs by former employers. Only 3 of the entire 694 jobs were secured through the public employment service.[6]

There are no adequate studies showing what methods get jobs for workers since the coming of unemployment compensation. Unemployment benefit claimants must register with the public employment service. Consequently, most nonagricultural workers, when unemployed, use that service as one way of looking for work. Do the unemployed now rely primarily upon the public employment office for placement? Or do they depend upon the older, traditional methods? To this there is no adequate answer.

We know that, compared with the thirties, the public employment service is today a far more effective oganization. The ratio of public-employment-service manufacturing placements to accessions to the number of manufacturing employees was over two and one-half times greater in the years 1946 and 1947 than it was ten years earlier. But even in 1946 and 1947 less than one out of every five accessions to the manufacturing work force represented placements by the public employment service. The other workers got there in other ways.

Although such ratios are substantially accurate, they fail to give the employment service its due. Ratios of placements to accessions are loaded against the employment service because they include, among the accessions, workers called back by employers from lay-off periods. These make up a substantial but indeterminable group. Ratios of claimants to placements are similarly biased because workers on short layoffs are counted among the claimants.

These workers often do not remain claimants long enough to be referred to employment. Although such laid-off workers are numerous, the available statistics do not separate them from other applicants.[7]

Direct Application

The fact remains that workers continue to apply directly to employers — and many do get jobs that way. It may be well to note here some of the reasons why workers and employers as well often prefer to do business in this fashion.

Hiring at the gate is usually an easy method for an employer. He has only to wait for the right man to come along. When there is a labor shortage the employer is unlikely to be satisfied with such waiting. In ordinary times, however, he may expect enough workers to apply to give him a fair selection. If a job shortage exists he may be overrun by applicants. To be sought after by job applicants is often a source of pride and satisfaction to an employer. Many employers trust no outside agency—particularly one manned by public servants — to do their picking and choosing. It should also not be overlooked that the employer who hires at the gate can interview many work seekers, get the information he wants from them on their qualifications and history, without disclosing what he has to offer.

From the worker's standpoint, direct application is often a matter of necessity. Other methods may have failed. Or he may apply directly because he wants to work in a particular plant. Furthermore, job seekers often try to be early birds. If they apply at a plant without waiting for a referral, a newspaper advertisement, or a call, they may be on the ground when an opening occurs.

Applications made at places of former employment involve other impelling personal factors. The worker is familiar with the job, the pay, the other workers and the working conditions. The employer knows him, his ability, and his habits. For this reason employers who need workers often canvass their former employees directly, without using any other agency. An employee so requested to return to a job may feel a certain pride that his old boss wants him back.

Aid of Friends and Relatives

Applying for work through friends and relatives is another method that workers use and upon which employers are apt to rely. The unemployed worker tends to turn first for assistance to the people he knows best. Utterly aside from the "influence" or "pull" (often an important element in his thinking) he may hope they can and will use to help him, the job hunter is apt to think of this method as a friendly, "homey" way to overcome the usual impersonality and red tape of the hiring process. He may think this approach gives him a higher social status both as job seeker and new worker. He is not just another worker looking for a job or starting in at the shop; he is Jack Smith's cousin or Jack Smith's friend who is looking for work or coming into the plant.

Many employers make a point of hiring upon the recommendation of their workers. Not only do they believe it makes for good employee morale; they also feel that their workers will not risk their own standing by making unworthy recommendations. This is especially true in small establishments. Even in large plants, however, foremen and other supervisors tend to help workers get their friends into the plant.

Commercial Agencies

Before the depression the United States had some three to four thousand fee-charging employment agencies.[8] The last Census of Business, however, showed 1424 private employment agencies that operated in 1939 with total receipts for the year of over 7.8 million dollars. The actual and potential abuses by fee-charging agencies have often led to public pressures for their regulation. Excessive fees, fees obtained by misrepresentation and fraud, fee-splitting with employers and their supervisory staffs, were but some of the evils that led to state regulation. Although complete regulation of the activities of such agencies, including the fees they may charge, has been sanctioned by the United States Supreme Court, the protections of the Fourteenth Amendment prevent their abolition or the destruction of their power to charge a fee.[9]

As profit-making ventures, fee-charging agencies have necessarily confined themselves to those communities and those industries and occupations where money could be made. As a result, in many cities and some states there are no such agencies. In a number of Southern states, laws designed to curtail recruitment of unskilled labor for out-of-state work have prevented the spread of private employment agencies. In addition, since they are private ventures, independently operated and usually individually owned, they work separately from each other and sometimes at cross-purposes.

Nonprofit Agencies

Fraternal, religious, and philanthropic organizations have sponsored nonprofit employment agencies, often in connection with relief activities. Such agencies have helped to counteract the abuses of the commercial ventures and to develop public interest in placement, but they have never covered a significant portion of the labor market. Furthermore, the stigma of charity has too often vitiated their enterprise. The workers and the jobs they have handled have often been low grade. Their activities have been worker slanted. Most of their work has been in periods of heavy unemployment, helping men find jobs. Helping employers find workers has not been a continuing part of their operation. Their efforts in placing workers laboring under disabilities — the physically handicapped, ex-convicts, older workers, Negroes, and labor force entrants — have been educational and have often exceeded the efforts of the public employment service.

Nonprofit agencies have also been operated by schools, colleges, and professional societies. Excluding the junior placement activities of public schools, these have generally operated in the professional and managerial occupations. Except for the commercial teachers' agencies, nurses' registries, and a few specialized commercial agencies in our largest cities, these nonprofit agencies have had little organized competition. In recent years, however, the public employment services have been reaching into these fields.

Unions and Employer Organizations

Trade unions function both as organized and unorganized employment mediums. All of them share the purpose of trying to keep their members in employment. In some instances they have sought to discharge that purpose through formal employment bureaus. In the main, however, the work is done informally by the business agent. From the working members and from his employer contacts he learns of openings for unemployed union brothers. In unionized industries the union becomes a major placement agency. In the building trades, for example, contractors ordinarily call the union office for new workers. The West Coast longshore hiring halls are union operated.

On the employer's side, trade associations have, in turn, sponsored employment bureaus. These have seldom been broad enough to dominate an industry. In the past, such bureaus have often been motivated by antiunion bias and have attempted to operate blacklists of "union agitators." [10]

Newspaper Advertising

Newspaper advertising is frequently used by employers seeking help. During the years 1932–1936 the Philadelphia newspapers carried a total of over 2.7 million lines of help-wanted advertisements. Over the same period the Philadelphia offices of the State Employment Services received a total of 67,561 job openings and made 47,415 placements.[11] In New York City, in 1940, the State Employment Service made over 159,000 private placements. In the same year three New York City newspapers (the *Times, Herald-Tribune,* and *Journal-American*) carried well over 214,000 help-wanted advertisements.[12]

Employers use newspaper advertising for a variety of reasons — to get quick results, to get and keep a constant flow of applicants, to obtain favorable advertising, to get applicants without telling too much about the job being offered. That such advertising may often produce considerable labor turnover has been recognized in both world wars when employer and government action of a "voluntary" nature was taken to regulate it. In addition newspaper advertising is expensive and, of course, tends to increase the waste that goes with gate hiring. Workers are sometimes wary of newspaper advertisements because of a feeling that there is a "catch" to them. Although newspaper advertising has at times been abused, many established and respectable employers use it regularly as a major device for attracting new workers.

Public Employment Offices

When World War I began there were ninety-six public employment offices. These were municipal and state enterprises. There had been little effective federal activity. During World War I the United States Employment Service was administratively created. By the time of the Armistice the U.S.E.S. was operating over eight hundred offices.

With the end of World War I the United States Employment Service was rapidly shorn of its power, its personnel, and its purse. The 1919 expenditures had been close to 5.7 million dollars. From

1921 to 1930 the annual appropriation never exceeded $225,000. A third to a half of this money went to the states in cash subsidies for public employment offices. The rest was devoted to gathering and publishing labor-market information and operating the Farm Labor Bureau. Until the passage of the Wagner-Peyser Act of 1933 the United States Employment Service remained in the doldrums. In 1931 the Department of Labor undertook to expand and reorganize the Federal Service. This was done, however, with little regard for existing state facilities. Although expenditures for the Federal Service were increased, because of the duplication of service that resulted, there was little real gain.

Wagner-Peyser Act

The Wagner-Peyser Act, which became law in June 1933, was the culmination of many years' effort to achieve a national employment service on a federal-state basis. This law provided for apportionment of federal moneys to the states upon the basis of their population. No payment was to be made to a state unless it made the same amount available to its employment service. To get the benefits of the act, states were also required to designate an agency to coöperate with the United States Employment Service, submit and have approved by the director of that service plans for operating the state's public employment office system.

Certifications might be revoked or withheld upon a finding by the federal agency that a state agency had not properly spent its money under the approved plan. It was accordingly also the duty of the Director of the United States Employment Service to prescribe rules, regulations, and standards of efficiency for the conduct of state employment offices and to ascertain whether such offices were being operated according to those rules and standards.

Upon the United States Employment Service were placed the duties of developing a national system of employment offices, for men, women, and juniors, and of maintaining a veterans' employment service and a farm placement service. It was clear, however, that the role of the federal agency was one of aiding and fostering. Direct placement work was to be the province of the states. Coördination, development of standards and procedures for operation, gathering and publishing information on employment, and maintaining a system for interstate clearance of labor — these were the active roles the federal agency was directed to assume.

At the time the Wagner-Peyser Act was passed there were 23

state employment services operating 192 offices in 120 cities. Within two years all these state systems but one became affiliated with the United States Employment Service. With the advent of unemployment compensation, after the passage of the Social Security Act in 1935, the other states soon organized employment services and affiliated them with the federal agency. By the end of 1938 all the states had been brought within the orbit of the system.

During this period the United States Employment Service carried on an extended program of occupational research. Begun in 1935, these studies bore real fruit in 1940. In May 1940 the *Dictionary of Occupational Titles* was published. This historic reference book listed 29,744 occupational titles and defined each in terms of what the worker does. An *Occupational Code,* based upon a decimal classification, grouped the occupations in terms of successive levels of industrial and skill combinations. Job descriptions were prepared which give the information about the essential content of each occupation. These were intended to help in identifying the occupational characteristics of work applicants and of specific job openings. They outlined the items of information that should be recorded about applicants in order to anticipate the requirements that an employer would be likely to demand. Proficiency tests for experienced or trained workers were also developed. In 1940, trade questions for 139 occupations were installed in 358 offices, work-sample tests in 214 offices. Aptitude test batteries for 48 occupations and 3 groups of occupations were also developed.

Social Security Act

The growth of the unemployment compensation system during these years and the close integration it required with employment service resulted in the merger of the two systems, in most states, in a single agency. The needs of the state employment offices for efficient service to unemployment compensation claimants were recognized by the Social Security Board which made grants to the states, separate from Wagner-Peyser funds, for expansion and operation of the state employment offices. Social Security grants soon became the principal source of revenue of the state employment services, being several times as great as the federal money supplied under the Wagner-Peyser Act. As a result, state agencies soon complained of the necessity of dealing with two different federal organizations. In 1939, by presidential order, the United States Employment Service was transferred to the Social Security Board.

The United States Employment Service then became a division of the newly organized Bureau of Employment Security, under the Social Security Board.

World War II

World War II began the same year that the United States Employment Service was transferred to the Social Security Board. In March 1941 the Bureau of Employment Security began a voluntary registration of workers for national defense. Twelve days after the Pearl Harbor attack, President Roosevelt requested the states to submit their employment services to nationalization. In January 1942 the fifteen hundred public employment offices were under federal operation.

At the same time the Director of the Bureau of Employment Security became the Chief of the Labor Supply Branch of the Office of Production Management. This proved but one of a series of interim organizational steps. Before the year 1942 was out the President, by executive order, created the War Manpower Commission, and, in September, transferred the United States Employment Service to it. In December the Selective Service System also became a part of the manpower agency.

Throughout the war the primary task of the employment service was what it had always been: placement. But the war brought it into new fields. The emphasis was upon service to war industry. As a natural result, nonwar employers were neglected. In many areas, these "nonessential" employers received no service from the employment offices for the duration of the war. Since many of the unemployment compensation claimants of the time were older men and women with no usable war-work skills, the employment offices were often criticized for failing to refer claimants to suitable job opportunities.

Various expedients were adopted to achieve employment stabilization. The occupational deferment from military service became a prodding tool to keep war workers in their jobs and get other workers with war-work skills into war jobs. Attempts were made to channel all war-work hiring through the employment offices. War workers who left their jobs without the approval of the War Manpower Commission were limited in their reëmployment opportunities.

The war-time achievements of the employment service are all the more remarkable when it is realized that, of all the major participants in the war, ours was the only country that had no national-service legislation. The employment services came out of the war expanded and strengthened. In the last year of the war almost 600 new local offices were added. The staff numbered 23,000. As the nation turned to reconversion, the United States Employment Service sought to emphasize a six-point program: labor market analysis and information, employment counseling, personnel management services to employers, placement service, special services to veterans, and coöperation with other community organizations and services.

Reconversion

The war ended in August 1945. The following month the War Manpower Commission was dissolved. The United States Employment Service was transferred, but not to the Social Security Board. Instead, it went to the Department of Labor. President Truman fought hard to continue the nationalized service during the reconversion period, at least through the first six months of 1947. He was defeated in this, and employment offices were returned to the states in mid-November 1946.

In an effort to strengthen the Labor Department, the President made two attempts to extend the wartime location of the United States Employment Service in the Labor Department. Both these reorganization plans were defeated by the Eightieth Congress. By rider to the 1948–49 appropriation bill, over the President's veto, the Congress forced the return of the U.S.E.S. from the Labor Department to the Social Security Administration's Bureau of Employment Security. The Eighty-first Congress reversed this action and approved a Presidential reorganization plan which in August 1949 transferred the Bureau of Employment Security, including the U.S.E.S., to the Labor Department.

EMPLOYMENT SERVICE AND UNEMPLOYMENT
COMPENSATION

Work Test

The effective operation of the public employment service, it has always been recognized, is essential to the unemployment compensation program. The functions of the public employment offices are, to be sure, not limited to serving the unemployment compensation system. Neither is their unemployment compensation service, properly understood, a mere application of a work test.

The main value of employment service to unemployment compensation lies in its ability to reduce the number of beneficiaries by the prompt filling of openings. To the extent that it can speed up the re-employment process by shortening the interval between the time when an opening arises and the time when it is filled, the employment service will lessen the drain upon the compensation fund.[13]

It is obvious that ordinarily no country wishes to pay benefits to claimants without having some reasonable assurance that they are being fully exposed to existing opportunities for suitable work. It is also generally agreed that the right to unemployment compensation should be limited to workers who are unemployed primarily because of their inability to find such work. The most satisfactory way of determining whether a claimant meets such a test is by offering him suitable work.

For several reasons this is often impossible. One reason is that there may be more unemployed workers than available jobs. This is a year-round phenomenon in depression times. Seasonal unemployment brings it yearly to many trades and many communities. Second, the employment office may be unaware of many of the available job openings. We have noted that in peacetime the public employment offices make a fifth or less of the placements and that jobs offered through other media may equal or exceed the openings communicated to the employment service. Third, if the public employment service is to keep and to increase the number of its employer-customers, it must send only well qualified applicants when it fills employers' orders. When there are more men than jobs this is likely to mean no referrals for the poorly qualified.[14]

A review of the occupations of over 39,000 applicants in the Saint Louis office in 1933–34 showed that 71 per cent were in 4 occupational groups — clerical, sales, building trades, and laborers. At the time there were 5 applicants for every clerical job, 4 for every sales job, 5 for every job in the building trades, and 12 for every laborer's job.[15]

More recently, a study made in August 1946 of unemployed workers and job opportunities in Rhode Island showed three experienced claimants for every skilled-crafts job and twenty-one experienced claimants for every professional or managerial job.[16] In 1946 the employment service in Rhode Island had a choice of referring many skilled workers to less skilled jobs or not referring them at all. In 1933–34 the Saint Louis office had no choice in the case of many laborer-applicants. It had nothing for them.

This situation would produce a dilemma if the work test were made the exclusive test of availability for work. The well qualified claimant would get the job referrals. If he refused such referrals, as he sometimes would, he would run the risk of benefit disqualification or ineligibility. The poorly qualified claimant, who is more likely to be on the fringe of the labor force, would receive few or no job referrals. His willingness to work would be untested and, if he chose, he might draw his benefits without ever trying to get a job. This dilemma can never be completely avoided in unemployment compensation. Three general methods have been employed to combat it. Two have operated from the unemployment compensation side of the administration. These have been (1) interviews and questionnaires concerning the claimants' circumstances and willingness to work, and (2) requirements that claimants make an independent search for work. The third method has been the indirect one of trying to increase the number of job openings referred to the employment service.

The foregoing comments have indicated the public employment service policy of basing job referral priorities solely upon registrant qualifications. This has been true ever since the public employment service, as we know it today, has been in operation. That fitness for the job is the criterion for referral is an achievement that can be appreciated only when previous practices in public employment offices are recalled. This has meant that employed and unemployed registrants are given equal consideration. No referral priority is given to unemployment compensation claimants or to claimants most in need of work or longest unemployed. These are policy decisions that are warranted to increase an employer's confidence in the public employment service as a supplier of competent workers. But it does mean that additional or special employment assistance is necessary to aid those claimants who, because of this policy, do not get a fair number of referrals.

A North Carolina survey of 5384 veteran claimants reporting in August 1946, all of whom had been unemployed for 20 or more consecutive weeks, revealed that 3935 of them (67.4 per cent) had received no referral during their entire unemployment. It would seem that, aside from the availability problems involved, such claimants were not receiving the employment counseling and assistance they needed. The period of the survey was one of job plenty. The claimants' civilian occupations were, in one-fifth of the cases, agriculture, forestry, or fishing, in one-fourth of the cases, semiskilled work, and in a little less than a fourth, unskilled work. By military occupations, 27.5 per cent were semiskilled and 40.9 per cent were unskilled. Very few of them had been interested in job training — less than 1 out of 6 had either completed or was attending or awaiting job training. Such circumstances raise real questions as to the effectiveness of the employment service.[17]

Placement Effectiveness

The percentages of manufacturing hires that are effected through the employment service have already been noted. It should be stressed that the record here is one of improvement. It has been estimated that in 1935–36 employment services placements were only 5 per cent of total factory accessions and 8 per cent in 1936–37.[18] During the late war it hovered around 50 per cent; in 1946 the ratio was 18.4 per cent and in 1947 it was 19.3 per cent.

There is good reason to suppose this ratio will improve. Before the war, the public employment offices were the recruiting agencies for the service industries, especially domestic service, and for unskilled labor. In 1933–34 manufacturing absorbed but 18.4 per cent of the nonagricultural private placements of the public employment offices (excluding forestry and fishing); in 1935–36 it accounted for 19.8 per cent. During the war manufacturing placements were the bulk of the employment service's work. It was then that the personnel of the employment service established working relationships that should stand the peacetime system in good stead. That manufacturing employers, at least in the first flush of peacetime reconversion, relied upon the employment services for assistance in getting workers, was indicated by the fact that over half of the nonagricultural placements (excluding forestry and fishing) made in October to December 1945, were in manufacturing. In 1946, manufacturing placements were 40.2 per cent of nonfarm placements; in 1947, they were down to 34.8 per cent.[20]

The effectiveness of the employment service may be measured in other ways. One is by analyzing the reasons for canceled openings. Such studies seldom appear in print. One of the few that have been released covered canceled openings in the public employment offices of New York State in 1935. In that year 26.7 per cent (39,329) of the openings in private industry placed with the public offices for filling were canceled. Analysis of the reasons for these cancellations showed that in 4868 cases (12.4 per cent) no applicant was referred by the office and the opening was filled through other sources. In 12,001 cases (30.5 per cent) the office referred an applicant but the opening was filled from another source. In 4595 cases (11.7 per cent) the opening was withdrawn by the employer and the job not filled. In 2613 cases (6.6 per cent) there was no qualified applicant available and the office canceled the opening. Other reasons included: insufficient time to contact the applicant (2.8 per cent), inability to interest the applicant because of the distance to the job, poor working conditions or pay (30.8 per cent), applicant referred by the office but failed to report to the employer (0.1 per cent).[21]

Labor-Market Information

An especially important aspect of the work of the public employment office is in the field of labor-market information and analysis. This work is necessary not only for efficient internal operation; it also fills a basic need of employers and workers. It is, moreover, a key element in availability determinations which must be geared to the current labor-market situation.

One important and controversial phase of labor-market analysis is determining prevailing wages, hours, and other working conditions. State unemployment compensation laws and the Social Security Act enjoin the denial of benefits to claimants who refuse jobs that offer them substantially less than the wages, hours, or other conditions prevailing for similar work in the locality. Unemployment compensation agencies have, in administering this provision, generally relied upon the employment offices (1) not to make referrals to jobs that did not offer prevailing wages, hours, or other conditions, and (2) to furnish information in contested cases as to what wages, hours, and other conditions prevail for the work in the locality. Real doubts exist as to how well the employment offices have discharged these responsibilities. In many instances, it seems clear, the employment service's advice has been based primarily upon the openings reported to it which are likely not to represent a fair sample of the jobs in the locality.

As a result, the federal Bureau of Employment Security has attempted to point out to state unemployment compensation agencies that there are other informational sources that may and should be used in determining prevailing work conditions.[22] In New York the unemployment compensation agency has recently made this a special, continuing project of its Bureau of Research and Statistics. Although the task is difficult, studies such as these would seem a responsibility of the employment service, which has a duty both to workers and employers to be able to give them reasonably accurate and complete labor-market information. Other governmental agencies do have responsibilities in this field but they generally operate on a state, regional, or national basis. Industrial groups gather information as well. The employment service, in President Roosevelt's words, the "corner grocery store" of employment, must have this information, properly dated and packaged, on its shelves.

Job Counseling

Hand in hand with the labor-market informational task goes the job counseling function. Often an unemployed worker's greatest need is sound advice, impartial and informed. This is obviously true in the case of inexperienced workers. Its truth is underlined in every period of labor-market turmoil. During the last week of September and the month of October 1946, the New York State Employment Service conducted a veterans job-counseling survey. Questionnaires had been sent to 44,000 veteran-claimants in the New York City area who had drawn 20 or more benefit checks. On the basis of their returns 6100 of these veterans were held unavailable for work. From the remainder 6500 were selected for concentrated job counseling during the period named. During this time 14 per cent of *all* veteran claimants interviewed in the New York City area were referred to jobs and 6 per cent were placed. Of the 6500 who had received special counseling, 50 per cent were referred to jobs and 20 per cent were placed.[23]

Employment Office Routine

Exposure of unemployment compensation claimants to suitable work opportunities, the best test of availability for work, depends upon employment office success in a number of different operations, some of them of a routine nature. Taking employers' orders over the telephone is an exercise in tact, imagination, and occupational knowledge.[24] Getting complete, detailed information about job requirements is essential not only for filling the employer's order but also for determining later whether the claimant who refuses the job is refusing suitable work. All too often the only information available on the jobs which a claimant has refused consists of the employer's name, the job title, the pay, and the hours. This much information the worker can get from a help-wanted advertisement. The employment office should be able to tell him the plant conditions, the general state of the equipment, what steps have been taken to prevent accidents, the sanitation facilities, and so on.

Another employment office operation, even more basic for availability administration, is good interviewing and coding. Without it proper referral is impossible. The public employment service, as we have noted, has the tools to do the job. Sometimes it does not have the people — since 1941 personnel turnover in the public employment offices has been large and constant. Sometimes the employment offices lack the time to do the job. A member of the staff of a California local office has described the impact of demobilization:

We were already taxed to the limit with the huge numbers of displaced war workers who had been crowding into the office since shortly after V–J day. To cope with the problem of handling loads far out of proportion to our office space, facilities, and personnel, we planned and devised various means. Registration interviews were scheduled by appointment. Monitored and self-registration methods were adopted. Streamlined, almost skeleton applications were taken. Speed became the watchword.[25] [But the results were] a huge number of veteran applicants being incorrectly or inadequately classified and coded.

A review of 5104 veteran cards in the active file showed, by the internal evidence of the cards, about one-fifth (906) that were inadequately or improperly classified and coded. When the time cannot be found, as it fortunately was in this case, to reinterview such registrants, their opportunity for proper referrals can be practically written off.

Early in 1948, the New York Advisory Council complained that the New York City employment offices were not actually registering claimants for work. Instead the employment offices were merely checking claimants' insurance cards to show that they had reported. This procedure reduced the employment service's file of job applicants and made it impossible to "call in" claimants to refer them to available jobs.[26]

GENERAL CONCLUSIONS

At this juncture the following points should be stressed:

1. The real business of a public employment office is proper placement. The burden of testing the good faith of a benefit claimant should not be its primary task. When such a test takes place — and it should happen often — it is as a by-product of the main job of the employment service. In some cases there will be few or no referrals. The unemployment compensation agency must then decide the claim on other bases.

2. The public employment office is not the only or the major way to a job. It has a substantial but not a preponderant number of the total job openings. Its placements appear to be a substantial percentage but not nearly a majority of the total hirings. There is a great deal of difference here among occupations and industries about which we have almost no information.

3. The public employment office is a major source of labor-market information. This is important for employers. It is even more important for workers and for unemployment benefit administration. By the labor-market information it gathers and dispenses, the employment office may do much to control worker mobility. Its data on the labor market are the basic prerequisites for determining whether or not a claimant is available for work.

4. The public employment office is the most important social device we have for improving the hiring process. It is intended and, on the whole, operated to place workers in the jobs for which they are suited. To the extent that it does this, the employment service makes a valuable contribution to employment stability. As such the employment service has a right to expect that unemployment compensation will be so administered as to strengthen rather than weaken the public employment offices.

CHAPTER V

STATUTORY PROVISIONS

UP TO THIS POINT we have centered our attention on what may be termed, in a broad sense, the economic and social background of availability for work. This and the remaining chapters will deal specifically with availability for work as a legal requirement to be eligible for unemployment benefits. This will involve discussions of statutory provisions and of "principles" or "doctrines" that are derived by interpreting the statutory provisions.

The availability requirements that affect unemployment benefit claimants in the United States and its territories are state and territorial laws. Each of the forty-eight states has an unemployment compensation law, passed by its state legislature. Alaska and Hawaii operate under unemployment compensation laws passed by their territorial legislatures. Only in the case of the District of Columbia did the federal Congress provide an unemployment compensation law. The Social Security Act and the federal unemployment tax provisions of the Internal Revenue Code, which prompted almost all the state unemployment compensation laws, make no provision for payment of benefits to claimants. Neither do they establish any eligibility requirements which claimants must satisfy.

Instead the federal laws provide for a 3 per cent tax on the payrolls of employers of eight or more, with certain employments excluded from tax. Employers covered by the federal tax are allowed to use the taxes paid by them under a state unemployment compensation law, which has been approved by the Labor Department, as a credit, up to 90 per cent, against the federal tax. In order for a state law to be approved for this purpose it must contain certain provisions specified in the Internal Revenue Code. Of these provisions the only ones that affect state laws and administration on availability problems are those which protect labor standards (discussed later in this chapter) and those which provide that all compensation must be paid through public employment offices or such other agencies as the Labor Department may approve.

To each state with a law approved for federal unemployment tax credit purposes, the Social Security Act further provides that federal grants shall be made of the amounts necessary for proper and efficient administration of the state's unemployment compensation law. In order to qualify for such grants, the Social Security Act specifies, among other provisions, that the state law must provide methods of administration that are "reasonably calculated to insure full payment of benefits when due." Furthermore, if the Labor Department finds that in the administration of a state law benefits are denied, in a substantial number of cases, to individuals who are entitled to benefits under the state law, administrative grants may also be denied to the state. Such provisions may bring the influence of the Labor Department into availability administration as, for example, in a case where a state agency refuses to pay benefits to claimants who were clearly available under the state law, as interpreted by the highest state authority. As is obvious, such instances are so rare that they almost never occur.

The practical result is that determination of availability for work under American unemployment compensation laws is exclusively a state function. Necessarily, then, we shall discuss the pertinent provisions of numerous state laws. In addition to those provisions which deal specifically with availability, other portions of the statutes which have a bearing upon availability and its administration will also be considered.

It should be noted that, except where otherwise indicated, the reference is to laws in effect November 30, 1949.

ELIGIBILITY PROVISIONS

Aside from the requirement that a claimant be available for work, the unemployment compensation laws, in general, require him to meet the following eligibility conditions: (1) he must have worked in insured employment; (2) he must have earned, within a fixed and recent period of time, a specified amount of wages in such employment or been employed a specific number of weeks (sometimes both); (3) he must register for work at a public employment office.

These statutory conditions are directly connected with labor-force attachment.[1] They have, in addition, other purposes. The first two, which deal with earnings or employment in insured work, stem from the financing methods used for unemployment compensation. They are intended to make and keep a close tie between the sources of unemployment compensation funds and their expenditure. Claimants receive no compensation unless a fixed minimum premium has been paid on their account. The compulsory registration for work adds to the effectiveness of the public employment service. It ensures the employment office a supply of workers to help meet employer orders. In the case of all three requirements, however, the measurement of labor-force attachment is an important element. The insured wage and employment requirements seek to measure past labor force attachment. The registration for work is a practical test which the claimant can meet only by an overt act.

Covered Employment

What is insured work is, in general, determined by two types of statutory provisions — specific exclusions of certain kinds of work and size-of-firm requirements. Under the first category, the pattern is largely set by the Federal Unemployment Tax Act although there have been numerous individual state variations. The federal law does not apply to such types of work as agricultural labor, domestic service, service for certain relatives, government employment, service for certain nonprofit organizations, casual labor which is not in the course of the employer's business, commission insurance agents and solicitors, and newsboys under eighteen years of age. Maritime employment has also in the past usually been excluded. The Social Security Act Amendments of 1946, however, extended the federal tax to private maritime employment and authorized the states to make similar extensions.

From the start, the federal tax has been applicable only to those employers (in covered employment) who had at least eight workers for at least one day in each of twenty weeks during the tax year. In most of the states coverage has gone beyond this. In twenty-two states, including about 30 per cent of the insured workers, the eight-worker coverage base is used. Eight states are on a four-worker base. These contain about 24 per cent of the insured workers. Sixteen states, including almost 30 per cent of the covered workers, are on a one-worker basis.[2] Size of payroll is used as an additional test of coverage in four states, as an alternative test in six states, and as the sole test in two states.

The excluded employments and the size-of-firm provisions in the laws bear little relation to any reasonable measure of labor force attachment. Other considerations explain their presence in the statutes. In the main, they were prompted by a desire to ease the initial administrative burdens of installing unemployment compensation systems in this country. Regardless of the reasons for them, however, these portions of the laws create artificial definitions of past labor-force attachment which a claimant must meet. Having been a steady worker for a government agency will do the claimant no good when he seeks benefits. Nor, in most states, will it be any help to him to demonstrate years of service in a one-employee grocery store.

During the year ending June 30, 1947, unemployment compensation coverage extended to some 32 million workers — 30.4 million under state unemployment compensation laws, 1.6 million under the Railroad Unemployment Insurance Act. It has been estimated that an additional 12.4 million wage earners, well over a quarter of the national total, are excluded from coverage.[3]

Earning and Employment Qualifications

Base Period

The earnings requirement to qualify for minimum benefits is the most important test used by American unemployment compensation laws to determine past labor-force attachment. The earnings considered for benefit eligibility are those of a specified period of time (usually called the base period) preceding the date when an insured worker files a claim for benefits.

In fourteen states a uniform base period is used with yearly beginning and ending dates fixed in the law for all workers.[4] Usually it is a calendar-year period. The other states have an individual base period, whose beginning and ending dates depend upon when an insured worker first files a claim for benefits. That first filing begins a one-year period which is called the benefit year.[5] In all but six of the states using an individual base period, the base period is the first four of the last five calendar quarters that precede the benefit year. Missouri has the longest base period, the first eight of the last nine calendar quarters preceding the benefit year. The shortest are in Nebraska and Utah (the four most recently completed calendar quarters) and in Michigan and Wisconsin (the one-year period immediately preceding the benefit year). California has a modified individual base period. For benefit years beginning November 1 to January 31 it is the four calendar quarters ending the preceding June; for benefit years beginning February 1 to

March 31 the base period is the four calendar quarters ending the preceding September, and so on.

No state, it will be seen, goes back more than two and a half years in determining benefit eligibility. In most states whether or not a worker has been attached to the labor force is determined by his wage record during a period no further back than eighteen months. Administrative expediency explains the brevity of the base period. With all proper regard for the administrative burdens of unduly increasing the base period, good reason exists for some lengthening. Certainly it should be done in the case of workers who have been incapacitated for prolonged periods or who can demonstrate that they have worked in noncovered employment.

In Oregon the base period is extended for incapacitated workers, with no such base-period extension going beyond four calendar quarters. Some justification also exists for counting weeks of benefits as part of the qualifying period of labor-force attachment. If this is done such weeks should be given less value than periods of employment — four or three weeks of benefits being considered the equivalent of one week of employment.

Earnings Qualifications

In the fifty-one jurisdictions operating unemployment compensation systems under the Social Security Act the base-period earnings required to qualify for minimum benefits are $100 or lower in seven cases; requirements in fifteen states are in the $101–$150 bracket; in six they are in the $151–$200 bracket; in nine they are in the $201–$250 bracket. One state requires $270 and eleven require minimal base-period wages of $300 or more.[6] How fair a measurement of labor-force attachment are these earnings requirements? Obviously nowhere are they high enough to eliminate the occasional worker. As earnings qualifications are made higher, however, they eliminate more of the poorly paid but steadily employed workers.

Employment Qualifications

Most early American unemployment compensation laws required, in addition to the qualifying earnings, that the claimant should have worked in insured employment for a certain number of weeks within the base period. This has disappeared from all the state laws except those of Michigan, Ohio, Utah, and Wisconsin. Ohio requires, in addition to minimal base period earnings of $160, employment in at least twenty calendar weeks. Wisconsin requires employment in fourteen weeks within the fifty-two preceding the end of the most recent week of employment. In Utah nineteen weeks of employment in the base period are required. Michigan requires fourteen weeks' employment within the year preceding the benefit year, each at an average weekly wage exceeding $8. *

Missouri requires earnings in at least three calendar quarters of the base period. Seven states require earnings in at least two calendar quarters — Arizona, Connecticut, Florida, Idaho, Indiana, Texas, and Utah. The remaining states impose no limitations upon the time which the nonseasonal worker need be employed in the base period.[7] He qualifies for benefits if he earns the required minimum amount, whether he takes one week or twenty weeks in the base period to do it.

Desirability of Length-of-Employment Test

The abandonment after 1936 of weeks of employment as a measurement of eligibility was based upon considerations of administrative expediency. Today the tide seems to be going the other way. In discussing one of two proposed plans for changing benefit formulas and simplifying wage records, the Bureau of Employment Security has stated: "Employment provides a better test of prior attachment than earnings, because it is more uniform in its application." [8]

There seems little doubt that this is the case. We raise earnings requirements to eliminate high-paid occasional workers, at the same time eliminating low-paid, steady workers whose benefit need is greatest. If we lower the earnings requirement to include more of this latter group we reap a claim harvest from the sporadically employed. Committed as we are to a system of basing benefit amounts upon the amount of prior wages, we cannot eliminate some type of worker-wage record. It does not follow, however, that the qualification requirement for minimum benefits need be stated wholly or partly in terms of a specific amount of earnings.

It has been argued that making weeks or days of employment the basic test of qualification would mean paying some low-wage workers a higher minimum benefit than the average weekly wage they ordinarily receive. In many, if not most, American states minimum benefits are already set high in relation to the average weekly wage of claimants who barely qualify so that they sometimes receive more in weekly benefits than they did in wages.[9] Whether this is undesirable is an open question. It is certain that if benefits higher than wages are to be paid to some claimants more should be done to ensure that these payments go to individuals who are ordinarily workers or seekers of work. It is preferable that they, rather than the occasional worker, should receive the benefits.

Workers without Dependents

The history of unemployment compensation has repeatedly demonstrated the differences in the labor-force attachment of claimants who have dependents and those who do not. Under state unemployment compensation laws, married women, and under the Servicemen's Readjustment Act, unmarried veterans have furnished a highly disproportionate number of the claimants held unavailable for work. In part this may be explained by the greater ability of claimants without family obligations to get along on the weekly benefit amount. But shuttling in and out of the labor force has always been characteristic of workers without dependents. It does not stem from unemployment compensation.

A number of states have tried to prevent this from draining off unemployment compensation funds by special statutory disqualifications. These make little individual differentiation. Instead they usually bar certain classes of claimants from drawing benefits — students, pregnant women, women who quit work because of a marital obligation, and so forth. A more fruitful and just approach may be found by dividing claimants into two broad classes — those with dependents and those without. The latter might then be required to furnish greater evidence of past labor-force attachment during the base period in order to qualify for minimum benefits — more wages or, preferably, more days or weeks of employment. A longer base period for claimants without dependents may also be in order — one hundred days of employment in each of two years for such claimants, as against one hundred days in one year for other claimants, for example.

It should be stressed that, difficult as it is to arrive at a satisfactory measure of past labor-force attachment, once a test is agreed upon, its application can be mechanical and objective. This is entirely in keeping with the concept that unemployment compensation is intended to be a routine operation. Improving criteria of previous labor-force attachment decreases the burden on availability administration, which can never be as routine as the business of determining if a worker has enough days or dollars to qualify.

Registration for Work

Every unemployment compensation law requires claimants to register for work at a public employment office and to report to such an office regularly, as required. To a limited degree, this is a test of physical ability. The claimant must be physically capable of coming to the office to register. As we have noted earlier, registering for work also requires of the claimant that he perform an overt act leading to his exposure to work opportunity.

Much of the thinking on availability for work has centered upon the precise effect to be given this work registration. Is it perfunctory compliance with a statutory requirement or is it evidence of a desire to obtain work? Without going into an extended discussion at this point, it may be said that the fact that it is required as a condition of benefit entitlement does not make a claimant's registration for work meaningless. Whatever his purpose in registering, the result is to put the claimant in the way of some job opportunities. This must be granted even as we realize that a claimant does not necessarily betray an avid desire for work when he registers at the employment office in connection with his benefit claim.

Registration for work can create no more than a presumption of availability. The evidence of a claimant's availability must be found in the sum of all his circumstances — his work history, his separation from employment, his personal situation, his statements, his activities toward getting work. Most important of all, we need to look to his reaction to specific opportunities for suitable employment.

DISQUALIFICATIONS FROM BENEFITS

The distinction often made in discussions of unemployment compensation, between "ineligibility" and "disqualification," is technical and frequently fictitious. The usual statement of this distinction is somewhat as follows: an eligibility requirement is a statutory condition which a claimant must meet before being entitled to receive benefits; a disqualification is a postponement, reduction, or cancellation of the benefit rights of an already eligible claimant.

The major "standard" disqualifications are those for voluntarily leaving work without good cause, discharge for misconduct connected with work, refusal of suitable work without good cause, and unemployment due to a stoppage of work is caused by a labor dispute. In a number of American laws one or more of these is phrased in terms of "ineligibility" rather than "disqualification." [10] When a disqualification extends for the duration of a claimant's unemployment it becomes, in a sense, an availability provision. The claimant who is disqualified for the duration of his unemployment is barred from benefits until he demonstrates his labor-force attachment by a new period of employment.

"Duration" disqualifications for voluntarily leaving work without good cause under the law exist in ten states: Alabama, Delaware, Florida, Iowa, Maryland, Massachusetts, Michigan, Missouri, New Hampshire, Pennsylvania. Seven states apply duration disqualifications if the worker is discharged from employment for misconduct connected with the work: Delaware, Florida, Maryland, Massachusetts, Michigan, Missouri, Pennsylvania. Eleven disqualify workers for the duration of the unemployment if they fail to apply for or to accept work and lack legal justification: Alabama, Delaware, Florida, Iowa, Maryland, Michigan, Missouri, New York, Ohio, Pennsylvania, Wisconsin. Nebraska cancels all previous benefit rights of workers who, without good cause, fail to apply for or accept suitable work. Regardless of how these are technically termed, they are clearly bars to eligibility.

DURATION OF BENEFITS

American unemployment compensation is characterized by limited duration of benefits. No American law grants more than twenty-six weeks of benefits in a single benefit year.[11] In twenty-nine states maximum duration is between twelve and twenty benefit weeks. These are important considerations in availability administration. It means that most claimants are short-term unemployed — at least while they are applying for and drawing benefits. They are easier to place, their skills and work habits have not been lost by disuse, and their job-seeking morale is good. There are exceptions to this. Some are long unemployed. They wait through months of joblessness before claiming benefits and then apply as a last desperate resort. Some are able, because of employment in the lag between the base year end and the beginning of a benefit year, to apply for a second benefit year with no intervening employment. In some instances the intervening employment is barely enough for qualification. These two groups, however, are a minority of the claimants.

In sixteen states the minimum benefit duration for claimants who qualify is eight weeks or less. In Missouri it may be a little more than one week, five and a fraction in Massachusetts, Rhode Island, and Texas. This places a rigid time limit upon attempts to test the availability of the barely qualifying claimant. Yet long duration for these marginal beneficiaries brings problems of its own. There are fifteen states where benefit duration is uniform for all eligible claimants.[12] In nine of them the prescribed period of benefits is twenty or more weeks. In these states distinctions based upon amount of earnings remain in the weekly amount of benefits, but all claimants who qualify get benefits for the same number of weeks in the benefit year.

As a group, the uniform-benefit-duration states require somewhat higher earnings for benefit qualification than all states considered together. Their requirements, however, are not such as to eliminate the high-paid, occasional worker. A factory worker who was employed eight weeks out of fifty-two at average 1949 factory wages would easily qualify in any one of the uniform-duration states, so long as he took care to have three of those weeks in a single calendar quarter. With qualification determined by dollars rather than days of employment, long duration for the barely qualifying claimant raises availability problems. These problems would be eased by making the qualification a time test — days or weeks of employment rather than an earnings test.

UNIFORM BENEFIT YEAR

In most states the benefit year is individual. The fifty-two-week period begins to run when the worker first files a claim under which he is qualified for benefits. In thirteen states, however, the benefit year is the same for all claimants and is determined by calendar dates prescribed by law.[13] The usual beginning date is in the first week of April. During the one-year period following that beginning date insured workers may draw benefits, if unemployed, based upon their wages in the calendar year preceding the beginning of the benefit year.

The uniform base-period benefit year system has great advantages of simplicity and understandability. It does, however, create some problems in availability determination. These center around the time lag involved between base-period employment and benefits.[14] The minimum and maximum possible months of lag under an individual base-period benefit year system are: end of base period to initial claim — minimum three, maximum almost six; base period beginning to initial claim — minimum fifteen, maximum al-

most eighteen; base period end to benefit year end — minimum
fifteen, maximum almost eighteen.[15] For most uniform base-period
benefit year states the minimum months of lag are the same but the
maxima are higher for base-period end to initial claim (almost fifteen months) and base-period beginning to initial claim (almost
twenty-seven months) and lower for base-period end to benefit-
year end (fifteen months).

This greater potential lag of uniform benefit year may have an
adverse effect upon availability when earnings are falling. With
benefits based on the higher wages of over two years back the benefit amount may deter claimants from taking jobs. Furthermore this
lag has also permitted, under the uniform benefit year, some claimants to draw benefits after long periods of unbroken unemployment.

Workers who were laid off immediately after V–J Day (August
14, 1945) in states with a uniform April 1 to March 31 benefit
year drew benefits based upon 1944 wages. Without intervening
employment, such workers were able to file again in April 1946
and draw on their 1945 earnings. With an individual benefit year,
the same workers had to wait until August 1946 to file and, instead
of drawing on earnings from January 1 to August 14, 1945, could
draw only on wages accumulated in the period April 1 to August
14, 1945. By increasing the number of otherwise eligible claimants
among the long-term unemployed the uniform benefit year adds to
availability problems.

AVAILABILITY REQUIREMENTS

Just as the earnings (or employment) requirement is the major
test of the unemployment compensation of claimant's previous labor-force attachment so is the availability requirement the major
test of his current membership in the labor force. It shares this
function with the registration-for-work requirement. The latter,
however, can be met by a simple act on the claimant's part. There
is no single thing a claimant can do that will be accepted as a complete demonstration of his availability for work. It is a complex of
many elements, mostly subjective. This subjective aspect, as we
have previously noted, breeds dissatisfaction and controversy over
the availability requirement.

Underlying Assumptions

The prescription of an availability requirement in an unemployment compensation law implies the acceptance of certain basic as-

sumptions. It means, for example, agreement upon the proposition that not only past but current labor-force attachment should be probed, before benefits are paid out. Such a statement probably would command general agreement. It is not, however, entirely unassailable. Assuming that a physical-capacity test were retained, what need exists to apply a test of current labor-force attachment to workers who have established by their work history that they are ordinarily in the market for a job? Would not the work-refusal disqualification suffice to purge the rolls of claimants who will not or cannot accept suitable work? In the absence of positive work opportunities let these unemployed workers have the benefit of any doubts there may be.

There are appealing elements in such an argument. It should, however, be pointed out that, in reality, it is no argument against testing current attachment. Instead it makes previous work history the sole criterion of that present attachment. The use of the work refusal disqualification desirably accents the use of objective measures before depriving a claimant of benefits. But the work-refusal disqualification cannot be expected to keep the system clear of claimants who are in no position to take work. An example should make this clear. A claimant who refuses suitable work because he is taking care of a sick wife will ordinarily not be disqualified. He has "good cause." Under the availability requirement he will, however, be barred from benefits until he is again free to accept work.

A second basic assumption underlying the availability requirement is the belief that it is possible to make a satisfactory decision on a claimant's current attachment to the labor force. Actually, how true is that? We have some generalized agreements on the meaning of labor-force membership. Aside from those generalities and some open-and-shut cases we are embroiled in what often appears as hopeless controversy. Perhaps, for now, the assumption may be questioned. It should, however, be recognized how inexperienced we are in this field. The very term *labor force* is a product of the thirties. Before unemployment compensation our law knew no such phrase as "available for work." As we gain in experience with these questions, both in unemployment compensation operations and in other kinds of employment investigation we will reorganize our ideas and improve our knowledge of the labor force.

A third assumption is involved in the availability requirement. It is assumed that the unemployment compensation agency is the proper one to determine whether or not an unemployed worker is in the labor force. Among government agencies that might conceivably be picked for the job the unemployment compensation administration is undoubtedly well fitted for it. This is especially true when the public employment service is integrated with the unemployment compensation function. It may be questioned, however, whether testing availability is best done by governmental middlemen in the labor market. Would it not be done better by workers and employers who know claimants and jobs more intimately than government clerks ever can?

The contention has some force. Other workers and employers do have a fund of knowledge and experience which can be helpful in solving problems of availability determination. Under our concepts of government, however, we cannot delegate availability determinations on individual claims to worker-employer committees. Neither can great numbers of claims be efficiently handled that way. The constant committee changes would prevent that. If the committee personnel did not change its nongovernment professional standing would soon be lost. Our political concepts, however, do not bar, but instead encourage, the use of such groups in planning policy. That conclusion is underlined by a consideration of this third assumption.

Finally, it may be said that including an availability for work condition in an unemployment compensation law takes for granted that determining availability can be done as a routine job. Either it assumes that or else it accepts the limitation that no more than a routine job will be done of investigating availability. The concept of routine must not be overemphasized. Orderly administration of unemployment compensation requires attention to individual cases. The system is intended, however, for quick handling of mass claim loads.

Unlike the assistance programs, which require investigation of the precise need existing in each case, the compensation program is premised upon a broad presumption of need. It assumes that unemployed workers need cash. This assumption, it is recognized, is true for the great majority of cases, but not all. Neither is it true to the same extent for all claimants. The compensation system, however, in the interest of quick and honorable aid to the unemployed, equalizes these differences. To attain a desirable swiftness in satisfying claims it must perforce rely upon rough-and-ready methods. "The real distinction [between social insurance and social assistance] is between a *routine* service and a *needs* service and the difference does not necessarily depend on whether funds are raised by contributions or by rates and taxes." [16]

The "Gross Sieve" View of Availability

The role of the availability requirement (and the other eligibility conditions) in the unemployment compensation structure may be best conceived as a broad, rough test that the claimant must meet. It is a gross sieve designed to block the clearly unfit from entering or remaining in the benefit system. So operated, it becomes a routine check of the claimant's work history, the circumstances of his work separation, his more prominent physical and other personal circumstances, and his expressed work restrictions.[17] Some claimants will get past such a preliminary examination despite their actual unwillingness and inability to work. They will not be numerous. For them there is a secondary line of defense to prevent them from penetrating too deeply, a finer sieve. That is the test of offered suitable work. It is recognized that a work offer is not always possible and that the job of the employment office is placement and not policing. If that office is, however, doing its job well and the employment level is fairly high there will be work opportunities offered to most claimants.

The offer of suitable work, if rejected by the claimant, may reveal previously undisclosed aspects of his availability. The reason for the refusal may indicate that the claimant is not, in reality, sufficiently attached to the labor force. The unemployment compensation agency then discovers the error of paying him benefits and holds him ineligible. On the other hand, the claimant's reason for refusal may be entirely consistent with availability for work. In that case if the reason is not strong enough to be "good cause," the claimant is disqualified.

Limitations upon the Availability Requirement

Labor Standards Provisions

Although the unemployment compensation statutes generally make a positive requirement that a claimant must be "available for work," they also contain provisions indicating that something less than total availability is required. In compliance with section 1603 (a)(5) of the Internal Revenue Code, all state unemployment compensation laws provide that benefits may not be denied to an otherwise eligible claimant for refusing to accept new work under any of the following conditions: (a) if the position offered is vacant due directly to a strike, lockout, or other labor dispute; (b) if the remuneration, hours, or other conditions of the work offered are substantially less favorable to the individual than those prevailing for similar work in the locality; (c) if, as a condition of being employed, the individual would be required to join a company union or to resign from or refrain from joining a bona fide labor organization.[18] These are usually known as the labor standards provisions. They apply, not only to the operation of the work refusal disqualifications, but also to the availability requirement. Under them a worker may not be held unavailable for work by reason of his unavailability for work that falls within the proscribed conditions.

The Servicemen's Readjustment Act of 1944 extended the first two of these protections to applicants for readjustment allowances, but omitted the third.[19] The Railroad Unemployment Insurance Act applies all three of these bars to benefit denials, but extends them to all work (rather than new work). In addition, it prohibits denying benefits to claimants who refuse to accept work if (1) the wage rate is less than the union wage rate, if any, for similar work in the locality; (2) acceptance would require the claimant to engage in activities which violate the law or which, by violating the reasonable requirements of the constitution, bylaws, or regulations of a bona fide labor organization to which he belongs, would subject him to expulsion from that organization; (3) acceptance of the work would subject him to loss of substantial seniority rights under any collective bargaining agreement between a railway union and another employer.[20]

The Delaware and Ohio laws prevent the denial of benefits if, as a condition of being employed (in new work), the individual would be denied the right to retain membership in and observe the lawful rules of a bona fide labor organization.[21] The New York law also specifies that benefits may not be denied if the employment is at an unreasonable distance from the individual's residence or travel to and from work involves substantially greater expense than that required in claimant's former employment (unless the expense is provided for).[22] Delaware and Ohio have a similar provision, but their laws require both the unreasonable distance and the greater expense before the protection applies.[23] In addition, the New York statute bars denial of benefits when the pay, hours, or conditions offered "are such as tend to depress wages or working conditions." [24] The Kentucky law prevents a denial of benefits for work refusal when acceptance would be prejudicial to the continuance of an established employer-employee relationship to which the worker is a party.[25]

Suitable Work

In forty-eight state laws, the Railroad Unemployment Insurance Act, and Servicemen's Readjustment Act, the disqualification for work refusal hinges upon a finding that the offered work is "suitable." In New York a claimant is disqualified if he refuses, without good cause, to accept an offer of employment for which he is reasonably fitted. In Delaware the disqualification applies if the claimant refuses to accept an offer for which he is reasonably fitted or refuses a job referral from a local employment office. Wisconsin disqualifies the claimant who, without good cause, fails to apply for or accept work.[26]

What is suitable work is ordinarily not expressly defined. In a few instances monetary minimum standards are set. California requires that wages at least equal the claimants' weekly benefit amount. Connecticut requires that the offered work yield greater remuneration than the weekly benefit.[27] Michigan provides that an offer of work in the individual's customary occupation, under conditions of employment and remuneration substantially equivalent to those under which the individual has been customarily employed in that occupation, constitutes suitable work.[28]

The usual statutory practice in the United States has been to leave the term *suitable work* undefined, but to specify a number of criteria which must be considered in determining whether or not work is suitable. These criteria have ordinarily included the degree of risk involved to health, safety, and morals, the claimant's physical fitness, prior training, experience, and earnings, length of unemployment and prospects for securing local work in his customary occupation, and the distance of the available work from the claimant's residence.[29]

The Pennsylvania law contains one of the few American statutory definitions of suitable work. It is described as meaning "all work which the employee is capable of performing." The statute, however, directs the department to consider, in addition to the criteria enumerated in the paragraph above, the following factors: the reasons for the claimant's unemployment, the prevailing condition of the labor market generally and in the claimant's usual occupation, the prevailing wage rates in that occupation, and the permanency of his residence.[30]

The bars to benefit denial that have been described in the foregoing paragraphs are phrased in terms of work refusal. They affect the application of the work refusal disqualification most directly. Their effects are not, however, confined to that portion of the laws. They pervade the availability requirements. It would be obviously nonsensical to hold that claimants who refused unsuitable work were free from disqualification but at the same time unavailable for work by reason of such refusal. In general, the unemployment compensation laws have been interpreted to limit the availability requirement to suitable work. In some laws the tie between availability and suitable work has been spelled out — Arkansas, Colorado, Idaho, Kentucky, North Dakota, Ohio, Pennsylvania, Washington, and the Servicemen's Readjustment Act.

Nonstandard Availability Provisions

An examination of Table A in the Appendix (pages 264–282) will reveal that most of the state unemployment compensation laws phrase their availability requirement in substantially standard language. Usually it is "able to work and available for work." The nonstandard availability provisions contain several types of additional requirements or specifications. In some instances more than one type of additional specification is included in a particular law.

The most common type of added specification is a requirement that the claimant be seeking work. Such provisions now exist in the laws of twenty-two states: California, Colorado, Connecticut, Delaware, Idaho, Illinois, Kansas, Maine, Maryland, Michigan, Missouri, Montana, New Jersey, New Mexico, North Carolina, North Dakota, Ohio, Oregon, Vermont, Washington, Wisconsin, and Wyoming. Their purpose is to ensure that claimants add their own, independent job-hunting efforts to the placement work done by the public employment service in their behalf.

In six states — Alabama, Maine, Massachusetts, Michigan, Washington, and West Virginia — the required availability provisions are specified in terms of availability for work in an occupation, such as the usual occupation, an occupation for which the claimant is reasonably fitted by past experience or training, or an occupation in which the claimant has previously been employed and received wages. It may be said that such provisions set a ceiling upon the availability for work that is required and that no greater availability is demanded of a claimant than is specified. Difficulties have, however, arisen in cases where claimants, voluntarily or involuntarily, have sought to confine their availability to occupations in which they had not customarily worked.

Breadth of availability for work is specified by Colorado which demands availability for *all* suitable work and by Washington which requires availability for *any* suitable work. Availability for *full-time* work is specified in the laws of Michigan and West Virginia.

The Alabama, Illinois, Michigan, and Ohio laws include a concept of locale of availability. In Alabama the individual must be available either (1) at a locality where he has earned wages for insured work during his base period or (2) where it may reasonably be expected that such work may be available. (The "such work" relates to work which the claimant is qualified to perform by past experience or training.) The Ohio law is quite similar. The Michigan law is more onerous. The claimant must be available either (1) at a locality where he has earned wages for insured work during his base period or (2) where the commission finds that such work is available. (In the Michigan law the "such work" means full-time work which the claimant is qualified to perform by past experience or training and which is generally similar to work for which he has previously received wages.) This provision is so drastic that it has become the horrible example of availability provisions that restrict worker mobility.[31] The Illinois law, by 1949 amendment, renders a worker unavailable if, following his most recent work separation, he moves to and remains in a locality where work opportunities are substantially less favorable than those in the locality he left.

New York and Massachusetts tie into their availability requirement a specification that the claimant must be unable to obtain work in his usual occupation or any other for which he is reasonably fitted. Ohio and Oregon add "unable to obtain suitable work" to their availability requirement. Although the unemployment compensation laws in general require availability for work during the week for which benefits are claimed, Rhode Island calls upon the claimant to be available for work whenever duly called for work through the employment office. In Wisconsin he is required to be available whenever, with due notice, he is called on by his current employer to report for work that is actually available. The Washington statute says he must be ready, able, and willing *immediately* to accept any suitable work which may be offered to him.

It would be a mistake to picture the state laws which use the standard "able to work and available for work" provision as presenting a pattern of uniformity. In all but seven of these jurisdictions the basic availability provision is circumscribed in one way or another. The seven are Arizona, District of Columbia, Georgia, Louisiana, Mississippi, Texas, Virginia.

The additional statutory limitations in the other states upon the basic availability provision deal with such subjects as: separations from work because of marriage or approaching marriage, marital obligations, pregnancy and childbirth, attendance at an established school, voluntary leaving, work refusal, and misconduct. When "disqualifying" acts such as these result in complete cancellation of benefit rights or a prohibition of benefits for the duration of the worker's unemployment they are properly classified as ineligibilities and modifications of the basic law on availability.

SUMMARY AND CONCLUSIONS

The coverage provisions of American unemployment compensation laws are inadequate as measures of past labor-force attachment. They usually bar, as evidence of the past labor-force attachment needed to qualify for benefits, any work done for employers with less than a specified number of employees or any work done in certain "excluded employments," such as farming, nonprofit institutions, domestic service, and government. About a fourth of the wage earners are thus excluded from coverage.

Most state unemployment compensation laws require claimants to have earned a specified sum of money in insured work. Putting the qualification requirement on a money basis requires keeping it low so as to avoid excluding low-paid workers. Comparatively high-paid, occasional workers are thus permitted to qualify. Basing benefit qualification on weeks or days of employment will avoid this result. Scaling the claimant's benefit amount to the amount of his earnings could continue.

In most states, base periods are short. (Base periods are past periods of time that are considered in computing a claimant's earnings in insured work which determine the benefit amount and duration to which he is entitled.) Ordinarily the base period extends back less than eighteen months preceding an insured worker's initial claim for benefits. Long base periods create heavy administrative burdens, although this might not necessarily be so if we used less cumbersome wage record systems. In any case, the short base period works a special hardship on workers who become disabled for any substantial length of time or who work, for part of the base period, in noncovered employment. In such cases, provision could well be made to extend the base period.

Except, in some states, for seasonal workers, the same earnings qualification is required of all workers. It is suggested that the minimum for benefit qualification be made heavier for workers without dependents who, as a group, are less apt to be firmly attached to the labor force. This could be done, for example, by requiring a hundred days of insured work in the preceding year of workers with dependents and a hundred days of insured work in each of the preceding two years of workers without dependents. Admittedly, this would do only a rough kind of justice. It should, however, discourage many of the "special" disqualifications which may, for example, deny benefits to a woman who was discharged, as soon as she was married, because of her employer's no-married-women rule.

Registration for work with the public employment service is a condition of benefit eligibility in all state unemployment compensation laws. This requires an affirmative act by the claimant which perforce exposes him to the job opportunities available through the public employment office. Registration for work tends to show availability for work but is only one source of evidence on the question.

A substantial minority of the state unemployment benefit laws deny benefits until the worker is again reëmployed (or is reëmployed for a specified period or earns a designated sum) if his unemployment is due to a named disqualifying act or condition. Some of the acts and conditions singled out include: voluntarily leaving work without good cause; discharge for misconduct connected with the work refusing, without good cause, to accept suitable work; leaving work to attend school; pregnancy; separation from work because of marriage. Such laws, in effect, require the disqualified worker to bring additional evidence of his availability — reëmployment of the kind the laws describe.

Fifteen states provide for uniform benefit duration. Every claimant who qualifies, whether for the maximum weekly benefit amount or the minimum, may receive benefits for the same number of weeks in the benefit year. Since earnings needed to qualify for minimum benefits are low ($300 in a one-year period is the highest required) uniform duration permits casual workers to qualify for a fairly long period of benefits — from twelve to twenty-six weeks, depending upon the state. This puts a burden upon availability administration since such workers are likely to be loosely attached to the labor force.

In thirteen states both the base period and the benefit year are uniform for all claimants. The usual uniform base period is the calendar year. Commonly, the wages earned in the calendar year are considered in computing benefits on claims filed at any time during the one-year period following a fixed date (usually in the first week of April) in the next calendar year. Benefits paid for April 1949–March 1950 unemployment are thus based on 1948 wages. Benefits paid for March 1949 unemployment are based on 1947 wages. As a result, if claimants in March 1949 find that wages have fallen since 1947, they are less apt to take available jobs since their benefits are high, reflecting 1947 wages. Furthermore, uniform duration permits a claimant who earned twice the qualifying amount by working six months, from October 1947 through March 1948, to qualify in two benefit years. Uniform duration in this way permits benefit drains by the long unemployed.

The existence of the availability requirement in the unemployment compensation laws reflects certain basic assumptions: (a) Not only the past but the present labor-force attachment of claimants should be ascertained. (b) It is feasible to make a satisfactory determination of current labor-force attachment. (c) The unemployment compensation agency, with the aid of the employment service, is the proper agency to make such a determination. (d) Availability can be determined as a matter of routine without an exhaustive investigation in every case. Although acceptable, these assumptions do not have the compelling force of axioms.

The availability requirement, in statutory perspective, may be best viewed as a gross sieve designed to keep the patently unqualified from entering or staying in the benefit system. Thus it becomes a routine check of the claimants' circumstances. For claimants who pass this routine check there remains the more exact probe of the offer of suitable work.

All state unemployment compensation laws provide the labor-standards protections which the federal statute requires before taxes paid by an employer to the state can be used as a credit against the federal unemployment tax. These labor-standards provisions state that benefits are not to be denied to an otherwise qualified individual for refusing to accept new work under any of the following conditions: (a) if the job offered is vacant due directly to a labor dispute, (b) if the wages, hours or other conditions of the work offered are substantially less favorable to the individual than those prevailing for similar work in the locality. Claimants may not be held unavailable for work because they are unwilling to accept jobs that fall within the condemnation of the labor-standards provisions.

Availability for work is usually interpreted as requiring only availability for suitable work. The unemployment compensation laws seldom define *suitable work* but they usually designate certain factors to be considered in determining whether work is suitable. These most commonly include: the degree of risk involved to health, safety, and morals; physical fitness; prior training, experience, and earnings; length or unemployment and prospects for securing local work in the customary occupation; and the distance of the available work from the claimant's residence.

In a bare majority of American unemployment compensation laws the wording of the availability requirement is substantially the same, "able to work and available for work." The most common variation (contained in twenty-two state laws) is to add a requirement that the claimant should seek work. Other variations require availability in terms of a designated occupation (such as the usual occupation or work for which the claimant is reasonably fitted by past experience or training), or for full-time work or for work at a locality where the claimant has earned wages in insured work or can earn such wages.

CHAPTER VI

GENERAL PRINCIPLES

•

NEED FOR PRINCIPLES

IT HAS BEEN SAID that the administration of the availability requirement suffers, not from a lack of principles, but from a lack of standards to guide the application of those principles. Although the "little principles" for applying the "big principles" have been sadly missing, it is also true that the fundamental precepts have seldom been set down in orderly fashion. The ones that have been applied must be deduced from a mass of administrative decisions and a handful of court decisions.

Early in the American benefit program the Social Security Board issued a volume of selected benefit decisions of the British Umpire. The book contained a short statement of principles used by the umpire in applying the able-to-work and available-for-work requirement.[1] The effect was potent. Even today the language of many availability decisions reveals their British ancestry. It is some measure of the unimportance then attributed to the availability provision that the Social Security Board, in 1938 and 1939, issued statements of "principles," covering the work-refusal, voluntary-leaving, and misconduct disqualifications, but no statement was issued on availability for work.[2] This defect was not remedied until 1945, when the Bureau of Employment Security released a draft stating "the views of the technical staff of the Bureau's Interpretation Service Section on the *Principles Underlying Availability For Work*."[3] At about the same time in an issue of the *Yale Law Review,* devoted entirely to unemployment compensation, an article appeared on availability.[4] The effects of this article and of the bureau's statement are not yet entirely evident.[5]

More than one reason exists for this seeming neglect of the principles of availability. The original expectation had been that, aside from physical inability cases, little use would be made of the availability provisions of the American unemployment compensation laws. When no work was to be had no questions would be asked.

When work was available the work refusal disqualification and not the availability requirement would be applied to claimants suspected of being work shy. Our history, as it turned out, has been quite different.

The reluctance of unemployment compensation administrators to define the policies and principles governing claimants' benefit rights has been a retarding factor. This reluctance has been based upon a deep-rooted distrust of generalizations and a well-considered belief in the importance of deciding each case on its own merits. Thus the *ad hoc* approach to availability has had strong adherents and real merit. The chief value of this view is its emphasis upon deciding each case on its individual merits. This is not inconsistent with developing general but flexible rules of decision.

Without accepted basic principles the interpretation of availability for work is a morass of conflicting decisions. This makes it impossible to explain availability to anyone — claimants, employers, the interested public, and even the staff of the unemployment compensation agency. The following excerpt from a claimant's informational booklet is typical of the explanations given to workers: "After you have established a valid initial claim, in order to qualify for benefits for any week, you must . . . *Be able to work and available for work.* You must be able and available to accept suitable work if it is offered." Administrative decisions which seldom reveal their underlying premises have been the primary informational sources upon which interested groups have had to depend for understanding availability. General ignorance of the subject has been the not astounding result. Great uncertainties among unemployment compensation staff members have flowed easily from this lack of the specific guidance of basic rules.

CRITERIA OF PRINCIPLES

What makes a good principle of availability? First let it be stated that we are using the word to refer to a basic doctrine from which specific applications of the availability requirement follow. Such a doctrine must be more than a controlling opinion. Because "available for work" is a statutory requirement, availability principles must function as rules of action. The system of which these rules are a part necessarily is a large scale clerical enterprise manned by ordinary people and dealing with great numbers of other ordinary people who have no special knowledge of the subject. Such factors emphasize the need for rules that are understandable if not simple.

The cases that arise under the availability requirement are infinitely varied. The principles to be used for decision must be broad enough to encompass this variety of situation and sufficiently flexible for individual fairness. In addition, the major forces and trends in the labor force and the labor market must be recognized in formulating availability principles. Thus it is absurd to say that all women who leave work because of marriage are unavailable for work. It is possible, however, to defend this position: The woman who leaves her job to marry but does not change the locality of her domicile casts doubt upon her availability for work. Special inquiry should be made in her case to determine if that doubt still exists when she files her claim. Such a statement recognizes individual differences but takes into account the fact that many women leave the labor force when they marry.

The frame of reference for workable availability principles may not be narrowed down to the availability requirement. The entire unemployment compensation system must be taken into account. In particular, attention must be given to the relationship between the availability requirement and the earnings (or employment) qualification for benefits. So also the connections with the registration for work requirement and with the work-refusal disqualification are of key importance.

These are but a few aspects of the problem of measuring statements of availability principles. It is not to be supposed that they explain *how* such principles are developed. The Holmes dictum stands: "The life of the Law has been experience, not logic." The foregoing suggestions are intended to emphasize that we must use our experience to test both the law and the logic of availability decisions.

THE PRESUMPTION OF AVAILABILITY FOR WORK

An otherwise eligible claimant ordinarily should be presumed available for work. This is a deep-rooted and important presumption. Work is a universal and eternal fact for the overwhelming majority of adult humans, as true of primitive peoples as it is of the members of machine societies.[6] John Stuart Mill wrote: "The majority of Englishmen and Americans have no life but in their work; that alone stands between them and ennui. Either from original temperament, climate, or want of development, they are too deficient in senses to enjoy mere existence in repose; and scarcely any pleasure or amusement is pleasure or amusement to them." [7] Philosophy, religion, and tradition all have stressed the importance of work. Erich Fromm, for example, emphasizes the role of Luther and the Reformation in building up the cult of work.[8]

We need not belabor the subject of work incentives. The primary reason for work is economic need. Work also satisfies social and physio-psychological needs. When everyone else in the group works the sluggard is lonely, disliked, and disdained. His unsatisfied bodily hunger for purposeful activity may even make him prone to illness.

In the case of the benefit claimant we have more than these generalizations to support the presumption of availability for work. His work history shows recent labor force attachment. This is entitled to great weight. Upon the basis of that history we may even grade the strength of the availability presumption in each case. Until illness or infirmity overtakes him, the longer the claimant has been a steady worker the stronger is the likelihood that he will continue in the market for work.

Benefit Amounts and the Cost of Living

Critics of the unemployment compensation program have sometimes contended that unemployment benefits deter claimants from accepting work by making it unnecessary for them to earn a living. We need to examine this contention carefully; if it is true, it makes doubtful the suggested presumption of availability.

No doubt unemployment benefits make the claimant's need somewhat less acute. That is their purpose. Unemployment compensation is intended to protect workers from the destitution that unemployment otherwise brings. Does it do more than that?

In a much-neglected study, the Bureau of Employment Security compared living costs in thirty-three American cities with benefit payments. It concluded:

Many workers receiving maximum payments under present laws suffer not only a substantial wage loss but, for workers with dependents, a reduction in income below what is required for an emergency level of living. The average claimant (with one dependent) in many States cannot maintain himself and his dependents at a decent standard of living on his weekly benefits. In some States, a large proportion of claimants without dependents cannot maintain themselves at a decent living standard on present weekly benefits.[9]

There are regrettable deficiencies in this report. Although released in 1946, the budgets used (the WPA maintenance and emergency budgets) were last priced in June, 1943. These budget costs were compared with maximum state weekly benefits payable as of December 31, 1945, and with the average state weekly benefits paid in 1943 and June and November 1945. Since very few states pay dependents' allowances no figures were available showing benefit payments actually made to claimants as classified by their dependency status.

Limited as it was, this study showed some remarkable results. The average state weekly benefit payment in 1943 was below the weekly maintenance budget for a person living alone in twenty-four of the thirty-three cities. The average state weekly benefit even in November 1945 — with some legislative increases in benefits and war wage credits to be drawn on — fell below the 1943-priced maintenance budget for the single person in four cities: Jacksonville, Florida; Manchester, New Hampshire; and Norfolk and Richmond, Virginia. In Denver and Memphis this single-person budget equaled the November 1945 average state weekly benefit. For a man and wife, the June 1943 weekly maintenance budget cost was greater, in every city compared, than the November 1945 average state weekly benefit payment. A fortiori, the deficiency of the average benefit was even greater in 1945. In every city studied the 1943 weekly maintenance budget costs for a man, wife, and one child were higher than the *maximum* weekly benefit allowed under the state law on December 31, 1945. In all but four of the cases the difference was $7 or more a week. In ten cases it was $10 or more. In only two cities (Detroit and Seattle) were 1945 maximum weekly benefits high enough to pay the living costs of a man, wife, and two children at a June 1943 "emergency" level.

A later release by the Bureau of Employment Security contains this significant paragraph:

Since the end of the war, the average weekly benefit paid under unemployment insurance had decreased, while the cost of living and weekly earnings have risen. From $18.81 in July–September 1945, the average payment for a week of total unemployment dropped to $17.72 by July–September 1947, while the consumers' price index rose from 129 to 161, or 25 percent. In effect, therefore, the "real" value of the average weekly benefit decreased from $14.56 to $11.02. Although the maximum weekly benefit has been raised in many states, wages have increased to an even greater extent and consequently the ratio of average weekly benefits to average weekly wages has declined. In July–September 1947, this ratio was only 35 percent, compared with a ratio of 43 percent in July–September 1945.[10]

It is true that these figures are averages which gloss over individual differences. It is also true that many claimants are secondary earners whose needs-benefits comparison differs from that of other workers. The same thing may be true of single workers who receive comparatively high benefit amounts. Taking such factors into account, we must nevertheless conclude that benefit payments have yet to destroy the need to work. By and large, it can safely be said that unemployment compensation does no more than protect from destitution. In too many cases it fails to do even that.

Effect of the Work Registration

The registration for work when the claim is filed gives additional support to the presumption of availability. This has been attacked as a perfunctory act which is performed in order to get benefits. Undoubtedly if registration were not required many claimants would not use the employment service. To follow this line of reasoning, however, to a conclusion that work registration is meaningless neglects the realities involved. The fact is that regardless of their motives, claimants do register with the employment service. In so doing, they expose themselves to the job opportunities which the employment service has to offer them. When they are referred to jobs, the great majority of claimants accept the referral and go to the employer for an interview. In 1946 and 1947, for example, less than two out of every hundred workers who filed valid claims were disqualified for refusing work offers or job referrals.[11]

The Pennsylvania Superior Court has expressed its accord with the presumption of availability.

Registration for work is the first requirement, and ordinarily it will be presumed that a claimant who registers is able and available for work. By registering the claimant makes out a prima facie case of availability, which is of course rebuttable by countervailing evidence, e.g., refusal of referred work, illness, inability due to superannuation, and other conditions.[12]

Most unemployment compensation tribunals would agree that ordinarily registration for work by an otherwise eligible claimant raises a presumption that he is available for work.[13] That this presumption is rebuttable there cannot be the slightest doubt. It is true that: "Registration with a public employment office and an expressed willingness to accept work offered through such office does not of itself establish availability for work." [14] The very circumstances that occasion the worker's joblessness may cancel out the presumption or prevent it from arising. The worker who leaves a job because it is beyond his strength may be expected to explain what work he is physically able to do. The woman who leaves work because she finds herself unable to handle both her job and her housework at the same time ought to satisfy the administrator that there is some work she will be able to do while taking care of her home.

In recent years the presumption has been under attack. A week before this writing the New York Readjustment Allowance Agent, in finding a veteran unavailable for work, wrote: "Availability is not presumed — it must be shown to exist." [15] The objections to presuming availability from work registration are, however, more deep-seated. Like the presumption itself they stem from Great Britain. In 1930 a group of Welshmen participated in a "National Hunger March" upon London. One of them sought benefits for the period of the march but was held not available for work. In passing upon his appeal the British Umpire said:

It is submitted in the Grounds of Appeal to the Umpire that the fact that the claimant signed the register at the Employment Exchange whilst on the march shows that he was available for work. It shows that he was saying that he was available but it does not establish that he was so available.[16]

This approach is highly understandable and acceptable, especially in the circumstances of the case. On its way to this country, however, it underwent a sea change. In some cases the registration for work was separated from availability upon the ground that it was a "requirement of eligibility separate and distinct from the availability requirement." [17] In others the claimant's work registration was described as a perfunctory act.[18] The strongest blow, however, was struck by the Supreme Court of Georgia in the case of *Huiet* v. *Schwob Manufacturing Company*.[19] The claimant had quit her work to join her soldier husband near a military post beyond commuting distance from her old job. The only evidence as to availability was the work registration and her statement on the claim form that she was available for work.

The court was asked whether the commissioner was authorized to find such a married woman available for work. In giving a negative answer, the court characterized the claimant's statement as "a mere self-serving declaration without probative value. It is like the unverified allegations in any other pleading, which can not prove themselves, but must be sustained by evidence, in order for the pleader to prevail." As one result of this decision, the Georgia unemployment compensation agency made all claimants file their claim forms under oath.[20] The court has not had occasion, to this writing, to pass upon the legal efficacy of that procedure.

Burden of Proof

Closely associated with the attacks upon the registration presumption has been a legalistic doctrine that the burden is upon the claimant to prove availability for work. The Missouri Supreme Court has announced:

We think it is apparent that the burden of proof to establish a claimant's right to benefits under the unemployment compensation law rests upon the claimant . . . An unemployed individual is eligible to receive benefits only if the commission finds that the required conditions have been met. The claimant assumes the risk of non-persuasion and we think the general rule applicable to ordinary court proceedings applies.[21]

The same rule and language have been adopted by the Oklahoma, Tennessee, and Washington supreme courts.[22] Similar rulings have been made in other states.[23]

It should be emphasized that the burden of proving his availability for work is a heavy load upon a claimant. Were there some prescribed and clear course for a claimant to follow in showing his availability the imposition might not be so serious. But there is no charted way. A claimant may make an honest and diligent search for work and yet be held unavailable. This happened in Nebraska when a former laborer, no longer able to work at his old job, actively sought clerical work. Local employers paid $25 to $40 a week, and he asked for $35, which was considered an excessive wage demand because of his lack of clerical experience.[24] An active, independent search for work may even be considered evidence of unavailability. That happened to an unemployed movie extra in Hollywood who forsook Central Casting and made her own work canvass of the studios.[25]

In states where the burden of proving availability is cast upon the claimant his appeal rights may suffer. The Missouri Supreme Court, in the case quoted above, concluded that the Commission's finding that the claimant was not available "need not be supported by affirmative, substantial evidence tending to show that she was *not* available for work, because the burden was on her, as claimant, to show prima facie that she was entitled to the benefits claimed." (Original italics.)

When this is the rule appeal may become a futile formality. Unemployed workers, lacking, as is usually the case, the aid of legal counsel, may present their story but fail for lack of proper technical guidance to make out a prima-facie case. According to the Missouri Supreme Court, the commission may then freely decide against the worker even though no substantial evidence exists to support its decision. Fortunately the general rule is that substantial evidence is required to sustain the finding of the unemployment compensation agency.[26]

A more reasonable approach would place the burden of obtaining evidence necessary to support its decision upon the unemployment compensation agency. It is upon that agency that the laws place the burden of investigating and deciding claims for benefits. This does not mean that the unemployment compensation authorities must make an exhaustive investigation of every benefit claim. The great majority of claims are routine applications made by workers who are laid off from work, usually for short periods. Additional facts pertaining to their availability usually do not exist. Ordinarily, therefore, no amount of investigation will produce evidence for or against their eligibility. Their availability must necessarily be accepted on presumption or, if you will, on faith. The claimant whose availability has been questioned, either on the agency's own initiative or as the result of an employer's protest, presents a nonroutine case which requires investigation.

It is not suggested that a claimant's duty of coöperating with the unemployment compensation agency should be lessened in any way. He is bound to furnish full and complete information about himself and his circumstances. If he fails to do so he has no one but himself to blame if he is found ineligible for benefits. He is required to report regularly to the employment office and to respond to its directions. He must also follow any other instructions he is given to help make the agency's work easier and better and to improve his own job-getting chances.

The agency, however, is in a superior position to get the facts surrounding the individual's availability. It has legal powers and investigative facilities with which the claimant cannot compete. The agency can get needed information not only from the claimant, but also from previous and prospective employers and anyone else who may have it. Its informational pipe lines to the labor market will produce the necessary factual background.

The Idaho Supreme Court has taken a similar view.[27] The claimant, sixty years old and a band-saw filer long in the employ of a lumber company, became unemployed during the winter shut-down. His usual wage was $2.025 an hour. When he filed his claim and registered for work he was offered two jobs, firing a boiler at eighty-eight cents an hour and common labor at eighty cents an hour. He would have had to commute to get to these jobs. Because of his physical condition he did not accept the referrals. He appealed from the Industrial Accident Board's ruling that he was unavailable for work. The court found no evidence that he could not have returned to his former job or that work the claimant could have performed was not available near his home. It cited the rule in workmen's compensation that when a claimant has failed or overlooked submitting evidence establishing to what compensation he is entitled, it is the board's duty to call attention to that failure and see to it that the available evidence to establish that fact is presented.

The court concluded: "Where unsatisfactory evidence is furnished by a party claiming unemployment compensation benefits the same rule applies as in workmen's compensation cases. That is, the board should make further and individual investigation and, to that end, may subpoena and examine other witnesses than those furnished by claimant." A California District Court of Appeal, in remanding a cannery worker's appeal from an unavailability ruling, rested its decision upon the inadequacy of the evidence in the Appeal Board's hearing record. Quoting from the Idaho decision, the California court stated that it had been "strongly influenced" by that case.[28]

AMOUNT AND NATURE OF WORK

Availability must be for a substantial amount of suitable work. This principle means: (a) No claimant need be available for work that is not suitable for him. (b) In any case, the claimant must be available for a substantial amount of work. The first part of the rule need not detain us long. We have already noted that the Servicemen's Readjustment Act of 1944 and the laws of eight states (Arkansas, Colorado, Idaho, Kentucky, North Dakota, Ohio, Pennsylvania, and Washington) tie the availability requirement to suitable work. In seven state laws the kind of work is differently specified.[29] In most states interpretation has confined the availability requirement to availability for suitable work.[30]

The conflicts arise on two basic subordinate questions. What is suitable work? For what amount of suitable work must the claimant be available?

Suitable Work

The meaning of suitable work merits a book of its own. It is, however, so involved in availability for work that some general discussion cannot be avoided here. Defining suitable work is hazardous and seldom attempted.[31] The usual tactic has been (1) to label certain circumstances as making work unsuitable, and (2) to point to a number of variable criteria which should be taken into account in deciding if work is suitable. Chapter V lists these criteria.

Separating "good cause" for refusing work from "unsuitable" work is equally difficult.[32] It has been sometimes suggested that the first refers to the worker's personal situation and the second to the characteristics and circumstances of offered work. This is no more than a crude approximation. A woman who has someone to care for her children during the daytime only has good cause for refusing night work. Such work may also be unsuitable for her. A worker, laid off for a short, definite period, may be offered similar permanent work at the same pay, in the same locality, but with a different employer. Although the work may be suitable for him, his ties to his regular employer (seniority, insurance, and so on) would furnish him good cause for refusing the offer. "Good cause" and "unsuitable work" may be viewed as two concentric circles, with "good cause" the larger of the two. All unsuitable work is work which a claimant may refuse with good cause. There remains an area of work that is suitable but which the claimant has good cause for refusing.

The apparent inseparability of "good cause" and "unsuitable work" makes for a dilemma in applying a rule that availability means availability for suitable work. If suitable work refers only to the job and its accompanying conditions the worker gets little protection. A forty-eight-year-old woman who had eagerly searched for work in the factories in her neighborhood was held unavailable for work. Because streetcar riding made her sick, she had had to refuse referrals to any work beyond walking distance of her home.[33]

To make the rule mean availability for suitable work which the claimant has no good cause for refusing, opens the door for paying benefits to some workers who are not available for any work. Since 1944 a number of decisions have included this statement of the meaning of availability.[34] Taken literally, it means that a husband who is busy taking care of his sick wife so that he cannot accept any work is nonetheless available for work. He has good cause for refusing any work. It is obvious that the rule must be qualified by reference to a residue of work which must remain within the claimant's availability after eliminating all unsuitable work and all work which he may have good cause to refuse.[35] Omitting such qualification robs the availability provision of much of its force.

Amount of Work

"Amount of work" is used here in its broadest sense, to cover every possible limitation on a worker's availability, whether it be a restriction to a particular occupation or industry, neighborhood or locality, working hours or week, or temporary or permanent work.

Many views have been taken of the amount of work for which a claimant must be available. It has been expressed as "some form of work," "some kind of work ordinarily done under contracts for personal services," "all suitable work," or a "substantial amount of suitable work." The first two descriptions given usually appear in cases involving physical ability to work. In the Shorten case, for example, the Connecticut court said: "The test of availability for work . . . is that the man is capable of performing some sort of work for which there is a call in the general labor market." [36] The claimant's legs had been badly broken so that he could do no work which required walking.

Conflict apparently exists over the proposition that a claimant must be available for all suitable work. The Washington law specifies availability for "any suitable work," the Colorado statute for "all suitable work." In Oregon the *Manual of Precedents* says: "The claimant is considered to be available for work only when he is prepared to accept at once an offer of any suitable work brought to his notice." [37] Similar language appears in a number of decisions, both judicial and administrative.[38] Such statements, however, cannot be taken literally. To do so would mean that any refusal without good cause of a suitable job offer would make the claimant unavailable for work. The need for separate availability and work refusal provisions would be removed. The work refusal disqualification would function only as an added penalty.

In actual practice it is common to disqualify a claimant for refusing a specific job offer and, at the same time, to hold him available for work. A New Jersey Board-of-Review decision came to that conclusion in the case of a woodworking machine operator, 3½ months unemployed, who, because he wanted work in his trade at a dollar an hour, refused work at a naval base at a starting rate of eighty cents.[39] To report all the cases of work refusal disqualification without unavailability ruling would require many pages.

In the Grant case, the New Jersey Supreme Court tried, while using the language of availability for all suitable work, to avoid making the work refusal disqualification either meaningless or an additional penalty to be tacked on to an unavailability ruling. A sales clerk who had quit her job to be married returned to the labor market six months later and claimed benefits. She refused her old employer's offer of sales work because she wanted factory work which paid better. The claimant applied at fifteen different places and finally, after those months, got factory work. She was disqualified for the work refusal. The employer contended that she should also have been held unavailable for work.

The court said:

The applicant directly and continually shut herself off from a considerable field of suitable employment. By her purposeful and voluntary act she was not wholly available for suitable work, and thus she placed herself, in our opinion, outside of those who . . . were eligible for unemployment benefits. Participation in benefits is granted only to those who in addition to being able to work are available for work. It was not merely that the applicant had failed to apply for a designated job; she had made herself definitely unavailable for any position in that scale of employment.[40]

According to this decision, a claimant may, without being held unavailable, refuse individual suitable jobs unless (1) he expressly cuts himself off from a particular field of suitable work, or (2) he refuses enough jobs in such a field to make it plain that he will not do such work. Such a rule seems an unwarranted infringement of a claimant's freedom of occupational choice. Under it unemployed carpenters would draw benefits without question, but a claimant, skilled as both a carpenter and an electrician, would be denied benefits if he chose to be available for carpentry work only. It is not contended that the carpenter-electrician should not be disqualified if he refused offered suitable work as an electrician. To consider him unavailable for work, however, merely because he chose one of two trades may mean denying him benefits when he has been offered no work at all. It becomes mere meddling with the claimant's right to choose and change his occupation.

The better rule on the quantum of availability is stated by the Pennsylvania court in the Bliley case: "So long as the claimant is ready, willing and able to accept some substantial and suitable work he has met the statutory requirements.[41] This, too, is the view taken by the federal Bureau of Employment Security: "Availability for work does not require availability for all suitable work. All that is necessary is availability for a substantial amount of suitable work." [42] The Illinois Board of Review has held: "The mere fact that an individual places certain restrictions on the type of work he is willing to accept does not in itself make him unavailable for work within the intent and meaning of the Unemployment Compensation Act. It is only where the limitations and restrictions reduce his prospects of employment to such an extent that he no longer has a substantial amount of work opportunities left that he, in effect, removes himself from the labor market and is not available for work." [43]

What Is a Substantial Amount of Work?

"Substantial" is similar here in sense to such words as "considerable" and "material." Like availability itself, the word is intangible. It can be clarified in relative terms only. Three tests may help to determine if the work for which the claimant is available is of substantial amount.

1. *Benefit qualification.* If the claimant obtained work within his restrictions, would it ordinarily furnish him sufficient earnings or employment which, if earned or performed in insured work, would qualify him again for benefits? This test would extend the benefit qualification and use it as part of a test of current as well as past labor force attachment. Since earnings and employment quali-

fication for benefits are arbitrarily arrived at, such a test would need to be used cautiously.

2. *Work history.* Has the claimant in the past made his living by work of the kind to which he now limits himself? This is a test of availability as well as amount of work. On the latter count the work history measures the substantiality of the work amount against the claimant's own experience. Work history is ordinarily not a controlling test. The claimant who meets it gives some evidence that the work is substantial. Ordinarily, a claimant who fails to meet it cannot contend that he is available for a significant amount of work. Possession of the necessary training and a changed labor market may justify a different conclusion.

3. *The labor market.* What are the industrial practices and conditions in the labor market area where the claimant is available for work? Greatest reliance will probably be placed upon this test. First, the flexibility of "labor-market area" should be noted. The area varies with occupations and industries, wage levels, changes in transportation facilities, and other factors. Second, it is not intended to suggest that the availability *of* work should govern the determination.[44] To do so would defeat the basic purpose of paying benefits to unemployed workers when no suitable work is available for them.

Under the labor-market area test, what is a substantial amount of work is not determined by existing job vacancies. Instead the jobs, filled or unfilled, that ordinarily exist in the area are the criterion of what is a substantial amount of work. It would be futile to suggest a mathematical ratio as a definition of substantial amount of work. One per cent of the existing jobs may mean 500 jobs in a city of 100,000. It may mean one job in a small village community.

No precise statements can be made of what amount of work is substantial. Experience does, however, demonstrate that in most labor markets certain recognized trades and occupations may safely be considered substantial. The butcher and the baker are found everywhere, although the candlestick maker has become a rare figure. A basic list of such trades might well be constructed. Many labor markets contain occupations which predominate there although seldom found elsewhere. New York is one of the few American cities where a dress designer may find a job. A rubber industry worker may expect to find employment in Akron but not in Richmond. Separate lists of additional "substantial" trades can readily be made for separate communities. Trades omitted from such lists are not necessarily too "insubstantial" to support a claim of availability. Other tests than the normal community yardstick may show that the work in question is substantial in the light of the immediate circumstances or the claimant's history.

Such methods should provide the necessary differentiation among communities. What of the changes within a labor market? Some trades rise with the times, others — note the candlestick maker — fall. Fortunately the waning of a trade seldom presents an unemployment compensation problem. Trade disappearance is a long-run phenomenon. Unemployment benefits are distinctly short run, relating as they do to work performed in the preceding year or two. Violent economic changes — from peace to war and back, for example — raise painful problems of adjustment. They do not, however, erase the approach outlined here. As new industries move in and out of a community, lists and concepts of substantial work will change. It is not to be supposed that any occupation has an eternal, vested right to its economic position.

Length of Unemployment and Prospects of Work

It has often been suggested that the longer a claimant is unemployed the greater should be the field of his availability. The carpenter-foreman who is out of work may be expected after four weeks to take journeyman work, after ten weeks to take a laborer's job. The theory is simple and appealing. The unemployed worker has a right to stick to his "reasonable" restrictions but only for a "reasonable" time. As was the case before unemployment compensation so should it be now. Unemployment benefits, it is reasoned, are not intended to maintain any specific wage or skill standard for workers. Benefits are designed to help unemployed workers to maintain a decent standard in the face of unemployment, but claimants should expect to lower their sights as their joblessness continues. Unemployment compensation cushions the shock but does not remove it.[45]

To apply such reasoning to the availability requirement leads to error. If the premise is accepted that no more is required than availability for a substantial amount of suitable work, then there appears to be no room for tying availability to the kite of lengthening unemployment and deteriorating work prospects. Whether or not a specific type of work is "substantial" has no direct relationship to the length of claimant's unemployment. Neither is it related to the claimant's immediate prospects of getting such work. Some connections do exist. If a doubt of the substantiality of the work a claimant will take had been resolved in his favor, his continued unemployment may show that a mistake was made. The supposed market for the work did not exist. (The length of unemployment may also have a bearing upon assessing the worker's demonstration of availability and his efforts to find work. This, however, is not connected with the quantum of work.)

The claimant's work prospects are connected with the labor-market evaluation needed to determine if the work is substantial. There are, however, differences. The former ordinarily involves a short run look at the future; the latter is on a broader base. A bricklayer who limits himself to bricklaying will ordinarily be considered available for a substantial amount of work. Yet, during a particular period of unemployment, his immediate work prospects may be poor. The employment office may find that no brick work is expected locally for six months. Unless work prospects change so radically as to spell the end of a claimant's work in the locality for the foreseeable future, it is hard to say that poor work prospects will make the work insubstantial. (Here again, work prospects affect the assessment of the demonstration of availability. The claimant's activity in looking for work may be expected to vary with his work prospects.)

Let us be clear. It is not suggested that the bricklayer who limits himself to bricklaying may merely sit back and draw rocking-chair money in a period when he cannot expect bricklaying work for many months. The argument is simply that he ought not to be held unavailable for work. He is still obliged to accept offers of other suitable work. If he fails, without good cause, he should be disqualified.

At this point the length of unemployment and the work prospects become potent factors. At the outset of a claimant's unemployment his customary occupation or the work to which he restricts himself may be the only work suitable for him. As his joblessness continues, however, and his work prospects remain poor, less desirable work may become suitable for him. The employment office should be free to follow this downward trend and offer him jobs from this increasing pool. Whether the employment office actually does refer the claimant to less desirable work must be decided by other factors. When laborers are unemployed, no reason exists for offering laborer work to the bricklayer, regardless of his length of unemployment. (He may himself ask for it.) This would be poor placement, satisfying neither the claimant nor the employer. It should go without saying that the less desirable work offered must actually be available.[46]

Furthermore, it is not suggested that the reasonable adjustment period has no place in availability administration. It definitely has. The "substantial amount of work" rule cannot be applied with exactness. It is a rough test. In many instances the work to which the claimant limits himself is on the borderline. If the unemployment or the limitation is involuntary in origin, the doubt should ordinarily be resolved in the claimant's favor.[47] This need not be a permanent decision by the unemployment compensation agency. Instead it should be viewed as an allowance to the claimant of a reasonable period to find work within his limitations.[48]

What is the effect of separating the availability requirement and the work refusal disqualification and making them respond differently to long unemployment and poor work prospects? There are at least two. First, it confirms the availability requirement as the rough test of minimal labor-force attachment. As suggested in the previous chapter this is a gross sieve, a first line of defense. As such it should do no more than eliminate those who are obviously not in the labor force. It is not designed to measure eligibility in fine gradations.

The fine sieve is the work offer, the secondary line of defense. The available claimant who refuses it, when the work is suitable and he has no good cause, becomes subject to disqualification. Because the work offer should be carefully adjusted to the claimant and his circumstances, it is not to be wasted on one who is clearly not in the labor force. The suggested argument saves availability from overrefinement and puts the onus of more precise adjustment where it belongs — on the work refusal disqualification.

The second effect of the argument is to operate against unavailability rulings which are based upon hypothetical questions and situations. If the view is taken that the longer a claimant is unemployed the less desirable work he must be available to take, the way is open to use hypothetical questions to preclude him from benefits. The ten-week-unemployed bricklayer may be asked whether he would take laborer work and held unavailable if he says "No," even though he has not been offered any specific job. Under the view suggested here this is unlikely to occur.

Negative Aspects of the Rule

There are certain negative aspects to the statement of the availability requirement in terms of a substantial amount of work. More accurately, they are protective corollaries. These were succinctly summarized in the Bliley case:

> There is no requirement . . . that a claimant shall be available for work in any particular place, such as the locality in which he earned his wage credits or where he last worked or resided . . . Nor does our statute . . . require that the employe shall be available for full-time work, or for permanent, as distinguished from temporary, employment . . . By the same token, the availability rule does not necessarily require that a claimant be available for his most recent work or his customary work. It is sufficient if he is able to do some type of work, and there is reasonable opportunity for securing such work in the vicinity in which he lives.[49]

The great weight of administrative opinion may be said to support these conclusions.[50]

Some of the courts, however, have not been convinced. The supreme courts of Ohio and South Carolina have approved a rule that availability requires availability for the work the claimant has been doing.[51] In Massachusetts one district court has held a chambermaid unavailable for work because she was unable to work the new hours her employer had fixed.[52] Another held a shoe cutter ineligible because a foot injury prevented him from working his machine.[53] A Georgia superior court and a Michigan circuit court have held workers ineligible for benefits because they lost their transportation to their last employment.[54]

Situations do arise which require a ruling that a particular claimant is unavailable for work if he excludes work in a particular establishment, at specified hours, or in a designated locality. The worker who will not take work outside the one-company town is apt to be unavailable unless he is willing to accept the working conditions that go with working for "the company." This, however, is entirely different from a general rule that a worker must be available for work with a particular employer. Not only are such rules undesirable as destructive of worker mobility and freedom to choose employment, they are utterly unrealistic as definitions of labor force attachment.

THE DEMONSTRATION OF AVAILABILITY

To demonstrate his availability the worker must look for work, as instructed by the agency. This rule is intended to stress two points. Registration for work usually creates a presumption that the claimant is available. Ordinarily, however, better proof is obtainable. The agency should require it in the form of a guided but active search for work. This is no cast-iron rule. There are exceptions to which we will presently come. Second, the agency, from the point of view of both unemployment compensation and employment service administration, owes the claimant a duty of assistance and guidance in his search for work.

Justification for a "Guided, but Active Work Search" Requirement

The state which compensates unemployed workers for their unemployment has a right to demand that they make an effort to end their unemployment. No one will argue with that statement. The argument has been over the kind of effort the claimant should be required to make and, especially, whether all claimants should at all times be required to make an active search for work independent of the employment service.

It should be obvious, in view of the infinite variety of circumstances which different claimants, occupations, and labor markets present, that no flat "Yes" or "No" can be given to the question of the independent search. The claimant who has been laid off for two weeks while the plant is being repaired can hardly be expected to scurry about in search of a two-week job. When depression strikes and there is no work to be had, the independent search requirement is a mockery of misfortune. It not only embitters the claimant; it places an unfair burden upon the employers to whom claimants apply in making their "independent search" for work. Nothing could be more futile. Again, if the employment office has plenty of job openings in the claimant's field, what useful purpose does his independent effort serve? To apply such a requirement in those circumstances would do no more than weaken the employment service.

As we have seen, however, from our review of the employment service, it often does not have a plenitude of jobs for the claimant. This may be the case even when the employment level is high. Again, the claimant's occupation may be very specialized. In such instances, the public employment office may be expected to receive few job openings to fill. When these are the facts the worker should be required to make his own search for a job.

It is not enough, however, to reach this conclusion in a claimant's case and then hold him ineligible if he fails to look for work by himself. Simple justice requires that the worker be told (1) that his circumstances require an independent job-hunt, and (2) what there is in his situation that makes this requirement necessary. (In too many instances claimants, although never informed of a requirement of an independent search for work, have been held ineligible for failing to make such a search.[55] When the requirement is imposed the reason for it is seldom given.) But even this is not enough. To stop at that point means that the agency runs the great risk that the claimant's independent canvass may be purely *pro forma*. He will waste his time and the time of employers and be no nearer to a job. Furthermore, to tell a claimant he must do his own looking for work should not end the employment office's obligation to him. Even when the employment office has no referrals to offer him it owes him the duty of job assistance.

The assistance in such cases may take many forms. Here are some of the steps that may be involved. The claimant should be given *labor market information* — what is the job picture in his field in the particular locality and elsewhere. He should receive *job counseling*. He should be helped to an understanding not only of the other occupations open to him, but also of the other industries in which he may use the skills he already has. Long-run vocational guidance is definitely involved here. Most concretely and most important — *he should be helped in mapping out a definite plan for his job search.* The ordinary worker is not an expert job-hunter. Often he does not know where to look for work. He seldom knows how to sell his services. On both these counts he needs the expert help of the employment office. It may be said that all claimants are entitled to these aids. Although this is perhaps theoretically true in reality the time usually cannot be found for such careful service to all. In the case of claimants required to do their own job-seeking, such aids should be a condition of the requirement.[56]

American Attitudes toward the "Seeking Work" Question

Early Interpretations

The views outlined above depart somewhat from the opinions found in the earlier benefit decisions. Most states have always accepted an independent search for work as strong proof of the claimant's availability.[57] The general rule was, however, that no independent search for work is ordinarily required of a claimant. The Oklahoma Board of Review took the extreme position that a claimant's failure to seek work independently of the employment service is unimportant in determining availability since such a search is not required. Only where the claimant presented evidence upon the point in support of his eligibility would it be considered.[58]

To compel unemployed workers, as a condition for the receipt of unemployment benefits, to actively seek work would in effect reestablish an outworn, uneconomic, and discarded practice which the Unemployment Compensation Act was intended to eliminate.[59]

Similar opinions were occasionally expressed in other states.[60]

A more moderate view was set forth by the Indiana Review Board.

The Indiana Employment Security Act does not provide, as an eligibility requirement, that a claimant must actively seek work. On the other hand, mere registration for employment with the United States Employment Service cannot always be considered as full compliance with the eligibility requirement that a claimant must be able to work and available for suitable work. Unemployed persons, in order to be considered available for suitable work, must be willing to do those things in respect to securing work that reasonable persons would do under like or similar conditions.[61]

The New Jersey Board of Review held that a rule that a claimant was ineligible because he did not make any efforts to secure employment was justified in a community where employment opportunities are plentiful. Where opportunities were limited and the claimant made every reasonable effort to secure work where it was likely to be obtainable, the rule was to be applied less stringently.[62] A similar approach was taken in Utah.[63] A Florida referee took the position that, although an active search for work was not a substantive element of availability, a claimant's failure to conduct such a search might result in a failure to satisfy the tribunal that he was actually in the labor market.[64]

Postwar Opinion

Before 1946, a rule that an independent search must be made had seldom been stated in the benefit decisions. Since then an increasing number of tribunals have held that an active search for work is required to establish availability.[65] In most instances, reliance upon the employment service for placement has not been accepted as an "active search for work." By now, also, twenty-two states have modified their laws to require, specifically, that claimants seek work.[66] Sixteen of these amendments were made in 1947–49, clearly a reaction to alleged abuses of unemployment benefits.

Principles Underlying Availability for Work, a document sponsored by the Bureau of Employment Security, expresses opposition to "any general requirement that workers conduct an independent search for work." It recognizes an exception "when a claimant's placement through the public employment service, or some other approved placement agency, is extremely improbable because the agency does not usually receive orders for the particular job or working conditions the worker wants." [67]

"Active, but Guided Search" Requirement
a Middle Path

This brief survey of American practice on "seeking work" requirements indicates that it has been negative rather than affirmative in character. Two diverse and general approaches have been taken. One rests upon the questionable premise that the employment service will supply enough job offers to make the independent search unnecessary. Until the employment service does meet that obligation, it is reasonable to expect and to ask claimants to do their best to help themselves. As the Tennessee Board of Review has said:

Eligibility for benefits does not revolve solely upon the inability of the employment service to place the claimant. Otherwise, a person who never had any intention of working at all could draw benefits simply because the employment service could not place them [sic] in some job perhaps of an unusual type, when, as a matter of fact, of his own knowledge, on account of being a member of a very special and particular calling, he may know of many vacancies and apply for none.[68]

The other general approach has been to impose, as a universal requirement, usually statutory, that claimants must make an active search for work. This, too, seems undesirable. As suggested above, there are times when registration with the employment service should be sufficient. No general statutory requirement can honestly be interpreted to permit a claimant to rest his search for work with registration and acceptance of referrals. Reading the "want ads" is not enough to meet a statutory requirement of "actively seeking work." [69] Applying for work to a private employment agency or through a union have, however, been held acceptable.[70]

Even under such a requirement the number and kind of job applications necessary in any given time period will vary with the circumstances. In New Jersey, industrial workers who claimed benefits in 1948, after the law was amended to require an active search for work, were advised to apply for work every day. In Missouri, for example, it has been held that a woman worker who had originally quit work because of pregnancy and later applied to her old employer at least five times had met the statutory "seeking work" requirement when the employer had agreed to call her if it had an opening.[71] A worker who had become unemployed because of a reduction in force did not, however, meet the requirement by keeping in touch with the employer.[72] An experienced cigar bunch maker who applied to the only other cigar factory in the area complied with the law.[73] Two applications in "many weeks of unemployment" are not enough; three applications in a period of over two months and a total of four or five applications in three months have been held not enough.[74] The law was satisfied, however, by applications at four places (the only retail stores in the town) in three months, and by six to eight applications in a two-month period.[75] The North Dakota Commissioners, by contrast, have held that claimants must make at least one attempt each week for which they file benefit claims.[76]

Of the twenty-two state laws that specifically require a search for work to establish eligibility, all but seven are cast in terms of absolutes. Commonly they speak of "seeking work," "actively seeking work," or "diligently seeking work." In Connecticut, Kansas, Maine, and Maryland, the requirement is phrased in terms of "making reasonable efforts to obtain work." The work search provisions of the California, Vermont, and Wisconsin laws reveal a somewhat different approach. The California law, for example, tells the claimant "to make such effort to seek work on his own behalf as may be required in accordance with such regulations as the Commission may prescribe." The commission, in its regulation, has translated this to mean a "reasonable" effort as determined by the circumstances of the case. The commission designated certain active uses of union facilities, civil service applications, "want ads," private employment agencies, application to former employers, and so on, as presumptively reasonable efforts to seek work. The commission's regulation also declared that an independent search would not be necessary if circumstances showed that it would be fruitless to the claimant and burdensome to employers. The result has been that California's law and regulation achieve a reasonable and equitable result. This result, however, is one that every state may obtain by interpretation of a statute that contains no "seeking work" requirement.

It should be recognized that requiring a claimant to make an independent search for work is an admission that the employment service does not have a suitable job to offer him. Since it cannot give him the best help, it should, in those instances, give him the next best : aid in planning his own campaign for a job. Some of this has been done through counseling programs but not nearly enough. Too often claimants have simply been told, in broadside fashion : "Go out and look for a job."

Since the end of the war a number of state unemployment compensation agencies have sought to apply this rule : The longer the unemployment, the more active the search required. This neglects one of the basic truths about unemployment : The longer the unemployment, the poorer the worker's morale. A better rule would have been : The longer a claimant is out of work, the more help he needs in finding his way back to a job.

At the same time, it might be well to emphasize to claimants the advantages to them of self-help in finding work. The claimant who makes his own direct search for work is free to be more discriminating than when he is following employment-service channels. Failure to accept employment-service referrals or offers of work made by employers to whom the claimant has been referred may carry sanctions in loss of unemployment benefits. Practically speaking, such sanctions do not apply to a claimant's independent job search.

We should recognize that the suggestion that claimants be expected to try to find their own jobs is somewhat less than ideal. Candor, however, requires that we admit the present imperfect state of the employment services. As they improve, the need for independent job hunting by claimants will diminish.[77] "The inn that shelters for the night is not the journey's end. The traveler must be ready for the morrow."

CHAPTER VII

GENERAL PRINCIPLES (CONTINUED)

SUBJECTIVE VS. OBJECTIVE APPROACHES

THE PRECEDING CHAPTER developed an *objective* approach to availability for work. The principles it suggested look outward from the claimant's state of mind to such factors as his work registration, the work history, his overt acts in seeking work, and, principally, the amount of work he is willing and able to take. In this chapter we shall be concerned with the *subjective* aspect of availability.

The subjective approach emphasizes the claimant's willingness and personal readiness to work rather than the quantum of work for which he is available. A claimant is available for work if he is physically able and ready and willing to work at some recognizable labor ordinarily done for hire. If he has exposed himself fully to work opportunities, the subjective approach tends to discount involuntary circumstances that make it unlikely for the claimant to obtain work.

The subjective and objective approaches have often been placed in opposition.[1] Originally the subjective view was dominant. In more recent years, especially during World War II, the objective view has come to the fore. The contrasting approaches may be better seen in perspective by examining some pertinent cases.

Governmental Restrictions

Effect of Legal Custody

Claimants whose freedom to work has been curtailed by legal detention are usually held unavailable upon the theory that they are unable to accept an offer of work.[2] Both a county jail inmate convicted of larceny and a parolee from a state mental hospital who had not yet been restored to reason by court order have been held to lack the legal capacity to enter into or perform contracts of employment.[3]

An Ohio claimant who left the state in order to avoid paying for support of a minor child was held not available for work. The payment had been imposed by a court as a condition of suspending sentence in a criminal nonsupport proceeding. The referee said: "It must be assumed that employers if apprised of the facts would not hire the claimant; therefore, he is an unemployable person, and on that theory he is not available for work." [4] A West Virginia claimant was denied benefits while he was out of jail awaiting trial for statutory rape when he was afraid to return to his job because of public feeling against him. The reason given for denying benefits was that the claimant's plight was his own fault.[5]

It should be emphasized that actual detention, and not innocence or guilt, has been the controlling factor in these cases. (In the Ohio nonsupport case given above, the referee considered the claimant "technically incarcerated.") Thus a claimant who had been ordered deported was held available when an immigration inspector informed the referee that the order might be executed in a short time or delayed for years.[6] Also held available for work was a claimant whose prison sentence for a drunken brawl had been suspended upon condition that he leave the city.[7]

Wartime Alien Controls

Japanese Evacuation and Relocation. During World War II the West Coast Japanese, including both aliens and American citizens, were removed from their homes to government-operated centers. Several preliminary steps preceded the relocation — freezing of alien assets, designation of strategic zones prohibited to enemy aliens, and imposition of curfews and travel limitations upon Japanese and enemy aliens. In March 1942 the enforced physical relocation of the Japanese began, first into assembly centers, and later into the more permanent relocation centers. The latter were ten communities located in sparsely settled areas of Arizona, Arkansas, California, Colorado, Idaho, Utah, and Wyoming. In 1942 these communities housed over 65,000 evacuees, over 104,000 in 1943. The major movement into the relocation centers began in May 1942 and continued until November.

Some of the Japanese-Americans had wage credits and sought to file benefit claims when the war made them unemployed. Determination of these claims centered about the question of availability for work. The reported decisions show that only so long as they kept out of the assembly and relocation centers were the Japanese claimants held available for work. Freezing of Japanese assets and curfew travel regulations, it was held, did not necessarily destroy availability.[8]

In three key decisions, the California Employment Commission held relocation center residents unavailable because their liberty of movement was restrained by War Relocation Authority regulations. One claimant had had two months' leave from the center to harvest beets and had worked in the center as a power-shovel operator. The center had a United States Employment Service office.[9] Another claimant had worked from February to May 13, 1943, for the center camouflage net factory. On May 17, 1943, when he replied to the commission's questionnaire, he had already received an indefinite leave permit but had not yet left the center. This permitted him to remain outside the center indefinitely. (Other types of leave, all of which required War Relocation Authority permission, were: short-term leave, to attend to personal affairs; leave to participate in a work group for the duration of the work; daily work pass, to commute to work outside the center.)

In this second case the commission emphasized that until the evacuee actually left the center he was controlled by the War Relocation Authority. Despite the claimant's actual work in the center, the existing work opportunities both in the center and outside, and the War Relocation Authority's policy of encouraging the evacuees to leave the centers, the California Commission concluded that the area was "remote" and work opportunities were extremely limited.[10] Only an evacuee who had already left the center on an indefinite leave permit was held available.[11] The California reasoning was followed by the Hawaii referee in denying benefits to a Japanese alien who had been evacuated to an Arkansas relocation center.[12]

Other Wartime Security Controls. A Nevada decision considered the disabilities of a Japanese alien outside the coastal area. A Nevada war worker of Japanese citizenship was detained by the FBI and later paroled to a citizen-sponsor in Utah. He was subject to residence, travel, curfew, and employment restrictions. The Nevada Board of Review held the claimant unavailable for work and emphasized that availability required ability to accept any suitable job at any time. That the claimant's restrictions were not self-created made no difference. "A claimant must be free as well as willing to accept work; he is not free to do so when the consent of a Government authority is necessary and there is no assurance that approval will be forthcoming." [13]

In Indiana an alien discharged, upon War Department orders, after twenty-six years' employment in a steel mill was held unavailable for work. Although nothing in the facts indicated subversive activities, the referee was convinced that "the War Department does not act capriciously." The claimant was free to work on nonclassified contracts. The referee, however, believed that no employer would hire the claimant if he knew that his last employment was terminated on War Department orders.[14]

Equally arbitrary was the decision of the West Virginia Circuit Court of Kanawha County. Ichamaru, a Japanese citizen, was a cook or steward for the Island Creek Coal Company. On December 8, 1941, he was taken into custody by the FBI and detained for about six months. He was then paroled in the custody of a New York City church committee. He then filed a benefit claim. In denying benefits, the court stressed that claimant's inability to get work was created not by the West Virginia employer, but rather by the action of the country of which he was a citizen.[15] This and the Nevada decision show the extremes which may result from an objective approach to availability. They tend to make the requirement mean availability of work.

An entirely subjective view was applied by an Ohio court to the case of an enemy alien who was discharged from a war plant, on Army orders, solely because he was an enemy alien. The court considered neither the claimant's occupation and skills nor the work that might or might not be open to him as an enemy alien. Instead it made the claimant's actions as a war worker the test of his eligibility. Was he a dangerous person in a war plant? Had he in any way impeded war production? If so, then he was not entitled to benefits. If, as the record showed, he was an honest and diligent workman who performed his duties and conducted himself as though he were a citizen then he was entitled to benefits.[16]

Even more striking is the decision by a New Jersey referee in the case of an American citizen of German descent. The claimant, a mechanical engineer in a war plant, was discharged in November, 1943, upon War Department orders, for subversive activities. The charge was later upheld in a hearing. The claimant did not get a job until January 29, 1944. While unemployed he wrote two hundred letters of application and applied personally to several employers. The referee held him available for work since he "complied with the statutory requisites." [17]

War Manpower Controls

In World War II workers in essential industries who left work without getting releases from their employers or "statements of availability" from the War Manpower Commission were not permitted to be hired for other work for a specified penalty period. The bar did not, however, prevent the employment service from referring them to work essential to the war effort or employers from hiring them for work in agriculture, domestic service, or government employment. These regulations aroused the sharpest conflict between the subjective and objective views of availability.

Decisions in at least nine states flatly denied benefits to workers who lacked statements of availability.[18] In other states this was somewhat softened. California and Illinois made exceptions in favor of the worker who quit with good cause.[19]

In some states the worker who was entitled to an availability statement but had, through error or ignorance, failed to get it was held eligible.[20] In both Missouri and North Carolina the determination of that entitlement was made by the unemployment compensation tribunal for itself.[21]

Most of the decisions denying benefits were based upon a policy of assisting the war effort. The rationalization offered, usually not clearly expressed, was the limitation on the work which the claimant could take. This was the explicit reason in cases where the claimant limited himself to work which he could not obtain without a statement of availability.[22] An Indiana referee evidently had this consideration in mind when he found that a claimant who quit his California job to return to Indiana was available for work. Although he gave no supporting facts, the referee said that the work limitations caused by the lack of an availability statement were insufficient to warrant a finding of unavailability.[23]

In five important industrial states — Connecticut, Michigan, New Jersey, Ohio, and Pennsylvania — a wholly subjective view was taken.[24] The most forthright statement came from the Connecticut Superior Court at New Haven County in the Mishaw case. Mishaw was a compositor of some thirty years' experience. He was hired as such by the Fairfield News but was actually assigned to tasks that were mostly those of a porter. He left the job and was denied a statement of availability. After stressing the need to look from the angle of the unemployed person to determine availability, the court said:

Availability for work is to be decided upon what the claimant does and not upon the existence of regulations, foreign to the act, which bar employers from hiring. And it makes no difference whether such regulations arise from agreements entered into by industry or imposed on it by federal authority. In short, the test of a worker's availability is subjective. As long as no provision of the act disqualifies him, he is entitled to its benefits, so far as the point under discussion is involved, when he has exposed himself unequivocally to the labor market.[25]

The last two sentences were later quoted with approval by the Connecticut Supreme Court of Errors.[26] The entire language was adopted by the New Jersey Board of Review.[27]

The language of the Mishaw case is sweeping. It lumps together all governmental hiring restrictions and all industrial limitations upon hiring as a single mass of irrelevant circumstances. It stresses the claimant as an actor in the labor market but makes no inquiry into the labor market in which he acts. So far as the court was concerned, the claimant, because of his lack of an availability statement, might actually have been barred from taking any work.

More moderate views were expressed by the federal Bureau of Employment Security. The bureau advised the states:

It remains for the State unemployment compensation agency to apply its interpretation of availability for work to all the circumstances of the individual cases, including the limitations on the worker's access to the labor market resulting from any lack of a statement of availability and his readiness, willingness, and ability to take work to which access is not limited by the plan.[28]

This was cited, in a detailed opinion, by the New York Appeal Board as the correct rule. The board concluded:

The failure of claimant to possess a statement of availability neither bars him from all employment, nor does it bar us from inquiring into whether he is available for employment under our Law.[29]

Government Licenses or Permits

It is generally agreed that availability for work means availability for work that is lawful. Availability for pandering would qualify no one for benefits. Women and minors, to be available for work, must be ready, willing, and able to do some work which is not legally barred to them.[30] If the law requires a license to practice the occupation, the claimant must be so licensed.[31] But what happens to his availability when he loses the license through no fault of his own and is unable to work at anything else?

Substantially, that is what is involved in the homeworkers' cases. The best known of these is *Smith* v. *Murphy*.[32] Maude Smith, fifty-two years old, was the mother of five children, the youngest being seven years old. She lived thirteen miles outside Gloversville, New York, and for thirty-five years she had been an industrial homeworker on gloves. Her husband worked in Gloversville and she was unable to leave her home to accept daytime outside work. In May 1942 the Industrial Commissioner denied her a homeworker's certificate. When she claimed benefits she was held unavailable for work when she refused work in a Gloversville factory. Both the referee and the Appeal Board disagreed with the determination and the Industrial Commissioner appealed to the court.

The court disposed of the appeal in these words:

Claimant became unemployed through no fault of her own. Now the State through the Industrial Commissioner with the one hand deprives her of the right to augment the family income through work which she can perform and compels her to be and remain unemployed and with the other hand would deprive her of the statutory benefit of being so unemployed. Claimant herself is able, ready and willing to accept employment at work which she has performed for some thirty-five years or at similar work. She is thus available for employment. Due to the State's refusal to permit industry to deliver work to her and to permit her to receive such work and the lack of similar work, she remains unemployed.

This may be compared with a previous decision by the same court denying benefits to a New York City homeworker who moved with her husband to Washington where there was no homework.[33] The claimant, who had one child, ten years old, refused a referral to work outside her Washington home on the ground that she had always worked at home and had to take care of her child.

An Illinois Board of Review decision, on somewhat different facts, allowed benefits to a homeworker during a period when she was not permitted to do homework. In this case, however, it was the employer, not the worker, who was required to have the permit. Benefits were allowed for a two-month period during which the claimant's regular employer was unable to employ her because of a delay in issuing the permit.[34]

More apropos is the decision of the New Jersey Board of Review. The claimant had been a homeworker for four years, always for the same employer. A federal ruling ended the relationship by prohibiting the employer from giving out any more homework. Although the claimant now lacked a homeworker's permit she would take no outside work because she suffered from recurrent attacks of lumbago which often disabled her. The board held her unavailable for work "because of the qualifications as to the type of work she will accept and the restrictions she has herself imposed." [35] Although the language used indicates a subjective approach, the facts bespeak objective measurement of availability solely in terms of the amount of work which the claimant was available to take. As such, it is in sharp contrast with the position taken by the same board on the effect of a lack of an availability statement.[36]

Other Involuntary Restrictions

Physical disabilities and lack of transportation to work come readily to mind as examples of involuntary circumstances curtailing availability for work.

Physical Inability

In physical inability cases the rule is clear that the claimant need not be available for all work or his last or customary work. He satisfies the law if he is available for some recognized kind of work that is ordinarily done for pay.[37] It is not required that such claimants be capable of competing with able-bodied workers, even in the field of work to which their disabilities restrict them.[38] Reluctance on the part of employers to hire epileptics,[39] cripples,[40] aged workers,[41] and others with disabilities detracting from their physical appearance or working powers[42] has been no bar to benefits.

The general rule has been that claimants suffering from physical disabilities must be able to work under the conditions that normally characterize employment. In a number of cases, however, claimants have been held eligible even though their disabilities required them to modify the usual working hours or conditions. A nervous bookkeeper-typist was granted benefits even though she could do no work outside her home.[43] Benefits have been allowed to disabled veterans who needed time off two or three times a week. In one case it was for medical treatments, followed by a few hours' rest after each.[44] In another it was because of recurring headache attacks.[45] Going home for meals because of a stomach ulcer[46] or eating every two hours[47] have also not prevented claimants from qualifying. An amputee in a wheel chair who could take no work involving stairs was also held able to work.[48]

In almost all jurisdictions more lenient standards have been applied to the claims of the physically disabled, although benefits have been denied to those utterly incapable of work lest the law become a health insurance measure.[49] The involuntary nature of the limitation is the main reason for this leniency.

Loss or Lack of Transportation

The benefit decisions present a somewhat different picture in the case of workers who, involuntarily, lack transportation to employment. These may be divided into two groups: (1) Workers who are stranded when their employer stops doing business or reduces his force and who have no transportation to other work; (2) Workers who once had but now have lost their transportation to work.

Few benefit decisions arise in the first category. This is to be expected since the workers fall in the precise class which unemployment compensation was intended to aid. Paying benefits to them presents only theoretical difficulties.[50] In practice benefits are paid and appeals are seldom taken. Consequently there are few benefit decisions.

In the second group appeals arise much more frequently. The weight of opinion is that workers who have lost their transportation to work are unavailable for work, if they live in communities where they have no work opportunities. Court decisions on the question base their conclusion upon the worker's obligation to supply himself with transportation.[51] They also contain a strong current of opinion to the effect that the claimant must be available for work at his last employment. Administrative decisions have ordinarily given little or no weight to the claimant's lack of fault for the loss of his means of getting to work.[52]

In a few states, a more sympathetic view has been taken. The Illinois Board of Review has held a claimant available for work when she was laid off, for lack of work, by the only employer to whose place of business she had transportation. The claimant had worked there for a year and a half and rode to work with her husband who had remained in the same employment. The employer had adopted a policy of not rehiring women. The board evidently assumed, however, that the claimant's continued unemployment was due, not to a lack of transportation, but to a lack of work.[53]

Decisions in Iowa, North Carolina, and Pennsylvania lay down a similar rule.[54] If the claimant has become unemployed for lack of work at the only place to which he had transportation he is held available for work although he is unable to get to other areas of work opportunity. The New York rule appears to be that the claimant without employment opportunities in his place of residence and without transportation to any place of possible employment may be held available for work. In order to qualify the claimant must be willing to work and must be making an honest effort to solve his transportation problem.[55]

RECONCILING THE SUBJECTIVE AND OBJECTIVE APPROACHES

It should be evident that no single approach to availability can be satisfactory in all cases. Mere willingness to work is not enough. The claimant must be free to work, physically and mentally capable of working and, ordinarily, in a position to get to some kind of work. By the same token, freedom to work, physical and mental ability, and access to a labor market area do not suffice. The will to work must exist. These factors add up to availability. We have said that to qualify a claimant for benefits, the sum should be availability for a substantial amount of work. Yet we may not suppose that even this general rule lacks its exceptions. Only through such exceptions can equitable results be generally attained.

Weighing Involuntary Unemployment or Work Limitation

If a claimant's unemployment or availability restrictions are involuntary in origin, he should be given the benefit of any reasonable doubt that the work for which he is available is of substantial amount.[56] The previous chapter suggested three tests to help in determining if the work for which the claimant is available is substantial in amount: the claimant's work history, qualification for benefits, and the labor market. These tests are not precise. In many instances their application will leave a real doubt: Has the claimant met the requirement? When this happens a subjective test should be used. How did the claimant become unemployed? Was it voluntary or involuntary? Why does he limit his availability? Is it mere whim or preference which motivates him? Or is it some "overpowering circumstance" which leaves him no real choice? If the unemployment or the limitation are involuntary in origin the doubt should be resolved in the claimant's favor.[57]

This principle applies the basic policy of unemployment compensation to resolve the conflict between the two fundamental approaches to availability. The laws of more than half the states declare that it is their purpose to benefit persons "unemployed through no fault of their own," combat the hazard of "involuntary unemployment," or do both.[58] Courts have commonly used these general purposes of unemployment compensation statutes as a guide in interpreting specific provisions.[59] They have done this even where the statute did not expressly declare that its purpose was to relieve involuntary unemployment.[60] In so doing the courts have followed an established rule of statutory construction, that is, in case of doubt as to the meaning of a statute, its general intent may be used to aid the interpretation.

Some cautions should be noted here. The reason for the unemployment or the availability limitation, whether voluntary or involuntary, has no direct bearing upon the question: Is the claimant available for enough work? Its use is suggested solely as a way of meeting a doubt. When no doubt exists no occasion arises, in measuring the amount of work the claimant can and will take, to consider the reason for his unemployment or work limitation. If it is clear that a claimant is available for a substantial amount of work it does not matter that he has voluntarily, even arbitrarily, limited the work he will take. If it is clear that the claimant is not available for a substantial amount of work it will, in most instances, make no difference that he is unemployed because of no fault of his own or that circumstances beyond his control force the work limitation.

Even when a doubt is so resolved in the claimant's favor, it does not mean that the question is permanently settled. Availability is a continuing test which the claimant must continue to meet. When other suitable work is available for him, the longer a claimant is unemployed because no work can be found within his restrictions the greater becomes the doubt that he is available for a substantial amount of work. The principle outlined above suggests allowing the claimant a reasonable period to find work within his limitations, when those limitations or his unemployment stem from causes beyond his control. If unemployment compensation is to furnish a bridge of benefits between jobs, it is essential that it give workers an opportunity to adjust to changed job conditions.

Involuntary Limitations: Personal and Impersonal

When involuntary, nonpersonal causes cut the worker off from suitable work opportunities he should be considered available for work despite his lack of access to a substantial amount of work. The length of the emergency adjustment period thus granted must be graded to the circumstances.

A real difference exists between involuntary work limitations based on the claimant's personal circumstances and those which are produced by nonpersonal causes. The worker is entitled to more time, in the latter case, to adjust to his new circumstances. It is not suggested that unemployment benefits should be restricted to instances where the unemployment is due to industry's failure to furnish work. Such a view tends to restrain worker mobility unduly and to lead to requiring that claimants be available for a particular job or at a particular place or time. Nonetheless, unemployment caused by impersonal factors, outside the control of the individual worker, is the major hazard against which the unemployment compensation is intended to operate. When that hazard strikes a worker, unemployment compensation should give the fullest kind of protection.

Normally, granting benefits in such circumstances is not inconsistent with requiring availability for a significant amount of work. From time to time, however, situations do arise which make such a requirement seem inconsistent with paying benefits. Such is the situation when the work a man does is abandoned, without reasonable likelihood that it will be resumed, and no other suitable work for him exists in his labor market area. This is the kind of result produced when the "company" leaves the one-company town. A similar question is presented by the worker, living in a community without suitable work opportunities, who has lost his access to such opportunities because he has been deprived of transportation facilities. Regardless of the rationale used, there can be no doubt that such workers should receive benefits. Payment may be justified as fulfilling the primary purpose of unemployment compensation. It may be defended upon the theory that no changes have occurred in the worker's willingness, readiness, or ability to work; only extraneous circumstances have been altered. Furnishing the worker a reasonable opportunity to explore job possibilities and to adjust to his new circumstances is an additional justification.

The result is not consistent with any "pat" theory. It does violence to both the "objective" and "subjective" views. In the cases suggested, willingness to work must be presumed for it cannot be tested. Only ability to work and personal circumstances affecting readiness to work can be measured at all, and then only hypothetically. Actually, the benefit payment is an emergency measure dictated by an emergency situation. The real problem is: How long does the emergency last? More accurately, when should the unemployment compensation agency tell the claimant: "You have had enough time to adapt yourself to your changed circumstance. You must now move or find a way to get to work if you wish to continue to be eligible for benefits."?

In answering this question it must be remembered that American unemployment compensation is a system of limited benefit duration. The most common maximum for weeks of benefits within a benefit year is twenty. Nowhere is the maximum higher than twenty-six. In most American states, benefit duration is variable, and a substantial number of claimants qualify for fewer than the maximum weeks of benefits.[61] The result is a fairly short period that the stranded claimant may be given, at public expense, to explore job possibilities.

It is not submitted that the entire benefit period should be granted without question to all or even most claimants in the group described here. The controlling factors should be (1) what the worker is doing to adjust himself, (2) what he reasonably can be expected to do, (3) his work history, and (4) his personal circumstances. The unmarried worker without family ties may reasonably be expected to move to a new community more readily than the family man who is a homeowner. The claimant who worked for twenty years in the plant which the company has abandoned needs more time to adjust than the one who had worked there a bare six months. The stranded worker who is making an effort to find a way out of his job difficulties is entitled to more assistance than the one who merely sits back and collects his checks.

Government Controls

We have seen that the power of the state may be used to curtail the individual's access to employment opportunity. When this prevents a worker from being available for a substantial amount of work, is he eligible for benefits? There is strong appeal in the New York court's argument that the state may not with one hand deprive the worker of a livelihood and with the other deny him the benefits of being involuntarily unemployed. Yet nowhere has that argument been effective enough to result in benefit payments to claimants who were illegally or innocently imprisoned.

To use the argument that government-imposed restrictions such as those which prohibit an employer from hiring an individual result in "constructive" imprisonment seems needlessly harsh.[62] As we have seen, thoughtful tribunals have rebelled against this view. Actually, it is based upon a mistaken assumption that prisoners are prevented "from being exposed to job opportunities and from accepting any job." [63] Although a prisoner may not be able to acquire the legal status of an employee,[64] he ordinarily works for hire during his imprisonment. He is not merely "exposed to job opportunities," he is forced to accept them. That element of compulsion, shown also in his legal inability to choose his work, makes the real difference between him and the free claimant.

None of the usual theories will rationalize the availability problems which government-imposed work restrictions raise. Fortunately, such problems are ordinarily infrequent. One approach which may be helpful (if not pressed too hard) is to distinguish the restrictions upon the basis of the government function involved. We may divide government operations into two very broad categories — political and socio-economic. Public safety, highway building, making war and peace are some examples in the first category. Tariffs, labor laws, price regulation are among those which belong in the second group. The original purposes of the state, this thesis suggests, are political. When the state, in fulfilling those purposes, curtails a worker's job opportunities so that he is not available for work he should not be entitled to benefits. His loss is part of the price of basic government functions. If, however, he is rendered unavailable for a substantial amount of work because of a socio-economic state operation he should be considered involuntarily unemployed, and in the same class as the victims of a sudden change in labor-market conditions.

Under such an approach prisoners would be held unavailable for work. During World War II it would also have meant that workers without availability statements who were unavailable for a substantial amount of work would have been considered ineligible for benefits. Homeworkers, however, who have been deprived of their permits, would be held available for work.

ELEMENTS OF AVAILABILITY

A logical order of exposition of the principles of availability would have made the "elements of availability" a starting point. By deferring that discussion until we had covered such subjects as the presumption of availability, amount of work, the demonstration of availability, and the conflicting subjective and objective approaches, some duplication has been avoided. The paragraphs that follow must be read in the light of the preceding discussion.

The usual statement of the elements of availability is that the claimant must be able to work, ready to work, and willing to work.

Able to Work: A more accurate term may be "qualified" to work. The eligible claimant is expected to have the qualities of the worker — physical and mental ability, skill, training, and experience sufficient to make him employable.

Ready to Work: "Freedom" to work better expresses this concept. "Ready" to work implies that the worker should be prepared immediately to accept offered work. Only one American statute, the law of Washington, specifies such immediacy. "An unemployed individual under the Unemployment Compensation Law is not presumed to be a minute man, standing at his door with his working-clothes on, his hand on the doorknob and his feet poised for a quick take-off in the event a job is offered him." [65] Literally, the word "ready" refers to preparedness, likelihood, opportuneness, and so on. This is somewhat inadequate. It is not enough that a claimant be prepared to work. Ordinarily, he must be free to work. Neither circumstances within his control nor those beyond his control must prevent him from being in a position to accept a substantial amount of work. Nor does the term "free" entirely cover the necessary ground. To be eligible the claimant must ordinarily have physical access to a labor market area where the work which he can and will do ordinarily exists.

Willing to Work: This is the most intangible element and the most difficult to test. How the claimant reacts to offers of work and his activity in looking for work are important as evidence. Often, however, there are no jobs to offer the claimant and it may be useless to expect the claimant to look for work. The claimant's previous work history and the circumstances of his separation from work may furnish the basis for inferences one way or the other as to his willingness. In many instances, however, the only recourse is to rely upon a general presumption of willingness to work.

SUMMARY

The principal points of this and the preceding chapter may be summarized as follows:

1. An otherwise eligible claimant ordinarily should be presumed available for work. Support for this presumption may be found in the following: (a) Most adult Americans work for a living. (b) The need to work is ordinarily not destroyed by benefits. (c) The claimant has demonstrated, by otherwise qualifying for benefits, a recent work history. (d) He has performed the overt act of registering for work.

The presumption is always rebuttable and not conclusive. Without the presumption, however, it is impossible to operate, especially when employment opportunities are few and work offers cannot be made. To require claimants to furnish affirmative evidence of availability because of any theory that the burden of proof of eligibility rests upon them loads them with a difficult and unfair task. Such doctrines have a place in court litigation. They do not belong in nonadversary proceedings such as the determination of unemployment benefit claims.

2. Availability must be for a substantial amount of suitable work. In general, a claimant should not be required to be available for work that is unsuitable for him, suitability of work depending upon his circumstances and the labor-market situation. At the same time, it is necessary that the worker be able and willing and in a position to accept a substantial amount of work. In determining whether the work within the claimant's limitations is of substantial amount, resort may be had to the criteria of benefit qualification, work history, and the local labor market area. The latter is the major test. The employment opportunities ordinarily existing in the labor-market area to which the claimant is available (where he lives or where he is willing and able to work) constitute the basic yardstick. Since availability for work, not availability of work, is involved, our concern is with the work ordinarily done in that locality and not with the job openings that happen to exist at the moment.

As a result, what is a substantial amount of work depends upon a long-run view of the labor market. It follows that a decision on whether a claimant is available for enough work is ordinarily not affected by the length of his unemployment or his prospects of work. Such factors, however, directly affect his sphere of suitable work. While remaining available for work, a claimant may, consistently, be disqualified for refusing without good cause a specific offer of suitable work lying outside his work restrictions.

The suggested test does not necessarily require a claimant to be available for his most recent work, his customary work, work at a particular place or time, full-time work rather than part-time, or permanent, rather than temporary, work. All that is necessary is that he be willing, able, and in a position to accept a substantial amount of suitable work.

3. To demonstrate his availability the worker must look for work, as instructed by the agency. An active, independent job search should be necessary only when and as administratively required. To codify this as a general statutory requirement leads to undesirable rigidity. When a claimant is required to make an independent search he should be told of the requirement and the reason and given assistance in planning his job hunt.

4. If a claimant's unemployment or availability restrictions are involuntary in origin, he should be given the benefit of any reasonable doubt that the work for which he is available is of substantial amount. Only when there is such a doubt does this principle apply. It tends to discriminate in favor of the involuntarily unemployed worker by giving him a longer period to explore job opportunities.

5. When impersonal factors, outside the worker's control, cut him off from access to suitable work opportunities he should be considered eligible for benefits even though he is unavailable for a substantial amount of work. The adjustment period granted to him will depend upon the particular circumstances. In some cases it may properly equal the maximum benefit duration. Some cases of curtailment of access to work because of government restrictions belong in this general category. A comprehensive rule is, however, difficult to formulate. One possible approach is to deny the benefit protection when the government function involved is political rather than, for example, socio-economic in its nature.

CHAPTER VIII

ABILITY TO WORK

BACKGROUND

AN INHERENT PART of availability for work is the physical and mental capacity to work. American unemployment compensation laws, however, are careful to specify that eligible claimants must be "able to work." In fact, the statutes place ability to work first and the requirement commonly reads "able to work and available for work."

The emphasis on "ability" reflects an effort to avoid health or disability compensation. To use insurance terms, it was intended to make unemployment due to physical or mental inability a non-covered risk. When American unemployment compensation was inaugurated compensating unemployment for economic reasons was considered more urgent. To cover the "lesser" risk in unemployment compensation was considered either too expensive or too daring. As a result, with four exceptions, American states cover workers for all types of involuntary unemployment except the most obvious kind. New Jersey, New York, Rhode Island, and California, the excepted states, have cash sickness insurance.

The failure to provide sickness compensation makes ability to work a crucial issue in unemployment compensation. It creates a need for careful, even meticulous distinctions between the "able" and the "unable" to work. The lack of sickness compensation produces conflicting pressures on unemployment compensation. On the one hand is a humanitarian desire to find ability to work in doubtful cases. On the other are the continuing efforts by claimants of questionable physical ability to try to "beat the system." Those efforts, sometimes successful, inevitably make administrators more watchful.

GENERAL DEFINITION

Based on the 1935–36 National Health Survey it has been estimated that, in 1940, over twenty-two million Americans, within the productive ages twenty to sixty-four, were handicapped by chronic disease or physical impairment, or had had some serious acute illness in the previous year.[1] Both the number of the physically weak and impaired and the infinite variety of jobs and their physical requirements compel a broad definition of ability to work.

Unemployment compensation authorities agree in general that "able to work" means no more than physical and mental ability to perform some services. They must be services that are ordinarily done for hire. And not only must the claimant be able to do some recognized work, he must also be able to do it under the conditions that ordinarily accompany that work. In other words, physically limited as the claimant may be, nonetheless he must offer sufficient physical and mental powers of labor to constitute salable services. Sometimes this has been stated in terms of a reasonable probability or expectancy of being hired. The cautionary statement is usually added that the claimant need not be able to compete with the physically able. Their economic competition may reduce his employability but they do not affect his ability to work.[2]

SPECIFIC PHYSICAL HANDICAPS

The foregoing general principles of benefit eligibility are substantially accepted throughout the country. The following sections consider some actual, illustrative rulings in cases of disease and disability.

Orthopedic Impairments

The 1935–36 National Health Survey defined an orthopedic impairment as a "permanent handicap which has been depriving the afflicted person of the natural use of some portion of his skeletal system." Estimates are that, in 1940, about 1.9 million Americans, 25 to 64 years old, had orthopedic impairments. Of these 1.6 million were not disabled. The survey showed, and it has been repeatedly demonstrated, that the incidence of unemployment is greater among such persons than among the physically whole.[3] The point hardly needs documenting. Significantly, unemployment compensation has been quick to accept such individuals as "able to work."

An Oklahoma referee's decision is illuminating. The claimant was a tailor. During his last employment he had the benefit of one leg and could use crutches. After he separated from his last job his other leg was amputated. As a result he was confined to a wheel chair. The referee said: "It is true he is limited by his physical handicap from accepting employment where it would be necessary to climb stairs, but it is also shown that there is employment in this area that he could perform; that he is in a position to accept such employment and physically able and capable of carrying on a full-time job in his customary occupation." [4]

Although most reported decisions have awarded benefits to amputees and others who have lost the use of their legs,[5] the Connecticut Shorten case is an exception. The claimant's legs were broken and he could not walk. The court found evidence to justify an ineligibility holding. According to the court, the test was ability to perform "some sort of work for which there is a call in the general labor market." That test is not met "if the only work which he is capable of doing is made work or work which might be offered to him for motives of sympathy or charity." [6]

Loss of an arm or its use has also seldom been a bar to establishing ability to work.[7] Thus, a veteran, rated 100 per cent disabled because of a bullet wound which paralyzed his right arm, was considered able to work. He testified that he could drive an automobile or truck and do any manual work requiring the use of only one arm.[8]

Blindness and Poor Vision

In general, American industry has treated the blind as unemployables. In 1935–36, for example, only 10 per cent of the blind (both eyes) were recorded as being employed. Although blindness of both eyes occurred in less than one-tenth of 1 per cent of the male population surveyed, ages fifteen to sixty-four, nearly 2 per cent of the "unemployable" males were blind.[9] Since the incidence of blindness climbs sharply with advancing years, it presents acute problems of occupational readjustment.

A Kansas case involved a sixty-one-year-old meat packer who had been retired because of age and failing eyesight. (He had nearly 20 per cent vision in both eyes.) He had worked in the meat packing industry for twenty-five years, before that in a newspaper circulation department. The claimant sought work actively but unsuccessfully. In awarding him benefits, the Kansas commissioner said:

Claimant has spent his life in useful employment. To say to such an individual that since he is unable to enter the general labor market for work of the type he previously performed, he is unable to work within the meaning of the Act, defeats the purpose of the Act in furnishing employment security in one of the most critical periods in claimant's life.[10]

Most unemployment compensation tribunals have been similarly inclined toward leniency in the case of blind claimants.[11] Weight has been given to the placement efforts of agencies for aid of the blind. The New Jersey Board of Review held that a blind claimant, pronounced employable by the State Commission for the Blind, could not be considered unable to work. The board also declared that a handicapped individual who was fitted for certain scarce types of work only was not to be expected to make the same general search for work as an unhandicapped individual.[12]

A different view appears in a Connecticut commissioner's decision. The claimant's poor vision made her need help to get about. During the war she did inspection work in a factory. Because of difficulty in obtaining a guide to bring her to work she left and obtained gauging work elsewhere. When the war ended she was laid off. At the time of her appeal she was able to get to her last employment and one other factory, but not to the plant where she had been an inspector or to the other large employers in the community. The commissioner acknowledged the claimant's interest in working but stressed that her inability to get to work at some of the places that could employ her definitely limited her availability for work. "Inasmuch as the Law makes no exceptions for persons in her handicapped condition, the same standards of availability must be applied to her as to everyone else." [13]

Ageing Workers

World War II cast the employment problems of older workers somewhat in the shade. Before the war those problems had been a serious national concern. The end of the war did not automatically revive the *status quo ante* for the elderly job seeker. The level of employment remained too high. Nonetheless, it was evident that older workers were no longer so welcome in postwar industry. Thus a special study in late 1946 of Oregon claimants who had been without steady work for more than two months showed that over half of the men were in the fifty to sixty-nine year age group. Over 8 per cent were seventy or more years old.[14]

The serious import of the placement difficulties of older workers is emphasized by the constant increase of the higher age groups within the population. In 1900 the United States had about three million people sixty-five years or older, representing 4 per cent of the population. In 1940 this group numbered nine million, a little less than 7 per cent of the population. Estimates are that in 1980 Americans sixty-five years or older will number twenty-two millions and constitute about 15 per cent of the population.[15]

To support so sizeable a group — whether by public or private funds — without receiving substantial productive services from them, will place an intolerable burden upon the economy. The only acceptable economic solution, in the absence of phenomenal strides in productivity, is to provide suitable and productive work for as many older people as possible. From the standpoint of their own health — both mental and physical — this is to the advantage of the older workers.[16] Usually it also accords with their own wishes.

In general, unemployment compensation tribunals have tended to find older workers both able to and available for work. This statement by the Indiana Review Board is typical: "The assumption that age *per se* renders an individual unavailable for work is untenable. All experience declares it false." [17] Most unemployment compensation tribunals would also accept the Virginia commissioner's view that, "One who is 67 years of age and shows a willingness to work within his limitations, does not have to meet the rigid requirements of a younger and more able-bodied man in order to establish availability for work." [18]

The claims of elderly workers often present this problem: They are no longer physically capable of doing their customary work, but they lack training and experience for other, lighter work. In the Anderson case, the claimant, seventy-two years old, had last worked in a wartime shipyard as a lead man fastener. According to him, his work was to mark places for others to bore holes. Before this job he had been a longshoreman for many years. Now he was no longer able to work in a ship hold although he could work on deck hooking on sling loads of lumber for hoisting. He had been referred to, but had refused to accept, three different laborer jobs. The Washington Superior Court agreed that these were beyond his strength and awarded him benefits.[19] Similar results have been reached in other jurisdictions.[20]

Another question is the effect of receiving pensions or old-age insurance. To what extent does it indicate unwillingness to work? Three jurisdictions, Hawaii, Montana, and West Virginia, by statute, bar recipients of primary old-age insurance benefits, under the Social Security program, from receiving unemployment benefits. In thirteen other states, only the excess, if any, of unemployment over old-age insurance benefits will be paid.[21] In all states, however, the view is taken that applying for old-age benefits or accepting an employer's pension may evidence an intention to retire from the labor force. Applying for or accepting such benefits are not, however, conclusive proof.[22]

A Pennsylvania referee's decision denied benefits to a sixty-five-year-old insurance office manager who retired on a monthly pension of $188.42 plus federal old-age benefits of $65 a month. He did not seek work independently and would accept only supervisory work at a minimum of $75 a week. The referee held that the claimant had not overcome the presumption, raised by accepting the retirement pension, that he intended to retire from the labor market.[23]

The Oklahoma Board of Review has held that a former oil-field worker, receiving monthly $33.66 in federal old-age benefits and $60 from an employer's retirement fund was "able," but not available for work. "Under the old-age plan of social security, he cannot be said to be in the labor market, so long as he receives funds from that fund." [24] This view is based upon a misapprehension. Old-age beneficiaries may and often do accept employment in preference to old-age benefits. Furthermore, they may, without loss of old-age benefits, earn up to $14.99 a month in covered employment and any amount in non-covered employment.

Contagious Diseases

In the case of claimants who are suffering from contagious diseases, a finding of inability to work is not always possible but the facts often show unavailability. If the ailment is quarantinable unavailability is usually automatic (except for homeworkers). Infectious skin ailments in food handlers or barbers, although barring them from their usual occupation, will not make them unavailable, if they may qualify for other kinds of work.[25] Syphilitic claimants are held eligible for benefits, if not infectious.[26] A Georgia referee explained this by saying that, if noninfectious syphilitics were generally not considered able to work and available for work, "many projects would have to stop for lack of labor." [27]

Tuberculosis has raised some difficult questions. Ordinarily, in active tuberculosis cases, medical opinion considers the victim infectious and unable to work. Benefits are usually denied in such cases.[28] Doctors may, however, disagree about a tubercular claimant's ability to work. They sometimes conflict in answering the question: Has the claimant's tuberculosis been arrested? A West Virginia coal miner, after a year's hospitalization for tuberculosis, reported back for work. The company doctor advised that his lungs might collapse at any time and he should not be rehired. The sanitarium doctors said he was not infectious and could do light work. The claimant was granted benefits.[29]

Sometimes the conflict is between the claimant and the doctor. a thirty-three-year-old carpenter was told, after a medical examination in October 1944, that he had pulmonary tuberculosis. He continued to work, running a bulldozer for four months and then seven months as a construction carpenter. This latter job proved too heavy for him and he left it in late November 1945. When he then claimed benefits, his doctor was asked for a statement. The physician advised that the claimant needed a complete rest for an indefinite period. In March 1945 the doctor had recommended hospitalization. This the claimant never underwent. The claimant's unemployment, except for some repair jobs, lasted until the end of April 1946, when he went to work on a full-time inside carpentry job. In finding the claimant able to work, the New York Appeal Board said:

It might have been advisable that claimant follow his doctor's recommendations in the best interests of his health. However, for reasons of his own he has not chosen to do so and apparently has not suffered any ill effects from adopting that course. In the light of his actual employment as a full-time worker, it must be held that claimant met the tests of availability for and capability of employment.[30]

PROOF OF ABILITY

Evidence concerning ability to work may be obtained directly from a claimant's own statements or behavior and appearance. The evidence may be the opinions of doctors, the observations of employers or fellow workers, or circumstantial evidence, such as the claimant's work and medical history, which raises reasonable inference. None of these constitute, in and of themselves, conclusive proof merely by falling in a particular category of evidence. The weight given to them must vary with the individual circumstances.

Claimant's Statements or Behavior and Appearance

A claimant's statement, in a contested claim, that he is able to work, is seldom given great weight. When little or no evidence exists that he is unable to work, the claimant's avowal of ability may be used to support the decision that he is eligible for benefits.[31] When, however, a claimant admits inability to work, as in a claim form or an application for sick benefits or disability compensation, that admission will usually be given great weight even though he later seeks to retract or modify it.[32]

The claimant's behavior or appearance before the tribunal or officer is bound to influence the decision. Thus, a painter who was so drunk when he reported on his benefit claim that the interviewer concluded that he could not work and might hurt himself if he tried was held ineligible by the New York Appeal Board.[33]

Ordinarily the claimant's behavior and appearance, like his avowals of ability, serve only as a check on other evidence.[34] A conclusion of sanity, based on medical testimony, a probate court proceeding, and a long employment record, is reinforced by the claimant's demeanor before the referee.[35] So also in the case of the claimant who continued to work even after he had injured himself, an appearance of good health aided the referee in concluding that the claimant was able to work.[36]

Medical Opinion

Unemployment compensation authorities recognize that ability to work is primarily the physician's province.[37] The usual practice, in questionable cases, is to direct the claimant to bring a doctor's certificate stating the claimant's physical condition and what employment limitations, if any, that condition requires. This, however, is not always satisfactory.

Some doctors do not accord such requests — whether made by the claimant or by the agency itself — the consideration they deserve. Sometimes the doctor fails to state in his certificate that he has examined or treated the claimant. This raises a suspicion that the doctor has simply written the kind of certificate that the claimant has requested. Often claimants bring medical certificates which say that they may do "light work" only. This is no help to the employment service which needs to know the claimant's specific physical limitations. Without such knowledge it is difficult to determine if a reasonable possibility exists of placing the claimant.

As suggested earlier, doctors sometimes disagree. Also, claimants, by their own actions in obtaining employment and keeping it, will at times disprove doctors' statements. A New Hampshire decision illustrates this. His physician described the claimant as a chronic asthmatic, unable to do work which required the same effort over regular workday periods. In the claimant's last job, in a shoe factory for an eighteen-month period, he had lost five weeks because of illness. Before that he had worked in a machine shop three years as a machinist. He was held able to work.[38]

In contrast is a Massachusetts decision. A meat cutter left work in February 1944 because of a heart attack. He first reapplied for his job in July 1944, and from then on three to five times a week until September when he was rehired as an over-the-counter salesman. He had been thus employed for two weeks at the time of the appeal hearing. He had filed a benefit claim in July shortly after he first reapplied for work. The claimant's doctor certified that the claimant, during the period in question, could do light work only. The decision denied benefits. "The claimant's brief employment in this case was not necessarily inconsistent with the doctor's diagnosis and therefore proved nothing as to the doctor's correctness. The employment may merely have indicated willingness to take a grave risk in spite of the doctor's advice." [39]

When a doctor predicts a date when the claimant will be able to return to work, that prediction may be outweighed by the claimant's statement, at an earlier date, that he is presently able to return to work.[40]

Employment History

Actual employment for hire is usually accepted as highly persuasive evidence of ability to work. It has sometimes been suggested that if ability to work has been questioned, evidence that claimant has worked will, in the absence of a change in his physical condition, remove all doubts of his ability.[41] An example is the case of a twenty-three-year-old claimant afflicted with arthritis since the age of three. He could walk with the aid of a cane. In his last job he had been employed for ten months at bench work mounting lenses in eyeglass frames. His arthritis became so severe that he had to leave. Earlier he had worked for nine months as a phonograph record-changer. The Illinois referee, in finding him able to work, pointed out: "Although claimant is crippled with arthritis, this same condition existed when he went downtown to work at his last job." [42]

Actually working, obtaining, or even seeking work have usually been considered strong evidence that a claimant who has been ill has recovered or that a claimant's disability is either nonexistent or limited to a specific kind of work. Thus, a Colorado coal loader who had "central nervous system syphilis" suffered from dizzy spells and short periods of lost consciousness. This made him unemployable in any mine operation. The fact, however, that he secured part-time work as a general dock laborer and that he was able to do such work on a full-time basis indicated his ability to work.[43]

A Nebraska epileptic quit his job to enter a hospital for special treatment, which neither helped nor hurt his condition. After he left the hospital he worked for about five months at an Army air base, before he became unemployed and claimed benefits. The appeal tribunal said: "He has best demonstrated his ability by working." [44]

Claimants sometimes engage in employment forbidden by their doctors. In such instances, the actual employment is ordinarily accepted as controlling evidence. Sometimes it has been said that to be considered physically able to work, a claimant must be able to work without endangering his physical condition.[45] Usually, however, assuming such danger, unless it may be a risk to others, it is considered a matter for the claimant alone to decide.

When a doctor treated a Massachusetts claimant for trench feet and certified inability to work for a minimum of six weeks, the claimant was nonetheless accepted as able to work after he found a job a week later and worked at it.[46] A North Carolina claimant was operated on for a double hernia. When he was discharged from the hospital his doctor told him not to work for two months. Instead the claimant applied for a job eight days later. He was not accepted. Within three weeks of his discharge from the hospital, however, he was working. He was held able to work.[47]

Claimants may also, by their work history, reveal physical inability to engage in sustained employment.[48] A history of absenteeism may suggest incapacity to work. A record of frequent job changes may also sometimes be associated with such incapacity. Caution is necessary in drawing inferences of inability from such circumstances. It need only be observed how difficult it often is for able-bodied workers to get work that is within their physical powers and at the same time suitable to their skills and training. When they accept, as they sometimes do, work that is not physically suitable, absenteeism and quits must be expected.

Disability Compensation

To apply for or receive sickness or disability benefits usually throws considerable light on alleged ability to work. Such benefits, however, are usually payable upon the claimant's inability to do his customary work. This permits some claimants to qualify under a disability benefit plan but yet be able to work within the meaning of the unemployment compensation law.

The most common disability benefit plan is workmen's compensation. The laws of five states — Connecticut, Massachusetts, Montana, Tennessee, and West Virginia — bar individuals who are receiving disability payments under workmen's compensation for a given week from receiving unemployment benefits for that week. In sixteen other states the disqualification is not total. Instead, recipients of workmen's compensation payments may receive only the excess, if any, of the weekly unemployment benefit amount over the weekly disability payment.[49]

An award or claim under workmen's compensation may raise a presumption of inability to work, but other facts may show that a conclusion of inability is not justified.[50] This has, however, been sometimes disputed on the ground that individuals should not be compensated twice for the same wage loss. The argument is particularly applicable to temporary disability. Even in that case, however, the compensated wage loss is not always marked by unemployment. A steeple jack may be injured at work and lose his sense of balance. He suffers a wage loss if he must then take lower-paid work. He may continue to receive workmen's compensation during a period when he cannot work as a steeple jack but can do other work. If he becomes unemployed during that time, should his disability benefits bar him from unemployment benefits?

The Indiana Board of Review has held that an award of sick benefits under a company plan was not "indicative" as to whether or not the claimant was thereafter able to work.[51] A Pennsylvania referee has held that a claimant who received sick benefits under a company plan was not able to work when her sick benefit application stated that she was totally unable to engage in any work, occupation, or business.[52] Essentially, then, as with workmen's compensation, the problem is one of coördinating with the unemployment compensation definition of ability to work.

Employer objections to hiring a claimant because he is a bad workmen's compensation risk have no bearing upon the claimant's ability to work, as that phrase is used in unemployment compensation.[53] This affects benefit claims filed by the physically handicapped who are often rejected for employment upon the ground, justified or not, that they are poor workmen's compensation risks.[54]

PHYSICAL STANDARDS

The mere fact that one employer, a group of employers, or even most employers would be reluctant to hire a claimant, does not affect his ability to work.[55] We have noted the greater incidence of unemployment among the physically disabled. The manpower utilization experience of World War II revealed again the great part prejudice plays in the joblessness of the disabled. Unemployment compensation tribunals have long been aware of this. By now it is accepted doctrine that "a physical disability, though lessening and perhaps even canceling a claimant's employment opportunities because of the unwillingness of employers to engage persons in claimant's condition, does not generally negative capacity to work." [56]

The view that availability for the last or customary work is not needed in order to meet the statutory requirement needs to be emphasized in the field of ability to work. It is stressed by the requirement in most state laws that, in determining whether offered work is suitable, the risk to the claimant's health and safety must be considered. Since physical ability wanes with the years and varies with changes in health, it is important that claimants should not be held to a requirement of ability to perform their last or usual work.

Unemployment compensation tribunals have, for the most part, been careful to accept ability to perform noncustomary work as satisfying the eligibility requirement.[57] A good statement of the prevalent view appears in a Kansas referee's decision:

A claimant may, because of some disability, be prevented from pursuing his usual occupation and yet retain sufficient powers of labor to render him capable of performing some gainful work in the labor market. If the claimant is ready, willing and able to accept some substantial, suitable work he should be held to have met the statutory requirement, so long as he had not so restricted the field of work for which he is available as to remove himself from the commercial labor market.[58]

Consistently, it has been held that a claimant may be able to work although he has failed to meet the physical standards of an individual employer.[59]

Disability for Part of a Week

All American unemployment compensation laws (except New York's) gear their benefits for total unemployment to "weeks" of joblessness. This raises the question: Is a claimant "able to work" during a compensable week if he has been ill during part of that week? The laws of Illinois, Indiana, Minnesota, and Washington reduce the weekly benefit by a fixed fraction for each work day of disability. The other states divide on the question. Some, like Utah, deny benefits for illnesses of three days or more and allow benefits for shorter illnesses only if the claimant did not, as a result of the illness, refuse work.[60] Others, like California, Oregon, Pennsylvania, and Texas, deny benefits if the claimant is unable to work for part of the week.[61] A few, like Missouri, allow benefits if the claimant's availability is not materially reduced.[62]

"Able though Disabled"

Six states (Maryland, Montana, and Nevada in 1945, Idaho and Tennessee in 1947, and Vermont in 1949) have borrowed, with some modification, a feature from the "GI Bill." Servicemen's readjustment allowances may be paid to an eligible veteran if he became unable to work during a period of continuous unemployment, and the unemployment had started before the disability came about. The state laws cited provide that, in such instances, "civilian" claimants may be paid benefits until they have been offered and have refused suitable work.[63]

Little evidence exists yet to show that these special provisos have made any real difference. Their theoretical justification is that, when lack of work initiates the unemployment it remains the basic cause for unemployment until suitable work is offered the claimant. Illness or disability occurring during the unemployment are not considered as the primary reasons for the continued joblessness. Whether or not this is sound reasoning, the reality is that

these provisos add a temporary disability insurance feature to unemployment compensation. This may be desirable, but the provisos
do lead to objectionable inequalities in treatment.

Suppose John Jones, a few days after being laid off and claiming benefits, rides in an automobile with Bob Brown. Both are disabled in an accident. Bob Brown, who works at the plant that laid
Jones off, gets his lay-off notice the day after the accident. Under
the provisos we have cited, Jones may receive benefits while he
is disabled but Brown may not.

Suppose instead that Mary White and Betty Gray, department
store salesclerks, are laid off on the same day. They come in together to file benefit claims. Two weeks later both girls, still unemployed, are disabled in the same automobile accident. Now both
continue to qualify for benefits under the proviso. Sometime later,
while both girls remain disabled, the local employment office offers
Betty Gray a suitable job but never reaches Mary White's name.
The result is that Betty is dropped from the unemployment compensation rolls as ineligible but Mary continues to draw benefits.
The real defect in the "able though disabled" provisos is not that
they give but half a loaf of protection; instead they give the worker
a lottery ticket for the half-loaf.

Temporary Disability Insurance

Three states — New Jersey, Rhode Island, and California —
have added disability insurance to their basic unemployment compensation systems. Other states are likely to follow suit. Rhode Island first instituted its Cash Sickness Compensation Act in April
1942. It is financed by 1 per cent deductions from wages. Coverage,
qualifying earnings, and administrative machinery are the same as
in unemployment compensation. Sick benefits, like unemployment
benefits, range from $10 to $25 a week, with benefit year potential
totals of $52 to $650. If unemployment is due to sickness resulting
from pregnancy, no more than fifteen weeks' benefits may be paid
to the claimant. Claimants may receive both workmen's compensation disability payments and sick benefits. If their sum exceeds
85 per cent of the claimant's average weekly wage at his last
regular employment, the weekly sick benefit amount will be reduced. Sickness is defined as the inability of an individual, because
of his physical or mental condition, to perform his regular or
customary work. The waiting period is one week. No sick benefits

are paid for any week for which the individual will receive unemployment benefits.

The California plan was enacted in March 1946. As in Rhode Island, financing is by a 1 per cent wage deduction, and coverage, qualifying earnings, and administrative machinery are the same as for unemployment compensation. Benefit amounts and totals are also the same as in unemployment compensation. In addition to disability benefits an individual confined to a hospital by his doctor's orders may receive $8 a day for not more than twelve days in any one benefit year. An individual may receive both unemployment and disability benefits in the same benefit year. Disability due to pregnancy is not compensable. The California definition of disability is the same as the Rhode Island definition of sickness. Only the excess, if any, of disability benefits over workmen's compensation will be paid to a claimant who otherwise qualifies for both. A worker who qualifies for unemployment benefits may not also receive disability benefits for the same weeks.

New Jersey enacted its temporary disability benefits law on June 1, 1948, benefits to become payable January 1, 1949. Qualifying earnings, coverage, administrative machinery, weekly benefits, and potential yearly totals are the same as in unemployment compensation. Financing is by a one per cent pay-roll tax, three-fourths from the workers and one-fourth from the employers. Benefits are barred for pregnancy, childbirth, miscarriage, or abortion. No benefits are payable for disability which is compensable under workmen's compensation. Disability is defined in two ways. An employed individual or one who has been out of employment for less than two weeks must be totally unable to perform the duties of his employment. An unemployed worker who meets all but the "able to work" qualifications for unemployment benefits must be totally disabled to perform any work for remuneration. A worker may not receive unemployment and disability benefits for the same week.

Both the California and New Jersey laws provide for election of private, voluntary plans instead of the compulsory one.

There has been little opportunity to accumulate experience with compulsory disability insurance. Rhode Island figures have shown an incidence of disability that is very close to the findings of the 1935–36 National Health Survey. Between 2 and 3 per cent of the eligible workers draw sick benefits each week.[64]

Coördinating unemployment and disability benefits has not been simple. The original definition of sickness in the Rhode Island Act was "unable to perform services for wages." This led to rulings that sick benefits could not be paid if the employee was able to do any work for which he could receive pay, whether or not it was his regular work.[65] The result was that the definition had to be changed.

Problems have arisen because workers have filed the wrong claim, asking for unemployment benefits when they were unable to work, or sick benefits when they were able to work. Apparently in Rhode Island the claimant must make an election, and at his peril.[66]

California tried to avoid this election by providing that the benefit year should be the same for disability and unemployment benefits and that filing of a valid claim for one should establish a valid claim for the other. (A valid claim requires that the individual be unemployed and have earned qualifying wages. Such a claim is necessary to start a benefit year.) The California Appeal Board has, however, decided that, if a claimant of disability insurance files a physician's certificate which does not conclusively establish disability but merely indicates questionable disability, he is ineligible for sick benefits. Not only is he ineligible for disability benefits, but also, according to the board, he does not have a "valid claim" sufficient to establish a benefit year. As a result, a claimant was denied disability benefits because he was able to work and unemployment benefits because he lacked a valid claim.[67]

In 1949 the New York legislature enacted a disability benefits law to be administered by the Workmen's Compensation Board rather than the unemployment compensation agency. Contributions begin January 1950 and benefits are payable for disabilities commencing on or after July 1, 1950. Although similar, coverage is not the same as in unemployment compensation. Benefits are one-half the average weekly wage of the last eight weeks of covered employment, with a minimum of $10 and a maximum of $26 weekly benefits. The total payable in any fifty-two consecutive week period or any one period of disability is thirteen weeks of benefits.

The plan contemplates two classes of beneficiaries: (a) workers disabled while engaged in covered employment or within four weeks after leaving such employment and (b) workers disabled while unemployed. Benefits to the first group are payable out of individual employer funds which the employer establishes by in-

suring with the state fund or with a private insurance company. If
he meets specified standards the employer may be his own insurer.
To pay the insurance cost the employer is authorized to deduct one-
half of one per cent, up to thirty cents a week, from his workers'
wages. Any costs of his workers' disability benefits that are not met
by such wage deductions are to be borne by the employer.

To be considered disabled, a worker in the first category mentioned above must be unable to perform the regular duties of his
employment or the duties of any other employment which his employer may offer him at his regular wages and which his disability
does not prevent him from performing. A worker in the second
category is considered disabled if he is unable to perform the duties
of any employment for which he is reasonably qualified by training
and experience.

The statute provides benefits for two groups of workers who are
disabled while unemployed. Workers whose wages qualify them for
unemployment compensation may, if disabled, draw disability benefits but only during the twenty-six week period immediately following separation from employment covered under the disability benefits law. Unemployed disabled workers who lack wages qualifying
them for unemployment compensation may also draw disability
benefits but only during a twenty-six week period following separation from covered employment and only if (1) they were paid
weekly wages of at least thirteen dollars in each of twenty weeks of
the thirty weeks preceding the last day they worked in covered employment and (2) they have, during their unemployment, evi-
denced their continued attachment to the labor market.

Benefits to unemployed disabled workers are not payable out of
individual employers' funds, but out of a special disability fund.
This fund is to be established out of employer and employee contributions during January–June 1950 and later replenished by such
annual assessments on the insurance carriers as the condition of the
fund requires.

CONCLUSIONS

All in all, the "ability" requirement in unemployment compensation has been administered with leniency. In part this is the
result of a catholic concept, derived from experience, of ability
to work. Employment service history emphasizes how few people
among the physically handicapped are actually unable to do some
kind of work for hire. In part, liberality on the score of "ability

to work" is a product of humanitarianism. Without disability insurance there is a reluctance to find a claimant unable to work and therefore ineligible for benefits.

The "ability to work" requirement, in the absence of disability insurance, is a constant threat to integrity of administration. Disabled unemployed workers need benefits even more than the able-bodied unemployed. This is the pressure for disability insurance. It is also the pressure upon those disabled workers to lie and cheat in order to get unemployment benefits. Many of them do cheat, and successfully. Except in the most obvious cases there is no assurance that they will be caught. The claimant whose arm is in a sling or who hobbles up to the claims counter on crutches will be questioned. If the employer or the claimant explains the work separation by some such statement as "too sick to work," "ill health," "job beyond strength," the claimant will be questioned. His ability to work will also be questioned if he refuses a job offer for reasons of health. If none of these occur, any real inquiry into the claimant's physical capacity is unlikely. Furthermore, no effective way exists to discover the nonobvious cases of disability. How can a claims clerk, without medical training, spot a tubercular claimant?

Disability insurance can remove the moral hazards involved in applying the "ability to work" requirement. To do this it must be coördinated with unemployment compensation. With such coördination there should seldom be ground for saying to an unemployed worker, "Benefits are denied to you because you filed your claim under the wrong program." Instead, if the claimant is otherwise ready and willing to work, he should receive benefits whether or not he is able to work. Disabled workers would draw benefits against the disability fund; "able" workers would draw against the unemployment fund.

We have seen that for unemployment compensation purposes a worker is "able to work" if he can perform some kind of recognizable work. It need not be his last or customary work. When this is the case, defining "disability" for disability insurance purposes as inability to do regular or customary work may be questioned. Two possible answers may be given. One would broaden the "disability" definition to mean inability to do any substantial work. This would mean that the claimant would have to rely on unemployment benefits unless he is utterly unable to work. Another answer would retain the inconsistent definitions of the two programs and bar recipients of benefits under one program from collecting under the other. This would allow claimants who are unable to do their regular work but able to do some other work to choose between the two programs.

A word needs to be said here of the importance of expanding the meaning of "ability to work" to keep pace with industrial and occupational change. Technological advance constantly reduces the need for brute strength in industry. Job reorganization makes it possible to adapt many jobs to the physically handicapped. Occupational trends of the past century and the predictable future show the increasing preponderance of the sales, clerical, and service occupations. These factors all point to a continued easing of the physical requirements for labor-force participation.

CHAPTER IX

WAGES AND WORK

WAGE RESTRICTIONS

A CLAIMANT'S WAGE DEMANDS and his restrictions upon the kind of work he will take are often related. This is usually not true when physical incapacity causes the work restriction. In other cases, however, the unemployed worker often tends to associate the wage he wants with the job he wants.

The wage specification is ordinarily only one aspect of the claimant's total job demand. The wage also has a social as well as a financial meaning. Not only does it relate to the worker's savings and security, food, housing, medical care, and ability to buy the things that may command social prestige — the wage itself carries prestige. Two dollars an hour connotes a higher social status than fifty cents.

In this chapter wage and kind-of-work limitations are considered under separate headings, but only because it makes for simpler treatment. The case situations will show that they are usually part of a single job demand.

Restriction or Preference

Mere expression of a preference for a certain wage or kind of work does not impair a claimant's availability for work.[1] A definite restriction may, however, be fatal. Whether a claimant is voicing a preference or imposing a restriction thus becomes important although often difficult to decide. Many claimants when interviewed in the local office feel they are bargaining for jobs. They tend to believe that the higher their demands the better job referrals they will get. Their vigor in setting those specifications often gives the mistaken impression that they will not settle for less. Later events often reveal that a claimant was merely bargaining. The claimant may apply for or accept work that does not meet his "specifications."[2]

Involved in the entire question of "restriction or preference" is a semi-procedural problem: In determining availability, what reliance should be placed upon mere questioning, oral or written in form, as compared with job referrals? Without attempting to discuss the question fully at this point attention may be called to the position taken by the New York Appeal Board. A claimant had been held unavailable partly because of a wage restriction. In reversing this holding, the board said, "In the absence of a definite, *bona fide* job offer and refusal because of the rate of pay, we cannot say that the claimant established her standard of a wage rate as a condition precedent to the acceptance of employment." [3] Since discussion of various job possibilities with an uncompromising claimant may prevent a referral and consequent offer, the New York position seems too sweeping. It does, however, put the emphasis where it belongs in this type of situation — upon the work referral rather than the hypothetical questionnaire.

Prevailing Wages

The "prevailing wage" concept has a double significance in availability for work. All American unemployment compensation laws prohibit benefit denial for a refusal to accept new work "if the wages, hours, or other conditions of the work offered are substantially less favorable to the individual than those prevailing for similar work in the locality." This is part of the "labor standards provisions," intended to protect unemployed workers from pressure to undercut established wage patterns. On the other hand, the "prevailing wage" concept functions as a ceiling as well as a floor. Availability interpretations have tended to deny benefits to workers who insisted on wages higher than those prevailing in the locality. Together these two views of "prevailing wage" seem to produce a dead level: The claimant may not ask for more but need not take substantially less than the prevailing wage.

"Similar Work"

The phrase "similar work" refers to job content and not job titles or work conditions. "Similar" points to a broader base of comparison than "identical." Except among the jobs in the offering establishment, precisely the same job will ordinarily not be found anywhere else. Differences exist among industries even in the same occupation. Being a vegetable cook in a cannery and being a vegetable cook in a hotel are very different. But some kinds of work are similar in all industries. A building watchman's job is much the same everywhere. Distinctions in kind of work may be based upon size of establishment, tools, processes, and materials used or customers served. The degree of skill, experience, knowledge, responsibility, and training involved in the work may also serve as criteria of classification. Whatever classification bases are used they must reflect differences among jobs in the performance required of the worker. Thus unionization is no proper basis to determine whether jobs are similar. Sex and age are in themselves irrelevant although they may be associated with true differences in performance requirements.

Although trade practice and collective bargaining agreements and, when those fail, the definitions and practices of government labor and employment agencies are of great assistance, similar work must necessarily remain a vague and unsatisfactory term.[4] The occupational classification of the employment service is what unemployment compensation administrators use to determine similar work.

"Locality"

One suggested definition of "locality" has been the "competitive labor market area in which the conditions of work offered by an establishment affect the conditions offered for similar work by other establishments because they draw upon the same labor supply." [5] This definition has the virtue of disregarding civil and political boundaries. (Except for the indirect effect of different taxes and government regulation, such lines have no real bearing upon wages or other conditions of work.) As a working definition, however, it seems overelaborate.

The quoted definition requires three subsidiary findings before an area surrounding a job site may be considered the "locality": (1) The offered work conditions affect the conditions offered by the other establishments in the suggested locality. (2) All establishments involved draw upon the same labor supply. (3) The interrelationship of work conditions in these establishments is caused by their common labor supply. Only the second proposition can ordinarily be proved. The other two, if they can be proved at all, require investigations that are beyond the scope of the employment security agency.

"Locality" may be defined more simply in terms of labor supply, as an area within which workers ordinarily seek jobs and from which employers ordinarily hire workers in "similar work."

When this is the case it is fair to presume that the establishments engaged in similar work in that area affect each others' working conditions. This definition is sufficiently flexible to include those occupations and industries where an establishment recruits its workers from a single town and those where the entire country may be the hiring area.

"Prevailing"

The term "prevailing" has reference to the work conditions under which employees are most commonly engaged in similar work in the locality. If over half the workers are paid substantially the same wage, that wage is prevailing. If the most frequent wage involves less than a majority of the workers but is received by a large percentage (30 to 50 per cent) it may nonetheless be considered the prevailing wage. In other situations a weighted average may be the fairest approach to the prevailing wage.[6] When no single wage or wage bracket predominates, even though some may represent large percentages of the whole, the weighted average is usually the best solution, if the wage distribution reveals a central tendency or is fairly evenly spread throughout the range. When two modes occur the prevailing wage may be said to include the wages they bracket.[7]

When the mode is used to determine the prevailing wage, it will be seen, as many as 70 per cent of the workers in similar work may be receiving other wages. When the weighted average is used, the prevailing wage obtained may be one that few or even no workers get. The oft-repeated proposition that a demand for wages higher than those prevailing is tantamount to withdrawal from the labor force cannot be very strong when a large percentage of the workers may be earning more than the prevailing wage. Demanding more than the prevailing wage may be consistent with labor force attachment when only a small percentage of workers are getting more than the prevailing wage. This may readily be the case during a growing labor shortage.

Equating every demand for higher than prevailing wages with unavailability for work becomes more dubious when we consider wage information sources used in unemployment compensation cases to establish prevailing wages. Customarily, major reliance is placed upon employment service reports. These, in turn, have usually been based upon the job orders received. Since the employment service has a limited employer clientele and since wages offered on job openings tend to be lower than those paid in filled jobs, job orders seem an inadequate basis for determining prevailing wages. In a labor shortage, entry wages and job orders may run ahead of prevailing wages. Furthermore, since "prevailing" refers to the conditions under which workers in similar work are actually working and not to the conditions being offered new workers, job orders are only indirect evidence of what is prevailing.[8]

This does not mean that job orders are valueless in determining prevailing wages. They are a fruitful source of information and often the only available source. It is not always possible, for a given type of work and locality, to secure superior information from such other sources as labor department surveys and employer and employee groups. Getting current information is also a real problem in this field.

"Wages"

The "labor standards" provision is protective and must be liberally construed. "Earnings," not mere wage rates, are what the law involves. To this end a number of factors must be considered in comparing an individual job with other similar work. Hours become part of the earnings computation. Paid vacations and sick leave may be calculated in wages. Where progressive wage scales are involved in an offered job, aside from the local prevalence of such scales, comparisons are required as to entrance wage, the bases for wage increases, the size of the increases, and how fast they take place. The wage payment methods may also be compared since they may affect the worker's earnings, their regularity or certainty, or the speed and tension of the work.

"Substantially Less Favorable to the Individual"

"Substantially" and "individual" are problem words. The first cannot be precisely defined. A minute difference between offered work conditions and those generally prevailing will obviously not meet the test of substantiality. A real and measurable difference is required that will place the worker in a position markedly inferior to that commonly occupied by other local workers doing the same kind of work. The Indiana Review Board did rule once that forty-five cents an hour was substantially less favorable than forty-seven cents, but most tribunals have required evidence of larger differentials, usually at least five or ten cents on an hourly rate.[9]

Wages below the minimum state or federal standards are *ipso facto* substantially less favorable, since they fall below the legally permissible prevailing wage. Wages and work conditions established by collective bargaining agreements are ordinarily held to be not substantially less favorable.[10] This is usually upon the theory that collective bargaining takes into account the local industrial practice.

The words "to the individual" have been given little importance. Wage comparisons seem to furnish small basis for individualization. Conceivably, however, a worker may be able to demonstrate by his previous experience that, despite the equality of earnings under a piece-rate and an hourly rate system, the former was substantially less favorable to him because of the work speed and tension involved.

Wage Restrictions above the Prevailing Wage

It has been common practice to hold claimants unavailable if they demand wages higher than those prevailing.[11] It is assumed, and sometimes expressly stated, that such claimants have removed themselves from the labor force. In exceptional cases workers of long experience or superior qualifications have been granted benefits despite specification of a higher-than-prevailing wage.[12] Even claimants who succeeded in getting the higher wage have been denied benefits.[13]

Benefits may be denied to claimants who demand higher-than-prevailing wages even though the work offers by which they have been tested lie outside their highest skills or even outside their experience. The California Appeal Board, for example, held that a claimant, registered as a ship rigger and oil-field rigger, who wanted a minimum of $1.25 an hour, was unavailable for work when he refused the following referrals: boiler fireman, $200 a month; construction laborer, .75 an hour; truck driver, $250 a month. To the claimant's contention that he lacked experience for these jobs, the board replied that no experience was required.[14]

A contrary view is expressed in a North Carolina decision. The claimant had been earning $30 a week. Less than a month after she became unemployed she failed to investigate a job opening paying $16 to $18 a week. The deputy said:

While it may be true that the work the claimant was told to investigate paid the prevailing wage for that sort of work, this would not be grounds alone for holding this claimant not available for work within the meaning of the Law. To hold otherwise would be, in effect, to hold not available for work the proverbial "Doctor, lawyer, merchant, chief," if he refused work as a bootblack, even though he could earn the prevailing wage ordinarily earned by a bootblack.[15]

When it is clear that local wages for similar work are highly standardized, insistence upon higher wages may render the claimant unavailable for any substantial amount of suitable work. Such wage standardization, however, is far from being the rule in American industry. Where it does not exist or wage information is inadequate, little basis exists for applying the prevailing wage doctrine of availability. Two more appropriate criteria are suggested: (1) Is the wage demand reasonably related to the claimant's prior earnings, training, skills, and experience? (2) Is the demanded wage actually being paid in a significant percentage of the local and similar jobs?

Relation to Previous Earnings

A claimant's past earnings have usually been considered only a part of his work history. Ordinarily, a claimant whose wage demands are out of line with his experience will be considered unavailable for work.[16] The mere fact that an individual grades himself upward has not, however, been conclusive evidence of unavailability.[17] Illustrations are the worker who has previously been underpaid or a period of sharp rise in wages.

The claimant's qualifications for the wage demanded are closely related to the criterion of previous earnings. The war and the reconversion period produced many cases of claimants who demanded wages that were reasonably related to their most recent earnings but were unattainable in the light of their peacetime qualifications.[18]

Whether a claimant is qualified for the wage he demands sometimes presents difficulties. In Ohio, a Negro veteran who fixed a minimum of $1900 a year was held unavailable for work. Before his military service, he was a stockkeeper for a government war agency at $1680 a year. Earlier the claimant had been a school-teacher, with highest annual earnings of $1875. He refused a referral to a government job as a stock clerk at $1704 a year, plus overtime. The referee said: "His work experience to date has not demonstrated that he has the capacity to earn the wages which he now requires before he will accept employment . . ." [19] The referee evidently gave little weight to the claimant's academic attainments.

How closely a claimant may adhere to the wage standards of his previous work has been made to depend upon the prospects for employment at such work and standards, leavened, in many instances, by allowing a "reasonable" period for adjustment and labor market exploration.

Work Prospects and Adjustment and Exploration Period

The work-prospects factor has become a standard test of availability.[20] Where recall to work at the customary wage is expected soon, a known demand exists for workers in the claimant's field, or the claimant succeeds in finding work at the specified wage, it may be held that the claimant's work prospects are good enough to justify the wage stipulation.[21] In some cases benefit denials based upon a lack of work prospects at the specified wage have, in practical effect, meant that the claimant was unavailable for work because no work was available for the claimant. One example is the disallowance of benefits to a former insurance company correspondent who wanted $30 a week. She had no other experience and the local insurance companies would not hire married women.[22]

Often a claimant will change his residence without adapting his wage demands to the new area. His consequent poor work prospects may lead to a finding of unavailability. Claimants who move from urban to rural areas and demand "city wages" are ordinarily denied benefits on this ground.[23] Similarly a claimant who has narrowed the area where he will take work will be held unavailable unless good prospects remain in the reduced area for work at his specified wage. For example, a Missouri carpenter who had worked at various construction jobs in Missouri and Kansas at pay rates of $1 to $1.50 an hour, was held unavailable for limiting himself to carpenter work at $1.25 an hour and within a 100-mile radius from his home. (This would include a territory equivalent in size to about 45 per cent of Missouri's square mileage.) [24]

The "labor market exploration period" allowed claimants has varied in length with individual circumstances.[25] Longer work experience at the wage demanded, union ties, and prospects of early recall to work at the usual wage have meant longer exploration periods. The time allowed before requiring the claimant to lower his wage sights has also varied directly with the wage and degree of specialized skill involved. A factory inspector in New Jersey with seven years' experience in her last job, who had last earned

$.95 an hour and set a minimum of $.85, was allowed three weeks.[26] A woodworking machine operator of twenty-five years' experience and a member of the union was held available in New Jersey throughout a three-and-a-half-month period when he insisted on $1 an hour.[27]

Living (or Profitable) Wage

Claimants at times will contend that they have fixed certain wage minimums because of their need for a living wage or a profitable wage. Most of the reported cases involve women workers who based their acceptable wage on what would be left over after they paid for care of their children or their households. Their contentions have seldom been successful.[28] There can be little doubt that a claimant is not available for work when, because of home conditions, she can accept only work which pays unusually high wages. Some of the situations presented by such claimants do, however, make the student of social insurance pause and consider.

A Minnesota case involved a widow supporting two small children, aged two-and-a-half and five years, respectively. She was widowed in 1942, about the time her youngest child was born. Shortly afterward she went to work in a war job, at $.75 an hour. This lasted eighteen months. Later she worked five months in another war plant at $1.02 an hour. In between she worked a month, during the Christmas season, as a salesclerk at $.40 an hour. She had no other work experience. She became unemployed immediately after the end of the war with Japan. At the time she filed her claim she was getting public assistance of $74 a month plus fuel. If she accepted work she would lose this aid, and it would cost her $10 a week to pay for the care of her children. She set a minimum of $.60 an hour. Work related to her experience was then paying $.55 an hour and involved a rotating shift. The claimant refused sales and cashier's jobs paying $20 to $25 for a forty-eight-hour week. She was held unavailable for work as of the day she first filed her claim.[29]

Mere unwillingness by claimants to accept substandard wages or wages that do not permit a minimum living standard has usually been viewed as consistent with availability. A woman in Kansas who left work because traveling twenty-eight miles a day for an hourly wage of thirty cents was not profitable for her was held available for work. She had a crippled husband and three children to support. The referee said:

A simple computation will show that at the hours and wages on said job she was making less than unemployment compensation benefits. It would seem reasonable to the referee that if industry cannot offer employment more attractive than unemployment compensation, that a worker is justified in refusing the employment.[30]

KIND OF WORK

Chapter VIII, "Ability to Work," covered the bulk of the situations where the claimant's availability for his most recent or customary work is, involuntarily, curtailed or destroyed. We are here concerned with those groups of claimants who (a) will accept no other than their customary work; (b) will accept their previous work only; (c) will take work with none other than a designated employer; or (d) limit their availability because of their union or nonunion status.

In all these cases one common feature exists — a conflict between the employee's interest in maintaining the work status he has achieved and the state's interest in getting him off the benefit rolls. The employer for whom the claimant worked regularly or most recently may not always share the state's fund-preserving interest. If the claimant takes other work, it affects the employer's labor pool. If, however, unemployment compensation is paid while the claimant awaits work with this employer, it helps to preserve that labor pool.

Limitation to Previous or Customary Work

In general, the tendency has been to sustain the eligibility of the worker who confines himself to his customary work. Determining factors have included: the worker's age and how long he has been engaged in such employment,[31] union affiliations, work prospects, and length of unemployment.

A leading Minnesota decision, *Berthiaume* v. *Director,* involved a boilermaker who was laid off, on October 5, 1943, because of lack of materials, from a job paying $1.70 an hour.[32] At that time he was told that he would be recalled as soon as material was available. He filed his claim on October 11. The same day the employment service offered him and he refused a referral to a truck-driving job at $.85 an hour. The claimant was a union member and did highly specialized work. His union business agent assured the claimant that he would soon be recalled to work in his usual trade and asked him to wait for such work. On October 18 the claimant was recalled to work. He appealed to the Minnesota Supreme Court from a decision that he was not available for work during that period. The Minnesota law then in effect required that a claimant be "available for work in his usual trade or occupation or in any other trade or occupation for which he demonstrates he is reasonably fitted."

Before the court was the question: Was the word "or" in the availability requirement conjunctive or disjunctive? Did the claimant have to be available for both his usual work and work in any other trade? Or, could he satisfy the law by availability either for his usual work or, alternatively, for other work he was reasonably fitted to do?

The court's answer was that availability interpretation must be guided by the statutory criteria of "suitable" work, which included the factor of prospects of securing local work in the customary occupation. If such prospects were reasonable, the availability requirement would be satisfied by availability for customary work. Otherwise the claimant had to be available for work in some other trade.

Determining Customary Work

Appeals from time to time concern what, in the particular case, is the claimant's customary occupation. One Michigan claimant had last worked as a salesman and, for ten years before that, as a salesman and purchasing engineer. He refused work as a die maker, a job which he had last performed seventeen years earlier. Since it was unreasonable to expect him to regain the skill he had so long neglected he was justified in refusing the work.[33]

Immediately after the war, it was common to pay little or no attention to claimants' wartime experience and to require availability for prewar work. For example, a District Court in Nebraska held that a former war worker who was unwilling to return to her prewar occupation of waitress was not available for work. The claimant also confined herself to a locality where, according to the court, there was no reasonable probability that she would secure the kind of work she had done during the war.[34]

Protecting Skill and Status

To protect and preserve the worker's skills and occupational status has motivated the rulings which hold a claimant available despite his unwillingness to work outside his most recent or customary occupation. A Mississippi decision says, "A skilled workman would not ordinarily be expected to accept work in which he could not utilize his skill and which might result in the loss to him of that skill." [35] And in Maine the referee has said, "Unemployment compensation, to my mind, intends to offer the involuntarily unemployed worker some protection against sacrificing skill, and intends to afford a reasonable waiting period during which, as long as a risk of re-employment exists, he might wait to resume his usual work upon which he has geared his individual economy." [36]

Work Prospects and Exploratory Period

What was previously said under the "Wage" headings, about the work-prospects and exploratory-period factors is equally applicable here. My own belief is that usually availability for one's customary work should be sufficient to establish availability for work. It is necessary only that the work ordinarily exist in the area of the claimant's availability during the time and under the conditions of that availability. This should not, however, prevent the disqualification of a claimant who refuses, without good cause, other suitable work.[37]

Work with One Employer Only

A claimant is ordinarily held ineligible if he limits his availability to work with one employer. Various exceptions, however, have been made in favor of laid-off workers who expect to be recalled soon. The availability of laid-off workers is closely related to the broader subject of employment stabilization. Most involuntary work separations are lay offs, rather than discharges. It has long been noted also that the proportion of layoffs that are temporary rather than permanent has been increasing.[38] Unionization, the seniority system, and changed managerial policies are immediate causes for this trend. More and more, workers tend to consider themselves as X Company employees and the X Company tends to share that view, both when the "employees" are in and out of work. The fact is that our concept of the employment relationship may be turning back from contract to status. Governmental and union contract regulation of hiring and firing and the drive for job security evidence such a change.

Strong pressures result to pay benefits to the worker who is laid off and waits for recall. But to do this may mean a considerable drain upon the unemployment compensation fund and a waste of manpower. Unemployment compensation authorities have taken diverse approaches to this problem. If the layoff is of indefinite duration the claimant has usually been held unavailable if he would take no other work. For example, the Missouri Supreme Court affirmed the denial of benefits to a laid-off glass company worker who refused other work. The claimant had worked three months for the glass company. When she was laid off she and other employees were told that they would be recalled but were given no assurance that it would be at any definite time in the near future.[39] Where recall is prompt, although the original layoff was for an indefinite period, appeal bodies tend to be lenient.[40] So also when a layoff is indefinite in length but bound to be short.[41]

Appeal bodies have disagreed on the availability of claimants who are laid off for short but definite periods and are willing to take temporary work only. The better and more usual opinion considers such workers eligible for benefits.[42] There have, however, been contrary decisions. An Alabama sewing machine operator was laid off by the employer for whom she had worked twenty-three years. When referred to other work she applied, as directed. She was not hired because she told the interviewing employer that she expected recall to her former job within two weeks. The referee said that the claimant "so imposed restrictions upon her availability for work as to render herself unavailable for work during the weeks involved." [43]

The suggestions made by Miss Olga Halsey in her article on the special unemployment compensation problems of laid-off workers are well taken.[44] She stresses the importance of adequate information, from the employer, both to worker and the unemployment compensation agency, concerning the probable duration of the layoff. After noting the common interest of the claimant and the employer in avoiding automatic benefit denials, she points to a policy of paying benefits to temporarily laid-off workers if they will take temporary work. As the layoff becomes more extended workers would be expected to accept other suitable, permanent work.

This writer leans toward the Vermont policy cited in the Halsey article: When an employer confirms the claimant's statement that he will be recalled within four weeks, the claimant may refuse any work during this period without loss of benefits. If the layoff is expected to be longer or lasts beyond the original four-week period the commission's local office may decide any eligibility question.[45] The period used may be too long, but the basic approach is reasonable. After the grace period has ended, claimants should be expected to accept other suitable work. That even then a claimant inserts the proviso that he will return, upon recall, to his former employer from whatever job he accepts hardly affects his availability. Every employer, when he hires a worker, takes a chance that the worker may leave to accept another job.

The importance of requiring laid-off claimants, who will not be recalled soon, to be available for interim work must not be minimized. Issues of total productivity, employment stabilization, and proper conservation of available funds are involved. It is an essential for any successful scheme of guaranteed wages.[46]

Labor Disputes

Workers unemployed because of labor disputes involving their employers are apt to be unwilling, until the dispute is settled, to take other work. Under most state laws, workers are denied benefits if they participate or are directly interested in the dispute or belong to the grade or class of workers which is participating in or directly interested in the dispute. This disqualification, in most states, continues so long as there is a stoppage of work due to the labor dispute. In some states, it remains in effect so long as the labor dispute is in active progress and causing the unemployment. Under all these laws "nonparticipant" workers, unemployed because of the dispute, may qualify for benefits. Ordinarily they have been awarded benefits despite their usual unwillingness to accept work anywhere else. This serves the common interests of the workers, the employers, and the community. As a result, appeals from such payments are not to be found.

A somewhat different situation exists under the laws of New York and Rhode Island. New York disqualifies workers unemployed because of a labor dispute for the duration of the dispute or for seven weeks, whichever is the shorter. Rhode Island applies an eight-week maximum. Until recently Louisiana, Pennsylvania, and Tennessee had similar laws. Under such provisions a question may arise: Must a claimant who has served out the disqualification but remains unemployed because of the continuing labor dispute be available for other work in order to qualify for benefits?

The question is somewhat of a dilemma. Not to require availability for other work seems to put the striker in a favored position. To deny benefits seems to disregard the very purpose of the limited disqualification. Strength is added to this latter view when it is considered that from 1927 to 1945 the average duration of work stoppages caused by labor disputes was only about sixteen days.[47] The life expectancy of a stoppage which has already lasted from four to eight weeks is short, bringing the situation close to that of workers laid off for a brief but indefinite period.

Few cases have been reported on this question. Most of the states that have had labor dispute disqualifications of limited duration agree that after the disqualification has been served, the claimants must hold themselves available for other work. Rhode Island alone dissents.[48]

Union and Nonunion Work

The eligibility of claimants who are restricted in their availability by union membership or nonmembership presents basic questions of public policy. The spread of collective bargaining and the growth of unionization have gone hand in hand with governmental recognition of the right to bargain collectively. Although collective bargaining seems secure, protracted and bitter struggles, even now not yet ended, have, however, marked the growth of this right. Consequently when union (or nonunion) status becomes an issue in unemployment compensation determinations, emotion is more often stirred than reason.

Suitability of Nonunion Work for Union Members

Only one court has yet passed upon the availability of a claimant who has excluded certain kinds of work because of his union status. A handful of cases have, however, been decided by the courts under the work refusal disqualification.[49] All involve union workers who refused work because acceptance, under the rules of their union would make them liable to suspension or expulsion from the organization. The courts have denied benefits in every instance.

Their opinions are, curiously, cast in terms of a kind of legislative competition between the unions and the state. Thus the Ohio Supreme Court writes that under an interpretation granting benefits to a union man who refused nonunion work "the right of the applicant for unemployment compensation would not be fixed or determined by the provisions of the statute but by rules adopted by organizations in which the applicant has membership." [50] In other words, unions would be taking over a governmental function. A second contention of the Ohio court is that paying benefits, in the circumstances, would result in an unconstitutional classification since a nonunion claimant would be disqualified for refusing the same work. "There can be no valid classification of persons based upon membership or non-membership in a labor organization, which would operate to differentiate rights to receive benefits under the unemployment compensation statute." [51]

It seems sufficient comment upon the second argument to note that the Ohio law provides:

No individual otherwise qualified to receive benefits shall lose the right to benefits by reason of a refusal to accept new work if: (1) As a condition of being so employed, he would be required to join a company union, or to resign from or refrain from joining any bona fide labor organization, or would be denied the right to retain membership in and observe the lawful rules of any such organization.[52]

The Ohio Court did limit this protection to an employment condition imposed by the employer. It did not, however, perceive any unconstitutionality in the quoted section because it extended to the union worker a protection which the nonunion worker did not receive.

A third argument, which comes closer to the basic issues, was supplied by the Pennsylvania Supreme Court:

The public policy of the Commonwealth does encourage membership in labor organizations but retention of membership therein is not a surrender to circumstances of the kind and quality which will turn voluntary unemployment into involuntary unemployment.[53]

This was by way of rebuttal to the majority opinion of the Pennsylvania Superior Court in the same case.[54] The lower court had found "good cause" for the claimant's work refusal. The loss of union status, it had said, with its attendant rights — which included the privilege of engaging in collective bargaining, an interest in sick and death benefits, and the opportunity to obtain and retain work within the member's trade at union rates — would be a substantial and irreparable harm.

This approach — from the standpoint of the individual claimant — would seem to be the beginning of wisdom in this field. A clear view of the unemployed union worker who applies for benefits may reveal him as being caught between two powerful forces. He is a citizen of the state and a member of the union. In theory, he controls the laws of one and the bylaws and regulations of the other. In reality, of course, he affects these controls to a slight degree only. For practical purposes, when they conflict, both are beyond his power to change. His only choice is to surrender either his union status or his claim for benefits. His union membership may (or may not) originally have been voluntary. With the passage of time, however, his commitment becomes too great for any truly voluntary withdrawal.

Admittedly, a rule that benefits will not be denied for refusing or excluding any work which is banned by union rules may open the door to abuse. Some union rules are arbitrary. Ways exist, however, to mitigate such results. One is by legislation. The Railroad Unemployment Insurance Act bars benefit denials when accepting the offered work would require violating a union rule or regulation, but only when the rule is "reasonable" and violation would result in expulsion.[55] Another is judicial. To be binding upon members, union rules must be reasonable and in accord with public policy.[56] A rule which is invalid by these criteria should not justify a claimant in refusing or excluding work. In passing, it may be noted that it is well established that a union rule forbidding members to accept nonunion work is valid.[57] Third, the protection given a claimant against nonunion work may, reasonably, vary directly with his commitment as a union member — how long he has been a union member and the union benefits to which he is entitled. Another relevant factor is the strength of the union in the labor-market area. In other words, what does the union member risk if he accepts nonunion work?

These considerations apply to the suitability of nonunion work for union members. Because availability is defined as requiring only that the worker be available for suitable work, they are an important part of our discussion. But they are only one part. Availability for work is a broader and looser requirement than the work refusal provision. A finding that nonunion work is suitable for a union member does not necessarily make him unavailable when he refuses to accept such nonunion work. Unless union work is insubstantial in amount within the area of his availability, there is no reason to hold him unavailable for work.

Local Conditions a Yardstick

Union strength in the trade and in the labor-market area involved thus becomes an important factor. A Florida painter, thirty-nine years a union member, stated that he would accept only brush work in a closed shop job at the union wage scale. According to the employment service, the area was highly unionized and a substantial majority of the work done in the painting industry was union work. The referee held him available for work, although pointing out that if the passage of time revealed little prospect for securing such work he would have to consider other jobs.[58] If the work involved is predominantly not unionized in the area, a claimant who confines his availability to nonunion work is usually denied benefits.[59]

Union Membership as Evidence of Availability

One significant element, seldom mentioned in the reported cases, is that union membership per se suggests attachment to the labor force. The first objective of union membership is obtaining and keeping suitable employment. In fact, in a highly unionized industry, availability for work may require union membership or willingness to join a union.[60] Oregon instructions to local offices for handling reconversion unemployment benefits for seamen stress compliance with union placement procedures as evidence of availability.[61] However, even when a union controls the local jobs, if it engages in discriminatory practices in admission to membership, those practices will not prevent a claimant who cannot obtain membership from getting benefits.[62]

Union Rules Hampering Availability

Instances do sometimes exist of clear unavailability because of the impact of a union rule or practice. Some of the larger locals of the musicians' union have required three to twelve months residence before a member can obtain steady work. Musicians attempting to transfer from other locals and willing to accept only musicians' jobs could expect that during the required residence period they would be able to get only one-night or fill-in jobs.[63] Some unions in seasonal trades prohibit members from accepting work in other trades during the off-season. If the slack season is of any real length, such a rule is bound to result in benefit denials to unemployed members.[64] Ordinarily, however, a claimant who limits himself to such work as he can take without exposing himself to union discipline or loss of union membership is held available for work.[65]

Freedom-of-Association Standard

This brings us directly to the positive protections of the labor-standards provisions contained in the state unemployment compensation laws. Their federal prototype, Section 1603(a)(5) of the Internal Revenue Code, bars the denial of benefit to an otherwise eligible individual for refusing to accept new work under the following condition: "If as a condition of being employed the individual would be required to join a company union or to resign from or refrain from joining any bona fide labor organization." With a few, but notable, exceptions, the state laws have followed this language word for word.[66] Under its terms, a claimant who refuses or excludes work where one of the proscribed conditions is a part of the employment, may not be disqualified or held unavailable because of his action.

A requirement to join a company union is a condition of the employment when the worker must join before becoming employed or must, in order to remain in employment, become a member within a prescribed period after starting work. State unemployment compensation agencies have been reluctant to make their own determinations of whether a union is company-dominated. Instead, they have preferred to rely upon the findings of the state and federal labor relations boards. A requirement that a worker resign from a bona fide union is "a condition of being employed," whether the resignation must take place before entering employment or within a definite period afterwards. When such a condition is imposed by the employer or by the union with which the employer has a closed-shop or union-shop agreement it comes within the condemnation of the statute. These interpretations have involved no controversy.

However, much controversy has been aroused over the applicability of this portion of the law to situations of the following types: (1) The claimant is a union member. Under his union's rules, he may be expelled or suspended or he must resign or withdraw if he accepts nonunion work. (2) The claimant is a member of Union A. Under his union's rules, he may be expelled or suspended or he must resign or withdraw if he joins another union. The employer has an agreement with Union B which requires new workers to join Union B. Neither the employer nor Union B compels such workers to withdraw or resign from or to refrain from joining any other union. In both these situations the question to be decided is the meaning of "condition of being employed."

The weight of opinion is that, in the situations described, the labor-standards provision provides no protection. The term "condition of being employed" refers to a condition imposed by the employer rather than to the result of the employment. The action of an outside agency, such as the claimant's union, which is precipitated by the claimant's employment, is considered a result and not a condition of employment.[67] The legislative history of the Social Security Act is consistent with such an interpretation.[68]

As suggested earlier, protection from benefit denial may nonetheless be based upon a finding that work involving loss of union status is unsuitable for the worker. This is not prevented by a narrow interpretation of "condition of being employed."

Police of Neutrality

Those who are interested in maintaining the neutrality of the unemployment compensation system in union questions would do well to consider the policy stated by the Iowa Employment Security Commission :[69]

It is advisable to guard against an unqualified interpretation that a requirement of membership in a bona fide union cannot affect the suitability of employment or constitute good cause for refusing or leaving employment. Certain safeguards and qualifications are necessary. Beyond these minima, the Commission in its judgment should erect further cautionary principles.

(1) The first qualification, which is perhaps unnecessary to state, is that in order to make the requirement a reasonable one as to claimant, he must be eligible for membership in the union and the union must be willing to accept him as a member.

(2) In the second place, claimant should be allowed with impunity to reject a requirement to join a union, even if it is a bona fide labor organization, unless there is a "closed shop" or "all union" agreement in existence with respect to the work. This principle is designed to assure that a requirement of union membership shall render work unsuitable or constitute good cause for leaving where there is no obligation on the employer to impose such a requirement. If that were not so, the Unemployment Compensation Law might be used to force men into a union not of the employees' own choosing.

(3) A requirement to join a union as a condition of being employed or being continued in employment should be deemed to render the

employment unsuitable or constitute good cause for leaving it, if claimant is a member of a rival bona fide labor organization and objects in principle to joining the new organization, or considers his obligation toward his own organization inconsistent with membership in the new organization, or would be required, as a condition of being employed or by the rules of the old or new organization, to give up his membership in the old organization in the event of so joining.

No statement better summarizes the desirable policies for applying the suitable work test to jobs involving union membership. Only the use of the worker's stake in his union as a criterion of the suitability of nonunion work need be added to cover practically all the suitable work questions that stem from union status.

SOME GENERAL CONCLUSIONS

Wise administration will avoid many of the problems we have discussed. Two things are involved: (a) As a matter of policy, whenever wage or kind of work limitations are at issue, determinations of unavailability should not be made upon the basis of response to questioning alone. Instead, primary reliance should ordinarily be placed upon the claimant's response to actual job offers. (b) Careful employment service practice should be observed. Skilled workers ought not to be referred to jobs below their qualifications when adequately qualified and lesser-skilled workers remain unemployed. When such cautions are taken comparatively few determinations will hold claimants unavailable because of wage or kind-of-work limitations.

The problems discussed in this chapter involve the sharpest kind of group frictions which the unemployment compensation program encounters. It is sheer foolhardiness for an unemployment compensation agency to carry alone the burden of meeting them. Neither is it desirable that questions of such real concern to the entire community should be settled without some form of community participation. If it were possible to give the administrative agency detailed legislative guidance such communal assistance would not be so important. Such is the nature of the subject, however, that it is impossible to spell out statutory guides except of the most generalized kind. Supplementation of those guides should be sought in advisory councils to aid the unemployment compensation administration in adapting its policies to the locality and to the times. Because availability and most other benefit eligibility and disqualification problems are usually local in their nature, it seems more important to have a network of local councils than a single state group. Participation of both labor and management is a prerequisite for their success.

CHAPTER X

HOURS AND OTHER TIME LIMITATIONS

THE SUBJECT OF TIME LIMITATIONS brings us close to the fringes of the labor force. Traditional economics thought of the marginal member of the labor force mainly in terms of wages. He sought work only when the offered wages rose enough to attract him. Unemployment compensation experience demonstrates that the locality of available work and the work time, as frequently as the wage, affect the decision to enter or to stay out of the labor force. Housewives, students, the aged, and the physically handicapped are often more concerned with the where, when, and how long of a job than with the wages it will pay.

How has unemployment compensation dealt with the claims of workers who limit themselves to work at certain hours of the day or portions of the week or year? Exceptions exist as in the case of the Seventh Day Adventist who rejects all Saturday work. All in all, however, it cannot be said that unemployment compensation has dealt leniently with time limitations. Such restrictions have usually been regarded critically.

TIME OF DAY

Most frequently women workers have been the claimants in benefit appeals concerning restrictions of availability to particular times of the day. In a later chapter, specific attention is devoted to the time limitations imposed by working mothers.[1] Here the treatment will be more generalized.

Availability for night work and for shift employment did not become an issue until the war. Some employments had always required night work or shift work, by their very nature: entertainment, hospitals, hotels and restaurants, utilities, transportation, and so on. Some plants were engaged in continuous processes that could not be halted. This was often the case in the iron and steel and chemical industries. In a few industries — textile and clothing or machine and machine tools, for example — some establishments gained a market advantage by voluntarily operating continuously. Before the war, however, most of our economy was on a straight day-work basis. Many prewar union contracts treated night work as emergency work and made no mention of multiple-shift operations.[2] During the war, most factories added evening and night shifts.[3]

Round-the-Clock Availability Rule

The war produced the round-the-clock availability rule. The Michigan Supreme Court phrased the rule in these words: "There is nothing in the statute to justify the conclusion that the legislature intended a claimant might limit his employment to certain hours of the day where the work he is qualified to perform is not likewise limited."[4] It may be noted, however, that although the facts before the court arose during the war, the court's decision was not rendered until 1947. There is evidence to indicate that the round-the-clock availability rule has persisted in some other states into the postwar period.

A case in point was decided by a Massachusetts Review Examiner. The claim was filed in June 1946. The claimant was a stockroom foreman with eighteen years of experience in his work. The claimant admitted that in the locality and industry in which he was customarily employed work opportunities existed on all three shifts. He had, however, always worked days and, because his wife and their new-born baby were in a precarious condition, he did not want night work. Evidence was also presented indicating that the claimant was actively attempting to find work. Nonetheless, he was held unavailable for work until he indicated willingness to accept night work.[5]

The case just cited and some others have denied benefits to workers who confined themselves to day work. Ordinarily, however, such claimants have been held available for work if good cause existed for refusing work at night or if the work involved was not usually performed at night.[6] It seems reasonable to expect that, as the war years recede, the round-the-clock availability rule will wane in importance. In a few states, however, a fundamental change will first have to take place in the decisions of the courts. The Michigan Supreme Court has already been mentioned. The court decisions in Connecticut, although not entirely clear, support a requirement of availability during all twenty-four hours. Courts in Massachusetts and West Virginia have accepted similar views.[7]

Availability for Hours of Previous Employment

The South Carolina Supreme Court has adopted a rule which requires claimants, in order to be eligible, to be available for the hours they had previously worked.[8] Similar in effect is the decision of a Massachusetts lower court.[9] This decision denied benefits to a hotel chambermaid who left work when her hours of 8:30 A.M. to 1:30 P.M. were changed to 1 to 6 P.M. Because of the care of an invalid husband she was unable to work the new hours. The court said that "the petitioner was not capable or available because her other duties prevented her from working the hours fixed for the employment." Such decisions are closely related to the more comprehensive rule that a claimant must be available for the work he has been doing.[10]

Availability for a Normal Work Period

Both rules mentioned are unnecessarily restrictive. When jobs are available both during the day and night or work is ordinarily performed during both periods, there is no occasion for a round-the-clock requirement. When a claimant is available for other employment than his last job, what reason can exist for tying him to the conditions of the last job? All that seems necessary is a requirement that there be a substantial amount of work for which the claimant is available and which is actually or ordinarily done during the hours he has stipulated.[11]

The fact that a claimant earned his wage credits or customarily worked during the hours he requires, is usually persuasive evidence that such work is normally done during those hours.[12] To accept without question, however, the proposition that availability for hours formerly worked constitutes eligibility would often lead to unwarranted benefit payments. Claimants who earned wage credits by working during unusual shifts instituted for short emergencies would then qualify for benefits without actually being available for normal employment.[13]

When claimants are available *only* for work in an industry or occupation in which seniority ordinarily dictates the work shift, the accord between their time limitations and seniority status will determine their benefit eligibility. A new worker, to be available, may have to be ready to accept work on one of the less favorable shifts. In a number of establishments, however, work on evening and night shifts is not distributed by seniority. Instead additional compensation, in one form or another, is used to attract workers to the unfavorable shifts. Restriction to a single shift, in these latter cases, should not necessarily mean unavailability.

AVAILABILITY FOR PART-TIME WORK ONLY

Many of the state unemployment compensation laws originally made special provisions for part-time workers. The usual definition of a part-time worker was : An individual (a) whose normal work is in an occupation in which his services are not required for the customary scheduled full-time prevailing in the establishment in which he is employed, or (b) who, owing to personal circumstances, does not customarily work the customary scheduled full-time hours prevailing in the establishment in which he is employed.[14] The unemployment compensation agencies, under these original statutes, were authorized to make rules applicable to part-time workers fixing methods of determining full-time weekly wage, qualifying wage, and appropriate minimum and maximum benefit amounts. These provisions were found unworkable and soon deleted by amendment. Only seven state laws retain such an authorization.[15] No rules adopted in these states in conformance with this portion of the statute can be found.

The New York law provides that a part-time worker may register as such and that the time which he "normally works in any calendar week shall be deemed his week of full-time employment." The definition of "part-time worker" is stated solely in terms of part (b) of the definition given above.[16] The laws of Michigan and West Virginia specifically require availability for "full-time" work, but do not define the term.

Labor force reports show that about 2 per cent of all the employed work less than fourteen hours in any given week and about 10 per cent work between fourteen and thirty-four hours. When it is considered that many of these less-than-full-time workers, in any one week, are not regular part-time workers but workers who are temporarily and partially unemployed, even the small percentages cited may be heavily discounted. They hardly warrant any elaborate and cumbersome administrative machinery to deal out precisely proportioned benefits to part-time workers.

In any discussion of part-time workers it should be stressed that high wages, high prices, and full employment attract part-time workers into the labor market. They need the work and employers need them. We should also note that with the steady decrease in

the length of the work week over the past half century the line between part-time and full-time work is becoming ever more difficult
to draw. When the agreed full-time week is thirty-five hours, as in
the ladies' garment industry, how part-time is thirty hours a week?
Twenty-five hours a week?

We may distinguish two groups of claimants who limit availability to part-time work, those with and those without a previous
history of part-time work. A number of tribunals have interpreted
the availability requirement to mean availability for full-time
work.[17] Under such interpretations, benefits will be denied to both
groups. A more liberal opinion, prevailing among other tribunals,
accepts as eligible claimants who have a previous history of part-
time work and restrict their availability to substantially those hours
previously worked. In a careful statement of its position on this
question, a Minnesota appeal tribunal expressed the following rule:
"An individual who has established a normal workday of less than
full-time and the wage credits on which his claim is based were
earned in short-hour employment, is deemed available for work if
he is available for similar work, and work of such a nature exists in
the locality and he has a reasonable possibility of securing said
work." [18] The California Appeal Board accepts this rule but with
the qualification that there must be good cause for the restriction
to part-time work.[19]

The favored treatment given to claimants with part-time work
histories, as distinguished from other claimants who limit their
availability to part-time work, is open to question. The theory
seems to be that benefits should be allowed if the claimant is available for work on the same basis as the one on which his wage credits
were earned. There is an unwarranted "insurance" ring to this
thesis. Earning wage credits in part-time work may be evidence that
sufficient part-time work ordinarily exists for the claimant to consider him available for work. It is hardly final proof.

The one-sidedness of allowing benefits to claimants with part-
time work histories appears when we consider some of the denials
of benefits to claimants who lack such work histories but limit their
availability to part-time work. In Connecticut a woman claimant
was ordered by her doctor to work no more than three hours a
day. She succeeded in finding such work but it did not affect the
decision.[20] So also in Minnesota, in the case of a sixty-three-year-
old streetcar cleaner, under doctor's orders to work part-time
only.[21] The California Appeal Board denied benefits to a seventy-

five-year-old janitor who wanted a six-hour day, upon the ground that there was no evidence that eight hours a day was beyond his physical capacities or injurious to his health.[22] In New York, the Appeal Board denied benefits to a sewing-machine operator who was customarily full-time employed. The claimant, after recovering from a stroke, was under medical instruction to work only two or three hours a day. However, despite his doctor's orders he was willing to work full-time.[23]

The concept of "once a full-time worker always a full-time worker" is highly unrealistic. Age, disability, the exigencies of personal circumstances — all create situations requiring a "full-time" worker to limit himself to part-time work. More than established part-time workers, the claimant with a full-time work history has demonstrated attachment to the labor force. To deny him benefits when, for good cause, he limits himself to part-time work of a kind which he can do and which is ordinarily done in the community cannot readily be justified. This evidently was the view of an Alabama lower court when it held that a seventy-year-old cloth inspector was available for work although she was physically incapable of working a full eight-hour day. Her eyes no longer met the standard required for inspectors, but her former employer was willing to rehire her as soon as she could meet the physical test for any of their jobs.[24]

A reasonable rule of availability for both groups discussed might be this: An individual who limits his availability to part-time work is eligible for benefits only if (a) there is good cause for the limitation, and (b) part-time work for which he is suited constitutes a substantial amount of the work actually or ordinarily existing in the locality.[25] Although such a rule will eliminate from benefits the claimants who want to work a half-day a week, some may prefer to add the apparent precision of a formula such as this: A claimant who limits himself to part-time work must be available for enough weekly hours of work to be able to earn, at the prevailing wage of his occupation, a sum equivalent to his weekly benefit amount.

AVAILABILITY FOR TEMPORARY WORK ONLY

Aside from seasonal workers, to be discussed later in this chapter, little is known about temporary workers, as a group. Workers who regularly confine themselves to temporary work are rare. Instead, such workers usually have a past history of working in or seeking "permanent" employment. Claimants who limit their availability to temporary work usually do so for one of two types of reasons — those connected with their employment status and those based upon personal circumstances. The first class includes such cases as: workers awaiting recall to their regular jobs (discussed in the preceding chapter), workers who are waiting to begin new jobs, claimants who are waiting to start or resume businesses of their own. In the second class are claimants who are waiting to move to a new locality, pregnant women, women who expect to be married at a fixed and future date and then leave employment, and students who will take vacation work only.

The tests of availability must be the same in both classes of cases. Continuing attachment to the labor force is, however, somewhat easier to find among the claimants in the first category. As noted in the preceding chapter, there is a strong tendency to find that workers awaiting recall within a definite period to their regular employment are available while limiting themselves to temporary work. So also in the case of claimants willing to accept temporary work only until they can begin or return to active operation of their own businesses.[26] The availability of claimants who are awaiting new jobs and meanwhile confining themselves to temporary work has been made to depend largely upon the certainty of the new job.

Workers whose limitation to temporary work has been based upon personal circumstances have not fared so well. Most of the reported decisions in this category have dealt with women claimants who were following their servicemen husbands from post to post.[27] In one such case, the Pennsylvania Superior Court held that the availability rule did not require availability "for permanent, as distinguished from temporary, employment." [28] The claimant had registered for work in Columbia, South Carolina, a city of 110,000 population and stated that she was available for a thirty-day period only. She was referred to work packing doughnuts but the employer, who wished a permanent employee, did not hire her. According to the court, all that was necessary was availability for "some substantial and suitable work."

In contrast is the decision of a Superior Court in Washington. Because her daughter might leave the locality, the claimant refused to accept permanent work as a nurse's aide. The claimant did not want to feel bound to stay in the event her daughter left. The court held that the work was suitable. Since the law of Washington required availability for any suitable work, the claimant was not eligible for benefits.[29]

A woman claimant who told a prospective employer that she would work only a few months, until her husband came back from service, was held available in Massachusetts.[30] A machinist in Indiana, however, was found unavailable because he intended to move to another locality as soon as he could find housing and meanwhile would accept only temporary work.[31] And the California Apppeal Board held the defendant in a wartime citizenship revocation trial unavailable for work. He had been ordered by the military to leave the West Coast pending the decision in his case. While in the state to which he had moved, he would take only temporary work, until he could again return to the West Coast.[32]

Why a claimant restricts his availability to temporary work bears upon his willingness to work. It is not, however, determinative of his availability. The occupation is important. If extensive on-the-job training is required to do the work, employers will not hire temporary workers. If such reluctance to hire is not a mere preference but the necessary result of the job requirements, it eliminates a market for temporary employees. In some jobs, however, usually unskilled, temporary work is common. In the light of such factors as these, the would-be temporary worker's qualifications and the labor characteristics of the locality must be examined, in order to determine the claimant's availability.

SABBATH WORK

Until the decision of the Ohio Supreme Court in the Kut case,[33] the law was settled that conscientious objections to work on the Sabbath made such work unsuitable[34] and that such objectors were nevertheless available for work. Whether the Sabbath in question fell on a Sunday[35] or, as in the case of Orthodox Jews and Seventh Day Adventists, on a Saturday[36] made no difference. Sabbath work was considered improper for religious observers for a variety of reasons: It constituted a "risk to morals," one of the criteria of suitable work found in the laws of most states. A contrary opinion would make the unemployment compensation law unconstitutional, as a violation of freedom of religion. Religious convictions, strongly held, are so impelling as to constitute good cause for refusal. Since availability refers to suitable work, religious observers were not unavailable because they excluded Sabbath work.

The Kut case is the first on this question to go to the courts. It is also the first availability case in which review by the United States Supreme Court has been sought. The claimant, Max Kut, an Orthodox Jew, was hired by Albers Super Markets in Cincinnati as an order clerk in June 1943. Later he was promoted to "checker." When the union objected to this on seniority grounds, the employer, rather than demote Kut, gave him his release. The claimant thus became unemployed on March 7, 1944. While in Albers' employ he had been permitted to work Sundays in lieu of Saturdays. While claiming benefits he continued to exclude Saturday work. Because of this two employers rejected him as a shipping clerk. This led to an unavailability ruling on March 24. On April 4 he obtained a job where he was not required to work on Saturday.

These are the facts as given in the lower court decisions. The Ohio Supreme Court, however, concluded from them that Kut's unemployment came about "by the refusal of the plaintiff to continue to perform the work assigned to him." The court mentioned the unsuccessful referrals, but not the duration of Kut's unemployment or his success in obtaining employment within his restrictions.

In upholding the denial of benefits, the court made three points:

1. Neither the statute nor its interpretation by the unemployment compensation agency in this case infringed the constitutional protection of freedom of religion.

The Ohio law then in effect required the claimant's availability "for work in his usual trade or occupation or in any other trade or occupation for which he is reasonably fitted." The court said this meant that the claimant "must be available for work on Saturday if this is required by his usual trade or occupation, as in this instance." (No reference was made to any evidence or finding that Saturday work was required in the claimant's usual trade or occupation. The facts reported reveal two employers who did not hire Kut because he would not work on Saturday, and two employers who hired him despite that limitation.) The court stressed that the claimant's choices of religion and occupation were voluntary. His choices, however, might prevent him from meeting the law's requirements.

This seemed plausible, but actually was somewhat misleading. The Ohio Courts had held that, to be available for work, a claimant was required to be available for the work he had been doing.[37] At the time of the Kut decision the established interpretation was that the Ohio law required a claimant to be available for work both in his usual trade and in any other trade or occupation for which he was reasonably fitted. In such circumstances a "voluntary choice" was illusory. Under the court's decision, Kut could not escape ineligibility by choosing to engage in a different "trade or occupation for which he was reasonably fitted" and which did not require Saturday work. He was pinned down by the court's words that he "must be available for work on Saturday if this is required by his usual trade or occupation." Incidentally, no findings were made that Kut confined his availability to some one occupation or excluded any but Saturday work.

Whether the Kut decision remains the law of Ohio is now open to question not only because the statute was amended in 1949 to require availability for "suitable work" but also because of the Ohio Supreme Court's decision in *Hinkle* v. *Lennox Furnace Co.* under the pre-1949 statute.[38] In the Hinkle case the court decided that a claimant's inability to engage in her former, customary occupation did not bar her from benefits so long as she was able and available for other work for which she was reasonably fitted. This raises the possibility that a Sabbath observer whose usual occupation requires Saturday work may meet the eligibility requirements by holding himself available for work in some trade for which he is reasonably fitted and which does not require Saturday work.

Unless it has been reversed by the Hinkle decision, the rule of the Kut case would seem to conflict with basic constitutional protections. If as the court specifically stated in the Kut decision, Sabbath observers are bound by the practices in their customary occupation, their only escape from ineligibility for benefits is to abandon their religious convictions. Such a limited "voluntary choice" is hardly consistent with freedom of religion. Had the facts in the Kut case indicated that the claimant was confining himself to work in which, in his chosen labor-market area, labor on his Sabbath was preponderantly required, the court's conclusion that he was unavailable for work would have rested on sounder constitutional grounds.

2. The court struck down as unconstitutional an Ohio regulation which required all claimants "to be available for each day of such week" (of compensable unemployment). This was on the ground that "the occupation" may not require availability for each

day of the week. Thus the court accorded a limited recognition to the constitutional rights of Sabbath-observing claimants.

3. In concluding its opinion, the court added other grounds for the benefit denial. It was held that Kut became unemployed when he refused the employer's offer of his original order clerk job "thus making himself unavailable for work — a direct violation of the statute which was not designed for the purpose of protection against unemployment that is voluntary."

Upon this portion of the decision, entirely nonfederal, the United States Supreme Court evidently based its dismissal of appeal. Two possible interpretations may be given the court's words: (1) a worker who leaves his job (without good cause) makes himself unavailable for work. This is judicial amendment of a law which provided a specific disqualification for such a leaving.[39] (2) Kut, who left his job, brought about his own situation of unavailability, that is, being an unemployed Sabbath observer in an occupation which required Sabbath work. This interpretation is so closely related to the first two holdings of the court that it cannot be separated and could defeat the nonfederal ground upon which the United States Supreme Court dismissed the appeal.

Aside from basic constitutional considerations, this subject raises questions of administrative policy. Not many claimants are involved, but the issues are explosive. Good administration ought not to kowtow to minority pressure groups. At the same time it is poor public-relations policy to offend minorities or other identifiable public groups gratuitously. The forms such ineptitude can take are illustrated by a case which occurred in Pennsylvania. The claimant was a rabbi, presumably Orthodox, who had earned his wage credits as a ritual slaughterer of animals. When he became unemployed and claimed benefits, he was referred to work as a laborer at $20 a week which required that he work on his Sabbath. When the rabbi refused the work he was disqualified for refusing suitable work without good cause. An appeal had to be taken to get the disqualification reversed.[40]

SEASONAL WORKERS[41]

Logically, the availability of seasonal workers may not fall under a heading of "Time Limitations." It is included in this chapter, however, because the subject has traditionally been classified under this main heading.

Seasonal Provisions

Paying benefits to seasonal workers has been the subject of considerable study and legislation. At the end of the 1949 legislative sessions twenty-one state laws had seasonal provisions.[42] All in all, thirty-five state laws have at one time or another included such provisions. Of the states which retain them several have never put them into effect. The laws of Delaware, Michigan, Minnesota, and Wisconsin apply the seasonal provisions to processors of agricultural products only. The others do not designate specific industries.

Considerable diversity may be found in the seasonal provisions. Seventeen states specify maximum annual operating periods for designation as a seasonal industry or occupation — ranging from fifteen weeks to one year.[43] Seasonal industries have also been measured by complete cessation of operations, and employment, man-hours, or payroll reduction of prescribed duration and percentage. Many and complicated formulas have been devised and used. These have employed varying methods of determining the peak and trough of employment. The percentage of decline required to make an industry seasonal has also varied, 40 per cent being the most common at present. Although study of the experience of an establishment or industry over a full business cycle is needed to measure its seasonal character, no state measures more than five years' experience. In most states a three year period is used.

Fixing the beginning and ending dates for a season is also required under the seasonal provisions and has provoked much controversy. When this is done on an industry basis, establishments will always be found within the industry that maintain high employment during the "off-season."[44] When it is done on an individual establishment basis, the administrative burdens become staggering.[45]

In most states with seasonal provisions, seasonal workers may draw benefits during the "season" only.[46] Nonseasonal wage credits are usually available for benefit purposes both during the active and off-season. Minnesota, however, makes seasonal wage credits available at any time but credits only that proportion of the seasonal wage as the active season bears to the calendar year. The definition of a "seasonal worker" has also presented difficulties. Although some laws have defined it in terms of percentages of earnings,[47] others refer to workers "ordinarily engaged in seasonal industry, and ordinarily not engaged in any other work." [48] In several states, a seasonal worker is anyone who has worked for a seasonal employer.[49]

Experience has demonstrated how ponderous and cumbersome the seasonal provisions are. The arguments in their behalf no longer seem so strong. States which pay off-season benefits to available seasonal workers have not made their funds insolvent. The predictability of seasonal unemployment has been demonstrated as a nice statistical average applicable to an industry, but unworkable for an individual establishment and its employees.[50] The high wages of seasonal workers within the coverage of the special provisions have been demonstrated to be mythical.[51] Under experience rating, seasonal employers who contribute heavily to unemployment get favored tax treatment as the result of special seasonal provisions which tend to exclude seasonal workers from benefits.[52]

The fact is that employees of firms with seasonal status are but a small percentage of the entire group of covered workers. Figures for twelve states, taken at various times before 1943, show that only in Alaska and Hawaii were such seasonal employees a high percentage of the total coverage, 50 per cent in Alaska before the war and 19.8 per cent in Hawaii in July 1941 (at season peak). The next highest was Oregon with 9.2 per cent in 1941 (season peak). All the others showed ratios of 5 per cent and lower.[53]

Many of these seasonal workers earn so little that they fail to qualify for benefits under the ordinary requirements. Of those who qualify only a minority claim benefits. Many regularly supplement their seasonal work with other employment, usually agricultural and not "covered." Most of them, men more frequently than women, but a majority in both sexes, want year-round work. Most of them, men more often than women, but a majority of both sexes, work over half the year. Such were the findings made from 1892 interviews of seasonal workers in four seasonal industries in California.[54]

Most states have concluded that case-by-case determination of the availability of seasonal workers during the off-season is not only the fairest but also the simplest and quickest way of handling the problem. The complexities of special seasonal provisions are beyond the understanding of most claimants and employers. Handling seasonal workers' claims under such laws takes twice as long as regular claims. Under the availability provision, the administrative burden is not eliminated but understandability of result can easily be achieved.

Seasonal Workers under Availability Provisions

The law is settled that, to be available for work, a seasonal worker must, during the off-season, be ready, willing, and able to take work outside his seasonal occupation.[55] The work history is an important tool in determining the out-of-season availability of such workers. It has been held "that where a claimant for benefits is a seasonal worker who has never, or has not for a long time been employed during the off-season of his customary seasonal occupation, there is created an inference that he is not available for work during such off-season." [56]

The Oklahoma Board of Review has, however, held that a cannery worker, whose community afforded no off-season work prospects, was available for work.[57] The board noted that this was different from the case of a claimant who moved from a locality of work opportunity to one where such opportunity was lacking. Although the canning season in the claimant's locality lasted only a few months, "Yet we cannot say that the legislature did not have in mind such situations. It might have been that it was fully recognized that in such businesses as the canning industry, the only way a supply of labor could be provided during the canning season was to contemplate the payment of unemployment benefits for a part of the year . . ."

The Oklahoma decision may be questioned as a rigid rule to be followed. It does, however, highlight the hardest availability problem to be solved in dealing with seasonal workers. A number of seasonal industries are located in areas which afford few or no work opportunities. They depend, in large measure, upon housewives, students, and migrants for their labor supply.[58] Food canning is a notable example. The seasonal workers living in these areas may or may not actually be able and willing to take off-season work. Their work histories are likely to show no off-season work because it is not to be had.

It can hardly be said that seasonal workers who confine themselves, during the off-season, to such areas have the required access to a labor market of substantial work opportunity. This is to be distinguished from the case of the nonseasonal worker, living in a locality of little work opportunity, who has become involuntarily unemployed because he has lost his transportation to work or his local employer has stopped doing business.

In any individual case, the foregoing conclusion ought not to be reached hastily. The injunction of the courts in the Garcia and Hagadone cases is important to remember.[59] In both cases, seasonal workers were involved. During the off-season they were referred to other work. In the Garcia case, a California cannery worker was referred to work ten miles distant from her home. In the Hagadone case, a sixty-year-old Idaho bandsaw filer was referred to unskilled work that, he claimed, would have been unsafe for him in view of his physical condition. In both cases, the courts remanded the determinations of unavailability upon the ground that evidence was lacking that local, suitable work was unobtainable.

STUDENTS

The availability problems raised by student claimants tend to fall in the "time" categories. Such claimants are apt to be unwilling to take work that will interfere with their studies. Limitation of availability to specific hours, part-time work, or seasonal work is characteristic. Although a readily identifiable group in the labor force and among benefit claimants, in neither category do students constitute a large group. During the war the number of students in the labor force reached unprecedented heights. In April 1944, about 1½ million young people, between the ages of fourteen and nineteen, were both attending school and in the labor force.[60] Even at that they constituted less than 3 per cent of the civilian labor force. In 1940 they had been less than 1 per cent of the labor force.

Special Student Provisions

Under American unemployment compensation laws students are often considered not employees for tax purposes and their employment not qualifying for benefit purposes. Under the laws of many states, student employment by an educational institution which is not exempt from federal income tax is excluded from coverage if the pay is not over $45 a quarter. In almost half the states, student employment by any organization exempt from federal income tax is excluded. Iowa, Kentucky, and Washington in different ways exclude services by a full-time or regular student. Illinois, Maine, Michigan, New Jersey, and Ohio exclude the part-time services of a minor student. New York excludes school year part-time and vacation period full-time service of a regular daytime student. South Dakota and Vermont collect taxes on the wages paid to students for short-time or vacation work, but will not consider such wages in determining benefit rights.

In twelve states student claimants are the object of special benefit disqualifications.[61] Most of these are addressed to students who are attending "established educational institutions." In Connecticut, Kentucky, and West Virginia the disqualification applies only if the student left work to attend school. Montana, North Dakota, and Ohio disqualify not only students regularly attending an established school but also individuals who leave work to attend school. Iowa disqualifies the student who fails to return to school during a period when he is customarily so engaged.

The justification offered for disqualifying students is the thesis that they are not a part of the labor force or, at least, not a part that ought to be entitled to unemployment compensation protection. If this argument is accepted, the best plan is to exclude students completely from coverage. To include their wages in the unemployment compensation tax base, while denying them benefits, as a class, is hardly honest. Actually, however, in terms of labor force membership and group need for protection against unemployment, there seems little basis for denying benefits to students as a class.

Another consideration in imposing legislative disqualifications for students has been "administrative difficulty." What this means is that student claimants raise more than their share of determination problems — usually availability problems. No figures have been collected to show how many or how few disputed benefit claims are filed by students. Most state unemployment compensation agencies, however, get along without a student disqualification. They rely upon the general availability requirement of their laws to settle the questionable cases. Much, if not most, student employment is, under present laws, not insured employment, as, for example, work for schools and colleges and on farms. These two factors cast doubt upon the need for special student disqualifications.

Student Claimants under the Availability Provision

Under the availability provision, there have been some decisions to the effect that full-time students, as such, are not available for work.[62] In some states, students have been held ineligible for benefits because they specified certain hours during which they would accept work.[63] These appear to be applications or extensions of the usual availability doctrines governing the availability of all claimants. In Massachusetts, for example, a war veteran enrolled in a full-time high school course in order to qualify for college entrance. Although he was willing to work after 3 P.M. on either the second or third shift, he was held ineligible because he was not available for work on all three shifts.[64] An Oklahoma high school student who had worked from 2 to 10 P.M. and who was unwilling to leave school to take work beginning before 2 P.M. was held unavailable for work by the Board of Review.[65] Leaving work in order to attend school has, in many cases, been considered evidence of unavailability while attending the school.[66]

It cannot be denied that the unemployment compensation agencies and appeal bodies have ever been suspicious of the availability of students. The principles they have followed, however, in determining their availability are the same principles they have applied to other claimants. Chief among them has been the requirement of willingness to accept suitable work.[67] An unemployed night club entertainer who was attending a secretarial school from 9 A.M. to 1 :30 P.M. was held available by a New York referee.[68] A similar result was reached by an Indiana referee in the case of full-time day students who had worked full-time while attending school and were laid off by their employers for lack of work. The referee, in this case, did not consider himself inhibited by the special disqualification of students contained in the Indiana law.[69] An unemployed cannery worker, engaged in a machine shop training course nightly from 7 to 10 P.M., was held unavailable by the New York Appeal Board when she refused to take daytime work in her usual occupation. She would take only work where she could use her new training although she lacked sufficient training to qualify.[70]

As in the Indiana case mentioned above, unemployment compensation tribunals have often looked to the student's previous employment history for aid in determining his availability.[71] A New Hampshire high school student who had earned his wage credits by working in a grocery store after school was held unavailable because additional studies had prevented him from getting to work on time and had led to his discharge by the employer.[72] Willingness to drop school to accept suitable work has often been a factor determining the availability of students.[73] The mere statement of such willingness to drop school in favor of work has, however, been viewed with some suspicion in the case of students who have paid tuition without prospect of refund.

Activity in search of work has been used as a criterion of student availability.[74] Willingness and ability to rearrange class hours in order to be able to accept work has, notably in the case of vocational students, also been often used as a test.[75]

Some distinctions have always been made, in practice, between the benefit claimant who is a vocational student and the claimant who is an academic student. The special student disqualifications, either specifically or by interpretation, are applied to the academic and not the vocational student. Under the general availability requirement also, the vocational student claimant has fared better than his academic brother. This was accentuated during the war period when vocational training became a key method for manning the war industries.[76] The public interest in "defense training" was declared in a number of decisions involving the availability of such trainees.[77] In some instances it was asserted that attendance at a defense training course did not impugn availability for work, but, instead, was evidence of such availability.[78]

The Michigan law provides extended benefits, if needed, for claimants who take courses to which they have been directed by the unemployment compensation agency or the employment service. Although such power must be used discreetly by a public agency, the need for it is clear. It is a necessary tool to secure the retraining of unemployed workers whose only skills are in overcrowded or obsolescent occupations. True, such subsidized retraining is seldom needed during periods of high employment and labor shortage. It is also true that retraining programs are often futile during depression periods. Between the boom and the bust, however, there is a real place for them. It is sobering to realize that Michigan is the only state which has equipped its unemployment compensation agency with a tool of this kind. The others have not yet touched the problem.

CHAPTER XI

RESIDENCE AND WORK LOCATION

PLACE LIMITATIONS UPON AVAILABILITY raise fundamental questions of social controls on mobility. Whether unemployment benefits will be granted or denied may not be the controlling element in individual decisions to move or not to move, to commute or not to commute. It seems reasonable, however, to assume — and individual claimant histories bear it out — that the effect upon benefit status of moving or not moving is a serious factor for many unemployed workers. An unemployed worker who is thinking of moving will feel more free to do so if he can count on a weekly benefit check while he is trying to establish himself in the new locality. If he is jobless and trying to get work at home he will resist moving elsewhere to get a job when he feels assured of his weekly benefits during his local job search. If it is correct to attribute such influence to unemployment compensation, its rules and practices need to be tied in closely to broad public policies for control of mobility and basic tenets of individual freedom.

This chapter will examine the unemployment compensation policies and rules which have been applied to "place" limitations on availability. When may a claimant restrict his availability to his home locality and continue to qualify for benefits? How does a claimant's removal to a new locality affect eligibility? What importance is assigned to the presence or absence of transportation to work?

Two general criteria present themselves for consideration in appraising the rules on place limitations. One is the effect of such rules upon desirable geographic labor mobility. The other is their effect upon individual liberty of movement. Both these yardsticks are vague. Not only is it difficult to find and measure the effects of availability policies in these terms, the terms themselves are hardly the subject of common understanding. For example, who determines what is desirable geographic mobility of labor? Yet the social concerns which the two suggested criteria express are the vital public stakes involved in decisions on place restrictions of availability. For that reason, although their application must be crude and intuitive, they cannot be abandoned as tests of the adequacy of existing rules.

RESTRICTION TO HOME LOCALITY

Unemployment compensation's basic approach has been that an unemployed worker ought not to be required to move from home as a means of qualifying for benefits. Every state statute but Nevada's and Wisconsin's makes the distance of the work from the claimant's residence a factor affecting the suitability of work. All but nine of the state laws make local work prospects a criterion in determining what is suitable work.[1] Such statutory provisions have yielded a strong tendency to find that the claimant who limits his availability to his home community and its environs does not make himself ineligible for benefits.[2]

Distance Criterion

A Pennsylvania Board of Review decision is a good illustration of how the "distance" criterion of suitable work is made to produce this result. The claimant lacked transportation to any other town. The main employment opportunities in her home town were with the employer who laid her off and one other employer. The board said: "In the present case the claimant is not the 'actor.' She has not moved to another locality but is remaining in her home community. Employment opportunities in such community may be limited but clearly are not nonexistent. In such a situation it appears to us that the usual rules for determining availability must be applied." Here the board pointed to the distance criterion in the Pennsylvania Law, stating that distance made work outside the claimant's town unsuitable because she lacked transportation. Thus the claimant had not excluded suitable work; therefore she was available for work.[3]

Temporarily laid off workers are commonly held available for work without regard to their unwillingness to take work involving extensive commuting or moving to another town. In *Porter* v. *Riley* a Washington lower court awarded benefits to a lumber-piler who limited himself to local work during a 2½ month seasonal layoff. He had a small farm with some stock which required his care during after-work hours and he refused work which was 101 miles away.[4]

Local Work History

The fact that the claimant earned his wage credits in his home locality has been given weight in some decisions. The Florida Board of Review, in the case of a saleswoman who had refused work in a town ten miles away because of difficult bus connections, phrased it in this way: "As long as an individual has some prospect of securing suitable work in his home locality where he has earned his wage credits, difficulties in getting to and from work in another locality operate more readily to prevent a claimant from being held unavailable for work.[5]

A Kansas referee was more positive. The claimant lived and had earned her wage credits in a rural area where work opportunities were limited. According to the referee, since she had earned all her wage credits there it was not unreasonable that she should limit her availability to that community. "The Kansas Unemployment Compensation Statute is not designed to drive claimants away from an established home to seek employment in a new territory on pain of losing their benefits. If a claimant's work history shows a habit of working in various parts of the State or country, then, and in that event, we may properly expect him to continue to do so if he wishes to meet the availability requirements of the Statute." [6]

Local Work Prospects

Most influential of all has been the element of local work prospects. It was here that the California District Court of Appeals parted company with the Appeal Board in the Garcia case.[7] The board had held a cannery worker unavailable for work, while seasonally unemployed, when she was registered for cannery or bottling work only and she refused a referral to cannery employment ten miles away to which she lacked transportation. The court said the record showed no evidence that the claimant was not qualified for and would not have accepted work other than that for which she was registered. Neither was there evidence that, in the claimant's home community, work was not available of the kind that claimant had previously done or was reasonably fitted to do. Lack of reasonable local work prospects underlies most of the decisions which hold claimants unavailable who have restricted themselves to their home communities.[8]

An interesting example of the effect given to local work prospects is this decision of the New Jersey Board of Review. Most of the large local employers in the claimant's line of work were strike-bound, making it impossible for her to find local work. The board held that she was available, but only for nine weeks. At that point, the board reasoned, it should have become plain to her that she could not find work in her own community and that she would have to seek employment elsewhere.[9]

Claimants with a history of accepting work in distant places are usually held strictly to that practice. If they limit themselves to local work they are ordinarily held ineligible.[10] This ruling has most commonly been applied to construction workers. The rule is readily justified when the claimant also limits himself to his customary work and little or no work of that kind is ordinarily done in the community. Sometimes, however, personal and subjective factors are given controlling weight.

An example is a decision by the Virginia Commissioner. The claimant, a West Virginia resident, had worked both in Virginia and Oregon during 1942 and 1943. He left an Oregon shipyard job to return to West Virginia because of his mother's illness. Having returned to his West Virginia home, he would now accept only work within commuting distance so that he might at all times be available to his mother. As an exception to the usual rule, he was held eligible for benefits.[11]

In contrast is the Illinois Board of Review's decision in the case of a construction foreman who had moved to a small community in order to accept a job. He remained there, unemployed, for eight months after the job ended. The board denied him benefits upon the theory that, if he had been genuinely in the labor market, he would have moved elsewhere, since there was a critical labor short-age in other areas.[12]

Restriction to Neighborhood

Restriction of acceptable work to establishments within walking distance or the immediate neighborhood of the claimant's residence has usually proved fatal to eligibility.[13] The fact that streetcar or bus riding makes the claimant sick has seldom had any effect upon the decision.[14] The Maryland Unemployment Compensation Board, in one case, where this claim was made and corroborated by a physician, said that it was "merely an excuse" that women were using to get benefits.[15] The limitation to the neighborhood or walk-ing distance occurs most frequently among women who have small children or other pressing domestic responsibilities. The usual result is benefit denial, although availability has been found in instances where the claimant lived in a busy industrial neighborhood.[16]

The Journey to Work

Involved in the entire question of restriction to the home locality is the reasonableness of commuting requirements. The importance of commuting to our industrial life cannot be doubted. Daily travel to and from work widens the labor market, making both workers and employers more independent. Workers get more flexibility in choosing their homes, and employers a wider choice of business locations. Socially, modern transportation and commuting have changed the nature of our cities. They are responsible both for decentralizing homes through suburbanization and partially decentralizing industry to suburban areas. Commuting also, it has been pointed out, tends to keep the family intact by enabling the various members to work in different localities while living in the same place.[17]

With all its importance, the daily journey to work has been little explored. Most unemployment compensation cases involving the reasonableness of travel time, distance or cost involved in offered work are decided on the basis of the "general information" which the administering agency has.[18] A 1934 survey of sixty-four American towns, ranging in size from twelve thousand to over a million inhabitants, showed that in twenty-one cities, 50 per cent or more of the family principal earners walked to work. In all places surveyed the great majority (over two-thirds) of the principal earners go to work in less than half an hour.[19] A New York City survey, made in the same year, showed that 57 per cent of the principal income earners reached their work in less than forty minutes. Only in the Bronx and Queens, was more than forty minutes' travel required by the majority of the principal earners.[20]

A 1936 study of thirty thousand employees of four auto factories in Flint, Michigan, showed that two-thirds got to work by car and that over 90 per cent had a ride of a half-hour or less.[21] In the sixty-four-town survey mentioned, in all but one city, at least twenty per cent of the principal earners used automobiles to get to work; in fourteen cities more than half used automobiles. A Utah survey in 1942 of over sixteen thousand workers in four of

the counties adjoining Great Salt Lake showed that a majority
(54.7 per cent) used automobiles to get to work.[22]

In 1935–36 it was found that American families with annual
incomes of less than $2500 spent from 1.6 per cent to 14.9 per cent
of their incomes on travel and transportation. These percentages
included, however, nonbusiness travel. Not only were the percentages spent on travel smaller with smaller incomes, but they also
varied somewhat with the size of the community. They were lowest in New York and Chicago, but in large cities like Columbus
and Denver they were a little higher than in small and middle-
sized cities.[23]

Another relevant consideration in assessing availability limitations to particular neighborhoods and localities is the apparent fact
that industrial workers ordinarily seek and find jobs and employers
recruit workers within a small and compact industrial neighborhood. Myers and Maclaurin, in a study of two adjacent New England cities, found that, although workers in one city had often been
employed in the other, 90 per cent of the job moves made, in the
1937–1939 period, among the thirty-seven firms studied were between establishments in the same city. Within each of these two
cities also there were neighborhood patterns of mobility. One small
woolen mill was located among a group of plastics and apparel
firms and geographically separated from the other textile firms.
Half the job movement between textiles, apparel and plastics involved this mill, but there was little or no interchange of workers
between it and the other local textile firms. A metal-products firm
in one of these cities found in 1942 that the greatest number of job
seekers came from the next-door women's shoe company. Forty-
three of the sixty-two workers hired by a cotton textile mill came
from firms located within a quarter-mile radius.[24]

Weighting the Worker's Choice of Locality

Until we are more adequately informed of the work location and
commuting mores of our communities, it would seem the better
part of wisdom to give considerable weight to the worker's selection of a locality in which he will seek to work. Surely this should
be our basic approach when a worker restricts his availability to
his home community. True, in no individual instance will such an
approach answer the relevant questions of the claimant's work history, his other job demands and his activity in pursuit of employ-

ment. Neither will it reveal the job opportunities normally existing in the area to which the claimant confines himself. When these factual inquiries are made, however, and the results assessed, the determination of the claimant's availability will often remain anything but clear-cut. When this occurs, the decisive factor may be furnished by giving weight to the claimant's own choice of work locality.

Making the claimant's choice a critical element springs not only from the lack of social and economic information already mentioned. It is based on a deliberate choice, in an area of doubt and lack of facts, to rely upon individual, not institutional, judgment. In an earlier chapter we reviewed the social ties that bind the worker to his community. In a social insurance system these must be given careful consideration. Pressure upon the worker to destroy or endanger those ties by going elsewhere to find work may increase rather than decrease social misfortune. Although not logically controlling, it may also be noted that the claimant who restricts his availability takes a greater chance than the unemployment compensation agency that pays him benefits. The agency stakes but a few dollars on its choice; the claimant stakes his livelihood.

REMOVAL TO A NEW LOCALITY

In a previous chapter we have noted the desirable purposes which may be served by the geographic mobility of labor. Such mobility can aid in equalizing wages and work conditions for comparable employments. It helps to distribute workers where the need is greatest. It may provide workers with an opportunity to use their capacities and abilities most effectively. In recent years about 10 per cent of the workers have, each year, made interstate moves. Many more workers have participated in intrastate moves. Although more common among non-covered (for example, agricultural) than covered workers, migration has been of sufficient importance from the very outset of the American unemployment compensation program to require special measures.

Interstate Benefit Plans

Because American unemployment compensation consists of individual state systems, it was evident soon after its inception that methods were needed to provide for workers who qualified for benefits under the law of one state but became unemployed while living in another state. The Interstate Benefit Payment Plan was developed in 1938 and is now used by all states. Under this plan workers who reside in one state and qualify for benefits from another may file their claims with their resident state. The state of residence then acts as an agent to accept the claim and work registration and to forward the claim to the liable state for determination and payment.[25]

More recently an Interstate Plan for Combining Wages has been set up to provide for the claimant who has worked in covered employment in more than one state, fails to qualify for benefits in any one of them, but would qualify in the state of residence if his wage credits were added together. Under this latter plan, now adopted by forty-five states, the state where the claim is filed gathers the information from the other states involved, determines and pays the claim, and later prorates the benefits paid among the other states.

The interstate benefit plans evidence that mere removal to another locality does not vitiate a worker's benefit eligibility. A host of unemployment compensation decisions attest to this basic principle. No argument is required to prove its soundness or desirability. As the unemployment compensation program has developed, however, some qualifications have been put upon this rule which, either in principle or in application or in both, are the subject of divided opinion.

Self-Created Distance

The laws of Alabama, Colorado, and West Virginia now provide, in effect, that a worker may be denied benefits for refusing work if he quits work without good cause connected with the job, moves to a new locality, and then refuses to return to accept an offered job in the old locality. The statutes of the states named provide that in such instances the work in the old locality shall not be considered as unsuitable because of its distance from the claimant's new residence.

The doctrine of these statutory provisions has had a limited reception.[26] Its origin was in a 1942 decision of the Alabama Supreme Court, *Ex Parte Alabama Textile Products Corporation*.[27] Mrs. Campbell, the claimant, quit her job in Andalusia, Alabama, and moved with her husband to Niagara Falls, New York. There she filed a claim for benefits. Her old employer promptly offered to return her to her old job. The claimant refused because she was living in Niagara Falls with her husband and could not return. The

Alabama law then in force specified that the distance of the offered work from the claimant's residence should be considered in determining whether or not the work was suitable. To this the Court said: "if her previous work is available and suitable and she . . . voluntarily puts distance between her and it, she cannot complain that such distance has rendered that job unsuitable."

The following year this view was adopted by courts in Georgia and West Virginia. The Georgia Supreme Court said that a woman worker who quit in order to get married and moved to a city 125 miles away "becomes the author of her own disqualification." If she is unable to find work in her new city and declines an offer of her former job, she "voluntarily renders herself unavailable for work . . . and cannot claim . . . distance as rendering the work unsuitable." [28] The West Virginia court applied the same reasoning in the case of three male claimants.[29]

Most states have considered the Alabama Textile Products Corporation doctrine an inequitable imposition of a double penalty. Under it the worker is disqualified once for quitting without good cause when he moves. After he has filed his claim in the new locality and receives and refuses an offer of his old job, he is again disqualified. In effect, he is given two separate disqualifications for the same act.

The 1948 amendments injected into the Missouri law a provision which combines features of the "self-created distance" doctrine with "removal to a remote area" doctrine. The Missouri law now provides that

if an individual has removed himself from the locality in which he actually resided when he was last employed to a place where there is less probability of his employment at his usual type of work and which is more distant from or otherwise less accessible to the community in which he was last employed, work offered by his most recent employer if similar to that which he performed in his last employment and at wages, hours, and working conditions which are substantially similar to those prevailing for similar work in such community, or any work which he is capable of performing at the wages prevailing for such work in the locality to which he has removed, if not hazardous to his health, safety or morals, shall be deemed suitable for him.

Removal to a "Remote" Area

There is virtual unanimity that the worker is unavailable who leaves a locality of industrial activity and moves to an area where little or no opportunity exists for work within his qualifications.[30] This is to be distinguished from the "self-created distance" principle. The two are alike only in placing responsibility upon the claimant for his own action; he made the move. Otherwise they are different. The self-created distance principle rests upon the claimant's leaving and refusing to return to a specific job or locality. No account is taken of the job opportunities in the new locality. The "remote area" doctrine makes everything hinge upon the work opportunities in the new locality. Whether or not there is a specific job offer waiting for the claimant in the old locality makes no difference.

Statutory amendment has imported the "remote area" doctrine into four state laws. The Alabama law makes benefit eligibility hinge upon availability for work which the individual is qualified to perform "either at a locality at which he earned wages for insured work during his base period or at a locality where it may reasonably be expected that such work may be available." In Michigan the individual must be available for full-time work which he is qualified to do and which is generally similar to work which he has previously done for wages. Furthermore, he must be available for such work at a locality where he earned base period wages in insured work or where the commission finds that such work is available.

By amendment in 1949, the Illinois law declares that a worker is unavailable for work if, after his most recent separation from employment, he has moved to and remains in a locality with work opportunities that are substantially less favorable than those in the locality he left. The Ohio statute was also amended in 1949. To qualify for benefits under the 1949 Ohio law, an unemployed worker must be available for suitable work and actively seeking work either at a locality in which he has earned wages subject to the unemployment compensation act during his base period or at a locality where such work is normally performed.

The most striking statement of the "remote area" doctrine occurred in the Teicher case, decided by the Pennsylvania Superior Court.[31] A department store saleslady quit her job in 1942 and moved to Alexandria, Louisiana, in order to be near her husband who was in training at Camp Claiborne near by. The court said that the claimant "deliberately became unavailable for work."

"She quit not only her employment, but all the existing areas of reasonable opportunity for employment and isolated or insulated herself from innumerable employers crying for the need of available employees."

The court distinguished this from the case of the person who becomes unemployed through no fault of his own. The community's duty to that individual is not discharged by requiring him to leave his established home. "But here, the claimant was the actor. In our opinion, the duty of the community is temporarily lost or suspended when the member voluntarily removes to another in which there is no employment available and no reasonable expectation of finding any."

Justifiable as this reasoning may have been, it received little support from the fact that Alexandria in 1940 had a population of over 27,000. The same Pennsylvania court, two years later, held that a war worker who followed her soldier husband to Columbia, South Carolina, a city of more than 110,000, was available for work.[32]

In the Reger case the Connecticut Supreme Court of Errors held that a New Haven bookkeeper who moved to Ozark, Alabama, to be near her soldier husband was available for work.[33] Ozark was a town of 4500. The largest town near by was Dothan, 25,000 in population and 28 miles away. The claimant was willing to accept any office work for which she was qualified, within a radius of 30 miles, to start at $15 a week, and to work any hours of the day.

Many of the local employers were unwilling to hire soldiers' wives. Of the 209 placements made by the Dothan employment service office during one of the 2½ months the claimant spent in the area only 5 were office workers. The claimant applied unsuccessfully for two local jobs. The court, relying upon a definition of "labor market" in terms of the "general performance," within the geographical area, of the type of services which the claimant is offering, found that the claimant had exposed herself "unequivocally to the labor market."

The decisions in the Reger and Teicher cases are not inconsistent in principle. They do, however, highlight a real problem. What is "an area of little or no work opportunity?" The better opinion seems to be that ordinarily the test must be the work that is usually performed in the locality and not the existing job openings. This was the opinion of the Connecticut Supreme Court of Errors in the Reger case. The Michigan Appeal Board, in applying the most stringent availability provision on the statute books, said:

"It is not necessary . . . to find that a specific job opening exists
for the individual, but it should be demonstrated that his chances
of securing employment in a new locality are at least approximately
the same as those existent in the locality in which the worker received wages during his base period." [34]

Measuring the labor market in terms of work ordinarily performed will not alone answer the question raised in the last paragraph. What volume of work, ordinarily performed within the
fields of the claimant's availability, marks the area of sufficient
work opportunity? Is it five jobs? or ten? or a hundred? The
answer must be that there is no precise answer. Manifestly, it
would be completely unfair to a claimant to say: "You have moved
to a locality where, over the past ten years, an annual average of
twenty people have been employed in the work for which you offer
yourself. This makes you unavailable for work, since there is too
little work opportunity in this locality to which you now confine
yourself." To this the claimant may reply by pointing to the small
size of the community. With a population of 500, for example,
twenty jobs may be the measure of an excellent work opportunity.[35] Or the claimant may say: "Yes, but the average has been
twenty workers in this field only because employers have been
unable to attract more qualified workers to this locality." Or the
claimant's line of work may be highly skilled and he may properly
contend that twenty jobs, for such skilled work, is indicative of an
area of sufficient work opportunity. These and other factors, must
be considered and analyzed before concluding that a given area has
so little work opportunity for a claimant that he makes himself
unavailable for work when he moves into it.

TRANSPORTATION FACILITIES

One of the elements of availability noted in an earlier chapter is
accessibility to a labor-market area. The claimant must be located
within reach of job locations. Ordinarily he cannot rely upon
transportation furnished by an employer. Some court decisions
have made a great point of this. A Georgia court used it as a ground
for denying benefits to a woman who lost her ride to work at her
last job. The court said: "Where there is no duty resting on the
employer from custom or contract express or implied, to furnish
means of transportation to his employee to and from work the
burden is cast on the employee to provide himself with such transportation. When he has this burden and is unable to provide him-

self with such transportation, even through no fault of his own, and the employer offers suitable employment, the employee is not available for work, I conclude." [36] The Supreme Courts of Ohio, Oklahoma, and Washington have relied upon this language.[37] Other courts have also indicated their agreement that transportation to work is a problem to be solved by the claimant.[38]

The complications of actual cases reveal, however, that casting the burden of transportation to work upon the claimant is no touchstone for determining availability. Difficult problems remain. An obvious exception, simple in solution, is furnished in an Indiana decision. A construction foreman returned to his home town where no job opportunities existed and there was no available transportation to nearby labor markets. He kept up his contacts with large contractors, however, and was willing to go anywhere in the country for work.[39]

A more involved case, from New Jersey, is that of a claimant in a rural community that lacked public transportation to surrounding industrial and commercial areas. The one local source of employment was a hat manufacturer employing about a hundred workers. The claimant had worked in the hat factory for a time and then found work in a town eighteen miles away to which she rode in another worker's car. She left this second job when she lost her "ride" and, after diligent search, was unable to find another. Although she applied for work at the hat factory she remained unemployed for six months until she got work with the hat establishment. The Board of Review allowed her benefits.[40]

The reasoning of the New Jersey Board of Review in such cases has been clearly stated:

Where an individual has a free choice as to his place of residence and chooses a place where there is no work rather than one where work can be found, it is reasonable to suppose that he does so because he is not anxious to work. That is not true in this case, however. The claimant is a married woman and is therefore legally bound to accept the domicile fixed by her husband. He is bound to this particular community by his work. His wife, the claimant, has no legal choice but must remain there with him. Therefore, in so doing, she displays no intent not to work.[41]

The decision in which this statement occurs passed upon the availability of a rural resident who lacked local work opportunities and both public and private transportation to the nearest community where work was obtainable. The board accepted the claimant's need to augment the family income as strongly persuasive of her intent to work if she could find a job.

The Alabama Board of Appeals took a similar view in the case of a farmer and his wife who lost their jobs and their only transportation to work when the employer, who had furnished the transportation, closed down. The claimants lived eight miles from a bus line.

The Board does not feel that claimants are required to change their homes to seek what would probably be a precarious living in the now competitive labor market or attempt to arrange for the purchase of an automobile in order to allow them to commute to and from their work . . . Claimants are just as willing to work today if some means of transportation is provided them as they were during the time when they held their jobs. They are no less accessible to the labor market today than they were at the time during which they were making contributions to the unemployment fund.[42]

The statement just quoted and the conclusion reached point to a desirable modification of the "accessibility" element in the availability requirement. When loss of transportation occurs simultaneously with a lay off or as the result of a lay off, the lack of transportation alone ought not to render a claimant unavailable for work. In areas where private transportation, such as car pools, are the only way for many workers to get to jobs, it is to be expected that a lay off will disrupt and sometimes destroy transportation arrangements. In such instances the unemployment is clearly due to economic circumstances rather than availability. Restoration of work opportunity will usually mean restoration of transportation.

A number of jurisdictions, including Illinois and New York, proceed substantially upon this basis in loss of transportation cases.[43] The Illinois Board of Review has gone so far in applying it as to allow benefits to a woman who was laid off by the factory where her husband, with whom she rode to work, remained employed. She had no transportation to other work and no prospects of suitable work in her community. Her last employer adopted a policy of not rehiring women.[44] The New York Appeal Board has extended benefits to claimants without employment opportunities in their places of residence and without transportation to any place of possible employment. It has been careful to require, however, that claimants must be willing to work and must be making an honest effort to solve their transportation difficulties.

TRAVEL STATUS

Benefits have ordinarily been denied to claimants who leave the locality to go on vacation, to visit friends or relatives, or for other personal reasons.[45] The reasoning has been that such individuals are engaged in personal business and either not interested in working or in no position to accept a job. Similarly, while claimants who are travelling are in actual transit the assumption has usually been made that they are unavailable. The difficulty of notifying them of job openings and their in-between status as work registrants in two different employment offices has led to this conclusion.[46] Unemployed workers who travel in search of work, however, have been held available for work.[47]

In some cases it has been held that workers who have been laid off for short periods and have good prospects of recall may take vacation trips without sacrificing eligibility for benefits. In such instances the worker must arrange for notice to reach him promptly that he has been recalled. He must also be able to return to the plant on short notice.[48] It has also been suggested that a distinction in the no-vacation rule may be made between salaried and wage workers on the theory that job offers for the former would not necessarily require the same immediate response.[49]

CONCLUSIONS

This chapter began by saying that, difficult to determine and vague as they were, the effects upon geographic mobility and upon individual liberty are important criteria in evaluating the rules on "place" restrictions. No finality is possible in this connection. Some suggestions can, however, be made.

1. The distance and time a claimant must be willing to travel to a job in order to qualify as being available, and the transportation cost he must be willing to pay, are expressions of a social standard of worker mobility. In practical terms, this standard tells the unemployed worker how much commuting the state expects him to do. This may be called either an intrusion upon individual liberty or one phase of our definition of that liberty. It may be considered either a partial statement or a reflection of social policy on many aspects of mobility: plant location, city planning, indus-

trial decentralization. The precise description is not so important as understanding the import of unemployment compensation decisions which turn upon the travel the claimant is prepared to undertake. Since such decisions are enmeshed in basic social policies of mobility and freedom, they need a solid base of information on travel times, distances, and costs for workers. This should be obtained on a local basis. In general, it is now lacking.

2. The "self-created distance" doctrine clearly fails on both counts. By making the worker ineligible for benefits, at a local employer's option, when he leaves and goes to another locality it creates a deterrent to worker mobility. The effect is to tie the worker, if he wishes to keep his protection against unemployment, to the one locality.

3. The "remote area" doctrine is more defensible although the strait-jacket provisions of the Alabama, Illinois, and Michigan laws cannot be condoned. By the test of effect upon desirable mobility, however, its wisdom as an immutable policy may be questioned. The reconversion period following World War II is a good instance of the possible weakness of this doctrine. When the war ended and the lay offs came, the workers who had been recruited from the small towns and the farms, it was hoped, would leave the industrial centers and go home. Many of them did. If they were unemployed when they got home and claimed benefits, they often found themselves denied compensation. The reason? They had removed themselves to areas of little work opportunity. This was bound to encourage these claimants to return to the war industry centers and to discourage other laid-off workers from leaving those centers. In such circumstances, application of the remote area doctrine is not consistent with desirable mobility. It may be that our reliance should be upon other social devices than unemployment compensation to induce workers to move from surplus labor areas. Should unemployment compensation act as a counterforce?

4. An unspoken assumption in many denials of benefits to claimants living in places of "little work opportunity" or "no transportation to work" is that the claimant is qualified and willing to do work in "covered" employment or industrial employment only. Often this is not the case, as investigation will show. People who live in such places, usually farm areas, are likely to be willing and able to accept farm work. Because farm placement has in so many cases been separated from the other employment services, there

has been a tendency to neglect the work opportunities it can give to benefit claimants. The result has been that unemployment compensation contributes to the pressures pushing workers, who have abandoned the city for the farm, back to the city again.

CHAPTER XII

WOMEN WORKERS

AS BENEFIT CLAIMANTS

AVAILABILITY ADMINISTRATION has no greater problems than those associated with women workers. No other group has occasioned more special legislation concerning their availability for work. Most state unemployment compensation laws contain special provisions aimed directly at women who seek benefits.

Adequate statistical information about women's claims is impossible to get. No national figures were gathered before 1946. During the period from 1946 to 1948, however, women claimants constituted a disproportionate segment of the claims load. Census labor-force estimates show women workers as a fifth of the unemployed in 1946, a quarter of the unemployed in 1947, and 31 per cent in 1948. During the same periods, women accounted for roughly four of every ten benefit claims, both initial and compensable.[1] Almost half of the claimants who exhausted their benefit rights during July 1946 to June 1947 were women. Of every dollar paid in state unemployment benefits during that period forty-two cents went to women claimants.

This is not necessarily a permanent or usual state of affairs. The war called forth an army of women workers. When the war was over, although many of them were reluctant to be demobilized, women workers bore the brunt of the postwar lay offs. Strategically, they were poorly placed in industry and their entrance poorly timed. Over three-fifths of the women workers added during the war went into manufacturing, over two-fifths into the major war industries. As wartime additional workers the women lacked seniority. When the work force reductions came after V–J Day the women were among the first to go.

During the last half of 1945 and in 1946 industry moved in the direction of prewar hiring patterns. In 1944 almost half the nonagricultural placements by the employment service were women workers. In the succeeding three years they have hovered around the 30 per cent mark. The drop was from 3.8 million placements in 1944 to 1.7 million in 1946. Just before V–J Day, of every 10 nonagricultural placements of women, 6 were in manufacturing, 3 were in trade and service. In the three years that followed this has been reversed, so that 3 of every 10 nonfarm female placements have been in manufacturing, and 6 in trade and service.

The wages being offered to women during this period were low. Of the job openings for women listed with the public employment offices in April 1946, which paid an hourly wage rate, over 70 per cent paid less than sixty-five cents an hour. Less than 28 per cent of the men's openings paid such low wage rates.[2] Understandably, many women claimants were unwilling to accept such jobs and unemployment compensation agencies, in many instances, paid them benefits — at least until it became clear that better-paying jobs were not to be found.

These facts give some perspective on the 1946 figures on women claimants. They do not, however, tell us anything about the "normal" load of women's benefit claims. The truth is that we know almost nothing about it. The American unemployment compensation system has been paying benefits for too short and turbulent a period.

Some "spot" surveys have, however, been made. A sample survey of claims filed in forty-seven states, during the second week of February 1943 showed that women were 38.3 per cent of all claimants. They were unemployed longer and drew more benefits than men.[3] Over a quarter of the Des Moines claimants who exhausted their benefit rights in the last half of 1939 were women.[4] Women beneficiaries constituted about 15 per cent of the Detroit claimants who filed claims in July–September 1938. They were about a fifth of the ones who exhausted their benefit rights.[5] Both of these area surveys also showed women as unemployed longer than men.

WOMEN AS PART OF THE LABOR FORCE

A fruitful avenue to study women workers in their relation to unemployment compensation is to consider them in relation to the labor force. No full-scale exposition can be attempted here, but some major trends and facts should be pointed out.

Feminization of the Labor Force

This has already been described in an earlier chapter. There we noted that in 1900 women were less than a fifth of the gainfully employed. In 1947 they averaged, over the year, as 28 per cent of the civilian labor force. The increase of the female work force has been most notable among twenty-five- to forty-four-year-old women. This group was 6 per cent of the total gainfully employed in 1900 and 12 per cent of the 1947 labor force. This is the age group which has accounted for over two-fifths of the increased percentage of women in the entire labor force. It is also the age group which contains most of the married women who are living with their husbands.

More Married Women in the Labor Force

Although labor force participation has increased among the entire female population the most phenomenal growth has taken place among married women. In 1890, 4 or 5 per cent of the married women were in the labor market. By 1947, about 21 per cent of all married women had joined the work force.[6]

The increasing tendency of married women to enter the labor force seems connected with the declining birth rate. In 1940, for each age group of married women (eighteen to forty-four years old), the percentage of women without young children (under ten years old) who were in the labor force was two to four times as great as among women with one young child and from two-and-a-half to more than six times as great as among women with two or more young children.[7]

It cannot be proven that the movement of women into the labor force has prompted a declining birth rate. The facts show only that the two go together. It would seem as reasonable to say that the falling birth rate has caused married women to enter the labor force. Whether cause or effect, in the view of the demographers, no real rise in the American birth rate is to be expected. The growth of the cities continues. The mechanizing and commercializing of home services continue. The demand for white collar workers in sales and office jobs, for professional and semiprofessional workers, for semiskilled industrial workers goes on growing. In all of these women are wanted. So long as these remain the facts we may expect more women workers, both married and unmarried.

It is not mere whim or even careerism that motivate married women to seek employment. "The majority of married women seek employment after experience has demonstrated the family need of their earnings; in about a third of the families the wife's or mother's earnings comprise one-half or more of all contributions to the family, and in a larger proportion of families they form from a fourth to a half of all contributions." [8]

A tabulation of married women in the 1940 labor force showed that among wives of husbands earning less than $1000 in wages or salary in 1939, a quarter to a third of those without young children (under ten) were in the labor force. Among wives whose husbands received $2000 or more in wages or salary in 1939, an eighth or less of those without young children were in the labor force. For women with young children, the percentage of labor force membership was also four or more times as great among the wives whose husbands earned less than $1000 as it was among those whose husbands earned $2000 or more in 1939.[9]

The ultimate outcome of the movement of married women into the labor force cannot be predicted. No end is foreseeable to the forces that have prompted and eased that movement. The American social and economic structure rests upon a continued stimulation of a widespread demand for more goods and services. By making necessities of luxuries we exert a social compulsion upon workers, their wives, and their families to bend every effort to achieve a higher material living standard. In many instances our system of distribution works in such a way that the stimulus for married women to work outside the home is a more primary one of basic need. Work as we may to destroy this more compelling stimulus there seems no prospect that we will do any damage to the equally powerful incentive of achieving a "desirable" living standard.

Irregularity of Women Workers

Women workers, on the whole, do not work as steadily as men. A survey of over three thousand women workers in Chicago showed that

some 48 per cent of the domestic workers, 46 per cent of the women in "other" occupations, and 40 per cent of the self-employed withdrew from the labor market for some period of time during 1937–41 . . . The lack of continuity in employment was particularly characteristic of the married women. Almost half of the married domestic workers and more than one-third of the single women left the labor market during the 54-month period; almost half of the married women in "other" occupations left the labor market at least once, while less than one-fourth of the single women withdrew.[10]

Women are much less likely to work a full week than men. During the 1940 census week 1.5 per cent of the men at work in non-agricultural jobs worked less than fourteen hours, 9.4 per cent worked between fourteen and thirty-four hours. During the same week, 2.6 per cent of the women employed worked less than fourteen hours, and 14.3 per cent worked between fourteen and thirty-four hours in nonagricultural employment. Census labor force estimates for 1948 show similar disparities among men and women who were at work in nonagricultural jobs. Among the men, 1.9 per cent worked less than fourteen hours and 10.8 per cent worked from fourteen to thirty-four hours; among the women 6.0 per cent worked less than fourteen hours and 12.8 per cent worked between fourteen and thirty-four hours during the week.[11]

Occupational and Industrial Distribution

Women workers have tended to cluster in the professional and semiprofessional, clerical and sales, semiskilled industrial, and service occupations. In 1947 these occupations accounted for almost nine out of ten employed women. In these occupational groups women have had, in recent years, a high percentage of representation. In 1947 women workers were about 27 per cent of the entire labor force, but they were well over two-fifths of the professional and semiprofessional workers, and of the clerical, sales and kindred workers, and almost two-thirds of the nonprotective service workers. In the semiskilled industrial occupations they were slightly more than a quarter of the labor force.

Some individual occupations are almost exclusively feminine. Nurses, stenographers, telephone operators, and domestic servants are examples of occupations that, in 1947, were filled, 90 per cent or more by women. In other occupations, such as teaching, dancing, laundry operators, office machine operators they also predominated and constituted more than 70 per cent of the 1947 workers.

The industrial distribution of women workers shows a similar picture. They seek and find work in manufacturing, trade, personal services, and professional and related services. More than eight out of every ten employed women workers in 1940 were in these industries. They filled a more than average percentage of the jobs in wholesale and retail trade; finance, insurance, and real estate; professional and related services; and personal services. Although they were less than a quarter of factory employees, they constituted more than half the workers employed in such industries as tobacco, knit goods, apparel and accessories, and miscellaneous fabricated textile products. They similarly predominated in general merchandise and limited-price variety stores, the telephone industry, the hotel and lodging industry, and domestic, educational, and medical and health service industries.

It is not yet possible to gauge the long-run effects of the war upon the occupational and industrial distribution of women workers. As of November 1946, women had managed to retain one million of the 2½ million additional production jobs which they acquired between October 1939 and the wartime peak of November 1943. About half the job increase from the prewar period has been concentrated in the durable-goods industries. What kinds of jobs women now hold in those industries is not clear, although there is evidence that they are being placed in unskilled and semi-skilled classifications. Postwar labor shortages have made it difficult to judge the depth and permanence of the penetration by women in the better-paying industries.[12]

It will be seen that the jobs at which women work are for the most part lighter than those that are predominantly male. Custom and tradition, as well as the lower strength of women, are responsible for this historic segregation of jobs by sex. In reality, it usually has little physiological basis, as the wartime experience on industry has demonstrated.[13] Nonetheless, distinctions between "women's jobs" and "men's jobs" remain widespread and are likely to persist for a long time to come. From the standpoint of unemployment compensation this has the unwholesome result of imposing often severe limitations upon the placement of women claimants. It constitutes one of the serious restrictions upon the testing of their availability for work.

Lower Earnings

One important reason for the lower earnings of women workers is their occupational and industrial distribution. The industries in which women work are low paying. We have noted, for example, that women workers are found in nondurable goods manufacturing rather than in durable goods industries. The average weekly earnings for durable goods workers in December 1946 were $49.51 while the average for workers on nondurable goods was $44.14. Average weekly earnings in such predominantly female industries as tobacco, knit goods, and shirts and collars were $5 to $11 below the average for the nondurable goods group.[14] Similar differentials appear in a comparison of average hourly earnings.

National earnings averages include many different plants and lump together the earnings of both men and women in an industry. The National Industrial Conference Board series of hours and earnings for production workers in twenty-five manufacturing industries shows that from 1920 to 1929 average weekly earnings for men were $10 to $14 more than women's average weekly earnings, $6 to $13 more from 1930 to 1940, and $16 to $23 more from 1941 to 1945.[15]

Within a single plant or industry the jobs to which women are assigned tend to pay less than men's jobs. Part of this is the result of discriminatory wage practices. In 6 telephone companies studied during the war men clerks were paid from $37.50 to $102.50 more per month than women clerks.[16] During World War II, of 148 plants which hired women for "men's jobs," 70 plants paid women lower starting rates than men.[17] In a few states sex discriminations in pay are prohibited by law.[18] "Equal pay for equal work" has been given effect in a number of union contracts and, during the war, by the War Labor Board. In principle, at least, it commands widespread acceptance today.

A more deep-rooted basis for sex differences in pay is the industrial practice of giving women the less skilled and more poorly paid jobs in an establishment. Here again it is custom and tradition which hold sway, although some plausible reasons exist. Women workers tend to be younger than men, with correspondingly less service and experience. Among workers with 1944 old-age insurance wage credits, the median age for men was 38.6, and 29.2 for women.[19] Women workers are sick more often and lose more time because of illness than men.[20] Their household and marital responsibilities are greater than those of men workers, contributing to higher absenteeism and quit rates.[21]

The pay women get affects their unemployment benefit status. During July 1946 to June 1947 the average weekly benefit paid for total unemployment was $18.82 for men claimants, and $17.08 for women. Fixed minimum and maximum benefit amounts prevent the disparity from being even greater. They also tend to make benefits for women a higher percentage of the weekly wage than in the case of men workers. As a result wages in jobs open to women are more likely to compare unfavorably with unemployment benefits. This is especially true of women with children who often deduct the cost of child care during the work day in their own calculation of their net wage. Falling wages or diminishing opportunities for employment at good pay aggravate this situation.

Personal and Domestic Responsibilities

Most working women hold down two jobs, the care of their homes and commercial employment. In 1947, over 45 per cent of the women in the labor force were married. Another 16 per cent were either widowed or divorced. Most of these married, widowed, or divorced women are burdened, outside their working hours, with household cares. In addition, an unknown but sizable number of single women workers have major domestic responsibilities for the homes they share with parents or other members of the family.

The care of young children is one important additional task of the working wife, widow, or divorcee. In 1940 over a fifth of the working wives living with their husbands had one or more children younger than ten years old. Over one-eighth of the working women with other marital status had one or more such young children. One out of every fourteen wives (husband present) in the labor force had one or more children, all under five years old.[23]

The growth of the nursery schools has done much to enable such women to enter employment. These, however, provide only day care and mothers often find it difficult to accept jobs involving night hours. Furthermore, because of their cost or location nursery schools are not available to all or even most working mothers. As a result — and this is the picture one gets from the unemployment benefit cases — most working mothers must rely upon other members of the family, maids, or sometimes friends and neighbors, to care for their children while they work.

The home responsibilities of women workers probably account for most of the availability problems they raise as benefit claimants. It is these situations that a number of the state laws have sought to reach by special disqualifications. These disqualifications attack separations to marry or to assume the duties of a housewife or because of marital obligations. Usually they bar the claimant from benefits until after she has been again employed or has earned a specified sum in reëmployment. Such disqualifications undoubtedly eliminate a number of would-be beneficiaries who have in fact left the labor force. At the same time, however, benefits are denied to many women whose domestic circumstances force them temporarily to stop working or to leave a particular job but not necessarily the field of gainful employment.

Rigorous as they are, the special married women's disqualifications do not even touch the major availability problem raised by the domestic burdens of women claimants — the limitations which they place upon the work they will accept. As we will see from the cases to be discussed in this chapter these limitations are extensive.

Because married women are usually secondary rather than primary earners their mobility as workers differs considerably from that of unmarried women and men. The push and pull of changing job opportunities has a blunted effect upon wives who work. When they leave their jobs to move to other localities it is usually in response to changed status for the husband or the family. When they remain in communities where jobs for them do not exist or have vanished it is for similar reasons. A few states have sought to solve some of the problems thus raised by disqualifying claimants who leave work to move to another locality to live with their husbands. Others achieve the same result by disqualifying women who leave their jobs because of a marital obligation, upon the theory that a wife is obliged by law to live with her husband in the place selected by him.

The disqualifications mentioned make no attempt to settle the cases of women claimants who, because of domestic considerations, remain in localities where there is no work for them. These have been left for decision under the general availability and work-refusal provisions.

Legal Status of Working Women

Women workers have long been a special concern of legislatures. Minimum wage laws and boards for women workers in various industries have been set up in twenty-seven American jurisdictions. The Fair Labor Standards Act which brought the federal government into the field provides that no sex distinction shall be made in its minimum wage orders. Nonetheless, waitresses and women laundry workers remain the concern of the state boards.

In all but five states some legal control exists of maximum work hours for women workers. In a large number of states laws or regulations provide for a weekly day of rest for women workers (twenty-four states) and meal and rest periods during the work day (twenty-eight states). Night work for women is subject to prohibition or regulation in twenty-three states. All states but Illinois and Mississippi have laws or regulations requiring the provision of seating facilities for women workers. All but seven states seek to regulate the toilet rooms furnished women workers.[24]

Various employments are prohibited to women, most commonly labor in mines (eighteen states). The Ohio Code lists twenty different occupations prohibited to women employees, including bowling alley pin setter, crossing watchman, and taxi driver. Oddly enough, only six states prohibit or regulate the employment of women in the periods immediately preceding and following childbirth.

Married women occupy an even more peculiar legal position as workers.[25] At common law a husband was entitled to the benefits of his wife's services — both in homemaking and commercial employment. Only by his agreement or misconduct did he forfeit such rights. Most Married Women's Acts specifically deprived the husband of the right to his wife's earnings in employment and made them her separate property. They did not, however, affect his right to her domestic services and her duty to render such services. The precise content of that duty depends upon the married couple's station in life. The marriage status also imposes upon both husband and wife a mutual duty of living together. This carries with it a correlative mutual right to each other's society and companionship — the legal right of consortium. A third legal aspect of married life which is important to wives as workers and claimants is the husband's right to choose and change the marital domicile.

These legal considerations have led at least one court to the conclusion that a working wife is a "conditional employee," her status as an employee "being conditioned from its inception upon his [the husband's] consent." [26] Manifestly, this is sheer nonsense. None of the marital rights and duties involved in the employment of a married woman are absolute. They are all subject to the qualifications imposed by "reasonableness" and "circumstances." It is difficult to conceive, in the case of the ordinary working wife, of the husband successfully bringing suit for separation or divorce upon the plea that his wife's employment had deprived him of her domestic services and consortium. Certainly the common law action for loss of consortium would never lie against the employer whose recruiting wiles enticed the wife out of the kitchen into his factory.

Similarly, the wife's legal duty to submit to the husband's choice of domicile and to follow him to a new domicile has gradually become more restricted. The husband may not exercise the right of domiciliary choice unreasonably or arbitrarily. He must have due regard for his wife's comfort, health, welfare, safety, and peace of mind. A wife who refuses, without just cause, to live at the home her husband selects is guilty of desertion. "Just cause" is, however, a broad concept. An unemployed or temporarily employed husband cannot establish desertion if his wife refuses to comply with his request that she come to another city.[27] Here the law seems to be slowly catching up with the facts: Family decisions on such important subjects as choice of a home — or whether a wife should work — are the province of both partners to a marriage rather than merely one.

The legal protections and regulations surrounding the employment of women as a group have, of course, an important bearing upon their job placement and their availability for work. Such laws, by restricting the employment of women, place special handicaps upon their availability that do not necessarily exist in the case of men. The effects of family law upon the availability of working wives differ little from the effects of their nonlegal household responsibilities. In the seven American jurisdictions, however, which impose special disqualifications upon claimants who quit because of "marital obligations," the legal meaning of such obligations becomes important.

Pregnancy and Childbearing

When women are pregnant they often leave or lose their jobs. These work separations may be the result of legal requirement, employer policy, or the worker's act. Ensuing benefit claims often raise difficult questions of availability. Oddly enough, although these questions have prompted 19 American jurisdictions to impose special disqualifications for pregnant women, we know very little about the number and proportion of pregnant claimants. Their number would seem to be small. The sample survey of early 1943, covering almost the entire country, listed only one-half of one per cent of the claimants as pregnant.[28] The 1940 census showed about 2.9 million women in the labor force who were within the childbearing ages and married and living with their husbands. The incidence of pregnancy among these women is unknown, although a 1943 report estimated that 3 to 6 new cases of pregnancy were occurring per month per 1000 workers.[29]

The ability of pregnant women to work is a recurring problem in unemployment compensation. The material on the effect of employment on pregnancy has been characterized by Baetjer as "contradictory and of questionable value." It does seem definite that traumatic injuries causing spontaneous abortions are very rare, but that premature births are higher among women employed away from home.[30] With properly controlled work conditions, however, women whose pregnancy is normal may perform certain types of work as efficiently as other women. Work that involves muscular strain, heavy lifting, constant sitting, standing, bending or stretching, continued carrying of appreciable loads, any strained position or good balance or exposure to toxic substances is generally considered unsuitable by medical and industrial experts. Regular work shifts, avoidance of night work, rest periods and facilities, adequate nutritional facilities are emphasized.

As to the prenatal leave required, Dr. Baetjer says: "This should be determined for each case individually, since this depends on the condition of the woman, her financial need, her home responsibilities and the availability of suitable work in the plant. In general, a minimum of six weeks' leave prior to delivery has been recommended. *There is, however, no convincing evidence that employment up to the time of delivery is harmful provided the physical condition of the woman is satisfactory and the work is suitable.*" [31] As to postnatal leave, the most common medical recommendation is six weeks. All medical and industrial health students stress the individual differences among pregnant women in their ability to work and the importance of relying upon the advice of the woman's physician.

As we have noted earlier, special disqualifications of pregnant claimants exist in a number of states. Most of these set specific periods before and after childbirth when a woman claimant is ineligible for benefits. Appendix Table C compares this latter group of disqualifications with the prohibitions in state laws upon the employment of pregnant women. From this table it will be seen that there is no real consistency between the general labor laws and the pregnancy disqualifications.

In general, the benefit denials prescribed by the special pregnancy disqualifications become operative when the claimant becomes unemployed due to pregnancy. Thus, the pregnant woman who is discharged or laid off because of pregnancy is denied benefits. Her ability and willingness to continue working make no difference. A fortiori, the pregnant woman who leaves her job is disqualified.

The pregnant worker who needs the job income is thus encouraged to hide her pregnancy as long as possible. Discovery and discharge mean the end of wages, with no prospect of unemployment benefits while she seeks other work. The pregnant worker who is doing work that is unsuitable to her pregnant condition is penalized if she leaves it to seek more appropriate work.

Except for pregnancy and childbirth, almost no type of availability limitation is peculiar to women. The limitations upon wages, hours, place, and nature of work that restrict the availability of women are also to be found among men. Differences do exist between men and women in the frequency with which they present certain limitations upon the work they will take and the reasons for those limitations. Thus men sometimes limit their availability because they must care for their children during certain hours. Women claimants, however, regularly interpose such restrictions. The section which follows, therefore, makes no attempt to cover all the availability problems that women claimants present. Instead a few of the situations which occur most frequently have been selected for discussion.

Pregnancy and Childbirth

Despite the special disqualifications in a number of laws, most American jurisdictions rely upon their basic availability provisions to determine the eligibility of pregnant claimants. Some tribunals have attempted to set down, as general rules, the periods during which pregnant women would be considered not available for work.[32] The better opinion seems, however, to be that each case must be decided on its own facts and that no rules can be laid down that may be rigidly applied.[33] As in all physical ability cases, medical statements have been extensively relied upon.[34] Activity in seeking work, the work history of the claimant's previous pregnancies, the kinds of jobs the claimant has done and is able to do, and the claimant's appearance and demeanor have been considered in determining the eligibility of a pregnant woman.[35] Performance of household duties during pregnancy has also been accepted occasionally as evidence of ability to work.[36]

The circumstances of a pregnant claimant's work separation have, understandably, been considered important evidence as to her availability. The General Counsel of the Florida Industrial Commission stated that women who leave work voluntarily because of pregnancy create a rebuttable presumption of nonavailability until two months after confinement.[37] No presumption of unavailability has ordinarily been inferred, in most jurisdictions, from a voluntary quit by a pregnant woman when it was shown that the work was too strenuous or opposed by the claimant's physician and that she was capable of other work.[38] Conversely, pregnant women who leave their jobs have been held ineligible when the work which they left was not strenuous or they were not able or available for other work.[39] When the reason for the leaving is the claimant's modesty, embarrassment, or distaste for being conspicuous, the usual finding is that the claimant is not available for work.[40]

This is not especially logical in a case where the claimant is able to do and has sought more secluded work that satisfies her delicate standards of sensibility. Claimants who can afford such standards are, however, not the most urgent concerns of social insurance.

In the absence of contrary evidence, women who are dismissed or laid off because of pregnancy are ordinarily considered available for work.[41] In one case, the South Dakota Unemployment Compensation Commission went so far as to hold that a pregnant woman who would take no other job than the one from which she had been dismissed was nonetheless available for work. The job involved was the only one the claimant had ever done. Her doctor advised her against doing any sort of work to which she was not accustomed. The only such work in the community was her old job. In her physician's opinion she was able to work. At the time of the lay off the claimant was two or three months pregnant.[42]

The reluctance of employers to hire pregnant claimants has usually not been considered fatal to their availability, since that would mean converting the requirement to one of availability *of* work.[43]

The application of the work-refusal disqualification in the case of pregnant women bears, of course, upon their availability for work. A Rhode Island referee's decision suggests that nothing in the law warrants judging a pregnant woman by a different set of rules than other women. The claimant was disqualified for refusing work in her regular line on the ground that it was too heavy for her because of her pregnancy.[44] This, however, is a minority opinion. No disqualifications have been assessed upon pregnant women who refused night work, work on alternating shifts or work that was too strenuous, too distant, or contrary to a physician's advice.[45] In Oregon a pregnant woman who refused a job in deference to her husband's wishes was held to have had good cause.[46]

For the purposes of the disability proviso of the Servicemen's Readjustment Act of 1944 (Section 700 (b)(4)), pregnancy was considered as an illness or disability. Veterans who initially qualified by being able to work and available for work at the time they filed for benefits, were permitted to continue to draw benefits although subsequently, during the same period of continuous unemployment, becoming unable or unavailable because of pregnancy.[47]

Care of Children

An over-all view of the treatment of married women's benefit claims shows that they have received no special consideration. The Connecticut Superior Court for New Haven County has stated bluntly a common judicial reaction. The claimant, Mrs. Anna Schaffnit, had worked for Winchester Repeating Arms Company during the war on the 11 P.M. to 7 A.M. shift. When she was laid off in February 1944 she refused to consider work on any other shift. The court said:

The plaintiff in this case is not a wage earner in the ordinary sense of the word. She is a housewife, living with her husband. She entered the labor market only because there happened to be work under abnormal conditions during the hours which suited her . . . Her excursion into the labor market was a detour. She is not within the class of persons for whom the legislature has expressed its solicitude — her continued unemployment is not due to lack of job opportunities but rather to her inability conveniently to accept such work as reasonably may be expected in the normal labor market.[48]

That the working wife and mother is not everywhere suspect was demonstrated by another Connecticut Superior Court judge in the Carani case. Mrs. Carani, in order to care for her seven children, limited her availability to work on the second shift, from about 3 P.M. until midnight. This was the shift on which she had last been employed. In holding her available for work, the court said:

This claimant ordinarily would not be required to work. Realizing that she is required to try to earn money in order to support and take care of her family, she is endeavoring to do what she thinks is her duty to her family. She meets it in the way which is most consistent with her desire to earn her living and, at the same time, to comply with her duty as the mother of these children . . . Her difficulty arises out of her attempt to meet all of these obligations in a way consistent with normal effort. This seems to account for her desire to work on the particular shift on which she has elected to work . . . The record does not show that any inconvenience or harm comes to anyone by reason of her election.[49]

Time Limitations

The entire problem of restrictions of availability for work to particular portions of the day has been a tangled one. Women who refuse specific jobs at particular hours because of the necessary care of children have only occasionally been disqualified for such refusals.[50] The decisions in these cases, in general, proceed upon the theory that maternal responsibilities that conflict with the hours of any specific job furnish good cause for refusing that job. At the same time, however, the tendency has been to find that such responsibilities, even though they may justify a particular job refusal, have the effect of making the claimant unavailable for work.

Day Work Only (or First Shift). Mothers who limit their availability, because of necessary care of children, to daytime work or work on the first shift are least apt to be held unavailable.[51] Availability is usually the finding when there is a daytime work history or most of the claimant's experience is in work that is mainly daytime employment. For workers in industries where the shift system prevails and seniority dictates who shall be employed on the day shift, a restriction to day work is usually synonymous with ineligibility for benefits. Yet no consistent rules can be formulated. Working mothers, limited in their availability to daytime work, have been denied benefits, in some cases, despite daytime work histories and work experience in office-clerical jobs. They have sometimes been considered available in spite of a night work history, or presence in a shift work industry.

Evening Work Only (or Second Shift). Almost all the reported cases in this category arose either during the war or in the period immediately following the war's end. Since the particular work day involved did not ordinarily exist in normal times, women who insisted upon it were usually held not available for work. Exceptions were usually based upon the need for a period to readjust and explore job opportunities, the current existence of work at those hours or the claimant's success in finding such work before the hearing of her appeal.[52] The Carani decision, quoted earlier, rested its holding of availability on broader grounds.

In view of the Schaffnit decision (also quoted above) and the decision of the Connecticut Superior Court for Fairfield County in the Vassallo case, it is questionable that the rule of the Carani case is the law of Connecticut. Mrs. Vassallo, a boxmaker on a 6 to 11 P.M. shift, lost her job while recovering from a back injury. She restricted her availability to the hours of 3 to 11 P.M. because her husband could care for their two children at that time. Because the claimant, during two months of unemployment, failed to arrange her affairs so as to permit acceptance of work during other hours, the court held that she was not available for work.[53]

The Michigan Supreme Court has ruled that a worker who limited herself to the second shift was not available for work.[54] Mrs. Koski had worked for Ford Motor Company on the second shift (3:40–11:40 P.M.). In October 1944 she was laid off, three months later she was recalled to the same shift. During the lay off she restricted her availability because she wanted to be at home mornings in order to awaken her sons, aged seventeen and ten, get their breakfasts, and start them to school. With this weak factual situation before it, the court tore apart the Michigan Appeal Board's efforts to get away from a round-the-clock availability rule. The Michigan statute requires the claimant to be available for "work of a character which he is qualified to perform by past experience or training, and of a character generally similar to work for which he has previously received wages."

The court said: "There is nothing in the statute to justify the conclusion that the legislature intended a claimant might limit his employment to certain hours of the day where the work he is qualified to perform is not likewise limited."

Night Work Only (or Third Shift). The war period, when night jobs were easy for women to get was a general exception. Special exceptions are also made for a few occupations in which women customarily work at night. Aside from these exceptions, working mothers who have limited their availability to night work have normally been held ineligible for benefits.[55] The Schaffnit decision was an example of leniency in its concession that women workers who had earned wage credits in night work were entitled to an adjustment period before being required to accept day work.

Other "Hours" Limitations. The South Carolina court in the

Judson Mills case laid down the rule that a claimant must be available for the work which he has been doing and — by implication — that the hours are part of the work.[56] The claimant was a third shift worker. Her four children, aged two to nine years, were cared for by a relative while the claimant worked. When the relative left and the claimant could find no one else to take care of the children, she left her job. Because of the necessary care of her children, the claimant limited herself to first or second shift employment.

The decision states the court's fear that the primary purpose of the experience rating tax system "would be greatly impaired, if not completely defeated, if benefits were paid to persons who become unemployed, not because the employer could no longer provide them with work, but solely because of changes in their personal circumstances."

A West Virginia court decision has held that married women who refused to accept rotating-shift work because they would be required to work on the night shift every other week, thus interfering with parental and home duties, were not available for work.[57] The West Virginia statute provided a special disqualification for workers who voluntarily left work to perform marital, parental, or family duties. From this the court, "with extreme reluctance," reached the conclusion that the legislature intended to deny benefits to claimants whose availability was limited because of parental and family duties. The legislature's failure to express that intent clearly and specifically by providing that such claimants were ineligible was evidently not considered by the court.

Part-Time Work Only. The common ruling that availability for work is synonymous with availability for full-time work falls with particular severity upon working mothers. Only in an occasional case, and usually one involving a woman with a history of part-time work, are benefits granted.[58] A decision by the New Jersey Board of Review is a refreshing exception.[59] The claimant, a factory worker, gave up her job in order to care for her children when their nursemaid left. She then took a sales job with hours of 1 to 5 P.M. and 7 to 9:30 P.M., six days a week, which allowed her to tend to her home duties. When she was laid off from this sales job she sought work with similar hours. At the same time she continued to seek a nursemaid. Ultimately she made arrangements for the care of her children which permitted her to return to her factory job.

In holding the claimant available for work during the period preceding her return to factory work, the Board of Review said:

There is nothing in the statutory condition that a claimant be "able to work and available for work" which bars an individual who has earned all of his wages in full-time employment from eligibility for benefits in periods when he can no longer accept full-time work but is ready and willing to take part-time employment. Nor does the Statute anywhere indicate that such was the legislative intent. We cannot find that the "work" for which the individual must be available is work of the kind in which he earned his wage credits, nor is it work that must be performed within certain hourly limits. From the expressed legislative intent in that benefits are to be paid to "part-time" workers [those with a history of part-time work; claimant did not meet the statutory definition], "totally unemployed" and workers "partially unemployed," we can only conclude that the Statute was enacted to extend its benefits to all those who are "unemployed after qualifying periods of unemployment" and who are genuinely present in the labor market; and the "work" for which the individual must be available will depend upon conditions in that labor market as well as the individual's own fitness and readiness to work.

Limitations as to Place of Employment

Women claimants have sometimes restricted their availability to a single employer or to the neighborhood in which they reside. Such restrictions commonly occur among women who are nursing infants or wish to get home to prepare lunch for their children. Almost always the finding is ineligibility for benefits.[60] Women whose maternal duties lead them to insist upon homework only have not been treated uniformly. The views of the New York Supreme Court's Appellate Division in the Smith and Salavarria cases have already been discussed.[61] Taken together, these two decisions say: Care of a child does not prevent unavailability when the claimant insists upon homework in a locality where it is not done. A woman who is burdened with care of children, and has long been a homeworker may continue to limit herself to such work without becoming unavailable for work, despite a governmental prohibition of homework by her.

In other states, the law is not clear.[62] Except in cases where the lay off is temporary, unemployed homeworkers seldom are considered available for work. Restriction to homework by a worker ordinarily employed outside the home is usually fatal to eligibility.

SOME RECOMMENDATIONS

Why women claimants are problems to an unemployment compensation system is not difficult to grasp. They are discontinuous workers. When they are unemployed the suspicion arises that they are not truly attached to the labor force. Often women are secondary workers. This has a tendency to make their need to work less compelling and strengthens the suspicion of their unavailability. Women, unlike men, customarily place family life before the job. Although it is steadily becoming less true, most women stop working when they marry, and most married women workers stop when they have a baby. Women are also subject to the special disabilities of pregnancy which often lead to their unemployment.

These statements are generalizations which do not necessarily apply to any individual working woman. It is this discrepancy between the mass and the individual which makes special statutory disqualifications — whether based on job separation because of marriage, marital obligations, or pregnancy — unacceptable as solutions of the problems of women claimants. Instead, it is suggested, the answers may be found in (1) broader social insurance, (2) aids to women workers, (3) better unemployment compensation administration, and (4) acceptance of the fact that women have a different labor force status from men, and should be treated differently as benefit claimants.

The first two approaches suggested lie outside the province of unemployment compensation. The availability problems of women claimants are more deep rooted than unemployment compensation. The unemployment benefit program focuses attention upon the problems of women's labor-force status; it does not create them and it cannot cure them. These two approaches — broader social insurance and additional aids to women who work — are, it will be seen, in a sense inconsistent. The first would offer incentives to women to retire, at least temporarily, from the labor force. The second would facilitate their continuing as workers. Not only is such inconsistency part of our traditional public policy; it is also part of a democratic approach that looks to greater freedom on the part of women, married women in particular, to choose whether or not they shall work.

Broader Social Insurance

A system of temporary disability insurance, with coverage similar to that of unemployment compensation, which provides benefits to pregnant women workers (both before and after childbirth) would practically eliminate unemployment benefit claims by pregnant women. In Rhode Island, which has a very large female labor force, the first two years of the Cash Sickness Compensation Plan saw about 17 per cent of the payments go to pregnant women. They constituted over 13 per cent of the cases.[63]

A flat system of children's allowance, payable regardless of need, would reduce the economic compulsion that often forces the mothers of young children to work. Almost two-fifths of the husbands of wives in the 1940 labor force who had children under 10 (in metropolitan districts of 100,000 or more) earned less than $1000 the previous year in wages or salary.[64] Under such a system mothers who went to work would be in a better position to secure competent care for their children and place fewer restrictions upon their availability.

More Aids to Women Workers

Broader provision of nursery school facilities, at suitable localities, rates and hours, we have learned, is important in retaining the services of the working mothers of preschool children. Little, however, has been done to relieve the burdens of mothers of school-age children. Women who work a full day usually get home two or three hours after their children are released from school. Communal facilities for the care and supervision of these children in their after-school hours make it easier for their mothers to be available for a full day's work.

Of major importance to the availability for work of women with domestic responsibilities is the further development of household conveniences and services. The vacuum cleaner and the pressure cooker play an important part in women's freedom to accept employment.

Better Unemployment Compensation Administration

To ensure that women who do not want to work or cannot accept work do not get benefits we need more careful administration. All the responsibility for this cannot be laid upon the unemployment compensation administrators. In part it rests upon employers who can help or hinder greatly by the kind of separation reports they make to the unemployment compensation agency. Unions have an especial responsibility to educate their women members in coöperating with the unemployment compensation authorities, rather than trying to "beat the system." The employment service has the major task in finding job openings for women claimants so that their availability may be put to the practical test. None of this removes the major burden of improved administration from the unemployment compensation authorities.

A few routine items that need emphasis in this connection are: (a) Careful check of the circumstances of separation in the case of every woman claimant (other than a mass lay off or a short, temporary lay off). (b) Special employment interview for every woman who is separated from work because of marriage, past or approaching, domestic responsibilities, or pregnancy. Questionnaires and written statements are of assistance primarily for a record. The oral interview, by a trained interviewer, is a more effective probe. Periodic reinterviews, to aid in determining continued availability, are important. (c) Previous work history is of particular importance in the case of women claimants — on the score of continuity in the labor force as well as reasonableness of availability restrictions. (d) Medical certifications of ability to work for all pregnant claimants. A single medical certificate given by the claimant's physician at the time of initial claim filing is not enough. The claimant should be required to furnish a monthly certificate of continued ability to work. At least once in the life of a claim that extends beyond a four-week benefit period, the certifying physician should be interviewed.

Acceptance of the Different Status of Women Claimants. Unemployment compensation is a form of social insurance. Its purpose is to protect society, as a whole, from some of the evils that go with unemployment. In the case of women workers one of those evils has always been their increased proneness to exploitation in jobs that offer hard work, bad hours, and poor pay, all damaging to them as wives and mothers. An unemployment compensation system that does not take these factors into account and brings pressure upon working mothers to accept work which conflicts with their jobs as mothers perverts its own purposes. At the same time, to lose sight of the lack of labor force continuity which most women display leads to unrealistic management.

a. The recommendation that the qualification for benefits should be more onerous for claimants without dependents has particular merit in the case of women workers. By requiring claimants without dependents — a class in which many women fall — to earn more or, preferably, work longer in the base period, much can be done to eliminate the sporadic woman worker as a claimant.[65]

b. There should be a flat declaration of administrative policy that pregnant women and mothers of preschool and school-age children will not be denied benefits for refusing to accept night work. Their position as mothers makes it important that they should be protected from unemployment compensation pressure to accept work that is potentially so harmful.

c. Women claimants who seek benefits after a period of conceded unavailability or whose availability may be in doubt — because of job separations or restrictions occasioned by marital or domestic responsibilities — should usually be required to give affirmative evidence of their availability. The requirement should be administrative, rather than statutory. The affirmative evidence may include such proofs as an active search for work, reëmployment (following a leaving of a job or the labor force), economic need to work, or rearrangement of marital or domestic cares to permit acceptance of work.

d. The moral and legal pressures upon married women ordinarily require a finding that the limitations upon their work availability which stem from their marital or domestic responsibilities are involuntarily imposed. Little or no real choice exists. As involuntary restrictions, they entitle the claimants to the benefit of any reasonable doubt that the work for which they are available is of substantial amount.

e. Most important is that greater recognition should be given to the viewpoint that women workers are different from men, not only in their physical attributes, but also in their social responsibilities. Our society is based upon the assumption that women will be able to fulfill those duties. Their maternal responsibilities are basic to our social order. Work that prevents their fulfillment should be considered unsuitable and refusing such work no basis for denying benefits. If our economic system invites and requires the employment of women, it must be ready to meet the risks that go with it.

CHAPTER XIII

SELF-EMPLOYMENT

UNEMPLOYMENT BENEFIT ELIGIBILITY

SELF-EMPLOYMENT, in a sense, is a mirror that reflects the short-comings and artificialities of unemployment compensation. Whenever unemployment compensation encounters the "own-account" worker it stubs its toe. On the tax side, no group has been involved in more litigation than such "own-account" employees as the commission salesmen and the insurance agents. In the matter of benefits, self-employment has occasioned few appeals to the courts but it has raised many and knotty problems for daily administration.

The difficulty stems from the artificial boundaries that surround unemployment compensation. The system is limited to individuals who have qualified by working for others. To qualify for benefits while unemployed they are required to be available to work for others again. Historically, unemployment compensation has had no place in its benefit structure for the small businessman or "own-account" worker who is out of work. Neither has it had room for the jobless employee who has entered and is operating a business of his own, even though the business is not yet a profitable venture. This closed system is in sharp contrast with the world of work, where unemployed workers sometimes go into business and small businessmen often fail and must seek work for hire.

As suggested above, the general rule has been that an individual is ineligible for benefits if he is engaged in a business of his own. Being engaged in business is, however, a matter of time, effort, investment, and many other variable factors. In this chapter we shall be concerned with the tests used in determining these variables and their effect on eligibility.

"Unemployment" and "Availability"

Some confusion in handling the claims of the allegedly self-employed arises from the blurred distinctions between "unemployment" and "availability," both of which are prerequisites for benefits. Unemployment is commonly defined in terms of failure to perform services or to earn wages with respect to a particular week. A typical statutory definition reads:

An individual shall be deemed "unemployed" with respect to any week during which he performed no services and with respect to which no wages were payable to him, or with respect to any week of less than full-time work if the wages payable to him with respect to such week are less than his weekly benefit amount.[1]

The words, "services" and "wages," are ordinarily interpreted broadly. Respectively, their given meanings are "labor," whether or not for hire, and "remuneration," whether or not earned in employment for another. As a result, a claimant who works at a business of his own, such as farming, may be denied benefits on the ground that he is not "unemployed." He may also be held unavailable for work upon the ground that he is not free to accept work because he is engaged in his own business.

The two concepts, it will be seen, are somewhat distinct. The same facts, however, are often relied upon in both instances and the results are similar. In practice, therefore, the two are often lumped together. Denials of benefits to self-employed claimants are commonly based upon a double finding that the claimant was "not unemployed and not available for work." [2]

Availability Criteria

Freedom to Accept Work

The basic availability test applied in the case of the "self-employed" claimant has been: Is he free to accept full-time employment? Benefits are usually denied if the self-employment takes up a substantial or major part of the claimant's time; if a minor or negligible portion of his time is involved benefits are usually granted.[3] For example, a carpenter who owned a farm operated by his family and a share cropper was held available for work and not self-employed when he usually did no more than plan the crop and buy the seeds and fertilizer. The claimant had helped his family on the farm since becoming unemployed because "he did not want to be idle." [4] An aircraft worker who bought and operated a small grocery store after he was laid off by the aircraft plant was held not available for work. The fact that he actively sought other work and would have withdrawn from active operation of the grocery store had he found work made no difference.[5]

A finding that a claimant worked a full work day or work week in self-employment is not necessary to support an ineligibility ruling. Working three or four hours a day in a grocery store in which the claimant owned a half-interest or working two or three days a week in a shop which the claimant owned have been sufficient to bar benefits.[6] Commission salesmen who worked less than a full day or week have been denied benefits because they were free, as masters of their own time, to work as much or as little as they chose.[7]

Claimants engaged in odd jobs or subsidiary work are usually not considered fully self-employed.[8] Thus sideline work such as selling insurance on Saturdays, occasional commission sales of a book, or giving private golf lessons from time to time have been held no bar to benefits. Odd jobs are ordinarily outside the claimant's customary employment and offer no reasonable prospect of a livelihood. A garage mechanic, for example, who rented a motion picture projector and educational films and, while he was out of work, gave a show two nights a week at a school was held unemployed and eligible for benefits, although he netted $5 to $7.50 a week.[9] (Although no bar to benefits, odd-job earnings over a fixed small sum, such as $2 or $3, are commonly deducted from the weekly benefit amount in calculating the claimant's benefits.)

A subsidiary test of freedom to accept work has been the importance of the claimant's presence to the business. Is he needed for continued operation? If it is a going business, did he replace someone in its operation? If he left, would it be necessary to hire a substitute?[10] If the answers to these questions are affirmative, benefits are ordinarily denied. A California shipwright, for example, who returned to his sixty-acre farm was denied benefits because it appeared that he was needed to do the farm work. He had quit his work to return to the farm when an older daughter who had been assisting his wife on the farm was married. The claimant's wife had four children, all under nine years of age, to care for. The claimant's livestock included nine milk cows, two hundred chickens, and twenty-five rabbits.[11]

Engaged in Self-Employment

A claimant is not considered unavailable for work merely because he owns, leases, or lives on a farm.[12] Neither will he be considered ineligible merely because he owns or has invested in a business.[13] His activity and interest in actually operating the business are determining factors.

In the Dellacroce case, where the Colorado Supreme Court had occasion to consider the meaning of "customary self-employment," this was a controlling element. The claimant had been denied benefits under a section of the Act which provided that a claimant who has failed "to return to his customary self-employment, when so directed" shall be disqualified. Dellacroce had been a coal miner for some 38 years. In 1923 he and his wife had bought 9¾ acres of farm land where they made their home. There they raised eleven children, four of whom were still living at home. During the nineteen years following the original purchase the claimant had added, by purchase and lease, additional acreage — a forty-acre tract on over half of which forage crops might be raised, and four hundred acres of grazing lands. The livestock consisted of twenty head of cattle and eight horses. All the work had been done by the claimant's wife and children. The claimant had not even supervised or planned any of it. Denying that mere ownership of the land made the claimant self-employed, the court reversed the commission's denial of benefits.[14]

Similarly, in the Siegrist case, a Michigan Circuit Court held that a machinist was unemployed during a lay off and eligible for benefits even though he owned a two hundred-acre farm, employed a hired man the year round, and drew a $35 monthly milk check. The facts showed that the claimant had taken in $754 from the farm operations, paid out $1138 during the year, and had to borrow money from a bank for living expenses.[15]

Whether or not a farmer or business operator is self-employed and ineligible for benefits during the business's slack season has been a disputed question. The Colorado referee has stated flatly: "Farming is considered an all-year occupation." The claimant in the case owned and operated a farm in Illinois. He had in recent years been engaged in industry in various parts of the country. In October 1943, he left industrial employment to return to his farm which was located at a place where there were practically no opportunities for employment in the occupation in which he had earned his wage credits. Benefits were denied.[16] Claimants have also been denied benefits during the slack season in the fish business, hotel business, and the carnival business.[17]

In the hotel case the claimant owned and operated a thirty-five-room hotel in Florida. She personally performed all the necessary services. At the time she filed her claim, late in May, the hotel had no guests and she had no work to do. The referee denied benefits upon the ground that the claimant was not unemployed even though she was performing no services. "There is a continuous holding-out to the public, in the same manner as a storekeeper or attorney presents a continuing offer to do business with the public."

A 1940 Alabama Counsel opinion has stated that farmers are unemployed after the crops have been laid by and no work but odd chores remains to be done.[18] This would also appear to be the rule applied in Illinois, Louisiana, Michigan, and Wyoming.[19] In Kansas, the rule that farming is an all-year occupation was relaxed when the facts showed that farming was not the claimant's primary occupation.[20] In Idaho the operator of a produce business has been held eligible for benefits during the off-season, as were a paint business operator in New Hampshire and a taxidermist and swimming-pool operator in Pennsylvania.[21] The better opinion would seem to lie with this latter group of cases. If the operator of a business makes himself available for such work as is ordinarily done in his community during the slack season of his business, no valid reason appears for denying him benefits.

Principal or Customary Occupation

One test used to determine if a "self-employed" claimant is in fact available for work for hire has been the test of principal or customary occupation. The tendency is to deny benefits if the self-employment is the claimant's customary or principal occupation and to alow benefits if it is not.[22] An illustration is the case of a South Carolina carpenter who owned and lived on a farm. He had about thirty acres under cultivation, principally in corn, cotton, and grain. The major farm work was done by hired labor, but the claimant did farm work himself between carpentry jobs. Cash earnings from the farm were estimated at not over $200 a year. When he did carpentry work the claimant earned over $50 a week. The tribunal found that his major interest was in the carpentry trade and that he met the availability requirement.[23]

A different result was reached by the Tennessee Board of Review in the case of a farmer who accepted war construction work in 1940 and in 1941 but quit each time to make a crop. The claimant filed for benefits after he finished working his 1942 crop but before the harvest. He explained that he would be available for work for a few weeks but would expect to return home and gather his 1942 crop. The Board said: "Operating this farm is the claimant's primary employment. His outside work is sporadic and limited to his personal convenience and to the time when he feels that he is not needed on his farm — to such times when such outside work will not interfere with the successful operation of the farm." Benefits were denied.[24]

Profit

A finding that the self-employment was profitable has never been considered essential for a denial of benefits.[25] Thus, commission salesmen without earnings, unsuccessful real estate brokers and oil prospectors, and operators of milk routes, language schools, and other businesses that failed to make a profit have been alike held ineligible for benefits.[26]

It has been suggested that the self-employment must be such that it offers a prospect of a livelihood or an ultimate profit.[27] This has been no rigid rule. Instead it has been used as a guide in the attempt to distinguish between a full-scale enterprise and one which is of the odd-job variety. Where the claimant is doing no more than trying to eke out an existence from some minor employment on his own account, this in itself has been no bar to eligibility. Attempts have often been made, for example, to distinguish between subsistence and commercial farmers.[28] Benefits are ordinarily denied to the latter but granted to the former class.

Preparing to Go into Business

Whether or not a claimant is eligible for benefits when he is preparing to go into business but has not yet established a going venture is ordinarily determined by the extent of his preparatory efforts and his willingness to accept other work. A hardware store manager was forced to resign when his employer learned that he planned to open a competing store. Although the store was not opened for business until two months later, the claimant was held unavailable from the date on which he, together with another individual, rented the premises. It was assumed that the claimant did not let his partner do all the work preparatory to opening the store.[29]

An attorney, who rented office space, had his name printed on the door and held himself available to any client who might seek his services, but received no remuneration from his law practice, was denied benefits in Massachusetts as not unemployed.[30] An Ohio attorney, however, who had rent-free desk space, did not have his name on the door or in any legal or other directory and had no office expense or clients was granted benefits.[31]

Benefits have also been granted, pending the commencement of actual and material services, to an investor and president of a new corporation, a beauty-parlor owner, and a chef who was an incorporator of a new restaurant corporation.[32] Similarly, a claimant who made a trip to see what fixtures he could buy for a retail silk business he wished to open was held available for work upon the theory that he was more interested in employment for hire.[33]

Another pertinent factor appears in the case of the unemployed truck driver who, according to the latter's records, told the employment service that he wanted to find his own job and that he might go into the service station business for himself. At the hearing on his appeal, the claimant said that he was trying to find a service station to operate but, in the meantime, he was willing to accept and was seeking work. Because "his statements to the employment service had the effect of eliminating him from consideration on referrals," the claimant was held unavailable for work until the date of the hearing.[34]

VETERANS' SELF-EMPLOYMENT ALLOWANCES

At the outset of this chapter it was stated that, historically, unemployment compensation has taken no heed of the joblessness of the self-employed. Although this is in general true, an interesting exception was created by the Servicemen's Readjustment Act of 1944 (the "G.I." Bill of Rights). Under Title V of this bill provision was made for readjustment allowances for military veterans of World War II. Unlike unemployment compensation, readjustment allowances used active military service and other than dishonorable discharge as the basis for qualification, rather than employment for hire. In other respects they were very similar to unemployment compensation.

Section 902 of the act added a novel feature by providing for allowances to the self-employed. A veteran who was fully engaged in self-employment and showed net earnings for the previous calendar month of less than $100 was entitled to receive the difference between $100 and his net earnings for that month.

Like the rest of the World War II veterans' benefits, the self-employment allowance program did not hit its stride until 1946. Over $11.6 millions were paid to self-employed veterans in 1945, and over $252.4 millions in 1946. This amount may be compared with the expenditure in 1946 of almost $1.5 billions for veterans' unemployment allowances. The average monthly number of veteran recipients of self-employment allowances in 1946 was 203,000, as compared with a monthly average of 1.4 million veterans receiving unemployment allowances. During the same year the monthly average of beneficiaries under state (civilian) unemployment compensation laws numbered 1.2 million and $1.1 billions were paid out in benefits.

Like the veterans' unemployment allowance program, allowances to self-employed veterans were administered by the state unemployment compensation agencies under the rules and regulations of the Veterans Administration. Because the entire self-employment allowance program was unprecedented, many new questions arose for decision. In the main, these stemmed from the specific provisions of the act. Thus it was necessary to determine what was meant by (a) "self-employed for profit," (b) "fully engaged" in self-employment, (c) an "independent" enterprise and (d) "net earnings."

Self-Employment for Profit

The state unemployment compensation agencies were directed to decide the applicant's status consistently with the definition of "employment" provided in the state unemployment compensation law.[35] Thus a beauty-shop operator who entered into an agreement with the shop owners to work as a regular employee until she could build up a clientele large enough to warrant opening her own shop was held not self-employed. The owners exercised definite control and direction over her services which were in the usual course and at the place of their business.[36] Similarly, a doctor working for a hospital, a share cropper working under the landlord's supervision, and a corporation officer or owner were held not in self-employment.[37]

A reasonable prospect was required, all the facts and circumstances considered, that a profit would be obtained from the enterprise within a not too distant future. The expected profit had to be large enough to furnish a livelihood. A mere side-line profit was not enough.[38]

Fully Engaged in Self-Employment

A veteran was considered fully engaged in self-employment during a given calendar month only if, throughout that month, he had engaged in self-employment to the exclusion of any services in an employment relationship.[39] To qualify the claimant had to be engaged in the self-employment for the entire month, not merely a major fraction of the month.[40] If the work was reduced because of a lack of business, seasonal or otherwise, the veteran might qualify if he did those things reasonably calculated to promote his enterprise.[41] The veteran's illness or disability which interrupted the active operation of the business for part of the month was no bar,[42] but he was not "fully engaged" if his continuing disability was such that he could operate only on a part-time basis.[43] Mere preparation to go into business did not meet the requirement.[44] Neither did absentee ownership without active services in the operation of the enterprise.[45]

Independent Enterprise

Since the program's purpose was to aid the veteran to establish or reëstablish himself in the profession or business of his choice, it was not expected that his enterprise would at the outset be financially independent. What was necessary was that the veteran be an owner of the business (although he might rent or borrow goods, equipment, or the premises) and that he should be free of supervision and control.[46]

Net Earnings

A veteran's net earnings from self-employment were computed by deducting, from his earnings during the month in connection with the self-employment, those expenses which he incurred during the month which were directly related to his self-employment. Reporting of income and expense was required to follow sound accounting practice but, so long as the method used was that best calculated to reflect the true "net earnings" and it was consistently used, either a cash or accrual basis was permitted. Personal or family expenditures were not considered deductible expense. The products of the enterprise which the veteran used to maintain himself and his family were included, at prevailing market prices, in his earnings.[47] Capital expenditures were not deductible expenses.[48]

Unemployment and Self-Employment Allowances

Veterans were required to choose whether they wished to apply for unemployment or self-employment allowances. The election was not permanent, but a veteran was not permitted benefits under both programs for the same month or different parts of the same month. A veteran who qualified for unemployment allowances for even one day of a month was denied self-employment allowances for the rest of the month.[49]

INSURANCE FOR THE SELF-EMPLOYED

The preceding sections of this chapter indicate the limitations put upon unemployment compensation for the self-employed and the bold steps which Congress took to provide assistance to veterans who attempted self-employment. The veterans' self-employment allowance program was limited in scope. It applied to veterans only and its benefits end two years after the last World War II veteran to be discharged is released from military service. Limited as it has been, the veterans' program points the way to a new possibility in unemployment compensation: A broad-scale, permanent program of insurance for the self-employed.

A full exposition of such a program is beyond the scope of this book. Because of the effects such a system would have upon our present availability concepts some attention is devoted to it here. First, is there a need for a self-employment insurance system? About nine million Americans and their dependents receive their basic support from operating farms, small businesses, and other unincorporated enterprises. About half of these are farmers. In addition about 3.4 million are professional people. Together, these groups comprised in 1940 a little less than one-fourth of our labor force, a substantial portion. In 1940, they received less than one-sixth of the national income. In fact, at no time during the sixteen-year period, 1929–1945, did the annual net income of proprietors exceed 17 per cent of the national income. In 1940, the net income of all proprietors was $950 per capita, $1045 for the nonfarmers, $823 for the farmers.

As a group, the self-employed are as subject to the vagaries of our economy as the wage earners. Dun and Bradstreet figures show that during 1940–1945 business liquidations ranged from 5.1 per cent to 18.1 per cent of all business enterprises. These figures fail to reveal the proportion of ownership transfers included, but they do indicate that even in the busy war years many businesses were forced out of existence. A United States Department of Commerce study of a representative sample of business sales and liquidations during the second quarter of 1946 shows: One-third of all sales and liquidations were because of economic failures. Of the entrepreneurs who failed, more than one quarter remained unemployed four to six months after the liquidation took place.[50]

The fact is that self-employment, especially among entrepreneurs without employees (over 45 per cent of our nonagricultural enterprises) is fraught with risk. From the point of view of both purchasing power and outlets for goods and services these enterprises are an unstable factor in our economy. As a matter of simple justice it seems absurd that the small businessman who fails can get no assistance from the state although the presidents of giant corporations like General Motors or United States Steel are eligible for unemployment benefits if they should become unemployed. From the standpoint of a public policy that seeks to encourage individual enterprise and stimulate small business rather than mammoth corporations, direct aid in stabilizing small enterprises is desirable.

Is it feasible to operate a self-employment insurance system? Our experience is limited to the veterans' program. That experience would seem to show that such a system of benefits need not be a grab bag. The field is new and the initial steps would have to be cautious. A program which limits benefits to entrepreneurs who qualify by a net income of at least $500 and not over $3000 in the previous calendar year and provides benefits for no more than four months of less than $100 net earnings should not be prohibitive in cost. It could be financed initially by a two to three per cent tax on the incomes of all proprietors earning over $500 and handled as an addition to their annual income tax. Because of the seasonal problems involved, it would seem advisable to exclude farmers from the program until additional experience has been gained.

To complete a self-employment insurance program a free two-way flow between employment and self-employment should be encouraged. A self-employed individual who had qualified for benefits under the suggested program should be permitted to draw benefits if he holds himself available for employment or is actively engaged in preparing a new self-employment venture. A claimant who has qualified for unemployment benefits by earning wages in employment should be granted benefits, when unemployed, if he is actively engaged in preparing or operating a self-employment venture. His earnings from the venture, if any, should be deducted from his benefit amount.

Present availability policies discourage the mobility of unemployed workers by denying them benefits if they enter upon full scale self-employment. This is more in keeping with a public policy of stratifying jobless workers into an employee caste. It is not consonant with a national policy of encouraging workers, employed and unemployed, to make the best and most fruitful use of their skills and talents whether in employment for others or for themselves.

Providing benefits to unemployed workers and self-employed when they are actively engaged in preparing a new self-employment venture would mean help to them when they need it most. As we have seen, neither the present unemployment compensation program nor the veterans' program have made such aid available. Such an addition to the benefit system needs to be worked out with care. It can be done, however, if evidence is required that the claimant is investing a major portion of his time and efforts and a reasonable amount of his available resources in furthering his project.

A program along the lines sketched so briefly here would destroy some of the artificiality of the present unemployment compensation definitions of "available for work." It would make those definitions come much closer to meaning "attached to the labor force." The present definitions divide the self-employed portion of the labor force from the workers for hire by a Chinese Wall.

CHAPTER XIV

CONCLUDING OBSERVATIONS

AVAILABILITY DEFINITION AND LABOR-FORCE MEASUREMENT

THE DISCUSSIONS of the preceding chapters have largely been devoted to the meaning, in unemployment compensation, of the term "available for work." Without attempting to summarize those discussions, it may be said that they show availability to be a vague concept. The meaning of availability becomes real on a case-by-case basis only. Since this is true of most abstract terms, we need not be discouraged in the use of "availability." Instead our analysis should emphasize the importance of getting general agreement upon the result in specific fact situations. It is of more use to us to know whether a worker who accepts a retirement pension from an employer is *ipso facto* unavailable for work than to be able to give a well-rounded definition of "available for work."

The case method of defining availability is necessarily a slow process. It does not lend itself readily to generalization. Although that is true, unemployment compensation experience in resolving availability cases has something to offer to labor force measurement. Two concepts of the unemployed labor force may be derived from the unemployment compensation cases in availability. One is classifying the unemployed on the basis of the employment terms they seek. Thus the unemployed labor force may be classified in terms of weekly hours of work, minimum hourly pay, maximum travel from home, and occupational category of work sought. A second and related approach views the unemployed labor force as not one but several labor forces of different degrees of labor-market attachment. Lines may be drawn, for example, between the unemployed who seek part-time work and those who seek full-time work, between the ones in search of occasional work and those who want steady work.

It must be recognized that labor-force measurement and availability in unemployment compensation reflect somewhat different considerations. Unemployment compensation, for example, has no primary concern with inventorying the nation's manpower potential. It offers no assistance in enumerating the untapped labor supply of students and housewives. To take another example, unemployment compensation has found no need to differentiate in its definition of total unemployment between claimants who retain some job attachment (that is, the temporarily laid-off) and those who have no such attachment (that is, the discharges, reductions in force, and quits).

For different purposes, labor-force measurement is concerned with both these questions. To determine our manpower potential it seeks to discover how many able-bodied students and housewives we have. To determine the extent of "real unemployment," labor-force studies try to distinguish unemployed workers who have no job attachment from those who do. Indirectly unemployment compensation experience aids such studies by offering information on the labor market behavior of those students and housewives who have recently accepted work and of unemployed workers both with and without job attachment.

WHAT WE DON'T KNOW ABOUT AVAILABILITY

The thought has often occurred to the writer that it is perhaps too soon for this book. The American unemployment compensation program is young. There are many basic things we have yet to learn about unemployment compensation. We lack much information about the things we are doing in the program. Availability is an excellent illustration of that lack. To cite a few examples:

1. We know how many claims are denied because of unavailability. We do not know, however, how many claims are challenged, whether by the unemployment compensation agencies or by employers, on grounds of possible unavailability. This is an important key to administration.

2. Although we now know the total number of benefit denials for unavailability in given periods we do not know the total number of different individuals involved in those denials.

3. We have no breakdown of benefit denials for unavailability by "race" or sex category, age grouping, or reason for unavailability.

4. We have no "follow-up" information on claimants who have been held unavailable. How frequently do such claimants succeed in finding work on their own terms? How soon after the benefit

denial does this happen? How frequently do "unavailable" claimants modify their demands to accord with the unemployment compensation agency's standards of availability? How soon do they do
this after the benefit denial?

5. At what point during the unemployment spell are claimants
denied benefits because of unavailability? In other words, how
many claimants are held unavailable at the time they first file a
benefit claim, how many are denied benefits after five weeks, after
ten weeks, and so on?

Until we start getting systematic information on such questions
as these we will remain in the dark about the actual operation of
the availability requirement. Compiling such information, if it is
to be useful, must be on a routine and continuing basis. The occasional "field study" or "survey" is tied too closely to the labor-
market conditions and administrative practice of the moment.

AVAILABILITY AND INDIVIDUAL LIBERTY

High on the list of what we do not know is the effect of the
availability requirement upon the liberty of benefit claimants. This
is closely connected with the question: How far should availability
policies go in tampering, albeit by indirection, with claimants' liberties? From time to time, in the foregoing chapters, various aspects of this question have been discussed. It has been pointed out
that they represent different phases of conflict between our aspira-
tions for security and liberty.

How is this dilemma to be resolved in the field of availability?
Three general methods may be suggested. One method is avoidance. This involves abstaining from policies that would breach a
claimant's liberty. Holding a claimant unavailable for work merely
because he changes his occupational choice and is unwilling to
accept his former type of work damages his freedom to choose and
change his occupation. Holding a claimant unavailable for work
solely because he has moved to another locality and is unwilling to
return to accept a job penalizes his freedom of movement. Abstaining from such policies avoids the conflict.

A second method is by information and guidance. Let us suppose that a carpenter-claimant abandons his carpentering and
decides that thenceforth he is a musician, an occupation in which
he is also qualified. To deny him benefits automatically, it has been
pointed out, violates his liberty. If the claimant has, however,

moved from an occupation with reasonable employment prospects to one which offers him no reasonable opportunity for employment there is, as we have seen, ground for denying him benefits. Even then we strike at his liberty. Much of this can be avoided if the pertinent labor-market conditions are adequately explained to claimants.

Broad informational programs are needed which will bring to workers a knowledge of labor-market conditions and their effects upon unemployment compensation policies. An even more profound need exists to educate our citizens, not only in their rights under the unemployment compensation and other social security programs, but also in the correlative duties which they have under those programs. Such educational and informational activities can do much to forestall conflicts between social policy as expressed in availability requirements and individual liberties.

In some instances the conflict cannot be avoided, and the best information and guidance program will soften but not remove the blow. A financial crisis occurs in the operation of a large plant in a small town. The factory closes down and the workers are laid off for an indefinite period. Other existing local industry cannot absorb them within the foreseeable future. Jobs are available for the laid-off workers in other cities, too distant for commuting. Ultimately the unemployment compensation agency is likely to reach the point of denying benefits to some of the workers who do not move. If it does, their right to stay home is made expensive.

That is an aggravated illustration of the need for a third method to settle conflicts of availability policy and individual liberty. This third method is one of democratic controls through local advisory committees of labor, management, and public representatives. The advice and aid of such committees, in local crises like the one described, may transmute the agency decision on benefits from a bureaucratic decree to a community plan of action.

Although many state laws expressly authorize the appointment of local advisory councils, American unemployment compensation has made no real use of community advisory committees. A Social Security Advisory Council exists at the federal level. In addition there are state advisory councils. The membership of these councils has been representative of labor, management, and the public. Their activity — and many of them have atrophied by inaction — has usually been centered upon recommendations for legislation.

Furthermore the state councils do not ordinarily operate or advise the unemployment compensation agency at the local community level.

In some states, labor and management representatives join a public representative or salaried referee to form a tribunal for deciding benefit appeals. The decisions of such tribunals are usually appealable to a higher administrative authority before a judicial review can be initiated. This method brings local labor and management representatives into local problems, but not until the agency has first made its decision and a claimant or employer takes an appeal. The tripartite tribunal also has other defects of costliness in time and money that have discouraged its use in most states as a hearing body for first-stage administrative appeals. In a large number of states tripartite tribunals are used as a final administrative appeals authority to decide benefit appeals. In such cases, the tribunal is a single body, established for the entire state. Its membership is not based upon or identified with the locality where the appeal arose.

One weakness of the American unemployment compensation system, it may be seen, is its failure to provide a continuing means to secure for its policies the advice and consent of the citizenry at the community level. Since unemployment compensation must necessarily deal mostly with problems as they occur locally, lack of local advice may be a serious defect. This defect, from the standpoint of democratic action, might not be so severe if it were possible to legislate unemployment compensation policy in detail. That, however, is usually not possible or desirable (for example, it is manifestly absurd to make benefit eligibility hinge, by statute, upon willingness to commute a minimum of ten miles a day). In fact, the opposite has usually been true. The legislatures have said that claimants must be "available for work" and then left it to the administrators, the referees, and the courts to build a new edifice of common law upon a generality.

When an administrative system is given great power to affect people's lives a post-review of its activity may be an inadequate guarantee of the discreet use of that power. Continuing advice on policy from the citizenry at the level of the geographic operating unit is in order, so as to help in keeping administration from becoming unresponsive bureaucracy.

Local advisory committees are not easy to organize or to operate. The idea requires selling, both to labor and management, before it can be put into effect. Once in operation, such committees and the administrative personnel who work with them have a narrow middle line to tread, between one extreme of inactivity and ineffectuality and the other of busybodiness and domination. The local office manager should be able to rely on his committee to give him the community viewpoint on questions of policy. It should be his task and objective to satisfy that viewpoint so far as possible within the limits imposed by the law and the decisions. The committee should be kept advisory and not become part of the administrative staff. It need not be stressed how valuable such committees can be in explaining to their communities what the unemployment compensation agency is doing.

No suggestion is intended here that our unemployment compensation agencies have abused the discretion which they have been given. On the contrary, they have discharged a difficult task with a judgment that was usually admirable. Their personnel would, however, be quick to concede the value to them of any feasible method of enrolling communal assistance to meet the problems of unemployment benefit administration. To date, little or nothing has been done to secure and organize such local assistance.

REDUCING AVAILABILITY RESTRICTIONS

Any exploration of the different kinds of limitations upon availability inevitably raises the questions: Why do workers impose such limitations upon their availability? Is there no way to curtail these limitations? Because these are basic questions, it may be well to sum up here the partial answers that are scattered throughout the foregoing chapters.

Although there probably are as many different reasons as there are restrictions on availability, these are some of the obvious factors which influence claimants to limit their availability: (1) illness and poor health, (2) family responsibilities, (3) union status, (4) attachment to a "regular" employer, (5) ignorance of labor-market conditions, (6) marginal attachment to the labor force; (7) ignorance of the meaning and effect of the availability requirement.

In addition there are certain more profound causes for availability restriction. One of these is the instability of our economic system which offers workers such little assurance of job security that a recent official paper (the "Latimer Report" on Guaranteed Wages) defined a guaranteed wage plan as one in which an employer assured a group of his workers a yearly minimum of three months' wages. Lack of job security creates in workers an inordinate fear of the loss of occupational standing. When he has no certainty that he will go back, after a "fill-in" job during a lay off, to his former work and pay, the claimant may be expected to resist even temporary downgrading. Lack of job security also leads the worker, whenever he thinks the market will permit, to insist upon his "price" in terms of pay, hours, and other working conditions. Our economic environment inspires him to grab what he can while he can.

Neither can this be cured by any system of full employment, desirable as it is, which guarantees a certain total number of jobs in the economy or even jobs for all who are able and willing to work. The lack which the worker feels is not the failure to assure jobs for everybody, but the failure to assure a suitable job for him. And it may as well be said again, that, as we noted in the introductory chapter, full employment may bring availability problems of its own by attracting marginal workers into the labor force and by giving the sellers of labor a bargaining advantage.

Availability restrictions are also fostered by our failure to meet the need of workers for satisfaction in their jobs. We do not equip our children, before they go to work, with enough information about themselves and about the job world so that they may make suitable work choices. We do not supply them, when they begin work and later, with the placement and personnel services to help them sufficiently to find the right job. When they are in a job they seldom find it so organized that they can derive from it a sense of personal participation and accomplishment in getting a desirable result. It is not surprising that availability restrictions often tend to run to pay, hours, and work location rather than to the kind of work.

In addition, it must be recognized that some benefit claimants who restrict their availability are trying to "ride" the program. They seek to collect benefits when they are actually not interested in working. Such claimants are a drain upon the resources of an unemployment compensation agency — its time, its money, and its prestige. To keep out all the work-shy claimants is difficult, if not impossible, without hurting many honest claimants who are anxious to go back to work. (Note, for example, the effects of laws that bar women from benefits, until they have been reëmployed, if they leave work because of marital responsibilities.) The result is that often we must depend upon a slower method, of weeding the malingerers out after they are inside the system and drawing benefits. This is expensive and can be damaging.

The unemployment compensation agency can do this necessary policing job. Education can, however, in time, reduce the size of that job. We accept the need to teach school children their rights and duties as citizens in a political democracy. Similarly, we need to teach them their rights and duties as participants in an economic democracy. Among the duties we must teach is the duty of the citizen, when he is a benefit claimant, to aid in protecting the unemployment benefit fund. Although the training of our people in economic citizenship ought not to end with their formal schooling, it ought to begin there. If the schools will accept this responsibility we may be able to reduce the number of the unemployment benefit "chiselers."

To give the reasons for availability limitations is almost equivalent to outlining what can be done to reduce them. Complete elimination of restrictions in availability is obviously impossible so long as both people and jobs differ so much. Even reducing the extent and number of availability restrictions is a task that is largely beyond the scope of the unemployment compensation agency. The unemployment compensation agency cannot stabilize employment and furnish job security to workers. Neither can it assure workers of satisfaction in their jobs. It is, however, within the competence of the unemployment compensation system to clarify for everyone concerned — employers, claimants, and the public — the relationship between availability problems and job dissatisfaction and insecurity. The employment service, by the quality of its placement work and by aiding vocational guidance of youth, can make an effective contribution in helping workers to job satisfaction.

Availability restrictions that stem from union status or attachment to a "regular" employer may, in many instances, be curtailed if the unemployment compensation agency will negotiate with the unions and employers involved. There have been interesting experiments in the State of Washington involving acceptance by unions of the responsibility of certifying to the availability of their unemployed members. During the war many unions agreed to the acceptance by their members, when no work in their line was to be expected, of other work, sometimes even under nonunion conditions. Negotiations with employers and unions have often made it possible for laid-off workers to take stopgap work without loss of status or seniority.

Claimant ignorance of labor-market conditions often leads to availability restrictions that are completely absurd. It is the special responsibility of the unemployment compensation agency and the employment service to give the claimant adequate labor market information so that he may make intelligent and realistic job demands. Implicit in this statement is the agency's need for complete and accurate knowledge of existing labor-market conditions and prospects. Implicit in it also is the need for a well-rounded program of job guidance and counselling to aid claimants in their search for work. In addition it is the special province and duty of the unemployment compensation agency to give the claimant a careful explanation of the meaning and effect of the availability requirement. This is not accomplished by merely telling him that he "must be able to work and available for work." In too many instances claimants are held unavailable for work without first being told why labor market conditions and the law make their availability limitations unreasonable.

Restrictions that are based upon health or illness are not within the direct power of the unemployment compensation agency to reduce. Health and disability insurance, however, can take many of these restrictions off the back of the administrative agency. The agency may properly point out the effect upon unemployment compensation of the lack of sickness insurance. It may also properly report the kinds of cases which would be covered under sickness insurance, and which go uncompensated under an "able to work" requirement.

All in all, then, the power of unemployment compensation administration to reduce the extent of availability restrictions is limited. It is largely confined to the indirect approach of supplying relevant information to the people concerned. Such an approach ought not to be underestimated. An energetic program to explain the availability requirement to workers, employers, and the public should have a salutary effect on availability limitations. It will not, however, remove more fundamental causes for claimants' restrictions, such as job insecurity and dissatisfaction.

BASIC POLICY IN AVAILABILITY

Since this is a book about a definition, the writer may perhaps be forgiven if, at the risk of some repetition, this concluding section is devoted to some of the factors involved in defining availability for work.

1. First we may note the purpose of unemployment compensation. That purpose is to pay benefits to unemployed people who ordinarily work for a living and who, but for their inability to obtain a suitable job, would now be working. We do this both for humanitarian reasons and because their uncompensated joblessness would have evil effects upon our society. Because we are concerned with the total effects of unemployment upon our society, the unemployment benefit system must be so operated that it will not foster greater evils than it is designed to overcome. Thus it is, for example, essential to guard against those claimants who would prefer benefits to suitable jobs.

2. The availability requirement is a test to discover whether claimants would, in actuality, now be working, were it not for their inability to obtain work that is appropriate for them. It is a generalized kind of test, serving to eliminate those claimants who obviously do not belong in the beneficiary class. It seems the path of wisdom not to press this test too far. When availability is in doubt it is usually preferable to consider the claimant eligible and to look to the results of actual referrals to suitable work for a more precise answer. When such referrals are not available, it violates the presumption of eligibility that is every claimant's due if the claimant of doubtful availability is denied benefits. The words "doubt" and "doubtful" must be stressed; the test is designed to exclude the clearly unavailable.

3. The presumption of availability has a sound foundation. It is based upon all we know of our people. They are bred to work. They need to work, for benefits will not ordinarily give them adequate support. Otherwise eligible claimants have met work or wage qualifications, proving recent labor-force attachment. They have also registered for work with the public employment service, thus exposing themselves to job offers. The presumption is readily rebuttable by contradictory facts. Without such a device as the presumption of availability it would be impossible to operate the unemployment benefit system during any period, such as a depression, when no job openings are to be had.

4. Although availability cannot be strictly defined, the concept in general describes a worker who is willing, able, and in a position to accept work that is substantial in extent and amount. He need not be prepared to take work that is not suitable for him, in the light of his individual circumstances and the existing labor market conditions. At the same time he must be prepared to accept work

that is reasonable in amount, as determined by the work opportunities ordinarily or presently existing in the locality where he is prepared to work.

5. There are two notable aspects of such a concept of availability. One is the stress that is placed upon the claimant's individual circumstances. The other is the force that is given to an understanding of the labor market in both its immediate and its long-run aspects. The administrative corollaries of such a view of availability are far-reaching. Case-by-case determination becomes the prescribed method. Class determinations of unavailability, whether by administrative interpretation or legislative act, are to be deemed undesirable. It is to be noted that decision of each case on its own merits involves most exacting personnel requirements. This is no small matter when millions of claims must be determined each year.

Another administrative corollary is the need to adjust availability determinations to changing labor-market conditions. This does not mean that availability policies should change with every ebb and flow of the demand for workers. Nor is it suggested that opportunism should be the basis of availability determinations. Availability determinations, in order to discharge the purpose of unemployment compensation, must cushion the shock of violent labor-market changes. They need also to be grounded in established principle if orderly and acceptable administration is to be achieved. Labor-market conditions will, however, control the application of the availability requirement. For example, they will determine whether available job openings exist to offer to claimants, thus putting their availability to the test. Labor-market conditions will also determine whether it is desirable and feasible to require claimants to seek work independently of the employment service. Thus changes in the labor market inevitably control the nature of availability administration.

It follows that unemployment compensation agencies have a continuing need for labor-market information and studies. Claims deputies and referees who decide availability cases need to know not only the pertinent facts of the current labor-market situation. They need also to be grounded in the historical background of the relevant occupation, industry, and labor-market area. Here again great demands are made upon administrative personnel.

6. Finally, we may point to certain attitudes or attributes of administration that are needed to do the job of defining availability day-by-day. One of these attitudes may be called an aversion to

legalism. This is another way of saying that each case must be decided on its own merits even though there are general concepts that are helpful. A second attitude that is required is humility. The claims deputy and the referee need to be impressed with the slender portfolio of facts upon which they must answer the question: Is this claimant prepared to take a suitable job or is he, in effect, just another loafer? They need also to give due weight to the comparative importance, in the claimant's eyes, of the decision which must inevitably be mere routine to the administrator. A third necessary attribute is courage. To award benefits to a union electrician who will not take a nonunion job or to an aircraft mechanic who will not take a salesclerk's job may invite severe complaints and even legislative investigations. Fair administration of the availability test is an impossibility, however, unless such risks are assumed.

APPENDIX

TABLE A

AVAILABILITY PROVISIONS

TOTAL BENEFIT DISQUALIFICATIONS[a]

State Unemployment Compensation Laws, November 30, 1949

State	Availability Provisions	Marital Condition or Childbirth	Total Disqualifications — Students	Other
Alabama......	Physically and mentally able to perform work of a character which he is qualified to perform by past experience or training and available for such work at a locality where he earned wages for insured work during the base period or at a locality where such work may be reasonably expected to be available	Women not able or available for 3 months before and 3 months after childbirth		No benefits until reëmployed if worker: (a) left work voluntarily without good cause connected with his work; (Exception for cases of sickness and disability if prescribed conditions concerning notice to employer, prompt return to work when able and compliance with employer's established leave policy are met. Further exception if worker quits old work and immediately takes another job at which he works eight weeks.) or (b) was discharged for dishonesty or criminal act connected with his work or for an act endangering the safety of others or for actual or threatened deliberate misconduct after written warning to him. No benefits until reëm-

ployed and has earned 20 times his weekly benefit amount if claimant fails, without good cause, to apply for or to accept available suitable work or to return to customary self-employment when so directed

Arizona........	Standard[b]	
Arkansas.......	Physically and mentally able to perform suitable work and available for such work	No benefits until reëmployed in paid employment for not less than thirty days if woman voluntarily left work to marry or to perform customary duties of a housewife or was separated from her customary occupation because of pregnancy
California.....	Standard; has made such effort to seek work on his own behalf as required by regulation	
Colorado......	Able and available for all suitable work; actively seeking work	

a "Total disqualifications" is used here to include disqualifications which deny benefits for the duration of the unemployment or the disqualifying condition or cancel wage credits completely.

b "Standard" refers to the common wording of the requirement, "able to work and available for work"; for purposes of this table, statutory provisions have been listed as "standard" if the language did not vary materially from the quoted provision ("physically and mentally able to work" in Connecticut and Indiana; "physically able to work" in District of Columbia).

TABLE A (Continued)

State	Availability Provisions	Marital Condition or Childbirth	Total Disqualifications — Students	Other
Connecticut....	Standard; has been and is making reasonable efforts to seek work	No benefits if unemployed due to pregnancy; women ineligible for 2 months before and 2 months after pregnancy	No benefits while attending school, college, or university as regularly enrolled student, if worker left work to attend	
Delaware.......	Standard; actively seeking work			No benefits until reëmployed if worker: (a) left last work voluntarily without good cause attributable to the employment; or (b) was discharged from his last employment for just cause connected with his work; or (c) refused to accept an offer of work for which he was reasonably fitted; or (d) refused to accept a referral to a job opportunity when directed to do so by a local employment office; or (e) became unemployed by reason of commitment to a penal institution
District of Columbia....	Standard			
Florida.........	Standard			No benefits until reëmployed and has earned 10 times his weekly benefit

State				
Georgia	Standard			amount if worker: (a) voluntarily left his last work without good cause; or (b) was discharged from his last employment for misconduct connected with the work; or (c) failed, without good cause, to apply for or to accept available suitable work
Idaho	Able to work, available for suitable work, and seeking work; claimant not ineligible if unable or unavailable due to illness or disability occurring after he filed a claim and registered for work and no suitable work has been offered him since illness or disability began	Woman who leaves work voluntarily to marry or perform customary housewife duties or leaves the locale to live with her husband deemed unavailable until she shows otherwise or becomes the main support of herself or her immediate family; no benefits during pregnancy if woman voluntarily left last work in customary occupation; woman ineligible for 6 weeks before and 6 weeks after childbirth	Not unemployed if attending a regularly established school, excluding night school	
Illinois	Standard; actively seeking work. Weekly benefit amount reduced one-third for each normal work day of inability or unavail-	Woman deemed unable to work and unavailable for 13 weeks before and 4 weeks after childbirth. Worker who left his		Worker is unavailable for work if after separation from most recent employing unit he has moved to and remains in a local-

TABLE A (Continued)

State	Availability Provisions	Marital Condition or Childbirth	Total Disqualifications — Students	Other
Illinois (*Cont.*)	ability for work. Individual deemed unavailable for work on any normal work day in which he fails to work because it is a religious or legal holiday or a customary holiday in his trade or occupation	most recent work voluntarily to marry is not available (Not applicable if worker becomes sole support of himself and his family) Worker who left work voluntarily because of marital circumstances is not available for work so long as such circumstances exist		ity where work opportunities are substantially less favorable than those in the locality he left. Worker who left work voluntarily because of filial or other domestic circumstances is not available for work so long as such circumstances exist All prior wage credits canceled if worker was discharged because of forgery, larceny, or embezzlement connected with his work and admits it or is convicted of it. Worker who has exhausted his benefits must earn 3 times his weekly benefit amount before he may begin a second benefit year; credited with weeks of employment in first benefit year
Indiana........	Standard Weekly benefit amount reduced by one-third for each normal work day of	Unavailable if unemployed due to pregnancy; all prior wage credits canceled if worker left work	Unavailable if attending regularly established training school, college, or hospital, excluding night	All prior wage credits canceled if worker: (a) left work voluntarily because of parental, filial, or

	inability or unavailability for work	voluntarily to marry or because of marital obligations (may be waived for good cause)	school or part-time training course	other domestic obligations (may be waived for good cause); or (b) was discharged from work for dishonesty connected with his work and has admitted it or been convicted for it
Iowa.........	Standard	No benefits if worker failed without good cause, when so directed, to return to customary duties as a housewife	No benefits if worker failed without good cause, when so directed, to return to customary occupation of being a student	No benefits if worker: (a) left work voluntarily without good cause attributable to his employer (exceptions: (1) left to accept better work and stayed in it at least 12 weeks; (2) after notifying temporary employer, left stop-gap work to return to regular employer; (3) left for necessary purpose of caring for injured or ill member of immediate family, accepted no other work, and returned to the employer as soon as the sick member recovered); or (b) failed, without good cause, to apply for or to accept available suitable work or to return to customary self-employment
Kansas........	Standard; making reasonable efforts to obtain work	Woman is not able to work or available to work during 2 months before		All prior wage credits canceled if worker was discharged for misconduct

TABLE A (Continued)

State	Availability Provisions	Marital Condition or Childbirth	Total Disqualifications — Students	Other
Kansas (*Cont*).		and 1 month after childbirth		connected with his work and convicted of a felony as a result of such misconduct
Kentucky.....	Physically and mentally able to work and available for suitable work	No benefits until reëmployed if worker quit most recent work to marry	No benefits until reëmployed if worker voluntarily quit most recent work in order to attend school	No benefits until reëmployed if worker: (a) voluntarily quit most recent work to become self-employed; or (b) was discharged for dishonesty in connection with most recent work
Louisiana......	Standard			
Maine..........	Able to work and available for work and in addition to registering for work and reporting at the public employment office is himself making a reasonable effort to seek work at his usual or customary trade, occupation, profession, or business, or in such other trade, etc. as his prior training or experience shows him to be fitted or qualified			
Maryland......	Standard; claimant not ineligible if unable or un-	No benefits if unemployed due to pregnancy;		No benefits if worker was discharged or given

State	Availability	Pregnancy/Childbirth	Disqualification
	available due to illness or disability occurring after he has registered for work and no suitable work has been offered him since illness or disability began (A claimant who has not actively sought work is to be disqualified for 1 to 10 weeks from the date upon which he was called upon to produce evidence of his efforts to find work. The Board is directed to consider whether the claimant's efforts to obtain work have been reasonable and are such efforts as an unemployed individual is expected to make if he is honestly looking for work. The extent of the effort required is to depend on the labor market conditions in the claimant's area.)	no benefits during 2 months before and 2 months after childbirth	indefinite lay off for dishonest or criminal act connected with or materially affecting his work or for willful act endangering the safety of others. All prior wage credits canceled. No benefits until reemployed and has earned 10 times the weekly benefit amount if worker: (a) is unemployed due to leaving work voluntarily and without good cause; or (b) is unemployed due to actual or threatened deliberate and willful misconduct connected with his work; or (c) failed, without good cause, to apply for or to accept available suitable work or to return to his customary self-employment
Massachusetts.	Capable of and available for work and unable to obtain work in his usual occupation or any other occupation for which he is reasonably fitted	No benefits if unavailable because of pregnancy; no benefits for 4 weeks before and 4 weeks after childbirth	No benefits until reëmployed if worker: (a) voluntarily left his last work without good cause attributable to the employer; or (b) was discharged from his last work solely for deliberate

TABLE A (Continued)

State	Availability Provisions	Marital Condition or Childbirth	Total Disqualifications Students	Other
Massachusetts (*Cont.*)				misconduct in willful disregard of the employer's interest
Michigan......	Seeking work; able and available for full-time work which (a) he is, by past experience and training, qualified to perform, and (b) is generally similar to work which he has previously done for wages; available for such work at a locality where (1) he earned base period wages in insured work or (2) the commission finds such work is available	No benefits until reëmployed if unemployed due to pregnancy		No benefits until reëmployed if worker: (a) voluntarily left work without good cause attributable to the employer; or (b) was discharged from work for misconduct connected with his work or for intoxication while at work; or (c) failed, without good cause, to apply for or to accept available suitable work or to return to customary self-employment
Minnesota......	Standard Weekly benefit amount reduced one-fifth for each day of inability to work or unavailability	No benefits until reëmployed in insured work for at least two weeks if woman worker: (a) separated from work because of pregnancy; or (b) voluntarily left work in order to visit or live with her husband or to assume the duties of a housewife		
Mississippi......	Standard			

Missouri........	Standard; has been and is actively seeking work		No benefits until reëmployed and has earned 10 times the weekly benefit amount if worker: (a) left work voluntarily without good cause attributable to the employment; or (b) was discharged for misconduct connected with his work; or (c) failed, without good cause, to apply for or to accept available suitable work or to return to customary self-employment
Mont'ana........	Standard; seeking work; claimant not ineligible if unable or unavailable due to illness or disability occurring after he has registered for work and no suitable work has been offered him since illness or disability began	No benefits until reëmployed and has earned enough new wage credits to qualify if claimant left her most recent work to be married	No benefits during school term or customary vacation periods within the school term if worker left his most recent work to attend an established educational institution or is a student regularly attending such an institution
Nebraska.......	Standard	Not available after voluntarily quitting work due to pregnancy; no benefits for 12 weeks before and 4 weeks after childbirth; wage credits earned before marriage canceled if woman's employment is discontinued on account of marriage	No benefits to students registered for full attendance at and regularly attending an established school, college, or university or to one who so attended during the most recent school term	All prior wage credits canceled if worker: (a) was discharged for gross, flagrant, and willful or unlawful misconduct connected with his work; or (b) failed, without good cause, to apply for or to accept available suitable work or to return to customary self-employment

TABLE A (Continued)

State	Availability Provisions	Marital Condition or Childbirth	Total Disqualifications — Students	Other
Nevada.......	Standard; claimant not ineligible if unable or unavailable due to illness or disability occurring after he filed initial claim for benefits and no suitable work has been offered him since illness or disability began	No benefits until reëmployed and has earned $50 in bona fide employment if worker left work voluntarily to marry	No benefits if worker is registered at and attending any established school, college, or university; night or vocational training schools excepted	
New Hampshire	Standard	Pregnant woman unavailable for not more than 16 weeks, beginning 8 weeks before expected childbirth; period may be ended before 16 weeks if, after childbirth, she earns in any week $3 more than her weekly benefit amount		No benefits until reëmployed and has earned weekly wages equal to $3 more than his weekly benefit amount, if worker quit work voluntarily without good cause. No benefits if worker was discharged for arson, sabotage, felony, or dishonesty connected with his work or for intoxication of such degree and rate of occurrence as to seriously hamper or interfere with his work
New Jersey....	Standard; has demonstrated that he is actively seeking work			

New Mexico...	Standard; actively seeking work		
New York......	"Total unemployment" defined as total lack of any employment on any day caused by the inability of a claimant who is capable of and available for work to engage in his usual employment or in any other for which he is reasonably fitted by training and experience		No benefits if worker, without good cause, refused to accept an offer of employment for which he is reasonably fitted by training and experience
North Carolina.	Standard; must establish that he is actively seeking work. Seasonal worker, during the off-season, must show that he is actively seeking work which he is qualified to perform by past experience or training during the off-season. Worker not available for any week (but not more than 2 in a calendar year) of unemployment due to a vacation. (Any pay roll week in which 60% or more of full-time working hours consists of a vacation period is a vacation week.)	Women not able or available for 3 months before and 3 months after childbirth; benefits not denied for this reason if child dies	
North Dakota..	Able to work and available for suitable work; ac-	Worker who voluntarily leaves work for indefi-	No benefits if worker left his most recent work

TABLE A (Continued)

State	Availability Provisions	Total Disqualifications — Marital Condition or Childbirth	Total Disqualifications — Students	Other
North Dakota (*Cont.*)	tively seeking employment	nite period to be a homemaker, because of marital obligations or approaching marriage, not available until availability is shown by some evidence in addition to registration for work and statement of availability. Woman is considered unable to work for 12 weeks before and 4 weeks after childbirth unless such facts as doctor's certificate or work history during previous pregnancies show otherwise	in order to attend an educational institution or is a student registered for full attendance at and regularly attending an established school, college or university or is on vacation within the school term (does not apply if worker is unemployed through no fault of his own and is attending school only because of lack of work and is willing to quit school to accept full-time work)	No benefits until reëmployed if worker: (a) quit work because of parental, filial, or other domestic obligations; or (b) refused without good cause to accept an offer of suitable work; or (c) refused to accept a referral to suitable work when directed to do so by a local employment office; or (d) advocates, or is a member of a party which advocates the over-
Ohio..........	Able to work and available for suitable work and actively seeking work either at a locality in which he has earned wages subject to the unemployment compensation act during his base period or at a locality where such work is normally performed; and is unable to obtain suitable work	No benefits until reëmployed if worker quit work to marry or because of marital obligations	No benefits until reëmployed if worker left his most recent work in order to attend an established educational institution or if he is a student regularly attending such an institution during the school term or customary vacation periods during the school term	

State			
			throw of our government by force; or (e) failed or refused to report as required by the rules of the unemployment compensation agency; or (f) became unemployed by reason of commitment to a penal institution; or (g) was discharged for dishonesty in connection with his work for which he was convicted or which he admitted.
Oklahoma......	Standard	No benefits until reëmployed if worker left work voluntarily to marry (May be waived or modified for good cause by appellate body)	No benefits until reëmployed if worker left work voluntarily to enter self-employment (May be waived or modified, for good cause, by appellate body)
Oregon.........	Standard; actively seeking and unable to obtain suitable work	Pregnant woman who leaves work is unavailable until 4 weeks after pregnancy ends	
Pennsylvania..	Able to work and available for suitable work		No benefits if unemployment is due to: (a) failure, without good cause, to apply for or to accept suitable work; or (b) voluntarily leaving work without good cause; or (c) discharge or tem-

TABLE A (Continued)

State	Availability Provisions	Marital Condition or Childbirth	Total Disqualifications		Other
			Students		
Pennsylvania (*Cont.*)					porary suspension from work for willful misconduct connected with the work
Rhode Island..	Physically able to work and available for work whenever duly called for work through the employment office				
South Carolna.	Standard				Not available for work if engaged in self-employment which returns or promises remuneration in excess of the weekly benefit amount
South Dakota..	Standard				
Tennessee......	Standard; claimant not ineligible if unable or unavailable due to illness or disability occurring after he has registered for work and no suitable work has been offered him since illness or disability began				
Texas.........	Standard				

Utah.........	Standard	No benefits while attending established school, night school, national defense or part-time training course (does not apply [a] if worker is unemployed through no fault of his own before enrollment and is attending school because of lack of work and actively seeking work and will quit school to accept full-time work during customary working hours or [b] major portion of base-period wage credits earned while attending school)
		No benefits during pregnancy if woman voluntarily left her last work in her customary occupation; no benefits for 6 weeks before and 6 weeks after childbirth; no benefits until re-employed and has earned $100 if woman voluntarily left work to marry, to perform the customary duties of a housewife, or to leave the locale to live with her husband (does not apply after change in conditions which makes her the main support of herself or her immediate family)	
Vermont......	Standard; no benefits for duration of unemployment is due to pregnancy	Commission may require, in addition to registration at an employment office, that the individual make such other efforts to secure suitable work as the commission may reasonably direct under the circumstances and to supply proper evidence thereof. If claimant fails, without good cause, to do so he is ineligible for each week such failure continues. Claimant not eligible if unable or unavailable due to illness or

TABLE A (Continued)

State	Availability Provisions	Marital Condition or Childbirth	Total Disqualifications	
			Students	Other
Vermont (*Cont.*)		disability occurring after he has registered and no suitable work has been offered him since illness or disability began		
Virginia.......	Standard			
Washington....	Able to work and available for work in any trade, occupation, profession, or business for which he is reasonably fitted; must be ready, willing, and able immediately to accept any suitable work which may be offered to him; must be actively seeking work; weekly benefit amount may be reduced by one-seventh for each day of unavailability for work. Worker considered unavailable for the entire week if unavailable for three or more days of the week			
West Virginia..	Able to work and available for full-time work for which he is fitted by prior training or experience	No benefits until reëmployed in insured work for 30 working days if unemployed because of preg-	No benefits if worker voluntarily quit work to attend an educational institution and is attending	No benefits until reëmployed in insured work for 30 working days if worker voluntarily quit to per-

West Virginia (*Cont.*)

form a parental or family duty or to attend to his person l business or affairs

No benefits to a worker while unemployed because of his own request or that of his authorized agent for a vacation period at a specified time that would leave the employer no alternative but to suspend operations

such institution or awaiting entrance to it or the beginning of a new term

nancy or worker voluntarily quit to marry or to perform a marital duty

Wisconsin......

Worker is ineligible if, with due notice, he is called on by his current employer to report for available work and he is unavailable for work or physically unable to do his work; in addition to registering for work, a claimant may be required at any time to make such other efforts to secure work as the commission may reasonably direct under the circumstances and to supply proper evidence thereof; failure, without good cause, to do so makes him ineligible so long as the failure continues.

No benefits until reëmployed within 4 different weeks and has earned 4 times his benefit amount if worker failed without good cause to apply for or to accept offered work (if failure is with good cause, but worker is physically unable to work or substantially unavailable, no benefits so long as inability or unavailability continues)

TABLE A (Continued)

State	Availability Provisions	Marital Condition or Childbirth	Total Disqualifications — Students	Other
Wyoming......	Standard; actively seeking work			
Alaska........	Standard	No benefits during 2 calendar months before and 1 month after childbirth		
Hawaii........	Standard	Woman considered unable to work for 2 months before and 2 months after childbirth unless such facts as work record during previous pregnancies or doctor's certificate show that she is able to work. Worker who, because of marital obligations or approaching marriage, voluntarily leaves work to engage in occupation of homemaker is not available for work until availability is shown by some evidence in addition to registration for work and statement of availability		

TABLE B

FACTORS CONSIDERED IN DETERMINING SUITABLE WORK

(STATE UNEMPLOYMENT COMPENSATION LAWS, NOVEMBER 30, 1949)

	Degree of Risk to Health, Safety and Morals	Physical Fitness	Prior Training	Experience	Prior Earnings	Length of Unemployment	Prospects of Securing Local Work in Customary Occupation	Distance of Available Work from Residence	Prospects of Obtaining Local Work
United States Total	47	46	47	47	40	45	42	45	7
Alabama.........	X	X	X	X	X	X	X	Xª	
Arizona..........	X	X	X	X	X	X	X	X	
Arkansas.........	X	X	X	X	X	X	omits "local"	X	X
Californiaᵇ.......	X	X	X	X	X	X	X	X	
Colorado.........	X	X	X	X	X	X	X	Xᶜ	
Connecticutᵈ.....	X	X	X	X		X			
Delawareᵉ........									
District of Columbia......	X	X	X	X				X	
Florida..........	X	X	X	X	X	X	X	X	
Georgia..........	X	X	X	X	X	X	X	X	
Idaho...........	X	X	X	X	X	X	X	X	
Illinois...........	X	X	X	X	X	X	X	X	

The "factors" indicated in the table and in these notes are in addition to those mentioned in the text of Chapter V as "labor-standards" provisions. Since the "labor-standards" provisions are overriding injunctions, the "factors" mentioned in these notes and in the table apply only if the work involved meets the "labor standards."

ª No work is deemed unsuitable because of its distance from the worker's residence, if that work is in substantially the same locality as his last regular place of employment and if the worker left that employment voluntarily without good cause connected with the employment.

ᵇ "Suitable employment" means work in the individual's usual occupation or for which he is reasonably fitted, regardless of whether or not it is insured work. Any work offered under the conditions checked in the table is suitable if it gives the individual wages at least equal to his weekly benefit amount for total unemployment. In any case in which the commission finds it impracticable to apply the statutory standards (checked in the table) it may apply any standard set by it which is reasonably calculated to determine what is suitable employment.

ᶜ Statute describes the factor as "the distance of the available local work from his residence."

ᵈ Work or self-employment is not suitable unless the administrator finds that it may reasonably be expected to yield a greater rate of remuneration than the worker's benefit rate for total unemployment. "Suitable employment" means either employment in the worker's usual employment or other employment for which he is reasonably fitted, regardless of whether or not it is insured work. The work, however, must be within a reasonable distance of the worker's residence or last employment.

ᵉ The worker is to be disqualified "if he has refused to accept an offer of work for which he is reasonably fitted, or has refused to accept a referral to a job opportunity when directed to do so by a local employment office of this State or another State." The statutory language makes no reference to "suitable" work or to "good cause" for refusing a job offer or referral. There is no disqualification for refusing a job offer of new work or a referral to a job opportunity if "the work is at an unreasonable distance from his residence, having regard to the character of the work he has been accustomed to do, and travel to the place of work involves expenses substantially greater than that required for his former work."

TABLE B (Continued)

	Degree of Risk to Health, Safety and Morals	Physical Fitness	Prior Training	Experience	Prior Earnings	Length of Unemployment	Prospects of Securing Local Work in Customary Occupation	Distance of Available Work from Residence	Prospects of Obtaining Local Work
Indiana..........	X	X	X	X		X	X	X	
Iowa............	X	X	X	X	X	X	X	X	
Kansas..........	X	X	X	X	X	X	X	X	
Kentucky........	X	X	X	X	X	X	X	X	
Louisiana........	X	X	X	X	X	X	omits "local"	X	X
Maine...........	X	X	X	X	X	X	X	X	
Maryland........	X	X	X	X	X	X	X	X	
Massachusetts....	X		X	X				X[f]	
Michigan[g]........	X	X	X	X	X	X	X	X	
Minnesota.......	X	X	X	X		X	X	X	
Mississippi.......	X	X	X	X	X	X	X	X	
Missouri[h]........	X	X	X	X	X	X	omits "local"	X	X
Montana.........	X	X	X	X	X	X	X	X	
Nebraska........	X	X	X	X	X	X	X	X	
Nevada..........	X	X	X	X	X	X	X		
New Hampshire..	X	X	X	X	X	X	X	X	
New Jersey......	X	X	X	X	X	X	X	X	
New Mexico......	X	X	X	X	X	X	X	X	
New York[i].......									
North Carolina...	X	X	X	X	X	X	X	X	
North Dakota....	X	X	X	X	X	X	omits "local"	X	X

[f] In addition to the factors checked in the table, consideration is given to whether the offered employment is located within reasonable distance of the worker's residence or place of last employment and does not involve travel expenses substantially greater than that required in his former work.

[g] An offer of employment in the worker's customary occupation, under conditions of employment and remuneration substantially equivalent to those under which he has been customarily employed in that occupation, is deemed suitable work.

[h] If a worker moves from the locality in which he resided during his last employment to a place where there is less probability of his employment at his usual type of work and which is more distant from or less accessible to the community in which he was last employed: (1) Work offered by his most recent employer is deemed suitable if it is similar to that which he performed in his last employment and at wages, hours, and working conditions which are substantially similar to those prevailing for similar work in that community. (2) Any work which he is capable of performing is deemed suitable, at the wages prevailing for such work in the locality to which he has moved, if it is not hazardous to his health, safety, or morals.

[i] The disqualification applies to a claimant "who without good cause refuses to accept an offer of employment for which he is reasonably fitted by training and experience." The statutory language makes no reference to "suitable" work. There is no disqualification if the offered "employment is at an unreasonable distance from his residence, or travel to and from the place of unemployment involves expense substantially greater than that required in his former employment unless the expense be provided for."

TABLE B (Continued)

	Degree of Risk to Health, Safety and Morals	Physical Fitness	Prior Training	Experience	Prior Earnings	Length of Unemployment	Prospects of Securing Local Work in Customary Occupation	Distance of Available Work from Residence	Prospects of Obtaining Local Work
Ohio............	X	X	X	X	X	X		X[j]	X
Oklahoma........	X	X	X	X	X	X	omits "local"	X	X
Oregon..........	X	X	X	X	X	X	X	X	
Pennsylvania[k]....	X	X	X	X		X	X	X	
Rhode Island[l]....									
South Carolina...	X	X	X	X	X	X	X	X	
South Dakota....	X	X	X	X	X	X	X	X	
Tennessee........	X	X	X	X	X	X	X	X	
Texas..........	X	X	X	X	X	X	X	X	
Utah............	X	X	X	X	X	X	X	X	
Vermont........	X	X	X	X	X	X	X	X	
Virginia.........	X	X	X	X		X		m	
Washington[n].....	X	X	X	X	X	X	X	X	
West Virginia....	X	X	X	X	X	X	X	X[o]	
Wisconsin[p].......									
Wyoming........	X	X	X	X	X	X	X	X	
Alaska..........	X	X	X	X	X	X	X	X	
Hawaii..........	X	X	X	X	X	X	omits "local"	X	

[j] There is no disqualification for refusing an offer of new work if "the work is at an unreasonable distance from his residence, having regard to the character of the work he has been accustomed to do, and travel to the place of work involves expenses substantially greater than that required for his former work, unless the expense be provided for."

[k] "Suitable work" means all work which the employee is capable of performing. In determining suitable work, the department is directed to consider, in addition to the factors checked in the table: The reasons for the unemployment; the prevailing condition of the labor market, generally, and particularly in the claimant's usual occupation; prevailing wage rates in his usual occupation; permanency of the claimant's residence.

[l] "Suitable work" means any work for which the worker is reasonably fitted, which is located within a reasonable distance of his residence or last place of work and which is not detrimental to his health, safety or morals.

[m] Substitutes "accessibility of the available work from his residence."

[n] In stating commissioner's authority to consider other factors which he may deem pertinent, statute specifically mentions "state and national emergencies."

[o] The distance of available or offered work from the worker's new residence is not considered in determining suitable work if that distance was created as the result of the worker voluntarily changing his residence to a new locality other than the one where he resided at the time he voluntarily quit his last employment without good cause involving the employer's fault.

[p] The disqualification applies "if an employe fails either to apply for work when notified by a public employment office or to accept work when offered him, and such failure was without good cause." The statutory language does not refer to "suitable" work or give any criteria of good cause for failure to apply for or to accept work.

TABLE C

SPECIFIC PERIODS OF INABILITY TO WORK FOR PREGNANT WOMEN IN
STATE UNEMPLOYMENT COMPENSATION AND LABOR LAWS

State	UC Disqualification Period		Employment of Women Prohibited		
	Before Childbirth	After Childbirth	Before Childbirth	After Childbirth	Employment or Industry
Alabama	3 mos.	3 mos.	.....	.....	....
Alaska	2 mos.	1 month	.....	.....	....
Connecticut	2 mos.	2 mos.	4 wks.	4 wks.	Any factory, mercantile establishment, mill, or workshop
Idaho	6 wks.	6 wks.	.....	.....	....
Illinois	13 wks.	13 wks.	.....	.....	....
Kansas	2 mos.	1 mo.	.....	.....	....
Maryland	2 mos.	2 mos.	.....	.....	....
Massachusetts	4 wks.	4 wks.	2 wks.	4 wks.	Laboring in mercantile manufacturing or mechanical establishment
Missouri	(No special disqualification)		3 wks.	3 wks.	Manual, physical, stenographic, or clerical work of any character in any manufacturing establishment, factory workshop, laundry, bakery, restaurant, any place of amusement, express, transportation or public utility business, common carrier, or public institution
Nebraska	12 wks.	4 wks.	.....	.....	....
New Hampshire	8 wks.	(None specified; total disqualification may not exceed 16 wks.)	.....	.....	....
New York	(No special disqualification)		.....	4 wks.	Factory or mercantile establishment
North Carolina	3 mos.	3 mos.	.....	.....	....
North Dakota	12 wks.	4 wks.	.....	.....	....
Oregon	.....	4 wks.	.....	.....	....
Utah	6 wks.	6 wks.	.....	.....	....

TABLE C   287

TABLE C (Continued)

State	UC Disqualification Period		Employment of Women Prohibited		
	Before Childbirth	After Childbirth	Before Childbirth	After Childbirth	Employment or Industry
Vermont.......	(No special disqualification)		2 wks.	4 wks.	Laboring in any mill' cannery, workshop, factory, manufacturing, or mechanical establishment
Washington....	(Regulation creates unavailability presumption when claimant's employment is terminated because of pregnancy. Presumption continues until doctor's certificate to the contrary designates periods of ability to do suitable work)		4 mos.	6 wks.	Any manufacturing or other mercantile establishment; laundry, drycleaning, or dye-works occupations

NOTES

EXPLANATION OF CITATIONS

THE *Unemployment Compensation Interpretation Service, Benefit Series (Ben. Ser.)*, published by the Social Security Administration, is a monthly compilation of noteworthy unemployment compensation decisions. Greatest reliance has been placed upon this publication for administrative decisions. Each published case is cited by number, by jurisdiction, and by a letter symbol signifying the type of tribunal or other body which rendered the decision. The absence of a letter symbol indicates an administrative interpretation or opinion of a state unemployment compensation agency. The letter symbols in use are as follows:

AG Opinion of an attorney general, as 704–Conn. AG

CC Opinion of a corporation counsel, as 1036–D.C. CC

Ct.D. Court Decision, as 870–Oreg. Ct.D.

A Decision of a lower appeal tribunal, as 189–Oreg. A

D Decision of a higher appeal body, considered, however, as an initial determination, as 741–R.I. D

R Decision of the highest administrative appeal body, as 194–N.Y. R

V Decision of a state appeal tribunal under the Servicemen's Readjustment Act of 1944. Note that cases in this last category were published in the *Benefit Series* in the issues of Vol. 8, No. 4 through Vol. 9, No. 9 only.

Administrative decisions of state unemployment compensation agencies other than those published in the *Benefit Series* have been cited in the notes as "unp." (unpublished). Readjustment Allowance Review Decisions made by the Veterans Administration, upon review of the decisions of the state Readjustment Allowance Agents under the Servicemen's Readjustment Act of 1944 are designated by the symbol "RAR–U" or "RAR–S" followed by a number. In the case of court decisions, a *Benefit Series* citation is given in addition to the conventional court reporting system citation.

NOTES

NOTES FOR CHAPTER ONE

1. "Able and available" was the issue in decisions of unemployment compensation referees and tribunals (first-stage administrative appeals) as follows: 1941 (six months) 22.5 per cent; 1942, 30.7 per cent; 1943, 42.1 per cent; 1944, 42.0 per cent; 1945, 44.0 per cent; 1946, 38.1 per cent; 1947, 39.7 per cent. (*Social Security Yearbook,* 1946, p. 33, and Bureau of Employment Security.)

2.

	"Able and Available" Denials	Other Disqualifications
1945	300,148	274,296
1946	589,895	526,925
1947 (first 9 months)	446,462	384,553

(*Social Security Yearbook,* 1946, p. 31, and Bureau of Employment Security.)

3. *Social Security Yearbook,* 1946, p. 31.

4. Hearings before the Committee on Ways and Means, House of Representatives, 79 Cong., 1 sess. on H.R. 3736, Aug. 30, 31, Sept. 1, 4, 5, 6, and 7, 1945, p. 31. Also pp. 46, 52 (testimony of Mr. John W. Snyder, then Director of War Mobilization and Reconversion), 73 ff. (testimony of Mr. Arthur J. Altmeyer, Chairman, Social Security Board), 165–67, 170 ff. (testimony of Mr. R. J. Thomas, then President, UAW–CIO), 358–369 (testimony of Mr. Stanley Rector, Chief Counsel, Unemployment Compensation Department, State of Wisconsin), 401–02 (testimony of Mr. Claude A. Williams, then Chairman, Texas Unemployment Compensation Commission), 447 (testimony of Mr. W. O. Hake, Commissioner, Tennessee Department of Employment Security).

Similar discussions appear in the Hearings before the Committee on Finance, United States Senate, 79 Cong., 1 sess. on S. 1274, Aug. 29–31, Sept. 1, 3, and 4, 1945, pp. 11, 80–189, 258, 272, 298, 546, 559, 562, 573; Hearings before the Committee on Ways and Means, House of Representatives, 79 Cong., 2 sess. on Social Security Legislation, Part I (Feb. 25–28 and Mar. 1, 1946) pp. 72–74; Part V (April 8–12, 1946), pp. 539–40; Part X (June 3–7, 1946) p. 1318 ff., 1348–1350, 1398 ff., 1421 ff.

5. June 26–30, July 1–14, 1946. The Baltimore *Sun* articles were, of course, not the first of their kind but they had the most widespread effect. The Los Angeles *Times,* May 9, 1946, had charged editorially that thousands were using unemployment compensation "as a vacation fund — a subsidy for idleness — the rule of availability is too loose to encourage applicants to seek employment . . ." On the same day the Newark (New Jersey) *News* editorially stated: "The requirement that beneficiaries register with the United States Employment Service and accept a comparable job, when offered, or be disqualified has not met the situation." Also, on May 9, 1946, the Seattle *Post-Intelligencer* editorially commended the Longview *News* for saying: "An abuse of the use of public funds has sprung up which has been allowed to go on for a length of time sufficient to make it appear to be standard, acceptable procedure. It should not be accepted.

A person should not be allowed to draw public funds merely because none of the jobs . . . suits his tastes or inclinations . . ." Similar editorials and articles appeared in the Indianapolis *Star* (May 17, 1946), the Dallas *News* (May 12, 1946), the New York *Journal-American* (May 31, 1946), and the Burlington (Vermont) *Free Press* (June 19, 1946).

6. New York *World-Telegram* (Aug. 5, 1946).

7. Providence *Journal-Bulletin* (Nov. 10–19, 1946). Quoted matter from the November 14 article.

8. For other newspaper articles and editorials, see the Hartford *Times* (Apr. 19, 1946), the Baltimore *Sun* (May 5, 1946), Portland *Oregonian* (July 21, 22, 1946; article by Paul F. Ewing who blamed "pure human cussedness" for the failure of unemployed workers to take jobs); Atlanta *Journal* (July 23, 1946, article by Mark Temple), New York *Sun* (Aug. 28–29, 1946, articles by Don Anderson), Roanoke *World-News* (Sept. 18, 1946), and the Tampa *Tribune* (Oct. 13–23, 1946, articles by Jim Killingsworth).

9. United States Bureau of the Census, *Sixteenth Census of the United States: 1940, Population, Volume III, The Labor Force, Part I,* 1943, Appendix: Population Schedule, Instructions to Enumerators for Population, p. 297.

10. Clarence D. Long, "The Concept of Unemployment," *Quarterly Journal of Economics,* Vol. 58, No. 1 (November 1942), p. 7.

11. Nuffield College Statement on *Employment Policy and Organization of Industry after the War.* Quoted in W. H. Beveridge, *Full Employment in a Free Society* (New York: W. W. Norton & Co., 1945), p. 18.

12. Alvin H. Hansen, *After the War — Full Employment,* National Resources Planning Board, February 1943, p. 3n.

13. Hansen, p. 125.

14. Beveridge, *Full Employment,* p. 173.

15. It may be argued that one of the essentials for a full employment program is that workers be discouraged from imposing any such substantial limitations upon their availability for work. This turns, however, upon what is "substantial" or, in reality, what is "reasonable." Not to anticipate too much the argument of Chapters VI and VII the answer to that depends largely upon the factors we have been discussing, particularly the state of the labor market. And if the limitations mentioned are not "substantial" or "reasonable" by that criterion, it seems inequitable to penalize the claimant.

16. Erika H. Schoenberg and Paul H. Douglas, "Studies In The Supply Curve of Labor: The Relation In 1929 Between Average Earnings In American Cities and the Proportions Seeking Employment," *Journal of Political Economy,* Vol. 45, No. 1 (February 1937), pp. 45–79.

17. Hansen, *After the War,* p. 3n.

18. *Social Security Bulletin,* Vol. II, No. 2 (February 1939), p. 41. The figures are not available for periods earlier than October 1944 to show the number of claims denied on the issue "able to work and available for work" and their ratio to insured claimants. There is no reason to suppose that before 1941 this ratio was any higher than 2 per cent. Compare this with the percentages given for periods in 1944–1946.

19. See the discussion and cases cited in Chapter VII on the effect of war manpower controls.

20. Michael Polanyi, *Full Employment and Free Trade* (Cambridge: Cambridge University Press, 1945), pp. 100–01.

21. Gertrude Williams, *The Price of Social Security* (New York: Oxford University Press, 1944).

22. Williams, p. 156.

NOTES FOR CHAPTER TWO

1. F. J. Roethlisberger, *Management and Morale* (Cambridge: Harvard University Press, 1946), pp. 22–26; F. J. Roethlisberger and Wm. J. Dickson, *Management and the Worker* (Cambridge: Harvard University Press, 1942), pp. 379–550; Carrie Glasser and Bernard N. Freedman, "Work and Wage Experience of Skilled Cotton Textile Workers," *Monthly Labor Review*, Vol. 63, No. 1 (July 1946), pp. 9, 12–14; John G. Gregory, Bureau of Vocational Counsel, Speech at Canterbury Club, Boston Daily *Globe*, January 27, 1946.

2. Joseph Tiffin, *Industrial Psychology* (New York: Prentice-Hall, Inc., 1946), pp. 4–8.

3. Roethlisberger, p. 23.

4. Ralph Presgrave, *Dynamics of Time Study* (New York: McGraw-Hill, 1945), pp. 144–194.

5. Morris S. Viteles, *Industrial Psychology* (New York: W. W. Norton & Co., Inc., 1932), p. 107.

6. *The Wealth of Nations* (edited from the fifth edition by Edwin Connan; London: Mathuen & Co., 1930), pp. 76–77.

7. "Recent Developments in Earnings in Slaughtering and Meat Packing," *Monthly Labor Review*, Vol. 63, No. 1 (July 1946), p. 53.

8. "Wage Structure of the Electric Light and Power Industry, July, 1945," *Monthly Labor Review*, Vol. 63, No. 3 (September 1946), p. 372.

9. "Wage Structure of the Hosiery Industry, January, 1946," *Monthly Labor Review*, Vol. 63, No. 6 (December 1946), p. 955.

10. Social Security Administration, Bureau of Research and Statistics, *Mobility of Workers in Employment Covered by Old-Age and Survivors Insurance*, Bureau Report No. 14, July 1946, Tables 6 and 9.

11. Carroll Dougherty, *Labor Problems in American Industry* (Boston: Houghton Mifflin Co., 1941), p. 173.

12. Dale Yoder, *Labor Economics and Labor Problems* (New York and London: McGraw-Hill Book Co., 1939), pp. 224, 227; Harry A. Millis and Royal E. Montgomery, *Labor's Progress and Some Basic Labor Problems* (*Economics of Labor*, Vol. I; New York and London: McGraw-Hill Book Co., 1938), pp. 199, 203. See also Emanuel Stein, Jerome Davis, and others, *Labor Problems in America* (New York: Farrar & Rinehart, 1940), p. 38.

13. Paul H. Douglas, *The Theory of Wages* (New York: Macmillan & Co., 1934), pp. 269–314; Erika H. Schoenberg and Paul H. Douglas, "Studies in the Supply Curve of Labor: The Relation in 1929 between Average Earnings in American Cities and the Proportions Seeking Employment," *Journal of Political Economy*, Vol. 45, No. 1 (February 1937), pp. 45–79; Sumner H. Slichter, *Modern Economic Society* (New York: Henry Holt & Co., 1928), pp. 620–629; Millis and Montgomery, pp. 181–188.

14. H. LaRue Frain, "Two Errors in Interpreting Wage Rate," *American Economic Review*, Vol. 19 (September 1929), pp. 378–92; "Wage Levels Between Firms," *American Economic Review*, Vol. 21 (December 1931), pp. 620–35; *An Examination of Earnings in Certain Standard Machine Tool Occupations in Philadelphia* (Philadelphia: University of Pennsylvania Press, 1929), p. 69.

15. Bureau of Labor Statistics, Bulletin No. 775, *Hourly Entrance Rates of Common Laborers in Large Cities, Spring and Summer 1943*.

16. "Wage Structure of the Hosiery Industry" (see note 9 *supra*), pp. 957, 961. For other recent examples: "Wage Structure of the Machine Tool Accessories Industry, January, 1945," *Monthly Labor Review*, Vol. 62, No. 3 (March 1946),

pp. 438–50; "Wage Structure of the Machine Tool Industry, January, 1945," *ibid.,* Vol. 62, No. 6 (June 1946), pp. 933–44; "Wage Structure of the Structural Clay Products Industry, October, 1945," *ibid.,* Vol. 63, No. 2 (August 1946), pp. 210–16; and "Wage Structure of the Electric Light and Power Industry" (see note 8 *supra*).

17. John W. Riegel, *Wage Determination* (Bureau of Industrial Relations, University of Michigan, 1937), pp. 7, 26.

18. *National Labor Relations Board* v. *Jones & Laughlin Steel Corporation,* 301 U.S. 1 (1937). See also *American Steel Foundries* v. *Tri-City Central Trades Council,* 257 U.S. 184 (1921) and the dissenting opinions of Mr. Justice Holmes in *Coppage* v. *Kansas,* Mass. 92, 44 N.E. 1077 (1896).

19. When business declines "union wages drop later and less than non-union. Sometimes union wages do not drop at all." Sumner H. Slichter, "Wage-Price Policy and Employment," *American Economic Review,* Proceedings, Vol. 36, No. 2 (May 1946), p. 306.

What effect has unionization had upon the demand for labor? Has labor paid for unionization in higher wages but a decreased demand for labor? Although no definitive answer can be given, it may be noted: (a) Average hourly earnings in this country rose over 500 per cent and the cost of living less than 140 per cent in the first forty-five years of this century. This would indicate that the demand for labor during this period of rising unionism was strong enough so that wages were more affected by competition than prices. (b) The higher wages that unionism brings, by increasing purchasing power, may help create their own demand for labor.

20. Charles A. Myers and W. Rupert Maclaurin, *The Movement of Factory Workers* (New York: John Wiley & Sons, 1943), p. 41.

21. "Extent of Collective Bargaining and Union Recognition in 1945," *Monthly Labor Review,* Vol. 62, No. 4 (April 1946), pp. 567–572.

22. In *Allen Bradley* v. *Local 3,* 325 U.S. 797 (1945) the New York electrical workers union by its contracts with local manufacturers and contractors was able not only to control workers' access to the New York market but also to keep out-of-town manufacturers and contractors from doing business in New York City.

23. Clyde W. Summers, "Admission Policies of Labor Unions," *Quarterly Journal of Economics,* Vol. 61, No. 1 (November 1946), pp. 66–91.

24. See Professor Richard A. Lester's testimony before a subcommittee of the Senate Committee on Education and Labor, Hearings on S. 1349, 79 Cong., 1 sess., p. 755. Also Riegel, pp. 2, 14, 22.

25. See, for example, *Shipowners Association of th Pacific Coast,* 7 N.L.R.B. 1002, review denied, *A.F. of L.* v. *N.L.R.B.* 308 U.S. 401 Aff. 103 F. (21) 933 (App. D.C.), *Mobil Steamship Assn.,* 8 N.L.R.B. 1297; *Federated Fishing Boats of New England,* 15 N.L.R.B. 1080; *Stevens Coal Co.,* 19 N.L.R.B. 98; *Kausel Foundry Co.,* 28 N.L.R.B. 906; *Alaska Salmon Industry, Ind.,* 33 N.L.R.B. 727; *Washington Metal Trades, Inc.* 43 N.L.R.B. 158; *Monon Stone Co.,* 10 N.L.R.B. 64; *Monterey Sardine Industries, Inc.,* 26 N.L.R.B. 731; *National Dress Manufacturers Assn., Inc.,* 28 N.L.R.B. 386; *Grower-Shipper Vegetable Assn. of Central California,* 43 N.L.R.B. 1389. See also Richard A. Lester and Edward A. Robie, *Wages Under National and Regional Collective Bargaining: Experience in Seven Industries* (Industrial Relations Section, Princeton University, 1946); "Collective Bargaining with Associations and Groups of Employers," *Monthly Labor Review,* Vol. 64, No. 3 (March 1947), pp. 397–410.

26. "Collective Bargaining with Associations and Groups of Employers," p. 26.

NOTES FOR CHAPTER THREE

1. Except where otherwise indicated labor force and population figures given in this chapter are based on the reports and publications of the United States Census Bureau, principally the following: *Population*, Vol. III, The Labor Force, Part I, United States Summary (Washington, 1943); Alba M. Edwards, *Comparative Occupation Statistics For the United States, 1870 to 1940* (Washington, 1943); *Estimated Future Population, By Age and Sex: 1945 to 1980*, Series P–3, No. 15, July 23, 1941; *Population*, Series P–10, No. 21, May 5, 1943; *Monthly Reports on the Labor Force*.

As indicated in the text of this chapter, the 1940 census was the first decennial census to use the "labor force" concept in enumerating employment status. Previous censuses had counted "gainful workers." The "gainful worker" count tended to exclude new workers, those seeking their first jobs; these were included in 1940. In other ways, however, the instructions to enumerators in the earlier censuses were more liberal than in 1940.

In July, 1945, other changes were made in the procedures. Beginning then unpaid family workers who worked more than 15 hours during the week were counted in the labor force. In addition more intensive methods were adopted to elicit from individuals, initially identified as students, housewives, or retired persons, information on any work or work-seeking they may have done. The Census Bureau estimated that these changes increased the July 1945 labor force figures by 1,470,000. The December 8–14, 1946, figures used in the text were probably not affected so much by the changes cited since December features bad weather and is a seasonally low month for agriculture and since the week in question preceded the usual school Christmas vacations. All these factors would tend to reduce materially the work activities of unpaid family workers, students, housewives, and retired persons.

2. *Year Book of Labour Statistics, 1943–44* (Montreal: International Labour Office, 1945), p. 5.

3. *Year Book of Labour Statistics, 1943–44*, p. 92.

4. W. S. Woytinsky, *Internal Migration During The War*, Research and Statistics Letter No. 68, Bureau of Employment Security, Social Security Board, November 27, 1944. The text of this letter (pp. 8, 10) states that New York lost in population during 1930–1940. Table 2, attached to the letter, however, shows a migration gain for New York in 1930–1940 of 382,675.

5. Lester M. Pearlman and Leonard Eskin, "State and Regional Variations in Prospective Labor Supply," *Monthly Labor Review*, Vol. 63, No. 6 (December 1946), pp. 851–871, Table 4, pp. 870–71.

6. Paul H. Landis, *Population Problems* (New York: American Book Co., 1943), p. 425.

7. Lester M. Pearlman, Leonard Eskin, and Edgar E. Poulton, "Nature and Extent of Frictional Unemployment," *Monthly Labor Review*, Vol. 64, No. 1 (January 1947), p. 2.

Charles A. Myers and W. Rupert Maclaurin, *The Movement of Factory Workers* (New York: John Wiley and Sons, 1943), p. 1.

9. In 1941–1943, according to records of the Bureau of Old-Age and Survivors Insurance, between 10.4 and 12.9 per cent of all male workers and from 5.8 to 9.0 per cent of female workers were multi-state workers. Franklin M. Aaronson and Ruth A. Keller, *Mobility of Workers in Employment Covered By Old-Age and Survivors Insurance*, Bureau of Research and Statistics, Bureau Report No. 14 (Washington, D.C.: July 1946), p. 26, Table 14.

10. Nathan Weinberg, "Workers' Experiences During First Phase of Reconversion," *Monthly Labor Review*, Vol. 62, No. 5 (May 1946), p. 717.

11. Ida C. Merriam and Elizabeth Bliss McClelland, "Employment Characteristics of Interstate Workers in Covered Employment in 1938," *Social Security Bulletin*, Vol. 4, No. 12 (December 1941), pp. 9, 10, 11. See also Aaronson and Keller, pp. 9–11 for 1939–1943.

12. Everette B. Harris, "Wartime Labor Force of St. Paul Propeller Plant," *Monthly Labor Review*, Vol. 62, No. 1 (January 1946), p. 98.

13. *Manpower For the Construction of Camp Albert H. Blanding*, Department of Research and Statistics, Florida Industrial Commission, September 1941, p. 15.

14. Petrim Sorokin, *Social Mobility* (New York: Harper & Bros., 1927), pp. 42, 46, 47.

15. Gladys L. Palmer, "The Mobility of Weavers in Three Textile Centers," *Quarterly Journal of Economics*, Vol. 55 (May 1941), pp. 460–485.

16. Anne Bezanson, et al., *Four Years of Labor Mobility: A Study of Labor Turnover In a Group of Selected Plants in Philadelphia, 1921–24*, Issued as Supplement Vol. 119, *Annals of the American Academy of Political and Social Science*, May 1925.

17. Myers and Maclaurin, p. 72.

18. Carrie Glasser and Bernard N. Freedman, "Work and Wage Experience of Skilled Cotton Textile Workers," *Monthly Labor Review*, Vol. 63, No. 1 (July 1946), pp. 8–15.

19. Seymour L. Wolfbein, *The Decline of a Cotton Textile City: A Study of New Bedford* (New York: Columbia University Press, 1944), pp. 38–55.

20. Tressa B. Manley, "Jack of All Trades — Master of Most," *Employment Service News*, Vol. 5, No. 4 (April 1938), pp. 12–13.

21. *Manpower for the Construction of Camp Albert H. Blanding*, p. 44.

22. Jacob Loft, *The Printing Trades* (New York: Farrar & Rinehart, 1944), p. 39.

23. Elizabeth W. Gilboy, *Applicants for Work Relief* (Cambridge: Harvard University Press, 1940), pp. 158–60.

24. Harold W. Metz, *Labor Policy of the Federal Government* (Washington, D.C.: Brookings Institution, 1945), p. 140.

25. Paul T. David, *Barriers to Youth Employment*, American Council on Education, 1942, p. 78.

26. Ralph Altman, "Defense Trainees and Availability for Work," *Social Security Bulletin*, Vol. 6, No. 7 (July 1943), pp. 25–30; Marvin Bloom, et al., "Unemployment Insurance and the Retraining of Unemployed Workers," *Social Security Bulletin*, Vol. 9, No. 4 (April 1946), pp. 16–20.

27. Olga S. Halsey, "Claimants Awaiting Recall — Their Special Problems of Availability and Suitability of Work," *Social Security Bulletin*, Vol. 9, No. 10 (October 1946), pp. 8–15.

NOTES FOR CHAPTER FOUR

1. *Monthly Labor Review* issues give Bureau of Labor Statistics labor-turnover figures based on a sample of manufacturing establishments. The total annual quit figures (per 100 employees) are 1943 — 62.3; 1944 — 61.0; 1945 — 60.9; 1946 — 51.5; 1947 — 40.7. No suggestion is here intended that the quit rate is determined primarily by methods of employee selection. It is affected by other internal plant conditions such as training, grievance procedures, and working conditions. The general business level, however, is probably the most potent determinant of the quit rate. Thus the 1939 annual rate was 9.5. But in 1920 the quit rate was over 10 per cent per month, a level never reached in World War II.

2. Emily H. Huntington, *Doors to Jobs: A Study of the Organization of the Labor Market in California* (Berkeley and Los Angeles: University of California Press, 1942), p. 43.

3. E. Wight Bakke, *The Unemployed Worker* (New Haven: Yale University Press, 1940), p. 235.

4. Dorothea DeSchweinitz, *How Workers Find Jobs: A Study of Four Thousand Hosiery Workers in Philadelphia* (Philadelphia: University of Pennsylvania Press, 1932), Table 15, p. 89.

5. Bakke, p. 231.

6. Charles A. Myers and W. Rupert Maclaurin, *The Movement of Factory Workers* (New York: Technology Press, 1943), Table 7, p. 47.

7. Projecting the manufacturing accession rate reported by the Bureau of Labor Statistics to the manufacturing employment figure will produce the estimated number of persons hired in manufacturing. A ratio may then be obtained between the manufacturing placements reported by the employment service and the derived figure of manufacturing work force accessions. This percentage was 18.4 in 1946 and 19.3 in 1947.

If it is assumed that all persons laid off in manufacturing during the year were rehired, the percentage may be adjusted by subtracting the layoff rate from the accession rate. This will yield a higher ratio of manufacturing placements to manufacturing work-force accessions — 22.5 per cent in 1946, 23.7 per cent in 1947.

(Manufacturing accession and layoff rates and employment figures as reported in *Monthly Labor Review* issues; manufacturing placements by the employment service as reported in issues of *The Labor Market*.)

8. Paul H. Douglas and Aaron Director, *The Problem of Unemployment* (New York: Macmillan Co., 1934), p. 266.

9. In *Adams* v. *Tanner*, 244 U.S. 590 (1917), the Court held that it was unconstitutional for the state of Washington to prohibit charging a fee for a job and that the private employment agency was a useful and legitimate business which could be regulated but not suppressed. In 1928, however, in *Ribnik* v. *McBride*, limits were set upon this regulatory power of the states, when the Supreme Court decided that New Jersey might not constitutionally regulate the employment agency fees to be charged employers and employees. The effect of this decision was finally wiped out in 1941 by the Court's opinion in *Olsen* v. *Nebraska*, 313 U.S. 862, when the Nebraska statute fixing the fees to be charged by employment agencies was upheld as constitutional.

10. A notable instance was the National Metal Trades Association whose constitution required each of the branches (27 in 1937) to maintain an employment bureau. Other cases are reported in *Industrial Espionage*, Senate Report No. 46, part 3, 75 Cong., 2 sess., 1937, and *Labor Policies of Employers' Associations*, Senate Report No. 6, part 4, 76 Cong., 1 sess., 1939.

11. Gladys L. Palmer, *The Search for Work in Philadelphia, 1932–36* (Philadelphia: WPA National Research Project, May 1939), pp. 41–43.

12. New York State Division of Placement and Unemployment Insurance, *Employment Review*, Vol. 2, No. 7 (July 1940), p. 300; Vol. 3, No. 5 (May 1941), pp. 220–222; Vol. 3, No. 8 (August 1941), p. 388.

13. Raymond C. Atkinson, Louise C. Odencrantz, and Ben Deming, *Public Employment Service in the United States* (Chicago: Public Administration Service, 1932), p. 40.

14. See E. Wight Bakke, "Public Employment Offices and Unemployment Insurance Systems: Some Hazards in Their Association," *Employment Service News*, Vol. 2, No. 10 (October 1935), p. 5; R. C. Atkinson, "The Employment Service and Unemployment Compensation Administration," *ibid.*, Vol. 4, No. 10 (October 1937), pp. 3, 4; Edgar B. Young, "Functional Relationship Between

Employment Service and Unemployment Compensation," *ibid.*, Vol. 5, No. 9 (September 1938), p. 5.

15. Leo McCarthy, "Supply and Demand of Applicants in St. Louis," *Employment Service News*, Vol. 2, No. 7 (July 1935), pp. 9–10.

16. John J. Corson, *Providence Journal,* November 13, 1946.

In mid-December 1945 the California employment offices had 1 job opening for every 4.4 benefit claimants (civilian and veteran). The 3 largest occupational groups among the California claimants were the skilled men workers, semi-skilled women, and unskilled women workers. For the first group, there was 1 job opening for every 3.4 claimants; for the second and third groups there was 1 reported opening for every 13 claimants. There were 23 skilled women workers for every job opening. Only in the case of women claimants registered for service jobs and clerical and sales jobs were there fewer than 2 claimants for each reported opening. *Characteristics of Claimants and Job Openings in Mid-December 1945,* Research Series No. 15, California Department of Employment, Report 383 #1, May 16, 1946, pp. 2–8, Reference Table No. 1.

17. Unemployment Compensation Commission of North Carolina, Bureau of Research and Statistics, *Special Survey of Veterans Readjustment Allowances for Claimants Who Have Been Unemployed for 20 or More Consecutive Weeks* (processed) Sept. 14, 1946, pp. 2–3.

18. Atkinson, Odencrantz, and Deming, p. 42.

19. It should be emphasized that these are national estimates. There was considerable variation among the states. The New Jersey Unemployment Compensation Commission has estimated that factory placements by the New Jersey employment service constituted the following percentages of accessions: 1942—11.9; 1943—20.7; 1944—27.6; 1945—22.3; 1946—8.7. See *Tenth Annual Report of the Unemployment Compensation Commission, New Jersey,* Calendar Year 1946, p. 68.

20. Percentages for 1933–34 and 1935–36 based on Atkinson, Odencrantz, and Deming, Table 5, p. 35. Percentages for October–December, 1945, and the years 1946 and 1947 derived from *The Labor Market.*

21. D. V. Varley and Molly H. Wilson, "An Analysis of Cancelled Openings," *Employment Service News,* Vol. 3, No. 2 (December 1936), pp. 5–10.

22. *Principles Underlying the Prevailing Conditions of Work Standard,* Unemployment Compensation Program Letter No. 130, Bureau of Employment Security, Jan. 6, 1947.

23. *Veterans Counselling Survey, New York City Area, September 23 — November 1, 1946,* New York State Employment Service (processed, undated, circ. Feb. 17, 1947).

24. Jimmie M. Morris, "My Job Is Order-Taking," *Employment Service Review,* Vol. 13, No. 6 (June 1946), p. 9.

25. Richard S. Alkire, "Reinterviewing Meant Recoding," *Employment Service Review,* Vol. 14, No. 1 (January 1947), p. 19.

26. *Report of the New York State Advisory Council on Placement and Unemployment Insurance for the Year 1947,* Jan. 30, 1948, pp. 14–17.

NOTES FOR CHAPTER FIVE

1. Other usual eligibility conditions, not directly connected with labor-force attachment, are: unemployment, filing a claim, serving a waiting period.

2. Except where otherwise indicated, the reference is to employment in 20 weeks. Percentages of covered workers mentioned in text refer to average monthly employment under state unemployment compensation in 1948.

Eight-worker minimum: Alabama, Colorado, Florida (or calendar quarter payroll of $5000 or more), Georgia, Indiana, Iowa (in 15 weeks), Kansas (also 25 or more workers in any one week during current or preceding calendar year), Maine, Michigan, Mississippi, Missouri, Nebraska (or calendar quarter pay roll of $10,000 or more), North Carolina, North Dakota, Oklahoma, South Carolina, South Dakota, Tennessee, Texas, Vermont, Virginia, West Virginia.

Four-worker minimum: Connecticut (in 13 weeks), Kentucky (8 workers in 20 weeks, or wages of at least $50 to each of 4 or more workers during each of 3 calendar quarters), Louisiana, New Hampshire, New Jersey, New York (in 15 days), Oregon (calendar quarter pay roll of $500 or more and four workers on any one day in each of six separate weeks during such quarter), Rhode Island.

One-worker minimum: Alaska (at any time), Arkansas (in 10 days), California (1 worker at any time and calendar quarter wages over $100), Delaware, District of Columbia (at any time), Hawaii (1 worker at any time), Idaho (coverage based solely on size of pay roll — $75 in calendar quarter), Maryland (at any time), Massachusetts, Minnesota, Montana (or calendar quarter pay roll over $500), Nevada (and calendar quarter pay roll of $225 or more), Pennsylvania (at any time), Utah (coverage based solely on size of pay roll — $140 in calendar quarter), Washington (at any time), Wyoming (and $150 calendar quarter pay roll, or calendar year wages of $500).

Other minimums: Two states are on a 6-worker basis: Illinois and Wisconsin (6 or more workers in 18 weeks or calender quarter wages of over $10,000 or, where employer records do not permit accurate count, total annual payroll of $6,000).

Two states are on a three-worker basis: Arizona and Ohio (three or more workers at any time). In New Mexico an employer is covered if he had a calendar quarter pay roll of $450 or more or if he had two or more workers within thirteen weeks.

3. *Unemployment Insurance Abstract:* Program Statistics and Legal Provisions 1937–47 (Supplement to *Employment Security Activities,* Vol. 3, No. 11 [November 1947]), Table 7, p. 14.

4. Colorado, Idaho, Illinois, Maine, Maryland, Massachusetts, New Hampshire, New York, North Carolina, Oregon, Rhode Island, Vermont, Virginia, Washington. Thirteen of these states (all but North Carolina) also use a uniform benefit year.

5. In the thirteen states with uniform benefit year, uniform beginning and ending dates are fixed by law for the one-year period during which workers may draw benefits against wage credits of a given base period. All uniform-benefit-year states also use a uniform base period.

6. Base-period wages required to qualify for minimum benefits:

$ 20 — Missouri (including wages in three quarters of eight-quarter base period)

90 — Mississippi

100 — Georgia (including $48 in one quarter and wages in two quarters), Iowa, Kansas ($100 in two quarters or $200 in one quarter), Rhode Island, Virginia

112.14 — Michigan (14 weeks of employment, during the one-year period preceding the benefit year, each at average weekly wage of more than $8.)

120 — Alabama (including over $75 in one quarter), Oklahoma

125 — South Dakota (including $60 in one quarter), Tennessee (including $50 in one quarter)

140 — North Dakota

150 — Alaska, Arizona (including wages in two quarters), District of Colum-

bia, Florida (including wages in two quarters), Hawaii, Louisiana, Massachusetts, New Mexico (including $78 in one quarter), South Carolina (including $100 in one quarter)

175 — Wyoming (including $70 in one quarter)
180 — Maryland (including $156 in one quarter), Vermont (including $50 in one quarter)
200 — New Hampshire, North Carolina, Texas (including wages in two quarters)
210 — Arkansas, Colorado, Delaware ($200 if 75 per cent of wages are seasonal), Montana
240 — Connecticut (including wages in two quarters), Ohio (and 14 weeks of employment), Pennsylvania
250 — Idaho (including wages in two quarters and $150 in one quarter), Indiana (including $150 in last two quarters)
270 — New Jersey
300 — California, Illinois, Kentucky, Maine, Minnesota, Nebraska, Nevada, New York (including $100 in one quarter), West Virginia
400 — Oregon
600 — Washington

Utah requires minimum base period wages equal to 16 per cent of the state's average annual wage and 19 weeks of employment. Wisconsin requires 14 weeks of employment. Employer's account is liable only if the average weekly wage equalled $12.

7. For limitations on benefit rights of seasonal workers, see Chapter X.

8. *Elimination of Wage Records From Unemployment Insurance Administration,* Unemployment Compensation Program Letter No. 126, Oct. 21, 1946, Attachment, "Plan I — A Benefit Formula and Reporting System Based Upon Recent Average Weekly Wages," p. 6.

Kidd and Wilson ("Employment and Earnings as Tests of Eligibility for Unemployment Benefits in South Carolina," *Social Security Bulletin,* Vol. 4, No. 5 [May 1941], p. 12), after examining the wage records of over twelve thousand South Carolina claimants, concluded that "virtually the same individuals were made ineligible by requirements stated as a multiple of the weekly benefit amount, as a flat dollar amount, or as weeks of employment . . ." Because of the greater fluctuation of earnings (rather than employment), the earnings requirement became more difficult to meet in less prosperous periods. Apparently they did not try to measure the effects of an employment test in terms of days of employment. They cast doubt upon the adequacy of a one-year base period and pointed to the length of the base period as more important in eligibility qualification than whether or not an earnings or time test is used.

9. Assuming that the average weekly wage is one-sixth the high quarter wages required for eligibility, in the following five states the minimum benefit amount is greater than average weekly wage of claimants who barely qualify: Alaska, Iowa, Oklahoma, Rhode Island, and Virginia. An additional twenty states are added to this list if it is assumed that the average weekly wage is one-eighth the required high quarter wage: Arizona, Arkansas, California, Colorado, Connecticut, Delaware, District of Columbia, Florida, Hawaii, Illinois, Louisiana, Massachusetts, Minnesota, Mississippi, Montana, New Jersey, North Dakota, Oregon, Pennsylvania, Texas.

10. Connecticut, District of Columbia, Idaho, Illinois, Indiana, Louisiana, Missouri, Ohio, Pennsylvania, Rhode Island, South Carolina, Utah, Wisconsin.

11. In Michigan benefits may be extended beyond the maximum 20 weeks for certain vocational trainees.

12. States and weeks: Arizona, 12; Georgia, 16; Hawaii, 20; Kentucky, 22; Maine, 20; Mississippi, 16; Montana, 18; New Hampshire, 23; New York, 26;

North Carolina, 20; North Dakota, 20; South Carolina, 18; Tennessee, 20; Vermont, 20; West Virginia, 23.

13. See note 4, *supra*.

14. *State Experience With Uniform Benefit Years and Base Periods,* Research and Statistics Letter No. 55, Bureau of Employment Security, July 3, 1944; also, under same title, Ruth Reticker and Margaret Dahm, *Social Security Bulletin,* Vol. 7, No. 6 (June 1944), pp. 17-24.

15. Assuming base period is first four of last five completed calendar quarters preceding the benefit year.

16. François Lafitte, *Britain's Way to Social Security* (London: Pilot Press, 1945), p. 23 (original italics).

17. I recognize that this is more than is done initially in the ordinary case in most offices. Partly this is because the availability test is of a continuing character.

18. In fact, most state unemployment compensation laws go beyond the federally required protection and say that "no work shall be deemed suitable and benefits shall not be denied" to any otherwise eligible worker for refusing to accept new work which violates these standards.

19. U.S. Code, Title 38, Chapter 11C, Sec. 696a (d) (2). The third provision, however, was operative as a result of the stipulation in the act that the state statutory standards should apply in determining what work was suitable.

20. U.S. Code, Title 45, Chapter 11, Sec. 354(c), especially (ii), (iv) and (v).

21. Delaware, Sec. 5(c)(1)(A); Ohio, Sec. 1345–6e(1). In both laws, by specific provision in Delaware and by court interpretation in Ohio, the "condition of being employed" must be one that is required by the employer.

22. Sec. 593.2(c).

23. Delaware, Sec. 5(c)(1)(C); Ohio, Sec. 1345–6e(3).

24. Sec. 593.2(d). This section also states "that no benefits shall be payable to a claimant who refuses to accept an offer of employment for which he is reasonably fitted by training and experience, whatever be the cause, if the circumstances show that such claimant has withdrawn temporarily or permanently from the labor market." The interpretation of this proviso has been that the finding that the claimant has withdrawn from the labor market must be based upon other evidence than his refusal or unwillingness to accept work that comes within the proscriptions of the law — those based upon Section 1603(a)(5) of the Internal Revenue Code and the specific additional proscriptions of the New York statute.

25. Sec. 341.100(1)(d).

26. Delaware, Sec. 5(c); New York, Sec. 593.2; Wisconsin, Sec. 108.04 (8)(a).

27. California, Sec. 13(a); Connecticut, Sec. 7508(1),

28. Sec. 29(1)(a).

29. See Appendix Table B.

30. Sec. 4(t). Other "definitions" of suitable work appear in the laws of California, Connecticut, Michigan and Rhode Island. See footnotes to Appendix Table B.

31. *Issues in Social Security,* Report by the Social Security Technical Staff to the United States Congress, House of Representatives, Ways and Means Committee, Washington, 1946, pp. 386, 709-10.

NOTES FOR CHAPTER SIX

1. Unemployment Compensation Interpretation Service, *Benefit Decisions of the British Umpire,* Benefit Series, General Supplement No. 1, June 1938.

2. *Principles Underlying Disqualification for Benefits in Unemployment Com-*

pensation: Research and Statistics Memorandum No. 32 (Refusal to Accept Work), August 1938, and Employment Security Memorandum No. 3 (Voluntary Leaving and Misconduct), November 1939.

3. Unemployment Compensation Program Letter No. 103, Dec. 10, 1945.

4. Louise F. Freeman, "Able to Work and Available For Work," *Yale Law Journal,* Vol. 55, No. 1, pp. 123–134.

5. *Reger* v. *Administrator* 46 A.(2d)844 (1946), 10780–Conn. Ct.D., *Ben. Ser.,* Vol. 9, No. 9 quotes and relies upon Mrs. Freeman's article. *Bliley Electric Co.* v. *U.C. Board of Review,* 45 A.(2d)898, 10754 Pa. Ct.D., *Ben. Ser.,* Vol. 9, No. 8, reveals (but without citation) the influence of the bureau's statement.

6. Melville J. Herskovits, *The Economic Life of Primitive Peoples* (New York and London: Knopf, 1940). "Primitive peoples, like ourselves, do as much work as they feel they must to meet the basic demands of getting a living, plus as much more as they desire to achieve any given end not encompassed by these basic demands . . ." (p. 78). Of work incentives in nonmachine societies: "One works because one must; because every one else works; because it is one's tradition to work." (pp. 97–98).

7. *Principles of Political Economy,* edited by J. W. Ashley (London: Longmans, Green & Co., 1909), p. 105n. Also see: Thorstein Veblen, "The Instinct of Workmanship and the Irksomeness of Labor," pp. 78–96 in *Essays In Our Changing Order* (New York: Viking Press, 1934).

8. Erich Fromm, *Escape From Freedom* (New York: Farrar, 1941).

9. "Unemployment Insurance and The Cost of Basic Necessities," Supplement to *Employment Security Activities,* March 1946.

10. "The Weekly Benefit Amount in Relation to Changing Prices and Wages," Supplement to *Employment Security Activities,* February 1948, p. 3.

11. There were 8.5 million insured claims in each of the two years, 1946 and 1947. In 1946, there were 134,000 work refusal disqualifications (1.6 per cent), and 113,000 in 1947 (1.3 per cent). During 1946, there were 589,000 determinations of unavailability or inability to work (6.9 per cent) and 565,000 (6.7 per cent) in 1947. The latter include many bona fide registrations for work by claimants who were later held unable to work. In both years more than 90 per cent evidently registered in good faith.

12. *Bliley,* etc., *supra,* note 5. Also see *Brilhart Unemployment Compensation Case,* 49 A.(2d)260 (1946); *Hassey* v. *U.C. Board,* 56 A.(2d)400 (1948), 12539–Pa. Ct.D., *Ben. Ser.,* Vol. 11, No. 6.

13. *Benefit Series:* 11451–Calif. R, Vol. 10, No. 5; 8877–Calif. AG, Vol. 7, No. 11; 825–Conn. R, Vol. 2, No. 2; *Goodman* v. *Administrator,* Superior Court, New Haven County, Connecticut, June 23, 1947, 12180–Conn. Ct.D., Vol. 11, No. 2; 12186–Del. A, Vol. 11, No. 2; 7988–Fla. A, Vol. 6, No. 6; 8889–Fla. A, Vol. 7, No. 11 (but special circumstances may cast doubt on genuineness of claimant's presence in the labor market); 9325–Ind. A, Vol. 8, No. 4 (presumption not rebutted by claimant's delay in reporting to United States Civil Service Commission for work that did not actually exist); 8026–Me. A, Vol. 6, No. 6; 5097–Mich. A, Vol. 4, No. 1 (although the claimant was disqualified for refusing to consider an offer of work, because she wanted to wait for her regular employer to recall her from a lay off); 7315–Mo. A, Vol. 5, No. 6 (although the claimant while on a temporary lay off went to a summer resort); 6511–Nev. R, Vol. 4, No. 10; 3591–N. Dak. A, Vol. 3, No. 6 (although claimant had quit work and moved to Minnesota to live with her hubsand and the former employer stated his opinion that she was not seeking work); 12853–Ohio R, Vol. 11, No. 10; 7042–Okla. A, Vol. 5, No. 2; 9457–Tenn. A, Vol. 8, No. 5 (despite school teacher claimant's intention to go back to her teaching job in the fall).

This is part of a larger presumption of the claimant's eligibility. See *Clinton* v. *Hake,* 206 S.W.(2d)887 (1947), 12634–Tenn. Ct.D., *Ben. Ser.,* Vol. 11, No. 7;

Boynton Cab v. *Geise*, 296 N.W. 630 (1941), 6312–Wis. Ct.D., *Ben. Ser.*, Vol. 4, No. 8; *Aragon* v. *U.C.C.*, 149 F.(2d)447 (1945) (C.C.A.9th), 9750–Fed. Ct.D., *Ben. Ser.*, Vol. 8, No. 9 reversed on other grounds, 67 Sup. Ct. 245, 91 L.Ed.143 (1946).

14. 11210–Ind. A, *Ben. Ser.*, Vol. 10, No. 2.

15. New York, RA–U–420–46, unp., Mar. 19, 1947.

16. Selected Decisions Given by the Umpire, Case No. 11161/30, Sept. 10, 1930.

17. 5638–Kans. A, *Ben. Ser.*, Vol. 4, No. 4. See also in *Benefit Series:* 6818–N.Dak. A, Vol. 4, No. 12; 6820–S.Car., Vol. 4, No. 12.

18. 5208–S.Car. A, *Ben. Ser.*, Vol. 4, No. 2.

19. 27 S.E.(2d)743 (1943), 8418–Ga. Ct.D., *Ben. Ser.*, Vol. 7, No. 3. See allso *Hunter* v. *Miller*, 27 N.W.(2d)638 (Neb.) (1947).

20. 8621–Ga., *Ben. Ser.*, Vol. 7, No. 7.

21. *Haynes* v. *U.C. Commission*, 183 S.W.(2d)77 (1944), 9246–Mo. Ct.D., *Ben. Ser.*, Vol. 8, No. 3. This quoted statement is a curious compound of three separate views. The first sentence, in the light of the entire opinion, is the court's real conclusion, that is, that the claimant must present affirmative and preponderant evidence to justify a finding that he is available for work. The second sentence is based on a generally accepted rule of administrative law: An administrative body or officer cannot act until it finds that the statutory conditions exist that are required for its action. The first clause of the third sentence follows Wigmore's language. It would suggest that, although no affirmative duty rests upon the claimant to put forth evidence of his availability, when he fails in this respect he assumes the risk of not convincing the commission of his availability. The second clause of that sentence denies that suggestion and reverts to the first sentence.

In support of its position the court cited *Queener* v. *Magnet Mills* (167 S.W.(2d)1 (1942), 8096–Tenn. Ct.D., *Ben. Ser.*, Vol. 6, No. 8). This Tennessee decision has little bearing upon the point for which it was cited. It was a labor dispute in which the issue was whether or not certain claimants came within the exceptions to the disqualification. Under the language of the Tennessee Statute the disqualification did not apply "if it is shown to the satisfaction of the Commissioner" that the claimants met the exceptions. The Tennessee court said, "By the force of the language used, the burden is on the claimants for compensation to bring themselves within the exceptions . . ." The Missouri law, at the time of the Haynes case, stated: "An unemployed individual shall be eligible to receive benefits . . . only if the commissioner finds" that he is available for work. In any case it is doubtful that even the Tennessee language quoted justifies the conclusion reached. Cf. *Toplis and Harding, Inc.* v. *Murphy*, 51 N.E.(2d)182 (1944), 8050–Ill. Ct.D., *Ben. Ser.*, Vol. 6, No. 7.

22. *Copeland* v. *Employment Security Commission*, 172 P.(2d)420 (1946), 10751–Okla. Ct.D., *Ben. Ser.*, Vol. 9, No. 8; *Clinton* v. *Hake, supra*, note 13; *Reese* v. *Hake*, 199 S.W.(2d)569 (1947) (Tenn.); *Jacobs* v. *Office of U.C. and Placement*, 179 P.(2d)707 (1947), 11832–Wash. Ct.D., *Ben. Ser.*, Vol. 10, No. 9; *Dwyer* v. *Appeal Board*, 32 N.W.(2d)434 (1948), 12903–Mich. Ct.D., *Ben. Ser.*, Vol. 11, No. 11 states a more careful view of burden of proof.

23. *Benefit Series: Dept. of Industrial Relations* v. *Tomlinson* 36 So.(2d)406 (1948), 12943–Ala. Ct.D., Vol. 11, No. 12; *Loew's, Inc.* v. *California E.S. Commission*, 172 P.(2d)938 (1946), 11689–Calif. Ct.D., Vol. 10, No. 8; 8808–Colo. A, Vol. 7, No. 10; *Vassallo* v. *Administrator*, Super. Ct., Fairfield Co., Conn., July 19, 1946, 11103–Conn. Ct.D., Vol. 10, No. 1; 10264–Md. R, Vol. 9, No. 2; *Foston* v. *Michigan U.C. Commission*, Circuit Court, Wayne County, Nov. 14, 1947, 12366–Mich. Ct.D., Vol. 11, No. 4; *Hunter* v. *Miller, supra*, note 19; *Kontner* v. *U.C. Board*, 76 N.E.(2d)611 (1947), 12914–Ohio Ct.D., Vol. 11, No. 11; Oregon U.C. Commission, *Manual of Precedents*, April 1946, Sec. 5230.

24. 11243–Nebr. R, *Ben. Ser.*, Vol. 10, No. 2.

25. 10311–Calif. R, *Ben. Ser.*, Vol. 9, No. 3.

26. *Dallas Fuel Co.* v. *Horn,* 300 N.W. 303 (1941), 7162–Iowa Ct.D., *Ben. Ser.*, Vol. 5, No. 4; *Craig* v. *U.C. Commissioner,* 121 P.(2d)303 (1942), 7268–Kans. Ct.D., *Ben. Ser.*, Vol. 5, No. 5; *Applegate* v. *Michigan U.C.C.,* Circuit Court, Wayne County, Docket No. 222, 303, Nov. 27, 1941, 7155–Mich. Ct.D., *Ben. Ser.*, Vol. 5, No. 4; *Berkowitz* v. *Weiss,* Circuit Court, Wayne County, Docket No. 221, 365, July 25, 1942, 7661–Mich. Ct.D., *Ben. Ser.*, Vol. 5, No. 11; *Mississippi U.C. Com.* v. *Avent,* 4 So.(2d)296 (1941), 6992–Miss. Ct.D., *Ben. Ser.*, Vol. 5, No. 2; *Meyer & Co.* v. *U.C.C.,* 152 S.W.(2d)184 (1941), 6614–Mo. Ct.D., *Ben. Ser.*, Vol. 4, No. 11; *Hartwig-Deschinger Realty Co.* v. *U.C.C.,* 168 S.W.(2d)78 (1943), 7605–Mo. Ct.D., *Ben. Ser.*, Vol. 5, No. 10; *Kellogg* v. *Murphy,* 164 S.W.(2d)285 (1942), 7751–Mo. Ct.D., *Ben. Ser.*, Vol. 6, No. 1; *S.S. Kresge Co.* v. *U.C.C.,* 162 SW(2d)838 (1942), 8342–Mo. Ct.D., *Ben. Ser.*, Vol. 7, No. 1; *Matter of Morton,* 30 N.E.(2d)369 (1940), 6421–N.Y. Ct.D., *Ben. Ser.*, Vol. 4, No. 9; *Matter of Electrolux Corp.,* 43 N.E.(2d)480 (1942), 7662–N.Y. Ct.D., *Ben. Ser.*, Vol. 5, No. 11; *Layman* v. *Oreg. U.C.C.,* 117 Pac.(2d)974 (1941), 7108–Oreg. Ct.D., *Ben. Ser.*, Vol. 5, No. 3; *Rahontis* v. *U.C.C.,* 136 P.(2d)426 (1943), 8263–Oreg. Ct.D., *Ben. Ser.*, Vol. 6, No. 12; *Leinbach Co.* v. *Board of Review,* 22 A.(2d)57 (1941), 6856–Pa. Ct.D., *Ben. Ser.*, Vol. 5, No. 1; *Iron Workers Union* v. *Ind. Comm.,* 139 P.(2d)208 (1943), 8321–Utah Ct.D., *Ben. Ser.*, Vol. 7, No. 1.

27. *Hagadone* v. *Kirkpatrick,* 154 P.(2d)181 (1944), 9580–Idaho Ct.D., *Ben. Ser.*, Vol. 8, No. 7. See also *Dwyer* v. *Appeal Board, supra,* note 22.

28. *Garcia* v. *Employment Stabilization Commission,* 161 P.(2d)972 (1945), 10241–Calif. Ct.D., *Ben. Ser.*, Vol. 9, No. 2. But see *Loew's Inc.* v. *Calif. E.S. Commission, supra,* note 23.

29. Alabama, Maine, Massachusetts, Michigan, Ohio, Washington, West Virginia. See Table 3.

30. *Garcia* v. *Employment Security Commission, supra,* note 28; *Reger* v. *Administrator, supra,* note 5; 10783–Fla. R, *Ben. Ser.*, Vol. 9, No. 9; Georgia, BR–436 (Nov. 20, 1946), unp.; *Hagadone* v. *Kirkpatrick, supra,* note 27; Indiana, 46–R–114 (Jan. 21, 1947), unp.; 10337–Kans. A, *Ben. Ser.*, Vol. 9, No. 3; *Berthiaume* v. *Director,* 15 N.W.(2d)115 (1944), 8909–Minn. Ct.D., *Ben. Ser.*, Vol. 7, No. 11; 11156–Miss. A, *Ben. Ser.*, Vol. 10, No. 1; 10741–Nebr. R, *Ben. Ser.*, Vol. 9, No. 8; *Hallahan* v. *Riley,* 45 A.(2d)886 (1946), 10819–N.H. Ct.D., *Ben. Ser.*, Vol. 9, No. 9; *W. T. Grant Co.* v. *Board of Review,* 29 A.(2d)858 (1942), 8160–N.J. Ct.D., *Ben. Ser.*, Vol. 6, No. 10; *Leonard* v. *U.C. Board of Review,* 75 N.E.(2d)567 (1947), 12461–Ohio Ct.D., *Ben. Ser.*, Vol. 11, No. 5; Oregon U.C. Commission, *Manual of Precedents,* April 1946, Sec. 5240.

31. *Principles Underlying the Suitable-Work Disqualification* (U.C. Program Letter No. 101, Bureau of Employment Security, Nov. 26, 1945) at no point suggests a definition.

32. *Principles Underlying the Suitable-Work Disqualification,* p. 12; Arthur W. Menard, "Refusal of Suitable Work," *Yale Law Journal,* Vol. 55, No. 1 (December 1945), pp. 138n., 147; "Issues Involved in Decisions on Disputed Claims For Unemployment Benefits," *Social Security Yearbook,* 1940, p. 41.

33. 8041–Conn. R, *Ben. Ser.*, Vol. 8, No. 1.

34. *Garcia* v. *Employment Security Commission, supra,* note 28; but see 12339–Calif. R, *Ben. Ser.*, Vol. 11, No. 4, in which the California Appeal Board gave this language the effect of the Grant case doctrine. See discussion of "Amount of Work" in this chapter. *Reger* v. *Administrator, supra,* note 5; 8889–Fla. A, *Ben. Ser.*, Vol. 7, No. 11; Florida Board of Review, B–R–193 (unp. Jan. 31, 1946); 10524–Fla. V, *Ben. Ser.*, Vol. 9, No. 6, aff. by VU–6–U; *Hagadone* v.

Kirkpatrick, supra, note 27; 10713–Ill. R, *Ben. Ser.,* Vol. 9, No. 8; 12109–Kans. R, Vol. 11, No. 1 (omits "suitable"); 8421–Miss. R, *Ben. Ser.,* Vol. 7, No. 3; 11156–Miss. A, *Ben. Ser.,* Vol. 10, No. 1; *Muraski* v. *Board,* 56 A.(2d)713 (1948), 12608–N.J. Ct.D., *Ben. Ser.,* Vol. 11, No. 7; *Leonard* v. *U.C. Board, supra,* note 30. In the Reger case, the Connecticut Supreme Court quoted this sentence from Mrs. Freeman ("Able to Work and Available for Work," p. 124) : "The availability requirement is said to be satisfied when an individual is willing, able and ready to accept suitable work which he does not have good cause to refuse, that is, when he is genuinely attached to the labor market." As the example given in the text indicates the two clauses may be inconsistent in specific cases.

35. The rule is so qualified in *Principles Underlying Availability For Work.* Also in Ralph Altman and Virginia Lewis, "Limited Availability for Shift Employment," *North Carolina Law Review,* Vol. 22, No. 3 (April 1944), p. 210.

36. *Shorten* v. *U.C. Commissioner,* 10 Conn. Supp. 186 (1941), 7242–Conn. Ct.D., *Ben. Ser.,* Vol. 5, No. 5. Other examples in the *Benefit Series* are: 293–Conn. R, Vol. 1, No. 3 (rubber factory work had affected claimant's health) ; 2692–Oreg. A, Vol. 3, No. 2 (elevator operator with paresis) ; 7309–Fla., Vol. 6, No. 6 (pregnancy) ; 7656–Ark. A, Vol. 5, No. 11 (hernia) ; 10202–Ohio A, Vol. 9, No. 1 (epileptic) ; 10246–Fla. V, Vol. 9, No. 2 (heart and artery condition) ; 10386–N.Dak. V, Vol. 9, No. 3 (spinal arthritis) ; 10901–Nebr. R, Vol. 9, No. 10 (broken jaw, preventing construction laborer from eating solid food; would not therefore accept usual work).

37. Sec. 5240. The Georgia Employment Security Agency, *Manual of Procedures For Claims Taking In Local Employment Offices,* Sec. 1410.0, makes a similar statement.

38. *Dinovellis* v. *Danaher,* 12 Conn. Supp. 122 (1943), 8201–Conn. Ct.D., *Ben. Ser.,* Vol. 6, No. 11; *Schaffnit* v. *Danaher,* 13 Conn. Supp. 101 (1944), 8956–Conn. Ct.D., *Ben. Ser.,* Vol. 7, No. 12; *Foss* v. *Danaher,* Superior Court, New Haven County, Conn., Apr. 17, 1945, 9657–Conn. Ct.D., *Ben. Ser.,* Vol. 8, No. 8; *Carwood Manufacturing Co.* v. *Huiet et al.,* Superior Court, Barrow County, Georgia, Docket No. 1855, June 5, 1943, 8417–Ga. Ct.D., *Ben. Ser.,* Vol. 7, No. 3; *Judson Mills* v. *U.C. Commission,* 28 S.E.(2d)535 (1944), 8525–S.C., Ct.D., *Ben. Ser.,* Vol. 7, No. 5. See also in *Benefit Series:* 7835–Kans. R, Vol. 6, No. 3; 11203–Ga. A, Vol. 10, No. 2; 5001–Miss. R, Vol. 4, No. 1; 10815–Miss. A, Vol. 9, No. 9; 12837–Mo. A, Vol. 11, No. 10; 6511–Nev. R, Vol. 4, No. 10.

39. 10195–N.J. R, *Ben. Ser.,* Vol. 9, No. 1. See also *In re Loeb,* 57 N.Y.S.(2d) 460 (1945), and, in *Benefit Series:* 10784–Fla. V, Vol. 9, No. 9; 11205–Ill. A, Vol. 10, No. 2.

40. *W. T. Grant Co.* v. *Board of Review, supra,* note 30. See also 12339–Calif. R, *Ben. Ser.,* Vol. 11, No. 4.

41. *Bliley Electric Co.* v. *U.C. Board of Review, supra,* note 5.

42. *Principles Underlying Availability For Work,* p. 14 (italics in original). Such a rule was suggested in Altman and Lewis, p. 211.

43. 11032–Ill. R, *Ben. Ser.,* Vol. 9, No. 12.

44. *Mishaw* v. *Fairfield News,* 12 Conn. Supp. 318 (1944), 8571–Conn. Ct.D., *Ben. Ser.,* Vol. 7, No. 6; *Reger* v. *Administrator, supra,* note 5; *Light* v. *Maryland U.C. Board,* Circuit Court, Washington County, Jan. 15, 1948, 12594–Md. Ct.D., Vol. 11, No. 7; *Smith* v. *Murphy,* 46 N.Y. Supp.(2d)774 (1944), 8643–N.Y. Ct.D., *Ben. Ser.,* Vol. 7, No. 7; *Canton Drop Forging & Mfg. Co.* v. *Zaharie,* Common Pleas Court, Stark County, July 7, 1944, 8926–Ohio Ct.D., *Ben. Ser.,* Vol. 7, No. 11. Also in *Benefit Series:* 10312–Calif. R, Vol. 9, No. 3; 7856–Colo. A, Vol. 6, No. 3; 10081–Fla. A, Vol. 8, No. 12; 6486–Ga. R, Vol. 4,

No. 9; 12580–Ill. R, Vol. 11, No. 7; 10008–Kans. A, Vol. 8, No. 11; 10743–N.J. R, Vol. 9, No. 8; 7993–N.Y. R, Vol. 6, No. 6; 9943–Oreg. R, Vol. 8, No. 10; 10487–Pa. R, Vol. 9, No. 4–5; 7428–S.Dak. R, Vol. 5, No. 7.

45. Such is the reasoning behind *Schaffnit* v. *Danaher, supra,* note 38; *Foss* v. *Danaher, supra,* note 38; *Berthiaume* v. *Director, supra,* note 30 (but here the statute required that the claimant be "available for work in his usual trade or occupation or in any other trade or occupation for which he demonstrates he is reasonably fitted and is actually seeking work.") ; *Hallahan* v. *Riley, supra,* note 30. Other examples in the *Benefit Series* are: 9392–Conn. R, Vol. 8, No. 5; 10707–Fla. R, Vol. 9, No. 8; 12099–Idaho A, Vol. 11, No. 1; 10714–Ill. R, Vol. 9, No. 3; 9325–Ind. A, Vol. 8, No. 4; 9151–Kans. A, Vol. 8, No. 2; 12676–Mass. A, Vol. 11, No. 8; 10904–N.J. R, Vol. 9, No. 10; 11005–Wis. R, Vol. 9, No. 11.

46. That considerations such as length of unemployment and work prospects should be guiding criteria in applying the work refusal disqualification has been well developed in *Suitable Work — Recommended Policies on Refusal of Work During Reconversion,* U.C. Program Letter No. 113, Bureau of Employment Security, Feb. 25, 1946. (Also in "Determination of Suitable Work During Reconversion," *Social Security Bulletin,* Vol. 9, No. 2 [February 1946], pp. 17–20). The Illinois Department of Labor's *Explanation of the Policy of the Division of Placement and U.C. With Respect to Refusals of Work During the Reconversion Period,* Aug. 17, 1945, states clearly: "The policy deals solely with the problem of refusal of work and does not in any way affect the application of any of the other principles of eligibility. Thus, whenever an issue arises concerning the readiness of a claimant to undertake full-time suitable work, the policy is inapplicable, and the issue is resolved solely on the basis of already established policy relating to availability for work." (See p. 3, attachment to U.S. Program Letter No. 97, Bureau of Employment Security, Oct. 29, 1945.)

47. See the discussion in Chapter VII. As suggested there, situations may arise where the entire substantial amount of work concept must be sacrificed to pay benefits to involuntarily unemployed workers.

48. The decisions are anything but clear in explaining whether they are based upon the theory of allowing time to explore work possibilities or upon the theory of downgrading as unemployment lengthens and work prospects do not improve. In general, they seem to proceed upon both theories. In addition to the cases cited in note 45, see the following examples: *Vassallo* v. *Administrator, supra,* note 23; *Benefit Series:* 10879–Maine A, Vol. 9, No. 10; 10792–Ill. R, Vol. 9, No. 9; 10867–Iowa A, Vol. 9, No. 10; 11045–La. A, Vol. 9, No. 12; 10979–Mo. A, Vol. 9, No. 11 (affirmed by commission, C–2379, unp.) ; 11244–Nebr. R, Vol. 10, No. 2; 11272–Vt. A, Vol. 10, No. 2.

49. *Bliley,* etc., *supra,* note 5. See also *Shellhammer* v. *U.C. Board of Review,* 57 A.(2d)439 (1948), 12789–Pa. Ct.D., *Ben. Ser.,* Vol. 11, No. 9.

50. Examples in the *Benefit Series* include: 10851–Ariz. A, Vol. 9, No. 10; 10853–Ark. A, Vol. 9, No. 10; 10779–Calif. R, Vol. 9, No. 9; 9207–Colo. A, Vol. 8, No. 3; 10607–Conn. R, Vol. 9, No. 7; 11201–Fla. A, Vol. 10, No. 2; 10437–Ill. R, Vol. 9, No. 4–5; 11211–Ind. A, Vol. 10, No. 2; 10722–Kans. A, Vol. 9, No. 8; 10725–Ky. V, Vol. 9, No. 8; 10877–La. R, Vol. 9, No. 10; 5894–Me. A, Vol. 4, No. 6; 7822–Mass. R, Vol. 6, No. 2; 10460–Minn. A, Vol. 9, No. 4–5; 10814–Miss. A, Vol. 9, No. 9; 11160–Mo. A, Vol. 10, No. 1; 10901–Nebr. R, Vol. 9, No. 10; 11068–N.H. R, Vol. 9, No. 12; 10743–N.J. R, Vol. 9, No. 8; 7992–N.Y. R, Vol. 6, No. 6; 5904–Okla. A, Vol. 4, No. 6; 2692–Oreg. A, Vol. 3, No. 2; 11263–Pa. R, Vol. 10, No. 2; 2394–Tenn. A, Vol. 3, No. 1; 10930–Va. R, Vol. 9, No. 10; 6703–Wash. A, Vol. 4, No. 12; 10931–W.Va. R, Vol. 9, No. 10, affirmed by *New River Co.* v. *Board of Review,* Circuit Court, Kanawha County, Mar. 28, 1946.

See also *Faulkenberry* v. *Dept. of Industrial Relations,* Circuit Court, Madison

County, Alabama, Mar. 21, 1944, 8657–Ala. Ct.D., *Ben. Ser.*, Vol. 7, No. 8; *Colvert* v. *Dept.*, same court, July 28, 1944, 8951–Ala. Ct.D., *Ben. Ser.*, Vol. 7, No. 12; *Shorten* v. *U.C. Commissioner, supra,* note 36.

51. *Brown-Brockmeyer Co.* v. *Board of Review,* 45 N.E.(2d)152 (1942), 7912–Ohio Ct.D., *Ben. Ser.,* Vol. 6, No. 4; (but see *Leonard* v. *U.C. Board of Review, supra,* note 30; *Craig* v. *Bureau,* Court of Appeals, First Appellate District, May 17, 1948, 12916–Ohio Ct.D., *Ben. Ser.,* Vol. 11, No. 11); *Judson Mills* v. *U.C. Commission, supra,* note 38. See also *Stevens* v. *Selby Shoe Co.,* Court of Appeals, Scioto County, Ohio, June 15, 1945, 9445–Ohio Ct.D., *Ben. Ser.,* Vol. 8, No. 5; Cf. *Canton Drop Forging & Mfg. Co.* v. *Zaharie, supra,* note 44.

52. *Daw* v. *Pickwick Hotel,* District Court, Central Berkshire, 5897–Mass. Ct.D., *Ben. Ser.,* Vol. 4, No. 6.

53. *Morse* v. *E.S. Division,* District Court, Marlborough, Middlesex County, Sept. 29, 1944, 9342–Mass. Ct.D., *Ben. Ser.,* Vol. 8, No. 4.

54. *Carwood Manufacturing Co.* v. *Huiet, supra,* note 38; *Woodall Industries* v. *Tracy,* Circuit Court, Oakland County, Michigan, Docket No. 26150, Sept. 17, 1941, 6836–Mich. Ct.D., *Ben. Ser.,* Vol. 5, No. 1.

55. In *Dwyer* v. *Appeal Board* (Docket No. 247,922, Sept. 9, 1947) this point was well made by the Circuit Court for Wayne County, Michigan. The Appeal Board had sought to bolster its contention that an independent work search was required of the claimant by citing figures obtained in a survey of manufacturers' use of the employment service. To this the court replied that the board had spent considerable time and money on the survey and that it would be unfair to require claimants to make such a survey themselves in order to determine whether they could rely upon the public employment service for placement. If an independent search was to be required of them, claimants needed to be told. In *Dwyer* v. *Appeal Board, supra,* note 22, the Michigan Supreme Court reversed this decision saying that the 1947 amendment to the Michigan law which inserted a "seeking work" provision was merely a clarifying provision.

56. An article by the manager of the Denver office of the Colorado State Employment Service speaks of "the failure of obviously well-qualified applicants to secure jobs with employers to whom they were referred. Analysis of these failures discloses in many instances that while a man or woman may be the best individual available for a particular position, he or she may be totally lacking in knowledge of personal salesmanship and the factors which make for a successful application or interview." In 1940 the Denver office arranged a series of classes in job-seeking techniques. William H. Lancaster, "Teaching Applicants How To Apply For Jobs," *Employment Security Review,* Vol. 7, No. 10 (October 1940), pp. 15–16.

57. There are far too many examples to permit a complete listing. The following cases in the *Benefit Series* are illustrative: 10851–Ariz. A, Vol. 9, No. 10; 10152–Ark. R, Vol. 9, No. 6; 10779–Calif. R, Vol. 9, No. 11; 11194–Conn. R, Vol. 10, No. 2; 10531–Ill. R, Vol. 9, No. 6; 10181–Ind. R, Vol. 9, No. 1; 10450–Iowa R, Vol. 9, Nos. 4–5; 10873–Kans. A, Vol. 9, No. 10; 11043–Ky. A, Vol. 9, No. 12; 11233–Mich. R, Vol. 10, No. 2; 10553–N.J. R, Vol. 9, No. 10; 11668–N.Mex. A, Vol. 10, No. 1; 11089–Tenn. R, Vol. 9, No. 12. Cf. 4844–Ill. A, Vol. 3, No. 12; 6820–S.C. A, Vol. 4, No. 12.

58. *Benefit Series:* 9637–Okla. R, Vol. 8, No. 7; 9940–Okla. R, Vol. 8, No. 10. See also 7742–Okla. R, Vol. 6, No. 1.

59. 8449–Mich. R, *Ben. Ser.,* Vol. 7, No. 3, but see *Foston* v. *Michigan U.C.C., infra,* note 65, and *Dwyer* v. *Appeal Board, supra,* note 22.

60. *Benefit Series:* 9740–Tenn. A, Vol. 8, No. 8; 9115–Wyo. A, Vol. 8, No. 1. (The Wyoming law has since been changed to include an "actively seeking work" requirement.)

61. 10181–Ind. R, *Ben. Ser.,* Vol. 9, No. 1.

62. 7740–N.J. R, *Ben. Ser.,* Vol. 6, No. 1.

63. *Benefit Series:* 7890–Utah A, Vol. 6, No. 4; 7891–Utah A, *idem.*

64. 8889–Fla. A, *Ben. Ser.,* Vol. 7, No. 11.

65. *Benefit Series: Dept. of Industrial Relations* v. *Tomlinson, supra,* note 23; *Broadway* v. *Bolar,* 29 So.(2d)687 (1947), 11685–Ala. Ct.D., Vol. 10, No. 8; *Loew's Inc.* v. *California E.S. Commission, supra,* note 23; 11691–Calif. A, Vol. 10, No. 8 (both antedate the amendment of the California law to require claimants to seek work in their own behalf) ; 12415–Colo. A, Vol. 11, No. 5; 12416–Conn. R, Vol. 11, No. 5 (precedes the effective date of Connecticut's "seeking work" requirement) ; 12021–D.C. A, Vol. 10, No. 2; 12263–Ga. R, Vol. 11, No. 3; 12098–Idaho A, Vol. 11, No. 1 (preceded "seeking work" amendment) ; 12109–Kans. R, Vol. 11, No. 1; *Foston* v. *Michigan U.C. Commission,* Circuit court, Wayne County, Nov. 14, 1947, 12366–Mich. Ct.D., Vol. 11, No. 4 (before Michigan's "seeking work" requirement went into effect; cf. *Dwyer* v. *Appeal Board, supra,* note 22) ; 12116–Mass. R, Vol. 11, No. 1; 11952–Miss. A, Vol. 10, No. 11; 12213–Nebr. R, Vol. 11, No. 2; 12763–N.J. R, Vol. 11, No. 9 (before the "seeking work" amendment; active search for work required after reasonable period (two months) of reliance on employment service) ; 11722–N.Mex. A, Vol. 10, No. 8 (before "seeking work" amendment to statute) ; 12456–N.C. R, Vol. 11, No. 5, affirmed by *U.C. Commission* v. *Dodson,* Superior Court, Orange County, N.C., Sept. 30, 1947; (before "seeking work" requirement went into statutory effect) ; 12462–Ohio R, Vol. 11, No. 5; 11744–S.C. A, Vol. 10, No. 8; 11829–S.Dak. R, Vol. 10, No. 9; 12473–Vt. A, Vol. 11, No. 5; 12076–Va. R, Vol. 10, No. 12; 12163–W.Va. R, Vol. 11, No. 1. Also the following, under statutes specifically requiring "seeking work": 12411–Del. A, Vol. 11, No. 5; *Wagner* v. *U.C. Commission,* 198 S.W.(2d)342 (1946), 11556–Mo. Ct.D., Vol. 10, No. 6; 12059–N.Dak. A, Vol. 10, No. 12; *Jacobs* v. *Office of U.C. and Placement, supra,* note 22; 11362–Wyo. A, Vol. 11, No. 3. Compare 12771–N.Y. R, Vol. 11, No. 9.

66. California, Colorado, Connecticut, Delaware, Idaho, Illinois, Kansas, Maine, Maryland, Michigan, Missouri, Montana, New Jersey, New Mexico, North Dakota, Ohio, Oregon, Vermont, Washington, Wisconsin, and Wyoming. See *Dwyer* v. *Appeal Board, supra,* note 55, in which the Michigan Supreme Court said that the amendment clarified but did not change the law.

67. U.C. Program Letter No. 103, Dec. 10, 1945, p. 11.

68. 10401–Tenn. R, *Ben. Ser.,* Vol. 9, No. 3. The claimant was a schoolteacher who had drawn benefits each summer for five successive years, never once applying for or being referred to a job. The sixth summer she was held ineligible for benefits.

69. 10371–Mont. A, *Ben. Ser.,* Vol. 9, No. 3. Also Missouri–A–3211–46, unp., Aug. 30, 1946.

70. *Private employment agency: Hunter* v. *State,* Superior Court, Spokane County, Washington, Docket No. 110198, 8316–Wash. Ct.D., *Ben. Ser.,* Vol. 7, No. 1.

Union: 11062–Mo. A, *Ben. Ser.,* Vol. 9, No. 12. See also in *Benefit Series:* 11043–Ky. A, Vol. 9, No. 12; 10851–Ariz. A, Vol. 9, No. 10.

71. 11242–Mo. A, *Ben. Ser.,* Vol. 10, No. 2.

72. A–4059–46, unp., Nov. 1, 1946.

73. 10466–Mo. A, *Ben. Ser.,* Vol. 9, No. 4–5. See also Missouri A–3553–46, Oct. 1, 1946, for a similar ruling in the case of a shoe factory worker.

74. 10465–Mo. A, *Ben. Ser.,* Vol. 9, No. 4–5; A–3808–46, unp., Oct. 31, 1946; A–3165–46, unp., Sept. 13, 1946.

75. 10978–Mo. A, *Ben. Ser.,* Vol. 9, No. 11; 10979–Mo. A, *Ben. Ser.,* Vol. 9, No. 11, affirmed by commission decision C–2379.

76. 12694–N.Dak. R, *Ben. Ser.,* Vol. 11, No. 8.

77. See Paul H. Douglas, *Standards of Unemployment Insurance* (Chicago: University of Chicago Press, 1932), p. 83.

NOTES FOR CHAPTER SEVEN

1. On April 3, 1944, the Planning Unit of the New York Division of Placement and Unemployment Insurance wrote ("Preliminary Disposition of Policy Referendum No. 1–44, *Statements of Availability,*" copy in writer's possession) : "We must decide whether availability is an *objective* fact, a *subjective* attitude on the part of the claimant, a simultaneous *combination* of both, or perhaps a *developing* condition depending on the duration of unemployment." (Original italics)

2. *Benefit Series:* 1965–Mich. A, Vol. 2, No. 9; 1219–N.Y. A, Vol. 2, No. 4; 4111–N.Dak. A, Vol. 3, No. 8; 11659–Pa. A, Vol. 10, No. 7; 12791–Pa. A, Vol. 11, No. 9; 5474–Tex. A, Vol. 4, No. 4; 3112–Wis. A, Vol. 3, No. 4. Also Oregon *Manual of Precedents,* Sec. 5270; New York Appeal Board 2573–40, unp.

3. *Benefit Series:* 4111–N.Dak. A, Vol. 3, No. 8 (larceny conviction) ; 9573–Colo. A, Vol. 8, No. 7 (paroled mental hospital inmate), but see 12787–Okla. R, Vol. 11, No. 9.

4. 4325–Ohio A, *Ben. Ser.,* Vol. 3, No. 9.

5. 8004–W.Va. R, *Ben. Ser.,* Vol. 6, No. 6. Cf. 12749–Mass. A, *Ben. Ser.,* Vol. 11, No. 9.

6. 4851–Ohio A, *Ben. Ser.,* Vol. 3, No. 12. But see 1219–N.Y. A, *Ben. Ser.,* Vol. 2, No. 4, where the claimant was in custody of the Immigration Service for purpose of deportation.

7. 3388–Ind. A, *Ben. Ser.,* Vol. 3, No. 5.

8. *Benefit Series:* 7594–Calif. A, Vol. 5, No. 10 (curfew regulations) ; 7513–Oreg. A, Vol. 5, No. 9 (asset freezing order) ; but see 8163–Wash. A, *Ben. Ser.,* Vol. 6, No. 10, affirmed by Commissioner in Review No. 286, unp. (evacuation imminent).

9. 8123–Calif. R, *Ben. Ser.,* Vol. 6, No. 9.

10. 8252–Calif. R, *Ben. Ser.,* Vol. 6, No. 12. Camouflage net factories were operated at the Colorado River, Gila River, and Manzanar centers; garment factories at Manzanar, Heart Mountain, and Minidoka; cabinet shops at Tule Lake, Manzanar, and Heart Mountain; sawmills at Heart Mountain and Jerome; a mattress factory at Manzanar; a bakery at Tule Lake; silk-screen poster shops at Granada and Heart Mountain; a model-warship factory at Gila River. All the centers had carpentry, furniture repair shops, and food processing plants. Over 7,000 center residents were employed by the trust association at Heart Mountain and the consumer coöperatives in the other nine centers. On September 30, 1942, approximately 33,000 evacuees were on the center pay rolls as workers. During 1942 about 10,000 evacuees left the centers for seasonal agricultural work. See U.S. Department of the Interior, War Relocation Authority, *WRA: A Story of Human Conservation,* 1946, pp. 32, 80, 98–100, 103–105.

In at least one benefit decision (8288–Oreg. A, *Ben. Ser.,* Vol. 6, No. 12, affirmed, U.C. Commission, No. 43–C–4, unp.) it was held that relocation center residents who worked a 5½–day, 44–hour week were not unemployed even though they earned less in such center employment than their weekly benefit amounts.

11. 8253–Calif. R, *Ben. Ser.,* Vol. 6, No. 12.

12. 8669–Hawaii R, *Ben. Ser.,* Vol. 7, No. 8.

13. 8312–Nev. R, *Ben. Ser.,* Vol. 7, No. 1, affirmed on rehearing by board of review, Appeal Case No. B–5, unp.

14. 8202–Ind. A, *Ben. Ser.,* Vol. 6, No. 11.

15. *Island Creek Coal Company* v. *Board of Review,* Dec. 30, 1943, 8529–W.Va. Ct.D., *Ben. Ser.,* Vol. 7, No. 5.

16. *Canton Drop Forging & Manufacturing Company* v. *Zaharie,* Common Pleas Court, Stark County, July 7, 1944, 8926–Ohio Ct.D., *Ben. Ser.,* Vol. 7, No. 11.

17. 8920–N.J. A, *Ben. Ser.,* Vol. 7, No. 11.

18. *Benefit Series:* 8569–Colo. A, Vol. 7, No. 6; 8747–Ga. A, Vol. 7, No. 9; 8822–Ky. R, Vol. 7, No. 10; (but not where the lack of an availability statement was not the claimant's fault, 9787–Ky. R, Vol. 8, No. 9) ; 8586–Md. A, Vol. 7, No. 6 (affirmed, U. C. Board, Maryland 832 unp.) ; 9224–Md. R, Vol. 8, No. 3 (affirmed in *Monches* v. *Bethlehem Sparrows Point Shipyard,* Baltimore City Superior Court, Oct. 17, 1944, unp.) ; 8526–S.C. A, Vol. 7, No. 5 ; 8651–S.C. A, Vol. 7, No. 7 ; 9747–Va. A, Vol. 8, No. 8 ; 8261–Wash. A, Vol. 6, No. 12 ; 9031–W.Va. R, Vol. 7, No. 12. Also Idaho–UC–934, June 3, 1943, unp.

19. *Benefit Series:* 8662–Calif. R, Vol. 7, No. 8; 9386–Calif. R, Vol. 8, No. 5; 9981–Calif. R, Vol. 8, No. 11; 8674–Ill. R, Vol. 7, No. 8. (Contra : 9486–Ill. A, Vol. 8, No. 6, where a purely subjective view was taken.) In Illinois however, the unemployment compensation agency made strong efforts to coördinate its rulings on "good cause" with those of the manpower authorities. No exception made in California in favor of the claimant who knew the effect of the lack of a release and was unwilling to accept agricultural or domestic work. (See 8802–Calif. A, Vol. 7, No. 10 and 9307–Calif. R, Vol. 8, No. 4.)

20. *Benefit Series:* 8518–D.C. A, Vol. 7, No. 5; 8701–N.J. R, Vol. 7, No. 8; 8842–N.C. R, Vol. 7, No. 10; 9087–N.C. R, Vol. 8, No. 1; 9088–N.C. R, *ibid.;* 8646–Okla. A, Vol. 7, No. 7. For the general rule in Oklahoma, see 8427–Okla. R, Vol. 7, No. 3; 9832–Okla. A, Vol. 8, No. 9.

21. *Benefit Series:* 9165–Mo. R, Vol. 8, No. 2; 9615–Mo. R, Vol. 8, No. 7; 9258–N.C. R, Vol. 8, No. 3.

22. *Benefit Series:* 8467–Calif. A, Vol. 7, No. 4; 8302–Conn. R, Vol. 7, No. 1; 9054–Ind. R, Vol. 8, No. 1; 8834–Nebr. R, Vol. 7, No. 10; (but not where the lack of an availability statement was not the claimant's fault, 9168–Nebr. R, Vol. 8, No. 2) ; 8598–R.I. A, Vol. 7, No. 6.

23. 9143–Ind. A, *Ben. Ser.,* Vol. 8, No. 2.

24. *Benefit Series:* 8517–Conn. AG, Vol. 7, No. 5; 8695–Mich. R, Vol. 7, No. 8; (dictum only; claimant held not available on other grounds) ; 8424–N.J. A, Vol. 7, No. 3; 8922–N.J. R, Vol. 7, No. 11; 8647–Pa. R, Vol. 7, No. 7. Ohio Board of Review, 429–BR–43, Oct. 13, 1943, unp.

25. *Mishaw* v. *Fairfield News,* 12 Conn. Supp. 318 (1944), 8571–Conn. Ct.D., *Ben. Ser.,* Vol. 7, No. 6.

26. *Reger* v. *Administrator,* 46 A(2d)844 (1946), 10780–Conn. Ct.D., *Ben. Ser.,* Vol. 9, No. 9.

27. 8922–N.J. R, *Ben. Ser.,* Vol. 7, No. 11.

28. *Guide for State Employment Security Administration,* Sec. 4701, 2b, Apr. 1, 1944.

29. *Benefit Series:* 9083–N.Y. R, Vol. 8, No. 1; 9084–N.Y. R, Vol. 8, No. 1.

30. *Benefit Series:* 12662–Idaho A, Vol. 11, No. 8; 11539–Ill. R, Vol. 10, No. 6; 10544–Mich. A, Vol. 9, No. 6; 7881–N. Y. R, Vol. 6, No. 4; 2235–W.Va. A, Vol. 2, No. 12. Connecticut, 137–B–45, unp. Compare 12784–Ohio R, Vol. 11, No. 9; 12852–Ohio R, Vol. 11, No. 10.

31. 10931–W.Va. R, *Ben. Ser.,* Vol. 9, No. 10, affirmed by *The New River Co.* v. *Board of Review,* Circuit Court, Kanawha County, Mar. 28, 1946, unp. Connecticut 28–B–44, unp.

32. 46 N.Y. Supp.(2d)774 (1944), 8643–N.Y. Ct.D., *Ben. Ser.,* Vol. 7, No. 7. The New York Appeal Board limits the rule of this decision to cases where the claimant will accept any suitable homework, whether or not in her line. N.Y. 14, 148–46, unp., Mar. 10, 1947.

33. *Salavarria* v. *Murphy,* 43 N.Y. Supp.(2d)899 (1943), 8426–N.Y. Ct.D., *Ben. Ser.,* Vol. 7, No. 3.

34. 10180–Ill. R, *Ben. Ser.,* Vol. 9, No. 1.

35. 8700–N.J. R, *Ben. Ser.,* Vol. 7, No. 8.

36. *Supra,* note 27.

37. *Shorten* v. *U.C. Commissioner,* 10 Conn. Supp. 1860 (1941), 7242–Conn. Ct.D., *Ben. Ser.,* Vol. 5, No. 5; *Anderson* v. *U.C. Commission,* Superior Court, Grays Harbor County, Washington, Nov. 15, 1945, 10408–Wash. Ct.D., *Ben. Ser.,* Vol. 9, No. 3; *Benefit Series:* 8610–Ala. V, Vol. 7, No. 7; 9207–Colo. A, Vol. 8, No. 3; 10246–Fla. V, Vol. 9, No. 2; 4689–Ill. A, Vol. 3, No. 11; 10534–Ky. V, Vol. 9, No. 6; 5003–Mo. A, Vol. 4, No. 1; 10901–Nebr. R, Vol. 9, No. 10; 9630–N.C. V, Vol. 8, No. 7; 10386–N.Dak. V, Vol. 9, No. 3; 9525–Ohio R, Vol. 8, No. 6 (but see *Brown-Brockmeyer Co.* v. *Board of Review,* 45 N.E.(2d)152, 7912–Ohio Ct.D., *Ben. Ser.,* Vol. 6, No. 4); 9840–Pa. R, Vol. 8, No. 9; 10054–Tenn. R, Vol. 8, No. 11; 8527–Wash. A, Vol. 7, No. 5. Also RAR–U–3.

38. *Benefit Series:* 10246–Fla. V, Vol. 9, No. 2; 9316–Ill. R, Vol. 8, No. 4; 2692–Oreg. A, Vol. 3, No. 2. Also British Umpire 6655/35.

39. 9204–Ark. R, *Ben. Ser.,* Vol. 8, No. 3.

40. 10963–Ill. A, *Ben. Ser.,* Vol. 9, No. 11.

41. *Benefit Series:* 9141–Ill. R, Vol. 8, No. 2; 10447–Iowa A, Vol. 9, No. 4–5; 9492–Kans. A, Vol. 8, No. 6; 10971–Md. A, Vol. 9, No. 11.

42. *Benefit Series:* 9207–Colo. A, Vol. 8, No. 3; 8743–Fla. A, Vol. 7, No. 9; 9182–N.C. A, Vol. 8, No. 2.

43. 11268–Utah A, *Ben. Ser.,* Vol. 10, No. 2.

44. 9358–N.Y. V, *Ben. Ser.,* Vol. 8, No. 4.

45. 9444–N.Y. V, *Ben. Ser.,* Vol. 8, No. 5.

46. 9043–Conn. R, *Ben. Ser.,* Vol. 8, No. 1.

47. 7738–N.J. A, *Ben. Ser.,* Vol. 6, No. 1.

48. 9185–Okla. A, *Ben. Ser.,* Vol. 8, No. 2.

49. *Shorten* v. *U.C. Commissioner, supra,* note 37; *D'Yantone* v. *U.C. Board of Review,* 46 A.(2d)525 (1946), 10923–Pa. Ct.D., *Ben. Ser.,* Vol. 9, No. 10. In 11960–N.J. R, *Ben. Ser.,* Vol. 10, No. 11 the view is taken that a blind claimant cannot be required to make the same general search for work as an unhandicapped individual. But see 12834–Mass. A, Vol. 11, No. 10.

50. See Freeman, Louise F., "Able To Work And Available For Work," *Yale Law Journal,* Vol. 55, No. 1 (December 1945), pp. 123–134. Having adopted a wholly objective view, she finds this is a difficult situation. "In terms of the labor market it must be said that since there is no suitable work for the individual and the labor market for an individual is limited to suitable work, there is no labor market for such individual in that locality unless he extends it by his willingness to take other work." (pp. 127–28) She resolves the difficulty by a retreat to general purposes. "It is questionable, however, that such individual is unavailable for work. He is not wilfully unemployed; the only reason he is not working is that no work is being performed which he can be reasonably expected to accept. Unemployment resulting from changes in labor market conditions would seem to fall within the unemployment that is intended to be compensated, for unemployment compensation is designed to assure a worker a reasonable opportunity to explore employment opportunitites in his locality and in other localities to which he is willing to move."

51. *Garwood Manufacturing Co.* v. *Huiet,* Superior Court, Barrow County, Georgia, Docket No. 1855, June 5, 1943, 8417–Ga. Ct.D., *Ben. Ser.,* Vol. 7, No. 3; *Woodall Industries* v. *Tracy,* Circuit Court, Oakland County, Michigan, Docket No. 26150, Sept. 17, 1941, 6836–Mich. Ct.D., *Ben. Ser.,* Vol. 5, No. 1; *Kontner* v. *U.C. Board,* 76 N.E.(2d)611 (1947), 12914–Ohio Ct.D., *Ben. Ser.,* Vol. 11, No. 11; *Davidson* v. *Hayes,* Common Pleas Court, Highland County, Ohio, Feb. 5, 1946, 10662–Ohio Ct.D., *Ben. Ser.,* Vol. 9, No. 7; *Copeland* v. *Em-*

ployment Security Commission, 172 P.(2d)420 (1946), 10751–Okla. Ct.D., *Ben. Ser.,* Vol. 9, No. 8; *Shellhammer* v. *U.C. Board of Review,* 57 A.(2d)439 (1948), 12789–Pa. Ct.D., *Ben. Ser.,* Vol. 11, No. 9; *Jacobs* v. *Office of U.C. and Placement,* 179 P.(2d)707 (1947), 11832–Wash. Ct.D., *Ben. Ser.,* Vol. 10, No. 9.

52. *Benefit Series:* 10232–Ala. A, Vol. 9, No. 2; 8736–Calif. R, Vol. 7, No. 9; 8619–Conn. R, Vol. 7, No. 7; 10080–Fla. A, Vol. 8, No. 12; 9888–Ga. A, Vol. 8, No. 10; 11936–Ill. R, Vol. 10, No. 11; 9599–Ind. V, Vol. 8, No. 7; 11854–Iowa R, Vol. 10, No. 10; 11312–Me. A, Vol. 10, No. 3; 9063–Md. A, Vol. 8, No. 1; 9065–Mass. A, Vol. 8, No. 1 (but see 9603–Mass. A, Vol. 8, No. 7 in which it was held that such a claimant should be held available during a reasonable period of adjustment) ; 10812–Minn. A, Vol. 9, No. 8; 11390–Nebr. R, Vol. 10, No. 10; 10549–N.H. R, Vol. 9, No. 6; 8699–N.J. R, Vol. 7, No. 8 (but see 10743–N.J. R, Vol. 9, No. 8 in which a married woman was held available because marital obligations prevented her from moving to a place of greater work opportunity) ; 9736–Tenn. R, Vol. 8, No. 8; 9462–Tex. R, Vol. 8, No. 5; 11184–Va. A, Vol. 10, No. 1; 10684–W.Va. R, Vol. 9, No. 7; 9113–Wis. R, Vol. 8, No. 1.

53. *Benefit Series:* 10713–Ill. R, Vol. 9, No. 8. Also see 10530–Ill. R, Vol. 9, No. 6; 9217–Ill. R, Vol. 8, No. 3. The Illinois general rule, however, remains that transportation facilities to work opportunities are needed for availability. See 11936–Ill. R, Vol. 10, No. 11.

54. *Benefit Series:* 10335–Iowa A, Vol. 9, No. 3; 10383–N.C. A, Vol. 9, No. 3; 10487–Pa. R, Vol. 9, No. 4–5.

55. New York Appeal Board No. 7222–42, unp., quoted in *Benefit Series:* 8776–N.Y. R, Vol. 7, No. 9 and 8923–N.Y. R, Vol. 7, No. 11. Contra: 8425–N.Y. R, Vol. 7, No. 3.

56. To similar effect, see *Principles Underlying Availability–For Work,* U.C. Program Letter No. 103, Bureau of Employment Security, Dec. 10, 1945, pp. 8, 9, and Ralph Altman, and Virginia Lewis, "Limited Availability For Shift Employment," *North Carolina Law Review,* Vol. 22, No. 3 (April 1944), pp. 209–10.

57. A good statement of the distinction between "voluntary" and "involuntary" is given in *Bliley Electric Co.* v. *U.C. Board of Review,* 45 A(2d)898 (1946), 10754–Pa. Ct.D., *Ben. Ser.,* Vol. 9, No. 8:

"'Voluntarily' and 'involuntarily' are antonymous and therefore irreconcilable words but the words are merely symbols of ideas, and the ideas can be readily reconciled. Willingness, wilfulness, volition, intention reside in 'voluntarily,' but the mere fact that a worker wills and intends to leave a job does not necessarily and always mean that the leaving is voluntary. Extraneous factors, the surrounding circumstances, must be taken into the account, and when they are examined it may be found that the seemingly voluntary, the apparently intentional, act was in fact involuntary. A worker's physical and mental condition, his personal and family problems, the authoritative demand of legal duties — these are circumstances that exert pressure upon him and imperiously call for decision and action.

"When therefore the pressure of real not imaginary, substantial not trifling, reasonable not whimsical, circumstances *compel* the decision to leave employment, the decision is voluntary in the sense that the worker has willed it, but involuntary because outward pressures have compelled it. Or to state it differently, if a worker leaves his employment when he is compelled to do so by necessitous circumstances or because of legal or family obligations, his leaving is voluntary with good cause, and under the act he is entitled to benefits. The pressure of necessity, of legal duty, or family obligations, or other overpowering circumstances and his capitulation to them transform what is ostensibly voluntary unemployment into involuntary unemployment." (Original italics.)

See also: 8846–N.C. AG, *Ben. Ser.,* Vol. 7, No. 10; *Principles Underlying*

Availability For Work, supra, note 56, p. 8; *Principles Underlying the Voluntary-Leaving Disqualification,* U.C. Program Letter No. 107, Bureau of Employment Security, Jan. 28, 1946, pp. 8–10; Ralph Altman and Virginia Lewis, p. 209n.

58. Arizona, California, Colorado, Delaware, Florida, Georgia, Idaho, Illinois, Indiana, Iowa, Kansas, Maryland, Michigan, Minnesota, Mississippi, Montana, Nevada, New Jersey, New Mexico, New York, North Carolina, Pennsylvania, South Carolina, Tennessee, Texas, Washington, Wyoming. (27)

A typical policy statement is that found in the Georgia law (section 2) : "As a guide to the interpretation and application of this Act, the public policy of this State is declared to be as follows : Economic insecurity due to unemployment is a serious menace to the health, morals, and welfare of the people of this State. Involuntary unemployment is therefore a subject of general interest and concern which requires appropriate action by the Legislature to prevent its spread and to lighten its burden which now so often falls with crushing force upon the unemployed worker or his family . . . The Legislature, therefore, declares that in its considered judgment the public good, and the general welfare of the citizens of this State require the enactment of this measure, under the police powers of the State, for the compulsory setting aside of unemployment reserves to be used for the benefit of persons unemployed through no fault of their own."

59. *Whitcomb Hotel* v. *Employment Commission,* 151 P.(2d)233 (1944), 9038–Calif. Ct.D., *Ben. Ser.,* Vol. 8, No. 1 ; *Carwood Manufacturing Co.* v. *Huiet, supra,* note 51 ; *Walgreen Co.* v. *Murphy,* 53 N.E.(2d)390 (1944), 8677–Ill. Ct.D., *Ben. Ser.,* Vol. 7, No. 8; *Bledsoe Coal Co.* v. *Review Board,* 46 N.E.(2d)477 (1942), 8052–Ind. Ct.D., *Ben. Ser.,* Vol. 6, No. 7; *Hutzler Bros. Co.* v. *U.C. Board,* Superior Court, Baltimore City, Sept. 29, 1943, 8460–Md. Ct.D., *Ben. Ser.,* Vol. 7, No. 3; *Chrysler Corp.* v. *Smith,* 298 N.W. 87 (1941), 6638–Mich. Ct.D., *Ben. Ser.,* Vol. 4, No. 11; *Courney* v. *Appeal Board,* Circuit Court, Genesee County, Mar. 15, 1945, 9613–Mich. Ct.D., *Ben. Ser.,* Vol. 8, No. 7; *Fannon* v. *Federal Cartridge Corp.,* 18 N.W.(2d)249 (1945), 9701–Minn. Ct.D., *Ben. Ser.,* Vol. 8, No. 8; *W.T. Grant Co.* v. *Board of Review,* 29 A.(2d)858 (1943), 8160–N.J. Ct.D., *Ben. Ser.,* Vol. 6, No. 10; *Board of Review* v. *Midcontinent Petroleum Corp.,* 141 P.(2d)69 (1943), 8213–Okla. Ct.D., *Ben. Ser.,* Vol. 6, No. 11; *Danzer* v. *State U.C. Commission,* Circuit Court, Multnomah County, Docket No. 135284, 5235–Oreg. Ct.D., *Ben. Ser.,* Vol. 4, No. 2; *Department of Labor and Industry* v. *U.C. Board of Review (in re Stewart),* 24 A.(2d)667 (1942), 7405–Pa. Ct.D., *Ben. Ser.,* Vol. 5, No. 7; *MacFarland* v. *U.C. Board of Review,* 45 A.(2d)423 (1946), 10751–Pa. Ct.D., *Ben. Ser.,* Vol. 9, No. 8; *Judson Mills* v. *U.C. Commission,* 28 S.E.(2d)535 (1944), 8525–S.C. Ct.D., *Ben. Ser.,* Vol. 7, No. 5; *John Morrell & Co.* v. *U.C. Commission,* 13 N.W.(2d)498 (1944), 8859–S.Dak., *Ben. Ser.,* Vol. 7, No. 10; *Keen* v. *Texas U.C. Commission,* 148 S.W. (2d)211 (1941), 6117–Tex. Ct.D., *Ben. Ser.,* Vol. 4, No. 7; *Bohannon* v. *U.C. Commissioner,* Superior Court, Yakima County, 8948–Wash. Ct.D., *Ben. Ser.,* Vol. 7, No. 11; *Goodwin* v. *Riley,* same court, 9028–Wash. Ct.D., *Ben. Ser.,* Vol. 7, No. 12; *Miners in General Group* v. *Hix,* 17 S.E.(2d)810 (1941), 7174–W.Va., Ct.D., *Ben. Ser.,* Vol. 5, No. 4.

60. *Department* v. *Drummond,* 1 So.(2d)395 (1941), 6429–Ala. Ct.D., *Ben. Ser.,* Vol. 4, No. 9 (Cf. *Carmichael* v. *Southern Coal & Coke Co.,* 301 U.S. 495 [1937], in which the United States Supreme Court held the Alabama law constitutional although, for lack of a legislative declaration of policy, it expressed no special intent to relieve involuntary unemployment) ; *Mishaw* v. *Fairfield News, supra,* note 25; *Barnes* v. *Hall,* 146 S.W.(2d)929 (1940), 6637–Ky. Ct.D., *Ben. Ser.,* Vol. 4, No. 11; *Board of Review* v. *Hix,* 29 S.E.(2d)618 (1944), 8798–W.Va. Ct.D., *Ben. Ser.,* Vol. 7, No 9.

See Gladys Harrison, "Statutory Purpose and 'Involuntary Unemployment,'" *Yale Law Journal*, Vol. 55, No. 1 (December 1945), pp. 117–123, for a valuable criticism of some of the cases listed in this and the foregoing note.

61. Because weeks of benefits in variable-duration states vary with the amount of qualifying wages, the percentage of claimants who qualify for less than maximum duration varies with employment conditions. Since the Bureau of Employment Security, until 1946, depended on a voluntary system for reporting potential benefit duration, figures are incomplete. Average potential duration was less than 15 weeks in 27 states, for benefit years ending in 1941 (37 states reporting), in 27 states for benefit years ending in 1942 (42 states reporting), in four states for benefit years ending in 1943 (19 states reporting, including only four variable duration states), in 19 states for benefit years ending in 1945 (39 states reporting), in nine states for benefit years ending in 1946 (50 states reporting).

Unemployment Insurance Abstract: Program Statistics and Legal Provisions 1937–47, Supplement to Employment Security Activities, Vol. 3, No. 11 (November 1947), p. 46, Table 30.

62. Cf. Louise F. Freeman, "Able to Work and Available for Work," pp. 131–32.

63. Freeman, "Able to Work and Available for Work," pp. 131–32.

64. Warren L. Hanna, "The Convict and the Compensation Law," *California Law Review*, Vol. 34, March 1946, pp. 167–185.

65. 5086–Conn. R, *Ben. Ser.,* Vol. 4, No. 1.

NOTES FOR CHAPTER EIGHT

1. David E. Hailman, *Health Status of Adults in the Productive Ages,* Reprint No. 2327, Public Health Reports, p. 15.

2. *Benefit Series:* 2352–Calif., Vol. 3, No. 1; 9207–Colo. A, Vol. 8, No. 3; 10246–Fla. V, Vol. 9, No. 2; 12957–Fla. A, Vol. 11, No. 12; 10447–Iowa A, Vol. 9, Nos. 4–5; 11945–Kans. R, Vol. 10, No. 11; 12602–Mass. A, Vol. 11, No. 7; 7694–Minn. R, Vol. 5, No. 12; 11713–Mo. A, Vol. 10, No. 8; 12980–Mont. A, Vol. 11, No. 12; 5174–N.J. A, Vol. 4, No. 1; 8707–Oreg. A, Vol. 7, No. 8.

"Issues Involved in Decisions on Disputed Claims for Benefits," *Social Security Yearbook,* 1940, p. 15.

British Umpire, Cases Nos. 308 (OW.D.), 6979, 1404/28, 6655/35; Respectively, BU–84, BU–2, BU–82 and BU–83 in *Benefit Decisions of the British Umpire,* Unemployment Compensation Interpretation Service, *Benefit Series,* General Supplement No. 1.

3. Bernard D. Karpinos, *The Physically Handicapped,* Reprint No. 2521, Public Health Reports, p. 6ff.

4. 9185–Okla. A, *Ben. Ser.,* Vol. 8, No. 2.

5. *Benefit Series:* 8471–Ky. A, Vol. 7, No. 4; 5466–N.J. R, Vol. 4, No. 4; 9357–N.Y. R, Vol. 8, No. 4; 9525–Ohio R, Vol. 8, No. 6; 12223–Ohio A, Vol. 11, No. 2 (affirmed by 1182–BR–47, unp.); 11824–Pa. A, Vol. 10, No. 9; 2390–R.I. A, Vol. 3, No. 1.

6. *Shorten* v. *U.C. Commissioner,* 10 Conn. Supp. 1860 (1941), 7242–Conn. Ct.D., *Ben. Ser.,* Vol. 5, No. 5.

7. *Benefit Series:* Eligible: 9782–Ind. A, Vol. 8, No. 9; 10877–La. R, Vol. 9, No. 10; 1537–Mich. A, Vol. 2, No. 5; 10463–Miss. A, Vol. 9, Nos. 4–5.

Benefit Series: Not Eligible: 6238–Calif. A, Vol. 4, No. 8; 4534–W.Va. A, Vol. 3, No. 10.

8. 10798–Ind. V, *Ben. Ser.,* Vol. 9, No. 9.

9. Rollo H. Britten, *Blindness, as Recorded in the National Health Survey,* Reprint No. 2332, Public Health Reports, pp. 22–24.

10. 11945–Kans. R, *Ben. Ser.,* Vol. 10, No. 11.

11. *Benefit Series:* 9316–Ill. R, Vol. 8, No. 3; 11543–Iowa A, Vol. 10, No. 6; 7877–Mo. A, Vol. 6, No. 4; 12515–N.H. R, Vol. 11, No. 6; 11960–N.J. R, Vol. 10, No. 11; 2878–N.Y. R, Vol. 3, No. 3. Compare 11694–Conn. R, Vol. 10, No. 8; 12096–Fla. A, Vol. 11, No. 1; 12834–Mass. A, Vol. 11, No. 10; 9516–N.H. R, Vol. 8, No. 6; 9856–W.Va. R, Vol. 8, No. 9.

Also see the following: *Colvert* v. *Department of Industrial Relations,* Circuit Court, Madison County, Alabama, July 28, 1944, 8951–Ala. Ct.D., Vol. 7, No. 12; 7561–Ark. A, Vol. 5, No. 9; 11291–Ga. A, Vol. 10, No. 3; 11701–Ind. R, Vol. 10, No. 8; 12125–Mont. A, Vol. 11, No. 1; 7245–N.J. A, Vol. 5, No. 5; 11432–S.C. A, Vol. 10, No. 4; 9744–Tex. A, Vol. 8, No. 8.

12. 11960–N.J. R, *Ben. Ser.,* Vol. 10, No. 11. Cf. 12834–Mass. A, *Ben. Ser.,* Vol. 11, No. 10. Note 12821–Idaho A, *Ben. Ser.,* Vol. 11, No. 10 in which the tribunal stated that the "actively seeking work" requirement in the law was intended to apply to casual and seasonal workers and implied that it was not intended to apply to older workers who had been in the labor market for a long time.

13. 11694–Conn. R, *Ben. Ser.,* Vol. 10, No. 8.

14. Oregon Unemployment Compensation Commission, Statistical Bulletin, Vol. 4, No. 2 (September 1946), pp. 5–6. Also see Nathan Weinberg, "Workers' Experiences During First Phase of Reconversion," *Monthly Labor Review,* Vol. 62, No. 5 (May 1946), p. 710. Cf. Mary T. Waggaman, "Employment and the Older Worker," *Monthly Labor Review,* Vol. 62, No. 3 (March 1946), pp. 386–391.

15. U. S. National Resources Committee, *The Problems of a Changing Population,* Report of the Committee on Population Problems, May 1938, U. S. Government Printing Office, Washington, pp. 25–26.

16. Michael T. Wermel, and Selma Gelbaum, "Work and Retirement in Old Age," *American Journal of Sociology,* Vol. LI, No. 1 (July 1945), pp. 16–21. Malford W. Thewlis, *The Care of the Aged,* third edition (St. Louis: C. V. Mosby Co., 1941), pp. 68–70.

17. 11853–Ind. R, *Ben. Ser.,* Vol. 10, No. 10.

18. 11606–Va. R, *Ben. Ser.,* Vol. 10, No. 6.

19. *Anderson* v. *Unemployment Compensation Commission,* Superior Court, Grays Harbor County, Washington, Nov. 15, 1945, 10408–Wash. Ct.D., *Ben. Ser.,* Vol. 9, No. 3. Under an earlier version of the Washington availability requirement, which demanded ability to work in the claimant's usual trade and occupation including the most recent employment, Anderson would probably have been held ineligible. See 7782–Wash. A, *Ben. Ser.,* Vol. 6, No. 2 (affirmed by commissioner in Review No. 308, unp.).

20. *Benefit Series:* 10506–Ala. R, Vol. 9, No. 6 (textile speeder hand); 7736–Calif. R, Vol. 6, No. 1 (longshoreman); 12567–Conn. R, Vol. 11, No. 7; 9989–Ga. R, Vol. 8, No. 11 (cement finisher); 12821–Idaho A, Vol. 11, No. 10; 10251–Ill. R, Vol. 9, No. 2 (miner); 9904–Ill. R, Vol. 8, No. 10; 11953–Ind. R, Vol. 10; No. 10 (steel mill and building trades laborer); 10453–Ky. R, Vol. 9, Nos. 4–5 (coal loader).

21. Disqualification applies to recipients of primary insurance benefits: Alabama, Arizona, Delaware, Kansas, Nebraska, New Mexico, Oklahoma.

Disqualification applies to recipients of old-age insurance benefits: Georgia, Iowa, Missouri, Ohio, Texas, Wyoming.

22. 7312–Mass. A, *Ben. Ser.,* Vol. 5, No. 6. Also see 12888 and 12890–Conn. R, *Ben. Ser.,* Vol. 11, No. 11.

23. 11737–Pa. A, *Ben. Ser.,* Vol. 10, No. 8. See also in *Benefit Series:* 9900–Ill. R, Vol. 8, No. 10; 11829–S.Dak. R, Vol. 10, No. 9.

24. 8847–Okla. R, *Ben. Ser.,* Vol. 7, No. 10.

25. *Benefit Series:* 9182–N.C. A, Vol. 8, No. 2; 9090–Ohio A, Vol. 8, No. 1; 12865–Pa. R, Vol. 11, No. 10; 8932–R.I. A, Vol. 7, No. 11; 9022–S.C. R, Vol. 7, No. 12. Cf. 3097–N.Y. A, Vol. 3, No. 6; 4112–Ohio A, Vol. 3, No. 8.

26. *Benefit Series:* 2352–Calif., Vol. 3, No. 1; 7902–Ga. A, Vol. 6, No. 4; 3087–Ill. A, Vol. 3, No. 4; (Cf. 3084–Ill. A, *ibid.*) 2671–Ind. R, Vol. 3, No. 2; 2229–Nebr. R, Vol. 2, No. 2; 2032–S.C. A, Vol. 2, No. 10.

27. 7902–Ga. A, *Ben. Ser.*, Vol. 6, No. 4.

28. *Wolpers* v. *U.C. Commission,* 186 S.W.(2d)440(Mo.) (1945).

29. 8949–W.Va. R, *Ben. Ser.*, Vol. 7, No. 11. Also see 9214–Ga. A, *Ben. Ser.*, Vol. 8, No. 3.

30. 11485–N.Y. R, *Ben. Ser.*, Vol. 10, No. 5.

31. 7736–Calif. R, *Ben. Ser.*, Vol. 6, No. 1.

32. *Standard Bleachery and Printing Co.* v. *Board of Review,* 40 A.(2d)558 (1945), 9518–N.J. Ct.D., *Ben. Ser.*, Vol. 8, No. 6; *Benefit Series:* 12288–Mo. A, Vol. 11, No. 3; 10571–Pa. A, Vol. 9, No. 6; but see: 7876–Miss. A, Vol. 6, No. 4; 9016–Pa. R, Vol. 7, No. 12.

33. 7941–N.Y. R, *Ben. Ser.*, Vol. 6, No. 5. Also see 8205–Md. A, *Ben. Ser.*, Vol. 6, No. 11.

34. *Benefit Series:* 4497–Del. A, Vol. 3, No. 10; 4088–Fla. A, Vol. 3, No. 8; 3478–Ill. R, Vol. 3, No. 5, affirming 3273–Ill. A, Vol. 3, No. 4; 6832–Ill. A, Vol. 5, No. 1; 2222–Ind. A, Vol. 2, No. 12; 2872–N.J. R, Vol. 3, No. 3; 2886—Oreg. A, Vol. 3, No. 3; 4700–W.Va. A, Vol 3, No. 11.

35. 7875–Mich. R, *Ben. Ser.*, Vol. 6, No. 4.

36. 11454–Del. A, *Ben. Ser.*, Vol. 10, No. 5.

37. *Benefit Series:* 10772–Ark. A, Vol. 9, No. 9; 6956–Ark. R, Vol. 5, No. 2; 12341–Calif. R, Vol. 11, No. 4; 9760–Del. R, Vol. 8, No. 9; 11292–Ga. A, Vol. 10, No. 3; 11299–Ill. A, Vol. 10, No. 3; 10796–Ind. R, Vol. 9, No. 9; 10258–Ky. R, Vol. 9, No. 2; 10877–La. R, Vol. 9, No. 10; 7875–Mich. R, Vol. 6, No. 4; 7878–Mo. A, Vol. 6, No. 4; 9172–N.H. R, Vol. 8, No. 2; 6958–N.Y. R, Vol. 5, No. 2; 7316–N.Car. A, Vol. 5, No. 6; 12224–Ohio A, Vol. 11, No. 2 (application for further appeal disallowed, 1183–BR–47, unp.); 11263–Pa. R, Vol. 10, No. 2; 7083–R.I. R, Vol. 5, No. 2; 11746–S.C. A, Vol. 10, No. 8; 11606–Va. R, Vol. 10, No. 6; 6982–Wash. A, Vol. 5, No. 2; 12938–W.Va. R, Vol. 11, No. 11; Cf. *Standard Bleachery and Printing Co.* v. *Board of Review, supra,* note 32; *Jackson Mills* v. *E.S. Commission,* Court of Common Pleas, Spartanburg County, South Carolina, Apr. 23, 1947, 11905–S.C. Ct.D., *Ben. Ser.*, Vol. 10, No. 10; 10589–WVa. R, *Ben. Ser.*, Vol. 9, No. 6.

38. 11871–N.H. R, *Ben. Ser.*, Vol. 10, No. 10.

39. 9604–Mass. A, *Ben. Ser.*, Vol. 8, No. 7.

40. 9505–Mass. V, *Ben. Ser.*, Vol. 8, No. 6; 10273–Mich. R, *Ben. Ser.*, Vol. 9, No. 2.

41. 8868–Va. R, *Ben. Ser.*, Vol. 7, No. 10.

42. 10963–Ill. A, *Ben. Ser.*, Vol. 9, No. 11; see also in *Benefit Series*: 9204–Ark. R, Vol. 8, No. 3; 9214–Ga. A, Vol. 8, No. 3; 9797–Md. A, Vol. 8, No. 9; 12125–Mont. A, Vol. 11, No. 1; 5464–Nebr. R, Vol. 4, No. 4; 12515–N.H. R, Vol. 11, No. 6; 12913–N.C. R, Vol. 11, No. 11; 10914–Ohio R, Vol. 9, No. 10; 11824–Pa. A, Vol. 10, No. 9; 11432–S.C. A, Vol. 10, No. 4; 8868–Va. R, Vol. 7, No. 10; 12869–Vt. R, Vol. 11, No. 10; 12941–Wis. A, Vol. 11, No. 11.

43. 9207–Colo. A, *Ben. Ser.*, Vol. 8, No. 3.

44. 11866–Nebr. R, *Ben. Ser.*, Vol. 10, No. 10, affirmed in *Alliance Times-Herald* v. *Miller,* Commissioner, District Court, Box Butte County, Nebraska, May 5, 1947. See also in *Benefit Series:* 9969–Ark. A, Vol. 8, No. 11; 11617–Conn. R, Vol. 10, No. 7; 10246–Fla. V, Vol. 9, No. 2; 11303–Ind. A, Vol. 10, No. 3; 10534–Ky. V, Vol. 9, No. 6; 8024–Me. A, Vol. 6, No. 6; 11229–Mich. R, Vol. 10, No. 2; 11160–Mo. A, Vol. 10, No. 1; 8924–N.C., Vol. 7, No. 11; 9368–Pa. R, Vol. 8, No. 4; 12545–R.I. R, Vol. 11, No. 6.

45. 9326–Ind. R, *Ben. Ser.,* Vol. 8, No. 4. Also 9604–Mass. A, *supra,* note 39.

46. 9505–Mass. A, *Ben. Ser.,* Vol. 8, No. 6.

47. 9631–N.C. V, *Ben. Ser.,* Vol. 8, No. 7. See also in *Benefit Series:* 292–Conn. R, Vol. 1, No. 3; 3085–Ill. A, Vol. 3, No. 4; 2683–Mo. A, Vol. 3, No. 2; 11871–N.H. R, Vol. 10, No. 10; 11486–N.Y. R, Vol. 10, No. 5; 2232–S.C. A, Vol. 2, No. 12, affirmed by commission 39–C–7, unp.; 296–Wis. A, Vol. 1, No. 3.

48. 9390–Conn. R, *Ben. Ser.,* Vol. 8, No. 5, affirmed by *Lombardo* v. *Danaher,* Superior Court, Hartford County, Conn., Feb. 5, 1945; 10749–Ohio V, *Ben. Ser.,* Vol. 9, No. 8.

49. Alabama, Colorado, Florida, Georgia, Illinois, Iowa, Maine, Missouri, Nebraska, New Hampshire, Ohio, Rhode Island, South Dakota, Texas, Vermont, Wyoming.

50. *Henry* v. *Ford Motor Company,* 289 N.W. 244 (Mich.); *Benefit Series:* 10853–Ark. A, Vol. 9, No. 10; 12572–Conn. R, Vol. 11, No. 7; 2665–Ill. A, Vol. 3, No. 2; 3579–Mich. A, Vol. 3, No. 6; 4693–Mo. A, Vol. 3, No. 11; 9016–Pa. R, Vol. 7, No. 12; 1266–S.C. A, Vol. 10, No. 2; Cf. 4095–Ky. A, Vol. 3, No. 8; 2364–Mass. R, Vol. 3, No. 1; 3092–Mich. A, Vol. 3, No. 4; 12786–Okla. A, Vol. 11, No. 9; 9956–Va. R, Vol. 8, No. 8; 433–Wis. A, Vol. 1, No. 4.

51. 9326–Ind. R, Vol. 8, No. 4.

52. 10571–Pa. A, Vol. 9, No. 6.

53. *Benefit Series:* 9485–Ga. R, Vol. 8, No. 6; 7148–Ky. R, Vol. 5, No. 4.

54. Robert C. Goodwin, "Slogan For The Year," *Employment Service Review,* Vol. 13, No. 10 (October 1946), p. 4; Millard W. Rice, "Jobs Better Than Pensions," *Employment Service Review,* Vol. 12, No. 11 (November 1945), pp. 17, 21.

55. *Benefit Series:* 11526–Ala. A, Vol. 10, No. 6; 11445–Ark. A, Vol. 10, No. 5; 9204–Ark. R, Vol. 8, No. 3; 11775–Calif. R, Vol. 10, No. 9; 12948–Colo. A, Vol. 11, No. 12; 8743–Fla. R, Vol. 7, No. 9; 9141–Ill. R, Vol. 8, No. 11; 10963–Ill. A, Vol. 9, No. 11; 10447–Iowa A, Vol. 9, Nos. 4–5; 9492–Kans. A, Vol. 8, No. 6; 10971–Md. A, Vol. 9, No. 11; 9432–Nebr. R, Vol. 8, No. 5; 9182–N.C. A, Vol. 8, No. 2; 11494–N.C. A, Vol. 10, No. 5; 9721–Ohio A, Vol. 8, No. 8; 8932–R.I. A, Vol. 7, No. 11; 11606–Va. R, Vol. 10, No. 6; 11760–W.Va. A, Vol. 10, No. 8.

In some lines of work employers are eager to hire the physically handicapped. The drop forge operator who is not at least partially deaf is assumed to be inexperienced.

56. 8743–Fla. A, *Ben. Ser.,* Vol. 7, No. 9.

57. *Benefit Series: Faulkenberry* v. *Department of Industrial Relations,* Circuit Court, Madison County, Alabama, March 21, 1944, 8657–Ala. Ct.D., Vol. 7, No. 8; 9866–Ala. R, Vol. 8, No. 10; 9207–Colo. A, Vol. 8, No. 3; 11201–Fla. A, Vol. 10, No. 2; 11291–Ga. A, Vol. 10, No. 3; 9458–Ga. R, Vol. 8, No. 6; 9904–Ill. R, Vol. 8, No. 10; 9326–Ind. R, Vol. 8, No. 4; 8519–Kans. A, Vol. 7, No. 5; 10453–Ky. R, Vol. 9, Nos. 4–5; 9337–Me. V, Vol. 8, No. 4; 8973–Ind. A, Vol. 7, No. 12; 8496–Minn. AG, Vol. 7, No. 4; 7694–N.C. R, Vol. 5, No. 12; 9089–Ohio R, Vol. 8, No. 1; 9090–Ohio R, *ibid.;* 9529–Ohio R, Vol. 8, No. 6; 9363–Okla. V, Vol. 8, No. 4; 11263–Pa. R, Vol. 10, No. 2; 10143–R.I. A, Vol. 8, No. 12; 8000–R.I. R, Vol. 6, No. 6; 9452–S.C. A, Vol. 8, No. 5; 9744–Tex. A, Vol. 8, No. 8; 11918–Va. R, Vol. 10, No. 5; 8527–Wash. A, Vol. 7, No. 5.

Contra: Brown-Brockmeyer Co. v. *Board of Review,* 45 N.E.(2d) 152 (1942), 7912–Ohio Ct.D., Vol. 6, No. 4; *Stevens* v. *Selby Shoe Co.,* Court of Appeals, Scioto County, Ohio, 9445–Ohio Ct.D., Vol. 8, No. 5. Cf. *Leonard* v. *U.C. Board of Review,* 75 N.E.(2d) 567 (1947), 12461–Ohio Ct.D., Vol. 11, N. 5; *Judson Mills* v. *U.C. Commission,* 28 S.E.(2d) 535 (1944), 8525–S.C. Ct.D., Vol. 7, No. 5.

58. 8519–Kans. A, *Ben. Ser.,* Vol. 7, No. 5.

59. *Benefit Series:* 9866–Ala. R, Vol. 8, No. 10; 10703–Colo. A, Vol. 9, No. 8;

9489–Ill. R, Vol. 8, No. 6; 9598–Ky. R, Vol. 8, No. 7; 10838–W.Va. R, Vol. 9, No. 9.

60. Utah Department of Employment Security, Division of Insurance, Claims Section, *Manual of Operations,* p. M303.12.

61. *Benefit Series:* 12342–Calif. AG, Vol. 11, No. 4; 9189–Oreg. A, Vol. 8, No. 2; 12238–Pa. A, Vol. 11, No. 2; 9953–Tex. A, Vol. 8, No. 10.

62. 11159–Mo. A, *Ben. Ser.,* Vol. 10, No. 1.

63. See in *Benefit Series:* 11053–Md. A, Vol. 9, No. 12; 11138–Md. A, Vol. 10, No. 1; 12211–Mont. A, Vol. 11, No. 2; Illustrative decisions under the SRA provision include: 9763–Fla. V, Vol. 8, No. 9; 9345–Mass. V, Vol. 8, No. 4; 9693–Mass. V, Vol. 8, No. 8; 9361–Ohio V, Vol. 8, No. 4.

64. David E. Hailman, *The Prevalence of Disabling Illness Among Male and Female Workers and Housewives,* Public Health Bulletin No. 260, 1941, p. 9; Helen L. Cowan, "Compensation for Sickness in Rhode Island," *Monthly Labor Review,* Vol. 60, No. 2 (February 1945), p. 231.

65. See *Fellela* v. *Rhode Island U.C. Board,* Rhode Island Superior Court, P.A. No. 2045, Nov. 3, 1943.

66. See Rhode Island, Referee's decision No. 3548, June 23, 1944, unp.; also No. 4669–AT, Jan. 11, 1946, unp., and 5231–AT, July 23, 1946, unp.

67. San Francisco *Labor Clarion,* Nov. 7, 1947.

NOTES FOR CHAPTER NINE

1. *Benefit Series:* 7147–Calif. A, Vol. 5, No. 4; 10531–Ill. R, Vol. 9, No. 6; 10868–Iowa A, Vol. 9, No. 10; 8835–N.J. R, Vol. 7, No. 10; 9524–N.Y. R, Vol. 8, No. 6; 10913–Ohio R, Vol. 9, No. 10; 10918–Okla. R, Vol. 9, No. 10.

2. *Benefit Series:* 8469–Ill. R, Vol. 7, No. 4; 9322–Ill. R, Vol. 8, No. 4; 9902–Ill. R, Vol. 8, No. 10; and the cases cited in note 1 *supra.*

3. 9524–N.Y. R, *Ben. Ser.,* Vol. 8, No. 6. The identical language supports the decision in 10868–Iowa A, *Ben. Ser.,* Vol. 9, No. 10.

4. John T. Dunlop, "The Economics of Wage Dispute Settlement," *Law and Contemporary Problems,* Vol. 12, No. 2 (Spring 1947), pp. 282–286.

5. Unemployment Compensation Program Letter No. 130, *Principles Underlying the Prevailing Conditions of Work Standard,* Bureau of Employment Security, Jan. 6, 1947, p. 7.

6. To obtain such an average: Multiply each wage involved by the number of workers receiving that wage and add the products. This sum is then divided by the total number of workers involved.

7. The determination of prevailing wage may be clarified by examining the following models, each of which shows a distribution of the wages of 100 workers.

Wage Rate	A	B	C	D	E
40–44.9¢			5	5	5
45–49.9			5	5	10
50–54.9		10	5	10	35
55–59.9		10	5	15	
60–64.9	5	20	5	10	
65–69.9	20	35	20	10	
70–74.9	55	15	15	10	5
75–79.9	20	10	25	15	20
80–84.9			10	10	20
85–89.9			5	10	5
Total	100	100	100	100	100

In models A and B the mode is clearly the prevailing wage. In C and D the weighted average would seem more suitable as a measure of the prevailing wage. Although the most common wage group in C is 75–79.9¢, the median occurs in the 70–74.9¢ bracket, and the weighted average is 69.5¢. Model D shows two separate modes, the 55–59.9¢ and the 75–79.9¢ brackets, but neither involve a large percentage and the distribution is rather even. The median is in the 65–69.9¢ bracket and the weighted average is 68.3¢.

Model E shows no central tendency and an uneven distribution. Two large groupings occur, one in the 50–54.9¢ bracket and one in the 75–84.9¢ brackets, with a central gap of three wage brackets. In reality there is no prevailing wage. For working purposes, however, 50¢ may be considered the floor and 84.9¢ the ceiling of the going wage. Such cases suggest a need to reëxamine the preliminary finding on "similar work."

8. *Benefit Series:* 9928–N.Y. R, Vol. 8, No. 10; 11396–N.Y. R, Vol. 10, No. 4.

9. 6563–Ind. R, *Ben. Ser.,* Vol. 4, No. 10. Other cases, reported in the *Benefit Series,* where it was found that wages offered were substantially less favorable than those prevailing include: 9572–Calif. R, Vol. 8, No. 7 (offered 55¢, prevailing 75¢); 8813–Fla. R, Vol. 7, No. 10 (offered $1.07, prevailing $1.25); 8817–Ill. R, Vol. 7, No. 10 (offered 33¢, War Labor Board minimum 40¢); 9891–Ill. A, Vol. 8, No. 10 (offered $15 a week, prevailing, $22–25); 7552–Mich. A, Vol. 5, No. 9 (offered $17 a week, prevailing $25); 9928–N.Y. R, Vol. 8, No. 10 (offered 60¢, prevailing 70¢); 10376–N.Y. A, Vol. 9, No. 3 (offered 90¢, prevailing 95¢–$1.05); *Ferguson* v. *Bureau of Unemployment Compensation,* Court of Appeals, Stark County, Ohio, No. 2207, Jan. 24, 1946, 10661–Ohio Ct.D., Vol. 9, No. 7 (offered $1, prevailing, $1.55); 9275–Tenn. R, Vol. 8, No. 3 (offered 70¢, War Labor Board suggested rate, 95¢).

10. *Benefit Series:* 9973–Calif. A, Vol. 8, No. 11; 7673–Conn. R, Vol. 5, No. 11; 8762–Mo. R, Vol. 7, No. 9 (affirmed, *Miller* v. *U.C. Commission,* Circuit Court, Jackson County, Missouri, Apr. 29, 1944); 7374–Pa. A, Vol. 5, No. 6 (affirmed, Board of Review, B–44–4–RD–847, unp.).

11. *Benefit Series:* 10943–Calif. R, Vol. 9, No. 11; 11285–Colo. R, Vol. 10, No. 3 (affirmed, *Bates* v. *Industrial Commission,* District Court for City and County of Denver, Sept. 16, 1946); 11999–D.C. A, Vol. 10, No. 2; 9669–Ill. R, Vol. 8, No. 8; 11308–Iowa A, Vol. 10, No. 3; 12505–Kans. A, Vol. 11, No. 6 (appeal dismissed, *Calvert* v. *Labor Commissioner,* Dist. Ct.; Sedgwick County, Kans., Jan. 2, 1948); 10013–Ky. A, Vol. 8, No. 11; 12431–La. R, Vol. 11, No. 5 (modifying 12110–La. A, Vol. 11, No. 2); 10350–Me. A, Vol. 9, No. 3; 13067–Mass. A, Vol. 12, No. 1; 10648–Mich. A, Vol. 9, No. 7; 10464–Miss. R, Vol. 9, Nos. 4–5 (affirmed, *Davis* v. *Mississippi U.C. Commission,* Circuit Court, Leaks County, Nov. 19, 1945); 12291–Nebr. R, Vol. 11, No. 3; 10127–N.J. A, Vol. 8, No. 12 (aff. BR–5981); 9940–Okla. R, Vol. 8, No. 10; 11428–Pa. R, Vol. 10, No. 4; 11431–R.I. R, Vol. 10, No. 4; 10585–Tenn. R, Vol. 9, No. 6; 9197–Tex. A, Vol. 8, No. 2; 12870–Va. R, Vol. 11, No. 10.

12. *Benefit Series:* 9652–Calif. R, Vol. 8, No. 8; 8955–Conn. R, Vol. 7, No. 12; 9219–Ill. R, Vol. 8, No. 3; 8990–Mo. R, Vol. 7, No. 12; 10994–Okla. A, Vol. 9, No. 11; 10680–Wash. A, Vol. 9, No. 7.

13. *Benefit Series:* 9669–Ill. R, Vol. 8, No. 8; 9921–Mich. A, Vol. 8, No. 10.

14. 10943–Calif. R, *Ben. Ser.,* Vol. 9, No. 11. See also *Benefit Series:* 8680–Kans. A, Vol. 7, No. 8 (refused trainee jobs); 9430–Nebr. R, Vol. 8, No. 5 (union carpenter, refused bridge builder helper-carpenter); 9351–N.H. R, Vol. 8, No. 4 (painter, foreman-estimator, refused straight painting); 10042–Ohio A, Vol. 8, No. 11 (appeal denied, 136–BR–45; bench hand, refused furniture finisher); 11428–Pa. R, Vol. 10, No. 4 (coner, refused trainee referral).

15. 10907–N.C. A, *Ben. Ser.,* Vol. 9, No. 10.

16. *Benefit Series:* 8730–Ala. R, Vol. 7, No. 9; 10242–Calif. R, Vol. 9, No. 2;

8304–Ill. R, Vol. 7, No. 1; 8914–Mo. A, Vol. 7, No. 11; 9433–Nebr. R, Vol. 8, No. 5; 9629–N.C. A, Vol. 8, No. 7; 9935–N.C. R, Vol. 8, No. 10; 9442–N.Y. R, Vol. 8, No. 5; 8236–Oreg. A, Vol. 6, No. 11.

17. E.g., 7598–Mo. A, *Ben. Ser.,* Vol. 5, No. 10.

18. *Benefit Series:* 9209–Colo. A, Vol. 8, No. 3; 8968–Ind. A, Vol. 7, No. 12; 9433–Nebr. R, Vol. 8, No. 5; 10471–Nebr. R, Vol. 9, Nos. 4–5; 11243–Nebr. R, Vol. 10, No. 2; 11402–Okla. A, Vol. 10, No. 4 (affirmed, Board of Review, 199–BR–46, unp.) ; 10402–Tex. R, Vol. 9, No. 3. Also see 9769–Ill. R, Vol. 8, No. 9; 8673–Ill. A, Vol. 7, No. 8.

19. 10390–Ohio V, *Ben. Ser.,* Vol. 9, No. 3.

20. See "Length of Unemployment and Prospects of Work" in Chapter VI.

21. *Benefit Series:* 10417–Ark. A, Vol. 9, Nos. 4–5 (affirmed Board of Review, BR–173) ; 9753–Calif. R, Vol. 8, No. 9; 9874–Calif. R, Vol. 8, No. 10; 8469–Ill. R, Vol. 7, No. 4; 10789–Ill. R, Vol. 9, No. 9; 9908–Kans. A, Vol. 8, No. 10; 11045–La. A, Vol. 9, No. 12; 7598–Mo. A, Vol. 5, No. 10; 10817–Nebr. R, Vol. 9, No. 9; 9524–N.Y. R, Vol. 8, No. 6; 11169–N.C. R, Vol. 10, No. 1; 9188–Oreg. A, Vol. 8, No. 2.

22. 7938–N.J. A, *Ben. Ser.,* Vol. 6, No. 5. Also see *Benefit Series:* 12947–Colo. A, Vol. 11, No. 2; 11244–Nebr. R, Vol. 10, No. 2.

23. *Benefit Series:* 10942–Calif. R, Vol. 9, No. 11; 9135–D.C. A, Vol. 8, No. 2; 9669–Ill. R, Vol. 8, No. 8; 8588–Mo. R, Vol. 7, No. 6; 11167–N.Mex. A, Vol. 10, No. 1; 10908–N.C. R, Vol. 9, No. 10 (affirmed, *State ex rel. U.C. Commission* v. *Burlington Mills,* Superior Court, Wake County, North Carolina, Apr. 19, 1946) ; 10048–R.I. A, Vol. 8, No. 11.

24. 8910–Mo. A, *Ben. Ser.,* Vol. 7, No. 11. (Appeal denied, U.C. Commission, C–1320, unp.; affirmed, Circuit Court, Ozark County, June 26, 1944, *Roberts* v. *Keitel, Sr.*)

25. *Benefit Series:* 9392–Conn. R, Vol. 8, No. 5 (four months) ; 10426–Conn. R, Vol. 9, Nos. 4–5 (at least seven weeks) ; 10707–Fla. A, Vol. 9, No. 8 (more than one week) ; 10714–Ill. R, Vol. 9, No. 8 (three months) ; 10716–Ill. R, Vol. 9, No. 8 (at least six weeks) ; 10867–Iowa A, Vol. 9, No. 10 (more than one week) ; 11214–Kans. A, Vol. 10, No. 2 (thirty days) ; 10641–Mass. R, Vol. 9, No. 7 (ten weeks more than reasonable time) ; 11244–Nebr. R, Vol. 10, No. 2 (six weeks) ; 13078–N.J. R, Vol. 12, No. 1 (two months) ; 10907–N.C. R, Vol. 9, No. 10 (less than one month not enough) ; 10394–Pa. R, Vol. 9, No. 3 (three months more than ample).

26. 10551–N.J. A, *Ben. Ser.,* Vol. 9, No. 6 (affirmed, Board of Review, BR–6091, unp.).

27. 10195–N.J. R, *Ben. Ser.,* Vol. 9, No. 1.

28. *Benefit Series:* 8880–Colo. A, Vol. 7, No. 11; 10320–Del. R, Vol. 9, No. 3; 10175–Ill. A, Vol. 9, No. 1; 8968–Ind. A, Vol. 7, No. 12; 9409–Iowa R, Vol. 8, No. 5; 10260–Me. A, Vol. 9, No. 2; 10350–Me. A, Vol. 9, No. 3; 12114–Mass. A, Vol. 11, No. 1 (adopted by Board Decision No. 19,266–BR; affirmed by *Abair* v. *Division,* District Court, Springfield, Mass., Apr. 28, 1947) ; 10546–Minn. A, Vol. 9, No. 6; 10042–Ohio A, Vol. 8, No. 11; 9940–Okla. R, Vol. 8, No. 10; 2395–Tenn. A, Vol. 3, No. 1; 7602–Tenn. A, Vol. 5, No. 10.

Compare: 10709–Ga. A, Vol. 9, No. 8; 7598–Mo. A, Vol. 5, No. 10; 10910–N.C. R, Vol. 9, No. 10.

29. 10546–Minn. A, *Ben. Ser.,* Vol. 9, No. 6. Also see, in *Benefit Series,* 9940–Okla. R, and 9945–Vt. A, both in Vol. 8, No. 10.

30. 10873–Kans. A, *Ben. Ser.,* Vol. 9, No. 10. See also in *Benefit Series:* 10416–Ark. A, Vol. 9, Nos. 4–5; 10509–Ark. A, Vol. 9, No. 6; 10543–Mich. A, Vol. 9, No. 6; 12920–Okla. A, Vol. 11, No. 11.

31. *Benefit Series:* 9759–Calif. R, Vol. 8, No. 9 (structural iron worker thirty-five years, refused laboring work) ; 9589–Ill. R, Vol. 8, No. 7 (fifty-eight-

year-old hat maker, eleven years with same employer, refused radio repairer trainee job); 13050–Ill. R, Vol. 12, No. 1; 10726–La. A, Vol. 9, No. 8 (machinist's helper, thirty years' experience, refused jobs as stationary boiler fireman and laborer); 8422–Mo. A, Vol. 7, No. 3 (musician thirty years, refused industrial work); 10195–N.J. R, Vol. 9, No. 1 (woodworking machine operator, twenty-five years' experience, refused helper's jobs); 10298–Pa. A, Vol. 9, No. 2 (fifty-five-year-old clerical worker, eighteen years in filing and general clerical work, refused cashier's job); 11520–Va. R, Vol. 10, No. 5 (sixty-seven years old, cable splicer over forty years).

Compare: 8812–D.C. A, Vol. 7, No. 10 (alteration tailor since age of fourteen, would take no other tailoring); 10252–Ill. R, Vol. 9, No. 2 (inside finish carpenter, union member thirty-eight years, only inside finish work, unemployed seven and a half months); 9780–Ind. A, Vol. 8, No. 9 (fur cutter, seventy-one years old, forty years' experience, would take no other work in off-season); 10338–Kans. A, Vol. 9, No. 3 (steam fitter, union member thirty-five years; allowed thirty days).

32. 15 N.W. (2d)115 (1944), 8909–Minn. Ct.D., *Ben. Ser.*, Vol. 7, No. 11.

33. 11322–Mich. R, *Ben. Ser.*, Vol. 10, No. 3.

34. *Scholle* v. *Miller, Comm.*, District Court, Gage County, Nebraska, May 10, 1946, 10982–Nebr. Ct.D., *Ben. Ser.*, Vol. 9, No. 11. See also in the *Benefit Series:* 10366–Miss. R, Vol. 9, No. 3; 10991–Ohio R, Vol. 9, No. 11; 10206–Okla. A, Vol. 9, No. 1.

35. 9162–Miss. A, *Ben. Ser.*, Vol. 8, No. 2.

36. 9420–Me. A, *Ben. Ser.*, Vol. 8, No. 5, affirmed by Commission, 44–CD–18 (unp.).

37. See the discussion in Chapter VI, under "Length of Unemployment and Prospects of Work."

38. Cf. Summer H. Slichter, "The Impact of Social Security Legislation Upon Mobility and Enterprise," *American Economic Review* (supplement), Vol. 30, No. 1 (March 1940), p. 44.

39. *Wagner* v. *U.C. Commission,* 198 S.W. (2d) (Mo.)342 (1946). See also in the *Benefit Series:* 10166–Calif. A, Vol. 9, No. 1; 9222–Kans. A, Vol. 8, No. 3; 10638–Mass. A, Vol. 9, No. 7 (affirmed, 12,568–BR); 12114–Mass. A, Vol. 11, No. 1 (adopted by board decision No. 19,266–BR; affirmed by *Abair* v. *Division,* District Court, Springfield, Apr. 28, 1947); cf. 12746–Mass. A, Vol. 11, No. 9; 11156–Miss. A, Vol. 10, No. 1; 12756–Miss. A, Vol. 11, No. 9; 8762–Mo. R, Vol. 7, No. 9 (affirmed by Circuit Court, Jackson County, Apr. 29, 1944, *Miller* v. *U.C. Commission*); 10818–N.H. R, Vol. 9, No. 9; 11892–Ohio R, Vol. 10, No. 10; 9745–Vt. A, Vol. 8, No. 8; *Bohannon* v. *U.C. Commission,* Superior Court, Yakima County, Wash., 8948–Wash. Ct.D., Vol. 7, No. 11; 11764–Wis. R, Vol. 10, No. 8. But see: 12954–Conn. R, Vol. 11, No. 12; 12975–Mass. A, Vol. 11, No. 12.

40. *Benefit Series:* 10421–Calif. R, Vol. 9, Nos. 4–5; 11620–Del. A, Vol. 10, No. 7; 10984–N. J. A, Vol. 9, No. 11; 11429–R.I. R, Vol. 10, No. 4; 13114–W.Va. R, Vol. 12, No. 1.

41. *Benefit Series:* 6172–Conn. R, Vol. 4, No. 7; 12901–Mass. R, Vol. 11, No. 11 (even though unexpectedly long); 9060–Me. A, Vol. 8, No. 1; 13075–Nebr. R, Vol. 12, No. 1; 10984–N.J. A, Vol. 9, No. 11; 11429–R.I. R, Vol. 10, No. 4; 12396–Utah A, Vol. 11, No. 4.

42. *Benefit Series:* 10513–Ark. A, Vol. 9, No. 6 (affirmed by Board of Review, 340–BR, unp.); 8734–Calif. R, Vol. 7, No. 9; 9972–Calif. R, Vol. 8, No. 11; 8953–Conn. R, Vol. 7, No. 12; 9764–Ga. R, Vol. 8, No. 9; 10965–Ill. R, Vol. 9, No. 11; 9060–Me. A, Vol. 8, No. 1; 10632–Me. A, Vol. 9, No. 7; 12063–Ohio R, Vol. 10, No. 12; 9018–Pa. R, Vol. 7, No. 12; 9267–Pa. R, Vol. 8, No. 3; 12396–Utah A, Vol. 11, No. 4; 11438–Wash. A, Vol. 10, No. 4.

43. 9865–Ala. A, *Ben. Ser.,* Vol. 8, No. 10. See also in the *Benefit Series:* 10783–Fla. R, Vol. 9, No. 9; 10172–Ga. A, Vol. 9, No. 1; 8931–Pa. R, Vol. 7, No. 11. Cf. 13075–Nebr. R, Vol. 12, No. 1.

44. "Claimants Awaiting Recall — Their Special Problems of Availability and Suitability of Work," *Social Security Bulletin,* Vol. 9, No. 10 (October 1946), pp. 13–15.

45. Vermont U.C. Commission, *Policy and Procedure With Respect to Determination of Suitable Work and Refusal of Referral,* Oct. 17, 1945, pp. 2, 3.

46. Office of War Mobilization and Reconversion, *Guaranteed Wages,* Report to the President by the Advisory Board, Jan. 31, 1947, pp. 101–124, 179–80.

47. Computed from Bureau of Labor Statistics, Bulletin No. 878, *Work Stoppages Caused by Labor-Management Disputes in 1945,* Table 1, p. 3.

48. *Clinton v. Hake,* 206 S.W.(2d)889(Tenn.) (1947), 12634–Tenn. Ct.D., *Ben. Ser.,* Vol. 11, No. 7; 10301–Tenn. R, *Ben. Ser.,* Vol. 9, No. 2. Other Tennessee Board of Review decisions, under the pre-1947 statute are cited by Commissioner W. D. Hake in his letter of February 27, 1947 to the writer: 46–BR–541; 47–BR–1; 47–BR–2; 47–BR–3 (all unp.). The letter of Thomas J. Donaghy, Administrative Assistant to the Pennsylvania Secretary of Labor and Industry, February 13, 1947, cites the decision of the Pennsylvania Board of Review in the Albright case (B–44–98–B–330, unp.). This decision holds that striking employees may be available for work while refusing jobs with the employer against whom they are striking. The New York position is stated unequivocally in a letter from Mr. Milton D. Loysen, Executive Director of the Division of Placement and Unemployment Insurance, January 16, 1947. New York claimants unemployed because of a labor dispute may not qualify for benefits while limiting their availability to their former employer. The Chairman of the Rhode Island U.C. Board, Mr. Mortimer W. Newton, in his letter of January 28, 1947 just as clearly takes the opposite position.

49. *Bigger v. U.C. Commission,* 53 A.(2d)761 (1947) (Del.), affirming 46 A.(2d)137 (1946); *Speer v. Industrial Commission,* Circuit Court, 11th Judicial Circuit, Dade County, Florida, Mar. 12, 1945, 9761–Fla. Ct.D., *Ben. Ser.,* Vol. 8, No. 9; *Chambers v. Owens-Ames-Kimball Co.,* 67 N.E.(2d)439 (1946), 10990–Ohio Ct.D., *Ben. Ser.,* Vol. 9, No. 11; *Barclay White Co. v. U.C. Board,* 50 A.(2d)336 (Pa., 1947). In *Donnelly Garment Co. v. Keitel,* 193 S.W.(2d)577 (1946), 10897–Mo. Ct.D., *Ben. Ser.,* Vol. 9, No. 10, the court disqualified the claimant for the work refusal and held her unavailable for work.

50. *Chambers v. Owens-Ames-Kimball, supra,* note 49.

51. *Chambers v. Owens-Ames-Kimball, supra,* note 49. For further comment, see "Withdrawal of Unemployment Compensation Benefits for Refusal to Accept Work in Violation of Union Rules," 56 *Yale Law Journal,* January 1947, pp. 384–395.

52. Section 1345–6(e)(1), Ohio General Code.

53. *Barclay White Co. v. U.C. Board, supra,* note 49.

54. 46 A.(2d)598 (1946), 10832–Pa. Ct.D., *Ben. Ser.,* Vol. 9, No. 9.

55. U.S. Code, Title 45, Chapter 11, Sec. 354(c). The New York Labor Law, Sec. 593.2.(a) extends broader protection and prevents benefit denial if acceptance of the employment "would interfere with his [claimant's] joining, or retaining membership in any labor organization."

56. 63 *Corpus Juris* 661, "Trade Unions," Section 10; 31 *American Jurisprudence* 856, "Labor," Section 43.

57. 31 *American Jurisprudence,* "Labor," Section 45.

58. *Benefit Series:* 9482–Fla. A, Vol. 8, No. 6; see also 9150–Kans. A, Vol. 8, No. 2; 11062–Mo. A, Vol. 9, No. 12. Compare 8912–Mo. A, Vol. 7, No. 11 (appeal denied by U.C. Commission, C–1358, unp.; union electrician refused to renew

registration with employment service). 13112–Tenn. R, Vol. 12, No. 1 (one who limits himself to union contract work is not available for work).

59. *Benefit Series:* 10942–Calif. R, Vol. 9, No. 11; 9532–Oreg. A, Vol. 8, No. 6 (one month exploratory period allowed); 11670–Tenn. R, Vol. 10, No. 7.

60. *Benefit Series:* 8082–Calif. R, Vol. 6, No. 8; 7932–Calif. A, Vol. 6, No. 5; 8124–Colo. A, Vol. 6, No. 9; 9635–Okla. A, Vol. 8, No. 7 (affirmed by Board of Review, 24–BR–45, unp.); 7447–Wash. A, Vol. 6, No. 1; 12162–Wash. A, Vol. 11, No. 1. Cf. 13087–Ohio R, Vol. 12, No. 1. Benefits were allowed in these cases: 9672–Ind. A, Vol. 8, No. 8 (referee found that employment in claimant's field was not closely controlled by any one union in area); 10336–Kans. A, Vol. 9, No. 3 (claimant experienced both as a painter and truck driver, actively seeking work, willing to take as little as 50¢ an hour); 7512–Oreg. A, Vol. 5, No. 9 (claimant's objections were on religious grounds).

Where "right-to-work" or anti-closed shop laws exist a somewhat different result may be obtained. See 9987–Fla. AG, *Ben. Ser.,* Vol. 8, No. 11. Willingness to join a union remained a factor under the Labor-Management Relations Act of 1947 (Taft-Hartley Law) which barred the closed shop, but left room for a union shop.

61. Oregon U.C. Commission, *Benefit Manual,* "Reconversion Unemployment Benefits For Seamen," June 19, 1947, Appendix F, Sec. 4800, II. A.2.f, p. 8. Title XIII of the Social Security Act providing for such benefits, to be paid through state unemployment compensation agencies from federal funds, was enacted in 1946.

62. 9352–N.J. A, *Ben. Ser.,* Vol. 8, No. 4.

63. *Benefit Series:* 9577–Fla. R, Vol. 8, No. 7; 7447–Conn. R, Vol. 5, No. 7; 9048–Ill. A, Vol. 8, No. 1.

64. *Benefit Series:* 8578–Ill. R, Vol. 7, No. 6 (fur finisher); 10338–Kans. A, Vol. 9, No. 3; 8964–Mo. A, Vol. 7, No. 2 (appeal dismissed by U.C. Commission, C–1303, unp.; hat worker); 8708–Oreg. A, Vol. 7, No. 8 (caterpillar operator-mechanic). *Contra:* 9601–La. A, Vol. 8, No. 7 (cement finisher, unemployed three weeks).

65. *Benefit Series:* 9128–Calif. R, Vol. 8, No. 2; 9482–Fla. A, Vol. 8, No. 6; 9221–Ind. A, Vol. 8, No. 3; 10112–Mich. A, Vol. 8, No. 2; 9247–N.J. A, Vol. 8, No. 3; 10196–N.J. R, Vol. 9, No. 1; 8771–N.Y. R, Vol. 7, No. 9; 10135–Okla. R, Vol. 8, No. 12; 10209–Pa. R, Vol. 9, No. 1; 8146–Va. A, Vol. 6, No. 9; 9115–Wyo. A, Vol. 8, No. 1.

Donnelly Garment Co. v. *Keitel, supra,* note 49, reaches a somewhat contrary conclusion but fails to hit the issue squarely. Claimant left Donnelly and then worked for Markay under a permit from the union. While she was unemployed Donnelly offered to rehire her. Claimant refused because she would have to join the Donnelly union and lose her status with the Markay union. The commission had said that the Donnelly job was suitable. (See 8343–Mo. R, *Ben. Ser.,* Vol. 7, No. 1.) This court accepted and then decided that in the light of claimant's "continuing" refusal of such suitable work she could not be available for work.

The commission also said that there was no evidence that the Donnelly union, which had a closed-shop agreement, was a company union. Throughout the history of this case, that union was under investigation by the National Labor Relations Board. At the time the commission made its decision (November 30, 1943), the National Labor Relations Board had issued a cease and desist order in which the union was characterized as a company union. See 50 N.L.R.B. 241 (C–1382), June 9, 1943. This order was later set aside by the U.S. Circuit Court of Appeals, 8th Circuit (151 F.(2d)854) but not until October 29, 1945.

66. Seven state laws have modified the federal language substantially: Delaware, Kansas, Massachusetts, New York, Ohio, South Dakota, and Washington.

In Delaware and Washington, the law refers specifically to a condition of being employed which is required by the employer. (Such language was inserted in the Minnesota law in 1943, declared by the State Attorney General, June 17, 1943, as not changing the previous meaning of the law, and deleted by amendment in 1945.) In Massachusetts and New York the phrase "condition of being employed" is omitted and the subject reference is to "acceptance" of such work or employment. In Massachusetts benefits may not be denied if acceptance of the work would "abridge or limit his right to join or retain membership" in a union. Similarly in New York, if it would "interfere" with such joining or retaining. Ohio bars benefit denials if the individual, as a condition of being employed, "would be denied the right to retain membership in and observe the lawful rules" of his union. Delaware also protects the worker from benefit denials if the employer denies him the right to retain such membership and observe such rules. In Kansas and South Dakota benefits may not be denied if, as a condition of being employed, the individual would be required to join or to resign from or refrain from joining any labor organization.

67. *Speer* v. *Industrial Commission, supra,* note 49; *Chambers* v. *Owens-Ames-Kimball Co., idem; Barclay White Co.* v. *U.C. Board, idem; Bigger* v. *U.C. Commission, idem. Benefit Series:* 8567–Ark. A, Vol. 7, No. 2; 8893–Ga. A, Vol. 7, No. 11; 10333–Ind. R, Vol. 9, No. 3; 9412–Kans. A, Vol. 8, No. 5; 8453–Va. A, Vol. 7, No. 3; 9853–Wash. A, Vol. 8, No. 9; 10679–Wash. A, Vol. 9, No. 7. *Contra:* 10415–Ark. AG, Vol. 9, Nos. 4–5; 9305–Calif. R, Vol. 8, No. 4; 8888–Fla. A, Vol. 7, No. 11; 11216–Ky. A, Vol. 10, No. 2; 7206–N.H. A, Vol. 5, No. 4; 10135–Okla. R, Vol. 8, No. 12; 7211–Tenn. A, Vol. 5, No. 4.

In the Bigger case, *supra,* note 49, the Delaware Superior Court took the view that "condition of being employed" included all the elements and incidents of the employment whether or not they were a contractual part of the relationship. The word "resign," however, was unequivocally different from "expel" or "suspend" and could not be stretched to cover them. In reviewing the case, however, the Delaware Supreme Court rejected this reasoning and adopted the more orthodox view.

The interpretation of the Social Security Administration (and its predecessor, the Social Security Board) is indicated by its acceptance of the Delaware and Washington provisions, as well as the Minnesota amendments of 1943, as meeting the requirements of Section 1603 (a) (5) of the Internal Revenue Code. See also: Unemployment Compensation Program Letter No. 101, *Principles Underlying The Suitable-Work Disqualification.* Bureau of Employment Security, Nov. 26, 1945, p. 11; Arthur M. Menard, "Refusal of Suitable Work," *Yale Law Journal,* Vol. 55, No. 1 (December 1945), p. 143.

68. U.C. Program Letter No. 101, *Principles Underlying the Suitable-Work Disqualification,* p. 11.

69. 8073–Iowa. R, *Ben. Ser.,* Vol. 6, No. 7.

NOTES FOR CHAPTER TEN

1. See Chapter XII, Women Workers, "Care of Children."

2. "Multiple-Shift Plant Operations," *Monthly Labor Review,* Vol. 46, No. 3 (March 1938), pp. 639–641; "Shift Operations Under Union Agreements," *idem,* Vol. 51, No. 4 (October 1940), pp. 860–872.

3. "Working Hours in War Production Plants," *Monthly Labor Review,* Vol. 54, No. 5 (May 1942), pp. 1061–1065.

4. *Ford Motor Co.* v. *Appeal Board,* 25 N.W.(2d) 586 (1947), 11553–Mich. Ct.D., *Ben. Ser.,* Vol. 10, No. 6. See also *Dinovellis* v. *Danaher,* 12 Conn. Supp. 122 (1943), 8201–Conn. Ct.D., *Ben. Ser.,* Vol. 6, No. 11; *Schaffnit* v. *Danaher,* 13 Conn. Supp. 101 (1944), 8956–Conn. Ct.D., *Ben. Ser.,* Vol. 7, No. 12; *Judson*

Mills v. *U.C. Commission,* 28 S.E.(2d)535 (1944), 8525–S.C. Ct.D., *Ben. Ser.,* Vol. 7, No. 5; *American Viscose Corporation* v. *Board of Review,* Circuit Court, Kanawha County, Apr. 14, 1944, 8725–W.Va. Ct.D., *Ben. Ser.,* Vol. 7, No. 8.

5. 11550–Mass. A, *Ben Ser.,* Vol. 10, No. 6. See also in the *Benefit Series:* 12559–Ala. A, Vol. 11, No. 7 (affirmed, B.A. Decision No. 862, unp.) ; Cf. 12171–Ala. A, Vol. 11, No. 2 (affirmed, B.A. Decision No. 855, unp.) ; *Rog* v. *Division of Employment Security,* District Court for Eastern Hampshire, October 31, 1946, 11475–Mass. Ct.D., Vol. 10, No. 5; 13071–Mich. R, Vol. 12, No. 1; 10903–N.H. R, Vol. 9, No. 10; 10916–Okla. R. Vol. 9, No. 10; 11079–Okla. A, Vol. 9, No. 12 (affirmed, Board of Review, 75–BR–46, unp.) ; 13110–S.C. R, Vol. 12, No. 1; 11184–Va. A, Vol. 10, No. 1.

6. *Leonard* v. *U.C. Board of Review,* 75 N.E.(2d)567 (1947), 12461–Ohio Ct.D., *Ben. Ser.,* Vol. 11, No. 5. See also in *Benefit Series:* 10514–Ark. A, Vol. 9, No. 6; 12724–Calif. R, Vol. 11, No. 9 (distinguishes 10239–Calif. R, Vol. 9, No. 2) ; 11287–Colo. A, Vol. 10, No. 3; 12815–Del. A, Vol. 11, No. 10; 7778–Del. R, Vol. 6, No. 2; 8698–Ind. A, Vol. 7, No. 11; 10722–Kans. A, Vol. 9, No. 10; 10970–La. A, Vol. 9, No. 11; 8694–Mich. A, Vol. 7, No. 8; 11149–Minn. A, Vol. 10, No. 1; 12979–Miss. A, Vol. 11, No. 12; 10367–Mo. A, Vol. 9, No. 3; 11060–Mo. A, Vol. 9, No. 12; 11066–Nebr. R, Vol. 9, No. 12; (allowed a nine-week period) ; 11329–Nebr. R, Vol. 10, No. 3; 12843–N.Y. R, Vol. 11, No. 10; 13086–N.C. R, Vol. 12, No. 1; 9183–Ohio A, Vol. 8, No. 2; 8711–Oreg. A, Vol. 7, No. 8; 10925–Pa. R, Vol. 9, No. 10; 12929–R.I. R, Vol. 11, No. 11; 11089–Tenn. R, Vol. 9, No. 12; 8938–Tex. A, Vol. 7, No. 11; 12477–Vt. R, Vol. 11, No. 5; 8164–Wash. A, Vol. 6, No. 10 (affirmed by Commissioner, No. 328, unp.) ; 11004–W.Va. A.R., Vol. 9, No. 11.

7. Connecticut: *Dinovellis* v. *Danaher, supra,* note 4; *Schaffnit* v. *Danaher, supra,* note 4; *Vassallo* v. *Administrator,* Superior Court, Fairfield County, July 19, 1946, 11103–Conn. Ct.D., *Ben. Ser.,* Vol. 10, No. 1; *Contra: Carani* v. *Danaher,* Superior Court, Hartford County, Docket No. 69595, 8416–Conn. Ct.D., *Ben. Ser.,* Vol. 7, No. 3.

Massachusetts: *Rog* v. *Division of Employment Security, supra,* note 5.

West Virginia: *American Viscose Corporation* v. *Board of Review, supra,* note 4.

8. *Judson Mills* v. *U.C. Commissioner, supra,* note 4.

9. *Daw* v. *Pickwick Hotel,* District Court of Central Berkshire, 5897–Mass. Ct.D., *Ben. Ser.,* Vol. 4, No. 10.

10. See Chapter VI, under "Negative Aspects of the Rule," and cases cited in notes 51–54 of that chapter.

11. U.C. Program Letter No. 103, *Principles Underlying Availability for Work,* Bureau of Employment Security, Dec. 10, 1945, p. 26; Ralph Altman and Virginia Lewis, "Limited Availability for Shift Employment," *North Carolina Law Review,* Vol. 22, No. 3 (April 1944), pp. 189–211; Louise F. Freeman, "Able to Work and Available for Work," *Yale Law Journal,* Vol. 55, No. 1, p. 130.

Note the following cases in the *Benefit Series:* availability limited to second (evening) shift; held eligible: 9875–Calif. R, Vol. 8, No. 10; 10313–Calif. A, Vol. 9, No. 3; 10794–Ill. R, Vol. 9, No. 9; 13055–Ind. A, Vol. 12, No. 1; 12283–Miss. A, Vol. 11, No. 3; 10028–Nebr. R, Vol. 8, No. 11; 11491–N.Y. R, Vol. 10, No. 5; 12316–Pa. R, Vol. 11, No. 3.

Availability limited to third shift or night work only; held eligible: 9753–Calif. R, Vol. 8, No. 9; 9208–Colo. A, Vol. 8, No. 3; 12731–Del. A, Vol. 11, No. 9; 11028–Idaho A, Vol. 9, No. 12; 9436–N.J. R, Vol. 8, No. 5; 12764–N.J. R, Vol. 11, No. 9; 6403–N.Y. A, Vol. 4, No. 9.

Also see: *Mees Bakery* v. *U.C. Board,* 56 A.(2d)386 (1948), 12541–Pa. Ct.D., Vol. 11, No. 6.

12. *Benefit Series:* 9296–Ala. R, Vol. 8, No. 4; 10313–Calif. A, Vol. 9, No. 3; 9614–Mo. A, Vol. 8, No. 7; 10367–Mo. A, Vol. 9, No. 3; 10028–Nebr. R, Vol. 8, No. 11; 9172–N.H. R, Vol. 8, No. 2; 9436–N.J. R, Vol. 8, No. 5; 9624–N.Y. R, Vol. 8, No. 7; 11089–Tenn. R, Vol. 9, No. 12; 10929–Tex. A, Vol. 9, No. 10; 8944–Va. R, Vol. 7, No. 11.

See also: *Lee* v. *Spartan Mills,* Court of Common Pleas, Spartanburg County, Apr. 3, 1944, 8717–S.C. Ct.D., *Ben. Ser.,* Vol. 7, No. 8 (While accepting the rule of the *Judson Mills* case, *supra,* note 4, this decision holds available a spinner, employed for thirty years on the first or second shift only, and for the last three years on a five-day week basis, who refused to accept third shift work on a six-day week basis.)

13. *Benefit Series:* 9126–Calif. A, Vol. 8, No. 2; 9225–Md. A, Vol. 8, No. 3 (affirmed by U.C. Board, No. 619); 9235–Mich. R, Vol. 8, No. 3; 10651–Nebr. R, Vol. 9, No. 7; 9525–N.Y. R, Vol. 8, No. 6; 11488–N.Y. R, Vol. 10, No. 5.

14. See Section 17.0828(5)(a) of the South Dakota Employment Security Act. Such a definition serves to distinguish "part-time work" from "partial unemployment" (working less than full-time and earning less than the weekly benefit amount in any one week with a regular employer) and "part-total unemployment" (working less than full-time and earning less than the benefit amount with a nonregular employer).

15. Colorado, Illinois, Indiana, Iowa, Massachusetts (omits part (a) of the definition given in the text), New Mexico, South Dakota.

In *Williams v. Commonwealth* (Fourth District Court of Berkshire, Aug. 5, 1948; 12977–Mass. Ct.D., *Ben. Ser.,* Vol. 11, No. 12) the court ruled that the authority given by the Massachusetts law to the Director of the Division of Employment Security to make special provision concerning the eligibility of part-time workers was discretionary and the director was not required to exercise that authority.

16. Sec. 597.3, New York Labor Law.

17. *Benefit Series:* 9986–Fla. A, Vol. 8, No. 11 (affirmed by Board of Review, No. 173, unp.); 9670–Ill. R, Vol. 8, No. 8; 12497–Ill. R, Vol. 11, No. 6; 9326–Ind. R, Vol. 8, No. 4; 9056–Ky. A, Vol. 8, No. 1; 8204–La. A, Vol. 6, No. 11; *Williams* v. *Commonwealth* (Mass.), *supra,* note 15; 12835–Mass. A, Vol. 11, No. 10; cf. 12514–Nev. A, Vol. 11, No. 6; 10561–N.C. R, Vol. 9, No. 6; 12617–N.Dak. A, Vol. 11, No. 7 (8 A.M. to 5 P.M. not a full workday); 3101–Ohio A, Vol. 3, No. 4; 9832–Okla. A, Vol. 8, No. 9; 6845–Oreg. A, Vol. 5, No. 1; 9190–Pa. R, Vol. 8, No. 2; 9946–Pa. R, Vol. 8, No. 10; 6978–Tex. A, Vol. 5, No. 2. Note 12766–N.J. R, Vol. 11, No. 9 on what is part-time work.

18. 10460–Minn. A, *Ben. Ser.,* Vol. 9, Nos. 4–5. See also in the *Benefit Series:* 12891–Del. A, Vol. 11, No. 11; 8521–Kans. A, Vol. 7, No. 5; 10550–N.J. A, Vol. 9, No. 6 (affirmed by Board of Review, BR–6094–D, unp.); 7093–N.Y. R, Vol. 5, No. 3; 9524–N.Y. R, Vol. 5, No. 3; 10211–R.I. A, Vol. 9, No. 1; 9450–R.I. R, Vol. 8, No. 5; 12396–Utah A, Vol. 11, No. 4.

19. *Benefit Series:* Available: 12341–Calif. R, Vol. 11, No. 4; 10238–Calif. A, Vol. 9, No. 1; 10775–Calif. A, Vol. 9, No. 9; 9568–Calif. R, Vol. 8, No. 7. Not available: 9751–Calif. R, Vol. 8, No. 9; 10423–Calif. R, Vol. 9, Nos. 4–5.

20. 9879–Conn. R, *Ben. Ser.,* Vol. 8, No. 10.

21. 9245–Minn. A, *Ben. Ser.,* Vol. 8, No. 3 (affirmed by director 6797–730, unp.).

22. 10423–Calif. R, *Ben. Ser.,* Vol. 9, Nos. 4–5.

23. 8775–N.Y. R, *Ben. Ser.,* Vol. 7, No. 9. See also 6960–N.Y. R, *Ben. Ser.,* Vol. 5, No. 2.

24. *Colvert* v. *Department of Industrial Relations,* Circuit Court, Madison County, July 28, 1944, 8951–Ala. Ct.D., *Ben. Ser.,* Vol. 7, No. 12.

25. Note three Connecticut Superior Court decisions: *Fratto* v. *Administrator*

(Fairfield County, May 29, 1947, 11844–Conn. Ct.D., *Ben. Ser.,* Vol. 10, No. 10),
holding that an arbitrary limitation to four hours' work in the middle of the day
(11 A.M. to 3 P.M.) destroyed availability; *Bunyan v. Administrator* (New
Haven County, June 24, 1947, 11845–Conn. Ct.D., *Ben. Ser.,* Vol. 10, No. 10),
holding that a married woman who limited herself to work between 1 and 6 P.M.
only because of the need to care for her son was not available when the normal
labor market did not provide suitable part-time work for her; and *Doerler* v.
Administrator (New Haven County, No. 70866, June 22, 1948), holding that a
summer season waitress who restricted herself to the hours she had most recently worked, 5 P.M. to 1 A.M., was not available when waitresses normally
worked a split shift, 12 noon to 2 P.M. and 5 P.M. to 1 A.M.

26. *Benefit Series:* 9776–Ill. A, Vol. 8, No. 9; 9331–Ind. A, Vol. 8, No. 4;
9696–Mich. A, Vol. 8, No. 8; 8461–N.J. A, Vol. 7, No. 7; 11510–Tenn. R, Vol.
10, No. 5; 10998–Tex. A, Vol. 9, No. 11. *Contra:* 9056–Ky. A, Vol. 8, No. 1;
8599–S.C. A, Vol. 7, No. 6; 7889–Tenn. R, Vol. 6, No. 4 (affirmed on rehearing
42–BR–57). See also Chapter XIII, "Engaged in Self-Employment" and "Preparing to Go into Business."

27. *Benefit Series:* Available: 8665–Calif. R, Vol. 7, No. 8; 9242–Minn. A,
Vol. 8, No. 3. Not Available: 8742–Fla. A, Vol. 7, No. 9; 9064–Mass. A, Vol.
8, No. 1; 8866–Va. R, Vol. 7, No. 10.

28. *Bliley Electric Co.* v. *U.C. Board of Review,* 45 A.(2d)898 (1946), 10754–
Pa. Ct.D., *Ben. Ser.,* Vol. 9, No. 8.

29. *Patterson* v. *U.C. Commission,* Superior Court, Clark County, Jan. 31,
1946, 10760–Wash. Ct.D., *Ben. Ser.,* Vol. 9, No. 8.

30. 10538–Mass. A, *Ben. Ser.,* Vol. 9, No. 3.

31. 8969–Ind. R, *Ben. Ser.,* Vol. 7, No. 12.

32. 8664–Calif. R, *Ben. Ser.,* Vol. 7, No. 8.

33. *Kut* v. *Albers Super Markets, Inc.,* 66 N.E.(2d)643 (1946), affirming
63 N.E.(2d)218 (1945), 9830–Ohio Ct.D., *Ben. Ser.,* Vol. 8, No. 9, which reversed Court of Common Pleas, Hamilton County, No. A–89738, Nov. 15, 1944.
Appeal dismissed, U.S. Supreme Court, 67 Sup. Ct. 86, rehearing denied, 67
Sup. Ct. 186.

34. *Benefit Series:* 7643–Calif. A, Vol. 5, No. 10; 6765–D.C. A, Vol. 4, No.
12; 11372–D.C. A, Vol. 10, No. 4; 10325–Ill. R, Vol. 9, No. 3; 9596–Ky. A,
Vol. 8, No. 7; 9007–N.C. A, Vol. 7, No. 12; 9537–Pa. A, Vol. 8, No. 6; 10491–
Pa. R, Vol. 9, Nos. 4–5; 11273–Va. A, Vol. 10, No. 2; 9851–Wash. A, Vol. 8,
No. 9 (but for a reasonable period only); 10514–Wis. A, Vol. 8, No. 12.

35. *Benefit Series:* 7054–Ga. R, Vol. 5, No. 2; 11459–N.C. A, Vol. 10, No. 5;
9007–N.C. A, Vol. 7, No. 12; 12796–Tenn. R, Vol. 11, No. 9.

36. *Benefit Series:* 10325–Ill. R, Vol. 9, No. 3; 10451–Kans. A, Vol. 9, Nos.
4–5; 8244–Mich. A, Vol. 6, No. 11; 11638–Nebr. R, Vol. 10, No. 7; 10197–N.Y.
A, Vol. 9, No. 1; 7600–Okla. A, Vol. 5, No. 10; 7512–Oreg. A, Vol. 5, No. 9;
10055–Tenn. R, Vol. 8, No. 11; 11273–Va. A, Vol. 10, No. 2; 9107–Wash. R,
Vol. 8, No. 1.
Contra: 8362–Mass. A, Vol. 7, No. 2; 9365–Pa. A, Vol. 8, No. 4; 9537–Pa. A,
Vol. 8, No. 6. Also see 12881–Calif. R, Vol. 11, No. 11.

37. *Brown-Brockmeyer Co.* v. *Board of Review,* 45 N.E.(2d)152 (1942);
motion to permit appeal overruled by the Ohio Supreme Court, Oct. 21, 1942;
7912–Ohio Ct.D., *Ben. Ser.,* Vol. 6, No. 4. Also see *Stevens* v. *Selby Shoe Co.*
Court of Appeals, Scioto County, Jan. 15, 1945, 9445–Ohio Ct.D., *Ben. Ser.,* Vol.
8, No. 5.

38. 83 N.E.(2d)521 (1948), 13410–Ohio, Ct.D., *Ben. Ser.,* Vol. 12, No. 5, overruling in principle the decisions cited in the preceding note.

39. At the time of Kut's separation from employment, the Ohio law provided
that individuals who left work voluntarily without just cause in connection with

their work should be required to serve an additional waiting period of three weeks and be subject to a reduction in the maximum amount of benefits equivalent to six times the weekly benefit amount.

The Ohio Supreme Court's report of the facts may also be questioned.

40. 10491–Pa. R, *Ben. Ser.,* Vol. 9, Nos. 4–5.

41. The most comprehensive study of American unemployment compensation experience with seasonal provisions is the Bureau of Employment Security's Research and Statistics Letter No. 70, *Special Provisions for Seasonal Employers and Seasonal Workers Under State Unemployment Compensation Laws,* December 18, 1944. The writer has relied extensively upon this monograph. It appeared in abridged form in Marianne S. Linnenberg, "Seasonal Employers and Seasonal Workers Under State Unemployment Compensation Laws," *Social Security Bulletin,* Vol. 7, No. 11 (November 1944), pp. 13–26.

42. Alabama, Alaska, Arizona, Arkansas, Colorado, Delaware, Georgia, Hawaii, Maine, Michigan, Minnesota, Missouri, North Carolina, Ohio, Oregon, South Carolina, South Dakota, Vermont, Virginia, Wisconsin, and West Virginia.

43. 15 weeks — Missouri
    25 weeks — Colorado
    26 weeks — Hawaii, Minnesota
    30 weeks — Michigan (except Great Lakes seamen)
    32 weeks — Alabama
    36 weeks — Arkansas, North Carolina, Ohio (except Great Lakes seamen)
    39 weeks — Michigan (Great Lakes seamen)
    40 weeks — Georgia, Maine, Ohio (Great Lakes seamen), Oregon, South Carolina, Virginia
    44 weeks — Arizona
    Less than 1 year — Alaska, Vermont

44. Research & Statistics Letter No. 70, pp. 38, 39.

45. For calendar year 1946, the Oregon agency listed 132 seasonal employers with 117 different seasonal periods. ("Change in Designation of Calendar Weeks on Seasonal Claims," Memorandum to all Oregon Local Offices, June 24, 1947.)

46. Alaska, Arizona, Arkansas, Colorado, Delaware, Missouri, North Carolina, Ohio, South Carolina, Vermont, Virginia.

47. *Colorado:* over 50 per cent of base-period wages from principal seasonal employer in a seasonal industry during the normal seasonal period or periods. *Hawaii:* over 25 per cent of base-period wages in seasonal industry. *North Carolina:* at least 25 per cent of base-period wages in seasonal employment.

48. Arizona, Delaware, Georgia, Missouri. In Alabama he is defined as an individual ordinarily employed in a seasonal industry.

49. *Arkansas:* if not in occupation in which employment continues throughout substantially all the year. *Maine:* earned any part of qualifying wage in seasonal industry. *Minnesota:* employed during the season by a seasonal employer, but not before or after the season during the quarter in which the season begins or ends. *Mississippi:* base period employment in a seasonal industry. *South Dakota:* engaged in a seasonal occupation. *Vermont:* unemployed person of a seasonal occupation.

50. In North Carolina, only five employers of over three hundred who applied for seasonality determinations were able to predict when they would lay off and recall their workers. *Seasonal Employment,* A Report to the Industrial Commissioner of the State of New York, Feb. 15, 1940, Committee on Seasonality, p. 15; Research and Statistics Letter No. 70, p. 9.

51. Research and Statistics Letter No. 70, p. 9.

52. *Seasonal Industries In Relation To Unemployment Compensation,* Ten-

nessee U.C. Division, Research and Statistics Section, June 1, 1944, pp. 29-30; McDonald K. Horne, Jr., "Seasonal Workers Under the Mississippi Unemployment Compensation Law," *Social Security Bulletin,* Vol. 2, No. 1 (February 1939), p. 14; Research and Statistics Letter No. 70, pp. 12-16; *Seasonal Employment,* A Report to the Industrial Commissioner of the State of New York, pp. 17-18.

53. Research and Statistics Letter No. 70, Table 1, p. 21.

54. *Seasonal Workers in California,* California Employment Stabilization Commission, Bulletin No. 21, Apr. 4, 1947, pp. 5-7.

55. *Benefit Series: Available for work:* 8733-Calif. R, Vol. 7, No. 9; 10067-Calif. R, Vol. 8, No. 12; 8953-Conn. R, Vol. 7, No. 12; 10082-Fla. A, Vol. 8, No. 12; 10087-Ga. A, Vol. 8, No. 12. Not available for work: 10070-Calif. R, Vol. 8, No. 12; 8734-Calif. R, Vol. 7, No. 9; 8736-Calif. R, Vol. 7, No. 9; 8745-Fla. R, Vol. 7, No. 9; 10080-Fla. A, Vol. 8, No. 12; 12353-Idaho A, Vol. 11, No. 4; 9780-Ind. A, Vol. 8, No. 9; 9058-La. A, Vol. 8, No. 1; 9924-Mo. A, Vol. 8, No. 10 (appeal denied, U.C. Commission, C-1951, unp.); 8708-Oreg. A, Vol. 7, No. 8; 6970-Oreg. A, Vol. 5, No. 2; 12319-S.Dak. R, Vol. 11, No. 3; *Bohannon* v. *U.C. Commission,* Superior Court, Yakima County, 8948-Wash. Ct.D., Vol. 7, No. 11.

56. *Benefit Series:* 12498-Ill. R, Vol. 11, No. 6; 12437-Nebr. R, Vol. 11, No. 5; 8708-Oreg. A, Vol. 7, No. 8; 6970-Oreg. A, Vol. 5, No. 2.

57. 9011-Okla. R, *Ben. Ser.,* Vol. 7, No. 12; see also *Seasonal Workers in California,* p. 16.

58. Research and Statistics Letter No. 70, pp. 4-9; *Seasonal Workers in California,* p. 18; William Papier, "Seasonality in Ohio Canning Establishments in Relation to Unemployment Compensation," *Social Security Bulletin,* Vol. 1, No. 10 (October 1938), pp. 8, 9.

59. *Garcia* v. *Employment Stabilization Commission,* 161 P.(2d)972 (1945), 10241-Calif. Ct.D., *Ben. Ser.,* Vol. 9, No. 2; *Hagadone* v. *Kirkpatrick,* 154 P. (2d)181 (1944), 9580-Idaho Ct.D., *Ben. Ser.,* Vol. 8, No. 7.

60. Lester M. Pearlman and Leonard Eskin, "Teen-Age Youth in the Wartime Labor Force," *Monthly Labor Review,* Vol. 60, No. 1 (January 1945), p. 8.

61. Connecticut, Idaho, Indiana, Iowa, Kentucky, Montana, Nebraska, Nevada, North Dakota, Ohio, Utah, West Virginia.

62. *Benefit Series:* 10427-D.C. V, Vol. 9, Nos. 4-5; 6398-Mont. A, Vol. 4, No. 9; 6112-N.Mex. A, Vol. 4, No. 7; 10398-Pa. V, Vol. 9, No. 3; 5473-Tex. R, Vol. 4, No. 4. See also RAR-U-23 and RAR-U-89.

63. *Keen* v. *Texas U.C. Commission,* 148 S.W.(2d)211 (1941), 6117-Tex. Ct.D., *Ben. Ser.,* Vol. 4, No. 7. *Benefit Series:* 10419-Ark. R, Vol. 9, Nos. 4-5; 5306-Fla. A, Vol. 4, No. 2; 9347-Mass. V, Vol. 8, No. 4; 5001-Miss. R, Vol. 4, No. 1; 9528-N.C. V, Vol. 8, No. 6; 11580-Ohio R, Vol. 10, No. 6; 9094-Okla. R, Vol. 8, No. 1; 10142-R.I. A, Vol. 8, No. 12 (affirmed by R.I. U.C. Board, No. 214, unp.); 7095-Tenn. A, Vol. 5, No. 3; 6121-Wyo. A, Vol. 4, No. 7.

64. 9347-Mass. V, *Ben. Ser.,* Vol. 8, No. 4.

65. 9094-Okla. R, *Ben. Ser.,* Vol. 8, No. 1.

66. *Benefit Series:* 5783-Ga. A, Vol. 4, No. 5; 7835-Kans. R, Vol. 6, No. 3; 5678-Ky., Vol. 4, No. 5; 5447-Mich. A, Vol. 4, No. 3; 6967-Ohio A, Vol. 5, No. 2; 5473-Tex. R, Vol. 4, No. 4; 7945-Va. R, Vol. 6, No. 5.

67. *Benefit Series: Available for work:* 9042-Conn. R, Vol. 8, No. 1; 12891-Del. A, Vol. 11, No. 11; 5200-Ill. A, Vol. 4, No. 2; 7692-Ill. R, Vol. 5, No. 12; 7509-Ind. A, Vol. 5, No. 9; 7871-Mass. A, Vol. 6, No. 4; 6403-N.Y. A, Vol. 4, No. 9; 7317-N.C. A, Vol. 5, No. 6; 6607-Ohio A, Vol. 4, No. 11; 6968-Okla. A, Vol. 5, No. 2; 5906-Oreg. A, Vol. 4, No. 6; 12068-Pa. R, Vol. 10, No. 12; 10929-Tex. A, Vol. 9, No. 10; 7097-Wash. A, Vol. 5, No. 3.

Benefit Series: Not available for work: 8081–Ariz. R, Vol. 6, No. 8; 5342–Conn. R, Vol. 4, No. 3; 8281–Minn. A, Vol. 6, No. 12; 7994–N.Y. R, Vol. 6, No. 6; 7999–R.I. R, Vol. 6, No. 6.

68. 6403–N.Y. A, *Ben. Ser.,* Vol. 4, No. 9.

69. 7509–Ind. A, *Ben. Ser.,* Vol. 5, No. 9.

70. 7994–N.Y. R, *Ben. Ser.,* Vol. 6, No. 6.

71. *Benefit Series:* 5196–Ark. A, Vol. 4, No. 2; 6510–Calif. R, Vol. 4, No. 10; 10313–Calif. A, Vol. 9, No. 3; 9042–Conn. R, Vol. 8, No. 1; 7509–Ind. A, Vol. 5, No. 9; 7597–La. A, Vol. 5, No. 10; 6694–Mo. A, Vol. 4, No. 12; 9359–N.C. V, Vol. 8, No. 4; 5902–Ohio A, Vol. 4, No. 6; 11514–Tenn. R, Vol. 10, No. 5; 10929–Tex. A, Vol. 9, No. 10; 11092–Tex. R, Vol. 9, No. 12; 11433–Utah A, Vol. 10, No. 4.

72. 7937–N.H. R, *Ben. Ser.,* Vol. 6, No. 5.

73. *Benefit Series: Available for work:* 8253–Calif. R, Vol. 6, No. 12; 5341–Conn. R, Vol. 4, No. 3; 12093–Del. A, Vol. 11, No. 1; 7055–Ill. A, Vol. 5, No. 2; 5678–Ky., Vol. 4, No. 5; 11043–Ky. A, Vol. 9, No. 12; 11857–La. R, Vol. 10, No. 10; 7871–Mass. A, Vol. 6, No. 4; 11233–Mich. R, Vol. 10, No. 2; 5898–Mont. A, Vol. 4, No. 6; 5899–Nev. A, Vol. 4, No. 6; 12442–N.H. R, Vol. 11, No. 5; 8551–N.Y. R, Vol. 7, No. 5; 7880–N.Y. R, Vol. 6, No. 4; 6965–N.Dak. R, Vol. 5, No. 2; 6408–Okla. R, Vol. 4, No. 9; 8161–S.C. A, Vol. 6, No. 10; 7094–Tenn. A, Vol. 5, No. 3; 5473–Tex. R, Vol. 4, No. 4; 8043–Va. A, Vol. 6, No. 6; 7097–Wash. A, Vol. 5, No. 3.

Benefit Series: Not available for work: 5342–Conn. R, Vol. 4, No. 3; 10427–D.C. V, Vol. 9, Nos. 4–5; 12034–Maine A, Vol. 10, No. 12; 7872–Mass. A, Vol. 6, No. 4; 6398–Mont. A, Vol. 4, No. 9; 8296–N.J. R, Vol. 6, No. 12; 7943–N.C. R, Vol. 6, No. 5; 9094–Okla. R, Vol. 8, No. 1; 12389–Pa. R, Vol. 11, No. 4; 6612–Tenn. A, Vol. 4, No. 1.

74. *Benefit Series:* 7642–Ark. A, Vol. 5, No. 10; 8253–Calif. R, Vol. 6, No. 12; 5198–Conn. R, Vol. 4, No. 2; 12093–Del. A, Vol. 11, No. 1; 11043–Ky. A, Vol. 9, No. 12; 6842–N.C. A, Vol. 5, No. 1; 6408–Okla. R, Vol. 4, No. 9; 7601–Okla. R, Vol. 5, No. 10; 5473–Tex. R, Vol. 4, No. 4; 11433–Utah A, Vol. 10, No. 4; 12003–W.Va. R, Vol. 10, No. 11.

75. *Benefit Series: Available for work:* 7642–Ark. A, Vol. 5, No. 10; 5200–Ill. A, Vol. 4, No. 2; 5206–N.J. A, Vol. 4, No. 2; 7976–N.Y. R, Vol. 6, No. 5; 11881–N.Y. R, Vol. 10, No. 10; 6842–N.C. A, Vol. 5, No. 1; 7601–Okla. R, Vol. 5, No. 10; 7696–Oreg. A, Vol. 5, No. 2; 7096–Tenn. A, Vol. 5, No. 3.

Benefit Series: Not available for work: 5885–Ill. A, Vol. 4, No. 6; 4999–Mich. A, Vol. 4, No. 1; 7997–Oreg. R, Vol. 6, No. 6; 7152–Tenn. R, Vol. 5, No. 4.

76. Ralph Altman, "Availability for Work of Defense Trainees," *Social Security Bulletin,* Vol. 6, No. 7 (July 1943), pp. 25–30.

77. *Benefit Series:* 7655–Ariz. A, Vol. 5, No. 11; 7970–Ariz. A, Vol. 6, No. 5; 7815–Calif. R, Vol. 6, No. 2; 7855–Calif. A, Vol. 6, No. 3, affirmed by E.S. Commission, C–1589, unp. (but see 7931–Calif. A, Vol. 6, No. 5) ; 7817–Fla. A, Vol. 6, No. 2 (cf. 7988–Fla. A, Vol. 6, No. 6); 7868–Ind. R, Vol. 6, No. 4 (but see 7869–Ind. R, Vol. 6, No. 4) ; 7693–Mass. A, Vol. 5, No. 12.

78. *Benefit Series:* 7873–Mich. A, Vol. 7, No. 1; 8088–N.J. R, Vol. 6, No. 8.

NOTES FOR CHAPTER ELEVEN

1. The excepted states are: Connecticut, Delaware, District of Columbia, Massachusetts, New York, Ohio, Rhode Island, Virginia, and Wisconsin.

2. *Garcia* v. *E.S. Commission,* 161 P.(2d)972 (1945), 10241–Calif. Ct.D., *Ben. Ser.,* Vol. 9, No. 2; *Porter* v. *Riley,* Superior Court, Yakima County, Washington, 9027–Wash. Ct.D., *Ben. Ser.,* Vol. 7, No. 12. *Benefit Series:* 9833–Ala. V, Vol. 8, No. 5; 12010–Ark. R, Vol. 10, No. 12; 7506–Calif. R, Vol. 5, No. 9;

12344–Colo. A, Vol. 11, No. 4; 12182–Conn. R, Vol. 11, No. 2; 10429–Fla. R, Vol. 9, Nos. 4–5; 9990–Idaho A, Vol. 8, No. 11; 9328–Ind. R, Vol. 8, No. 4; 9785–Kans. A, Vol. 8, No. 9; 9793–Md. A, Vol. 8, No. 9; 9697–Mich. R, Vol. 8, No. 8; 9432–Nebr. R, Vol. 8, No. 5; 5173–N.J. A, Vol. 4, No. 1; 11168–N.Mex. A, Vol. 10, No. 1; 12054 and 12055–N.Y. R, Vol. 10, No. 12; 705–N.C. A, Vol. 1, No. 6; 8709 and 8710–Oreg. A, Vol. 7, No. 8; 9943–Oreg. R, Vol. 8, No. 10; 12468–Pa. R, Vol. 11, No. 5; 10586–Tenn. R, Vol. 9, No. 6; 8940–Tex. A, Vol. 7, No. 11 (appeal dismissed, 1149–CA–44, unp.) ; 8942–Tex. A, Vol. 7, No. 11; 8652–Va. R, Vol. 7, No. 7 (a departure from the usual Virginia rule in such cases) ; 12479–Va. R, Vol. 11, No. 5; 8946–Wash. A, Vol. 7, No. 11.

3. 10487–Pa. R, *Ben. Ser.,* Vol. 9, Nos. 4–5. The board's language follows closely the phraseology of the *Court in Department of Labor and Industry. U.C. Board of Review and Teicher,* 35 A (2d)739 (1944) 8560–Pa. Ct.D., *Ben. Ser.,* Vol. 7, No. 5. See also 10488–Pa. R, Vol. 9, Nos. 4–5 to the effect that a claimant who is so situated must eliminate other obstacles to availability.

4. *Supra,* note 2. See also *Benefit Series;* 1018–Calif. A, Vol. 2, No. 3; 9990–Idaho A, Vol. 8, No. 11; 8709–Oreg. A, Vol. 7, No. 8; 9284–Va. R, Vol. 8, No. 8.

5. 10429–Fla. R, *Ben. Ser.,* Vol. 9, Nos. 4–5. See also *Benefit Series:* 12188–Del. A, Vol. 11, No. 2; 12198–La. A, Vol. 11, No. 2; 12479–Va. R, Vol. 11, No. 5.

6. 9785–Kans. A, *Ben. Ser.,* Vol. 8, No. 9.

7. *Supra,* note 2. See also *Benefit Series:* 7506–Calif. R, Vol. 5, No. 9; 10429–Fla. R, Vol. 9, Nos. 4–5; 9432–Nebr. R, Vol. 8, No. 5; 8710–Oreg. A., Vol. 7, No. 8; 10487–Pa. R, Vol. 9, Nos. 4–5; 12468–Pa. R, Vol. 11, No. 5; 10586–Tenn. R, Vol. 8, No. 6; 8946–Wash. A, Vol. 7, No. 11.

8. *Wiley* v. *Carroll,* 201 S.W.(2d)320 (1947), 11865–Mo. Ct.D., *Ben. Ser.,* Vol. 10, No. 10; *Scholle* v. *Miller,* District Court, Gage County, Nebraska, May 10, 1946, 10982–Nebr. Ct.D., *Ben. Ser.,* Vol. 9, No. 11; *Hart* v. *Miller,* District Court, Gage County, Nebraska, May 10, 1946, 11557–Nebr. Ct.D., *Ben. Ser.,* Vol. 10, No. 6; *Goodwin* v. *Riley,* Superior Court, Yakima County, Washington, 9028–Wash. Ct.D., *Ben. Ser.,* Vol. 7, No. 12. *Benefit Series:* 12091–Colo. A, Vol. 11, No. 1; 10863–Ga. R, Vol. 9, No. 10; 10100–Ind. A, Vol. 8, No. 12; 9595–Iowa A, Vol. 8, No. 7; 12121–Miss. A, Vol. 11, No. 1; 9169–Nebr. R, Vol. 8, No. 2; 9080–N.H. R, Vol. 8, No. 1; 10904–N.J. R, Vol. 9, No. 10; 8791–Tenn. R, Vol. 7, No. 9; 8945–Va. R, Vol. 7, No. 11; 12478–Vt. A, Vol. 11, No. 5; 4124–Wash. A, Vol. 3, No. 8.

9. 10904–N.J. R, *Ben. Ser.,* Vol. 9, No. 10.

10. *Benefit Series:* 8959–Ga. R, Vol. 9, No. 10; 10863–Ga. R, Vol. 9, No. 10; 9785–Kans. A, Vol. 8, No. 9 (distance) ; 9169–Nebr. R, Vol. 8, No. 2; 9430–Nebr. R, Vol. 8, No. 5; 8791–Tenn. R, Vol. 7, No. 9; 8945–Va. R, Vol. 7, No. 1; Cf. 10586–Tenn. R, Vol. 9, No. 6; 11272–Vt. A, Vol. 10, No. 2.

11. 8652–Va. R, *Ben. Ser.,* Vol. 7, No. 7.

12. 8675–Ill. R, *Ben. Ser.,* Vol. 7, No. 8. See also 8681–Ky. A, *Ben. Ser.,* Vol. 7, No. 8.

13. *Benefit Series:* 9569–Calif. A, Vol. 8, No. 7 (affirmed by Appeal Board, No. 3853, unp.) ; 9041–Conn. R, Vol. 8, No. 1; 9773–Ill. A, Vol. 8, No. 9; 8470–Ind. A, Vol. 7, No. 4; 9070–Mich. A, Vol. 8, No. 1; 11712–Miss. R, Vol. 10, No. 8; 11640–N.H. R, Vol. 10, No. 7; 10921–Pa. R, Vol. 9, No. 10; 9200–Wis. R, Vol. 8, No. 2.

14. *Benefit Series:* 9041–Conn. R, Vol. 8, No. 1; 10921–Pa. R, Vol. 9, No. 10. *Contra:* 10435–Ill. R, Vol. 9, Nos. 4–5 (many factories within walking distance) ; 12580–Ill. R, Vol. 11, No. 7 (bus or street car riding dangerous to claimant because of brain operation; active labor-market area) ; 8999–N.J. R, Vol. 7, No. 12 (sought and found work on her own initiative).

15. 10637–Md. R, *Ben. Ser.*, Vol. 9, No. 7.

16. *Benefit Series: Benefits denied:* 9041–Conn. R, Vol. 8, No. 1; 9773–Ill. A, Vol. 8, No. 9; 11156–Miss. A, Vol. 10, No. 1; 11640–N.H. R, Vol. 10, No. 7; 5113–Pa. A, Vol. 4, No. 1; 9200–Wis. R, Vol. 8, No. 2.

Benefit Series: Benefits granted: 10790–Ill. A, Vol. 9, No. 9; 12577–Ill. R, Vol. 11, No. 7; 10285–N.Y. R, Vol. 9, No. 2; 11587–Pa. A, Vol. 10, No. 6.

17. Kate K. Liepmann, *The Journey to Work* (New York: Oxford University Press, 1944), p. 10.

18. For an objective factual approach to one aspect of the commuting problem as it arises in unemployment compensation, see Illinois Division of Placement and Unemployment Compensation *Deputy's Manual*, Jan. 3, 1947, Principles of Investigation and Determination, Supplement No. 3, "Travel Time in Chicago, in Minutes by Type of Transportation," pp. i-xi.

19. "Travel Time in Chicago," pp. 118–19. Derived from *Real Property Inventory*, made by U.S. Department of Commerce, Bureau of Foreign and Domestic Commerce, 1934.

20. *Real Property Inventory*, p. 120. From *"Real Property Inventory of New York City,"* 1934.

21. *Real Property Inventory*, p. 65.

22. *Utah Employment Security Digest*, Vol. 3, No. 8 (December 1942), p. 3.

23. *Family Expenditures in Selected Cities, 1935–36,* Vol. VI, Travel and Transportation, U.S. Bureau of Labor Statistics Bulletin No. 648, 1940, p. 5.

24. Chas. A. Myer and W. Rupert Maclaurin, *The Movement of Factory Workers: A Study of A New England Industrial Community, 1937–39 and 1942* (New York and London: Technology Press, 1943), pp. 23–28.

25. A further development of the Interstate Benefit Payment Plan was the experimental Interstate Benefit Arrangement which was abandoned in 1949. Under the Plan all determinations and payments are made by the liable state under its law. Under the Arrangement the liable state acted on the initial claim in the benefit year, prescribed the duration and amount of benefits and determined any issues of disqualification or eligibility that are connected with the separation from work. All payments and subsequent determinations were made by the agent (resident) state under its own law. A clearing house operation was used for distributing benefit costs among the states.

26. See the following in the *Benefit Series:* 10331–Ind. R, Vol. 9, No. 3; 9422–Md. A, Vol. 8, No. 5; 8496–Minn. AG, Vol. 7, No. 4; 8829–Mo. R, Vol. 7, No. 10; 9184–Ohio R, Vol. 8, No. 12. Also *Brown-Brockmeyer Co.* v. *Holmes,* Court of Common Pleas, Montgomery County, Ohio, May 26, 1948, 12917–Ohio Ct.D., Vol. 11, No. 11, construing the bar against denying benefits if the work offered is at an unreasonable distance from the worker's "residence," says "residence" means the place where the claimant lived at the time he left his employment.

27. 7 So.(2d)303, 7482–Ala. Ct.D., *Ben. Ser.*, Vol. 5, No. 8.

28. *Huiet* v. *Schwab Manufacturing Co.*, 27 S.E.(2d)743 (1943), 8418–Ga. Ct.D., *Ben. Ser.*, Vol. 7, No. 3.

29. *U.S. Coal & Coke Co.* v. *Board of Review,* Circuit Court, Kanawha County, West Virginia, Apr. 3, 1943, 8147–W.Va. Ct.D., *Ben. Ser.*, Vol. 6, No. 9. See also *Feuchtenberger Bakeries, Inc.* v. *Board of Review,* same court, Apr. 15, 1943.

30. *Wiley* v. *Carroll, supra,* note 8; *Anthony* v. *U.C. Board,* Superior Court, Baltimore, Md., May 14, 1947 (affirming 11859–Md. A, *Ben. Ser.*, Vol. 10, No. 10); *Hunter* v. *Miller*, 27 N.W.(2d)638 (Neb.) (1947).

Benefit Series: 8875–Ark. A, Vol. 7, No. 11; 12881–Calif. R, Vol. 11, No. 11; 11928–Calif. R, Vol. 10, No. 11; 11614–Calif. R, Vol. 10, No. 7; 12091–Colo. A, Vol. 11, No. 1; 12094–D.C. A, Vol. 11, No. 1; 8746–Fla. R, Vol. 7, No. 9; 12966–Ill. R, Vol. 11, No. 12; 9220–Ill. R, Vol. 8, No. 3; 9673–Ind. A, Vol. 8, No. 8;

11855–Iowa R, Vol. 10, No. 10; 8679–Kans. A, Vol. 7, No. 8; 8681–Ky. A, Vol. 7, No. 8; 8026–Me. A, Vol. 6, No. 6; 9495–Md. A, Vol. 8, No. 6; 8689–Mass. A, Vol. 7, No. 8; 8511–Mich. R, Vol. 7, No. 4; 12124–Mo. R, Vol. 11, No. 1; 12290–Mont. A, Vol. 11, No. 3; 11717–Nebr. R, Vol. 10, No. 8; 11721–Nev. R, Vol. 10, No. 8; 9811–N.J. A, Vol. 8, No. 9; 11722–N.Mex. A, Vol. 10, No. 8; 12770–N.Y. R, Vol. 11, No. 9 (cf. 12688–N.Y. A, Vol. 11, No. 8, appeal dismissed, Appeal Board Decision No. 11612–47, unp.) ; 8705–Ohio R, Vol. 7, No. 8; 9636–Okla. R, Vol. 8, No. 7; 12465–Oreg. R, Vol. 11, No. 5; 7982–R.I. A, Vol. 6, No. 5 (affirmed by U.C. Board, R.I. 95, unp.) ; 11670–Tenn. R, Vol. 10, No. 7; 6879–Tex. A, Vol. 5, No. 2; 12635–Tex. A, Vol. 11, No. 7 (Commission Appeal denied, 3149–CA–48, unp.) ; 11269–Utah A, Vol. 10, No. 2; 11272–Vt. A, Vol. 10, No. 2; 9852–Wash. A, Vol. 8, No. 9 (affirmed by commissioner, C–592, unp.) ; 8796–W.Va. R, Vol. 7, No. 9; 11275–Wyo. A, Vol. 10, No. 2.

31. *Supra,* note 3.

32. *Bliley Electric Co.* v. *U.C. Board and Sturdevant,* 45 A.(2d)898 (1946), 10754–Pa. Ct.D., *Ben. Ser.,* Vol. 9, No. 8.

33. *Reger* v. *Administrator,* 46 A.(2d)844 (1946), 10780–Conn. Ct.D., *Ben. Ser.,* Vol. 9, No. 9.

34. 8760–Mich. R, *Ben. Ser.,* Vol. 7, No. 9. The Michigan law, Sec. 28(c), requires that the claimant be "able to perform full-time work of a character which he is qualified to perform by past experience or training, and of a character generally similar to work for which he has previously received wages, and he is available for such work, full-time, either at a locality at which he earned wages for insured work during his base period or at a locality where it is found by the commission that such work is available." See also *Benefit Series:* 12010–Ark. R, Vol. 10, No. 12; 11690–Calif. R, Vol. 10, No. 8; 12099–Idaho A, Vol. 11, No. 1; 9218–Ill. R, Vol. 8, No. 3; 11211–Ind. A, Vol. 10, No. 2; 12468–Pa. R, Vol. 11, No. 5.

35. Cf. 9139–Ill. R, *Ben. Ser.,* Vol. 8, No. 2.

36. *Carwood Manufacturing Co.* v. *Huiet,* Superior Court, Barrow County, Georgia, June 5, 1943, Docket No. 1855, 8417–Ga. Ct.D., *Ben. Ser.,* Vol. 7, No. 3.

37. *Kontner* v. *U.C. Board,* 76 N.E.(2d)611 (1947), 12914–Ohio Ct.D., *Ben. Ser.,* Vol. 11, No. 11; *Copeland* v. *Employment Security Commission,* 172 P. (2d)420 (1946), 10751–Okla. Ct.D., *Ben. Ser.,* Vol. 9, No. 3; *Jacobs* v. *Office of Unemployment Compensation and Placement,* 179 P.(2d)707 (1947), 11832–Wash. Ct.D., *Ben. Ser.,* Vol. 10, No. 9.

38. *Woodall Industries, Inc.* v. *Tracy,* Circuit Court, Oakland County, Michigan, Sept. 17, 1941, Docket No. 26150, 6836–Mich. Ct.D., *Ben. Ser.,* Vol. 5, No. 1; *Rog* v. *Division of Employment Security,* District Court, Eastern Hampshire, Massachusetts, Oct. 31, 1946, 11475–Mass. Ct.D., *Ben. Ser.,* Vol. 10, No. 5; *Davidson* v. *Hayes,* Common Pleas Court, Highland County, Ohio, Feb. 5, 1946, 10662–Ohio Ct.D., *Ben. Ser.,* Vol. 9, No. 7; *Shellhammer* v. *U.C. Board of Review,* 57 A.(2d)439 (1948), 12789–Pa. Ct.D., *Ben. Ser.,* Vol. 11, No. 9.

39. 11210–Ind. A, *Ben. Ser.,* Vol. 10, No. 2.

40. 8767–N.J. R, *Ben. Ser.,* Vol. 7, No. 9.

41. 10743–N.J. R, *Ben. Ser.,* Vol. 9, No. 8.

42. 11363–Ala. R, *Ben. Ser.,* Vol. 10, No. 4.

43. *Benefit Series:* 10530–Ill. R, Vol. 9, No. 6; 10335–Iowa A, Vol. 9, No. 3; 10383–N.C. A, Vol. 9, No. 3; 8776–N.Y. R, Vol. 7, No. 9; 8923–N.Y. R, Vol. 7, No. 11. *Contra:* 8425–N.Y. R, Vol. 7, No. 3.

44. 10713–Ill. R, *Ben. Ser.,* Vol. 9, No. 8.

45. *Benefit Series:* 10511–Ark. A, Vol. 9, No. 6; 5199–Ill. R, Vol. 4, No. 2; 2588–Ind. A, Vol. 3, No. 3; 6943–Ky. R, Vol. 5, No. 1; 6251–Mass. A, Vol. 4, No. 8; 3066–Mich. A, Vol. 3, No. 3 (affirmed *Partain* v. *Fisher Body Corp.,* Circuit Court, unp.) ; 12287–Mo. A, Vol. 11, No. 3; 5004–Nebr. R, Vol. 4, No.

1; 6399–N.H. A, Vol. 4, No. 9; 11725–N.Y. R, Vol. 10, No. 8; 4519–Okla. A, Vol. 3, No. 10; 4697–W.Va. A, Vol. 3, No. 11.

46. *Benefit Series:* 6244–Ga. A, Vol. 4, No. 9; 2025–Mich. R, Vol. 2, No. 10; 7510–Mich. A, Vol. 5, No. 9; 3583–Minn. A, Vol. 3, No. 6 (affirmed by director, 922–52, unp.); 11166–N.J. R, Vol. 10, No. 1.

47. *Benefit Series:* 3346–Ga. A, Vol. 3, No. 5; 5199–Ill. R, Vol. 4, No. 2; 11376–Ind. A, Vol. 10, No. 4; 12596–Miss. R, Vol. 11, No. 7; 9807–Mo. A, Vol. 8, No. 9; 4104–N.J. R, Vol. 3, No. 8; 1838–N.Y. R, Vol. 2, No. 8.

48. *Benefit Series:* 11108–Del. A, Vol. 10, No. 1 (to visit sick mother); 11948–Mass. A, Vol. 10, No. 1; 7510–Mich. A, Vol. 5, No. 9; 7315–Mo. A, Vol. 5, No. 6; 11993–Vt. A, Vol. 10, No. 11; 5848–Wash. A, Vol. 5, No. 1. Cf. 11455–D.C. A, Vol. 10, No. 5; 11725–N.Y. R, Vol. 10, No. 8.

49. 10997–Tex. A, *Ben. Ser.,* Vol. 9, No. 11.

NOTES FOR CHAPTER TWELVE

1. "Initial claim" covers both new and additional claims. A "new claim" is an application for determination of benefit rights (amount and duration) which certifies to the beginning date of a period of unemployment or its continuance into a new benefit year. An "additional" claim is an application which certifies to the beginning date of a period of unemployment, the first benefit period of which would fall within a benefit year in which a valid initial claim has already been filed. For Wisconsin, which has no provision for a benefit year, a new claim is one which requires a determination of benefit amount and duration, as well as eligibility for benefits, on a per employer basis. Texas has no provision for filing additional claims.

"Comparable claim" means an application for benefits which certifies to the completion of a period (usually seven days) for which benefits are paid or payable.

2. *The Labor Market,* June 1946, p. 12.

3. Arnold Steinbach and Philip Booth, "A Survey of Claimants for Unemployment Compensation in February–March, 1943," *Social Security Bulletin,* Vol. 6, No. 12 (December 1943), p. 9.

4. Homer J. Freeman, "Unemployment Benefit Rights and Beneficiaries in Polk County, Iowa, 1938–39," *Social Security Bulletin,* Vol. 5, No. 1 (January 1942), pp. 15–24.

5. Daniel Creamer and Arthur C. Wellman, "Adequacy of Unemployment Benefits in the Detroit Area During the 1938 Recession," *Social Security Bulletin,* Vol. 3, No. 11 (November 1940), pp. 3–11. Same title, Employment Security Memorandum No. 14, January 1941, p. 26.

6. U.S. Department of Labor, Women's Bureau, *Handbook of Facts on Women Workers,* Bulletin No. 225, 1948, p. 10.

7. John D. Durand, "Married Women in the Labor Force," *American Journal of Sociology,* Vol. 52, No. 3 (November 1946), p. 218.

8. *Women Workers in Their Family Environment,* United States Department of Labor, Women's Bureau, Bulletin No. 183, 1941, p. 14. Based upon a 1939 sample survey of 6000 women workers in Utah and Cleveland, Ohio. In 1928, of 311 married women who applied for work at a Denver Y.W.C.A. Bureau and gave their reasons for seeking a job, 90 per cent (281) said that economic necessity forced them to try to earn. Of those reporting on the point, 74 per cent (221) had no support from husbands (91 widows, 68 divorced, separated, or husband deserted, 52 others). Of 94 married women who applied in 1928 for work with a Denver department store and gave their reasons, 86 said they were forced by economic necessity to seek employment. "Why Married Women

Seek Employment," *Monthly Labor Review,* Vol. 30, No. 4 (April 1930), pp. 90–91.

9. John D. Durand, "Married Women in the Labor Force," p. 222, Table 4. Based on a tabulation of married women, ages 18 to 64, in metropolitan districts of 100,000 or more, whose husbands received not more than $50 in income other than wages or salaries in 1939. A survey of a random sample of Delaware claimants during the period December 1941–February 1942 showed that 73.2 per cent of the claimants with working wives had base year earnings of less than $1000. *The Dependents of Unemployment Compensation Claimants, Delaware, December, 1941–February, 1942,* Bureau of Employment Security, Research and Statistics Letter No. 31, September 11, 1943, Table 10, p. 18.

10. Erne Magnus, "Gainfully Employed Women in Chicago," *Social Security Bulletin,* Vol. 6, No. 4 (April 1943), pp. 10–11.

11. Sixteenth Census of the United States: 1940–Population, Volume III, *The Labor Force,* Part 1, United States Summary, Table 86; *Monthly Reports of the Labor Force,* 1948.

Because of changes in census techniques the 1940 and 1947 figures are only roughly comparable.

In considering the percentages it must be emphasized that they include workers who worked short-hour weeks because of illness, lack of work, or other causes beyond their control as well as those workers who voluntarily elected to work less than full-time weeks or at short-hour jobs.

12. "Postwar Labor Turn-over Among Women Factory Workers," *Monthly Labor Review,* Vol. 64, No. 3 (March 1947), pp. 411–419.

13. Anna M. Baetjer, *Women In Industry: Their Health and Efficiency* (Philadelphia: W. B. Saunders Company, 1946), Chapters 1 and 2.

14. "Trends of Earnings and Hours," *Monthly Labor Review,* Vol. 64, No. 3 (March 1947), pp. 544–547.

15. National Industrial Conference Board, *The Economic Almanac for 1946–47* (New York: 1946), p. 176.

16. *Equal Pay For Equal Work For Women,* Hearings before a subcommittee of the Committee on Education and Labor, United States Senate, 79 Cong., 1 sess. on S. 1178, Oct. 29–31, 1945, pp. 12, 64–82, 133.

17. National Industrial Conference Board, *Wartime Pay of Women in Industry,* October 1943, pp. 18–19.

18. Illinois, Massachusetts, Michigan, Montana, New York, and Washington.

19. George H. Trafton, "Age distribution of Workers in Industries under Old-Age and Survivors Insurance," *Social Security Bulletin,* Vol. 10, No. 3 (March 1947), Tables 1 and 2.

20. Anna M. Baetjer, *Women in Industry,* Chapters 4–7.

21. There are no adequate figures on quit rates among women as compared with men workers. Bureau of Labor Statistics data for July 1943–December 1946 indicate that women's quits in manufacturing industries have tended to be 35 per cent to 55 per cent greater than men's. (See issues of the *Monthly Labor Review,* beginning Vol. 57, No. 1, July 1943.)

22. Without fixed minimum and maximum weekly benefit amounts and under a benefit formula based on a fixed fraction of high-quarter or base period earnings, a smaller percentage of women than men would qualify for most present minima. At the same time a smaller percentage of women than men would qualify for benefit amounts greater than the present maxima.

The period for which men's and women's benefit amounts are compared is the only one for which the information at this writing is available. Undoubtedly however, the difference shown is smaller than one may ordinarily expect to find. The large proportion of women claimants still drawing benefits based upon wartime wages accounts and the proportionately greater unemployment among women rather than men ex-war workers kept the average benefit amounts for the two groups so close together. In states like Idaho, Maine, and North Dakota, which had few war workers, the average weekly benefit for men during this period was from $2.35 to $5.36 higher than the women's average benefit.

23. Sixteenth Census of the United States, 1940, Population: *The Labor Force* (Sample Statistics), *Employment and Family Characteristics of Women*, 1943: Table II.

24. U.S. Department of Labor, Women's Bureau, *Handbook of Facts on Women Workers*, Bulletin No. 225, 1948, pp. 46–51.

25. See *Corpus Juris Secundum*, Vol. 41, "Husband and Wife," Sections 7, 10, 11, 258, 261, and cases cited therein.

26. *Ex Parte Alabama Textile Products Corporation*, 7 So.(2d)303 (1942), 7482–Ala. Ct.D., *Ben. Ser.*, Vol. 5, No. 8. Also note 12067–Pa. R, *Ben. Ser.*, Vol. 10, No. 12, which held that a waitress who had been discharged at her husband's request because her work interfered with care of their three minor children was not available for work.

27. *Speak* v. *Speak*, 19 P.(2d)386 (Utah).

28. Steinbach and Booth, Table 9, p. 15.

29. Anna M. Baetjer, *Women in Industry*, p. 159.

30. Baetjer, pp. 174–177.

31. Baetjer, p. 188. (Italics supplied.)

32. See, for examples, the following in the *Benefit Series*: 4837–Ala., Vol. 3, No. 12 (30 days before childbirth and 30 days after) ; 2219–Ark. A, Vol. 2, No. 12 (one month before) ; 3828–Calif. A, Vol. 3, No. 7 (two months before) ; 4087–Fla. A, Vol. 3, No. 8 (one month before and one month after) ; 2675–Md. A, Vol. 3, No. 2 (three months before) ; 4321–N.J. A, Vol. 3, No. 9 (one month before) ; 2877–N.Y. A, Vol. 3, No. 3 (two months before) ; 4522–Pa. R, Vol. 3, No. 10 (three months before and four weeks after) ; 7887–Pa. R, Vol. 6, No. 4 (modifying previous rule) ; 7428–S.Dak. R, Vol. 5, No. 7 (three months before) ; 3365–Tenn. R, Vol. 3, No. 5 (30 days after) ; 4853–Tenn. R, Vol. 3, No. 12 (90 days before) ; 10404–Va. R, Vol. 9, No. 3.

33. *Benefit Series*: 6243–Del. A, Vol. 4, No. 8 (claimant held eligible until day before childbirth) ; 8743–Fla. A, Vol. 7, No. 9 ; 4343–Ill. R, Vol. 4, No. 3 ("The availability of an unemployed worker for benefits [sic] must be considered with respect to each week of unemployment of that worker. We cannot agree with the referee's attempt to fix an arbitrary time limit beyond which the claimant must be considered as being unavailable for work.") ; 10327–Ill. R, Vol. 9, No. 3 ; 12031–Ind. R, Vol. 10, No. 12 ; 8520–Kans. A, Vol. 7, No. 5 ("Every pregnancy case is different and each rests upon its own facts.") ; 7879–N.J. R, Vol. 6, No. 4 ("Practically every pregnancy case is different and each rests upon its own facts. They cannot be grouped under general rules, convenient and desirable as that might be.") ; 6840–N.Y. A, Vol. 5, No. 1 ("No hard and fast rule can be drawn in cases of pregnancy . . . Normally a pregnant woman is incapable of employment from the seventh month of pregnancy. This is not an inflexible rule but is the normal application in normal cases . . .") ; 7887–Pa. R, Vol. 6, No. 4 ("While experience in a majority of cases will not warrant an absolute rule with respect to all claimants irrespective of the facts in a particular case, average general experience does warrant holding that there is a strong presumption of unavailability during the period between the end of the sixth month of pregnancy and one month after the birth.") ; 10404–Va. R, Vol. 9, No. 3 ("Although as a general rule we feel that most women in such a condition would be unable to work and unavailable for work for approximately 90 days before confinement, yet each individual's claim must be examined to deter-

mine whether or not such individual comes within an exception to the general rule.").

34. *Benefit Series:* 9384–Ariz. A, Vol. 8, No. 5; 4082–Ark. A, Vol. 3, No. 8; 9388–Calif. V, Vol. 8, No. 5 (aff. RAR–U–19, unp.) ; 1502–Conn. R, Vol. 2, No. 5; 3653–Conn. R, Vol. 3, No. 6; 6243–Del. A, Vol. 4, No. 8; 10711–Idaho V, Vol. 9, No. 8; 4500–Ill. A, Vol. 3, No. 10; 5343–Ill. R, Vol. 4, No. 3; 13327–Ill. R, Vol. 9, No. 3; 12031–Ind. R, Vol. 10, No. 12; 9496–Md. V, Vol. 8, No. 6; 2682–Mich. A, Vol. 3, No. 2; 6877–Mich. A, Vol. 5, No. 1; 4505–Mo. A, Vol. 3, No. 10; 6814–Mo. A, Vol. 4, No. 12; 6070–N.H. A, Vol. 4, No. 6; 4321–N.J. A, Vol. 3, No. 9; 3845–N.Y. R, Vol. 3, No. 5; 6840–N.Y. A, Vol. 5, No. 1; 3592– Ohio A, Vol. 3, No. 6; 4518–Ohio A, Vol. 3, No. 10; 7887–Pa. R, Vol. 6, No. 4; 2397–Tenn. A, Vol. 3, No. 1; 10404–Va. R, Vol. 9, No. 3.

35. *Benefit Series: Activity in seeking work:* 9384–Ariz. V, Vol. 8, No. 5; 8743–Fla. A, Vol. 7, No. 9; 4443–Ill. A, Vol. 3, No. 9; 5343–Ill. R, Vol. 4, No. 3; 8520–Kans. A, Vol. 7, No. 5; 8830–Mo. R, Vol. 7, No. 10; 5467–N.J. A, Vol. 4, No. 4; 7879–N.J. R, Vol. 6, No. 4; 7887–Pa. R, Vol. 6, No. 4; 11749–Utah A, Vol. 10, No. 8; 10404–Va. R, Vol. 9, No. 3.

Benefit Series: Work history in previous pregnancies: 10327–Ill. R, Vol. 9, No. 3; 4518–Ohio A, Vol. 4, No. 10; 7887–Pa. R, Vol. 6, No. 4.

Benefit Series: Suitable work for claimant: 4082–Ark. A, Vol. 3, No. 8; 3073– Calif. A, Vol. 3, No. 4; 2354–Conn. R, Vol. 3, No. 6; 3563–Conn. R, Vol. 3, No. 6; 4315–Fla. A, Vol. 3, No. 9; 6245–Idaho A, Vol. 4, No. 8; 3836–Ill. A, Vol. 3, No. 7; 4500–Ill. A, Vol. 3, No. 10; 4989–Ill. R, Vol. 4, No. 1; 5343–Ill. R, Vol. 4, No. 3; 6106–Ill. R, Vol. 4, No. 7; 10327–Ill. R, Vol. 9, No. 3; 1692–Me. A, Vol. 2, No. 7; 2872–N.J. R, Vol. 3, No. 3; 5171–N.J. A, Vol. 4, No. 1; 5625–N.J. A, Vol. 4, No. 4; 2513–N.Y. A, Vol. 3, No. 1; 3592–Ohio A, Vol. 3, No. 2; 13249–Okla., Vol. 12, No. 3.

Benefit Series: Appearance and demeanor: 3836–Ill. A, Vol. 3, No. 7; 4505– Mo. A, Vol. 3, No. 10; 2373–N.Y. A, Vol. 3, No. 1; 3592–Ohio A, Vol. 3, No. 6.

36. *Benefit Series:* 6243–Del. A, Vol. 4, No. 8; 6877–Mich. A, Vol. 5, No. 1; 4321–N.J. A, Vol. 3, No. 9; 2397–Tenn. A, Vol. 3, No. 1.

37. 7309–Fla., *Ben. Ser.,* Vol. 5, No. 6. See also 4837–Ala., *Ben. Ser.,* Vol. 3, No. 12 (now superseded by special disqualification) ; 4989–Ill. R, *Ben. Ser.,* Vol. 4, No. 1.

Although it would seem unreasonable in cases where pregnant women leave work which is too strenuous for them or contrary to their doctors' advice, the weight of opinion is that a pregnant woman leaves work *voluntarily.* See: *Hutzler Bros. Co.* v. *U.C. Board,* Superior Court, Baltimore City, Md., Sept. 29, 1943, 8460–Md. Ct.D., *Ben. Ser.,* Vol. 7, No. 3; *John Morrell & Co.* v. *U.C. Commission,* 13 N.W.(2d)498 (1944), 8859–S.Dak. Ct.D., *Ben. Ser.,* Vol. 7, No. 10. *Benefit Series:* 6245–Idaho A, Vol. 4, No. 8; 6070–N.H. A, Vol. 4, No. 6; 7070– N.Y. A, Vol. 5, No. 2; 12708–Tenn. R, Vol. 11, No. 8; 8603–Tex. R, Vol. 7, No. 6. *Contra:* 12348–Del. R, Vol. 11, No. 4; 6494–Ohio R, Vol. 4, No. 9.

38. *Benefit Series:* 2219–Ark. A, Vol. 2, No. 12; 4082–Ark. A, Vol. 3, No. 8; 3073–Calif. A, Vol. 3, No. 4; 1502–Conn. R, Vol. 2, No. 5; 3006–Conn. R, Vol. 3, No. 3; 4315–Fla. A, Vol. 3, No. 9; 5343–Ill. R, Vol. 3, No. 3; 6106–Ill. R, Vol. 4, No. 7; 6070–N.H. A, Vol. 4, No. 6; 5171–N.J. A, Vol. 4, No. 1; 5625–N.J. A, Vol. 4, No. 4; 7879–N.J. R, Vol. 6, No. 4; 3592–Ohio A, Vol. 3, No. 6; 5907– Va. A, Vol. 4, No. 6 (tobacco factory, scent too strong).

39. *Benefit Series: Work not strenuous:* 4083–Calif. A, Vol. 3, No. 8 (greeting card sales clerk) ; 4087–Fla. A, Vol. 3, No. 8 (office cashier) ; 2386–Ohio A, Vol. 3, No. 1; 5467–N.J. A, Vol. 4, No. 4 (general office worker) ; 7070–N.Y. A, Vol. 5, No. 2 (office worker).

Benefit Series: Not able or available for other work: 4443–Ill. A, Vol. 3, No.

9; 1692–Me. A, Vol. 2, No. 7 (no other experience) ; 7942–N.J. R, Vol. 6, No. 5; 3355–N.Y. R, Vol. 3, No. 5.

40. *Benefit Series: Hutzler Bros. Co.* v. *U.C. Board, supra,* note 37; 2867–Mass. A, Vol. 3, No. 3; 4105–N.J. A, Vol. 3, No. 8; 2882–Ohio A, Vol. 3, No. 3; 4964–Okla. A, Vol. 3, No. 12; 12146–Oreg. A, Vol. 11, No. 1; *Contra:* 6814–Mo. A, Vol. 4, No. 12 (claimant would take any work except at the place where she was last employed).

41. *Benefit Series:* 5877–Ala. A, Vol. 4, No. 6; 8743–Fla. A, Vol. 7, No. 9; 555–Ind. A, Vol. 1, No. 5 (workmen's compensation insurance carrier prohibited employment of pregnant women in the factory) ; *Abbott* v. *Maryland U.C. Board,* Circuit Court, Allegany County, Mar. 19, 1948, 12669–Md. Ct.D., Vol. 11, No. 8; 3760–Mass. A, Vol. 3, No. 6; 4502–Mich. A, Vol. 3, No. 10; 6877–Mich. A, Vol. 5, No. 1; 9253–N.J. R, Vol. 8, No. 3; 9708–N.J. R, Vol. 8, No. 8; 10033–N.J. R, Vol. 8, No. 11; 3845–N.Y. R, Vol. 3, No. 7; 7053–Va. A, Vol. 5, No. 10. *Contra:* 4837–Ala., Vol. 3, No. 12 (rebuttable presumption, now superseded by statutory disqualification) ; 2677–Mass. A, Vol. 3, No. 2.

42. 7428–S.Dak. R, *Ben. Ser.,* Vol. 5, No. 7.

43. *Benefit Series:* 8743–Fla. A, Vol. 7, No. 9; 10327–Ill. R, Vol. 9, No. 3; 9496–Md. V, Vol. 8, No. 6; 10033–N.J. R, Vol. 8, No. 11. But see 9362–Okla. R, Vol. 8, No. 4 and 9187–Okla. A, Vol. 8, No. 2.

Indication that "appearance" and consequent unwillingness of employers to hire are factors to be considered may be found in 6840–N.Y. A, *Ben. Ser.,* Vol. 5, No. 1.

44. 6571–R.I. A, *Ben. Ser.,* Vol. 4, No. 10. See also 5098–Mich. A, *Ben. Ser.,* Vol. 4, No. 1.

45. *Benefit Series: Night work:* 2379–N.C. A, Vol. 3, No. 1.

Benefit Series: Alternating shifts: 8839–N.Y. R, Vol. 7, No. 10.

Benefit Series: Too strenuous: 2513–N.Y. A, Vol. 3, No. 1 (power machine) ; 6017–Ohio A, Vol. 4, No. 6 (former work).

Benefit Series: Too distant: 1803–Mich. A, Vol. 2, No. 7 (claimant would have been required to drive 52 miles through heavy traffic and weather).

Benefit Series: Against medical advice: 6769–Ill. A, Vol. 4, No. 12 (packing pickled pigs' feet — involving disagreeable odors, slippery floors, and climbing stairs) ; 5625–N.J. A, Vol. 4, No. 4 (machine work).

46. 4917–Oreg. A, *Ben. Ser.,* Vol. 3, No. 12.

47. RAR–U–19 (affirming 9388–Calif. V, *Ben. Ser.,* Vol. 8, No. 5). See also 10288–N.Y. V, *Ben. Ser.,* Vol. 9, No. 2.

48. *Schaffnit* v. *Danaher,* 13 Conn. Supp. 101 (1944) 8956–Conn. Ct.D., *Ben. Ser.,* Vol. 7, No. 12.

49. *Carani* v. *Danaher,* Superior Court, Hartford County, Docket No. 69595, 8416–Conn. Ct.D., *Ben. Ser.,* Vol. 7, No. 3.

50. *Benefit Series: Disqualified:* 6099–Calif. R, Vol. 4, No. 7 (night work; claimant, a waitress, had a 16-year-old son; had worked nights for a number of years) ; 11369–Del. A, Vol. 10, No. 4 (seamstress; clothing store work, 9:30 A.M.–6 P.M.; would work nights or no later than 5 P.M.) ; 2501–Me. A, Vol. 3, No. 1 (night work; claimant unemployed for five months, not diligent in devising ways and means to be able to resume work) ; 8995–N.H. R, Vol. 7, No. 12 (night work; claimant was a textile worker) ; 3454–N.C. A, Vol. 3, No. 5 (night work; would have been given day work if her husband would transfer to the night shift) ; 11655–Ohio A, Vol. 10, No. 7 (machine operator, 3–11 P.M.; five children) ; 2961–Pa. A, Vol. 3, No. 3 (7 A.M.–5 P.M.; claimant had to get her children ready for school) ; 6020–Pa. A, Vol. 4, No. 6 (three evenings a week; son 16 years old; claimant worked nights in previous employment) ; 2519–R.I. A, Vol. 3, No. 1 (3–11 P.M.; referee contended claimant could have put child in day nursery to be taken home by the husband after he stopped work at 5 P.M.) ; 7711–Vt. A, Vol. 5,

No. 12 (third shift; work in claimant's line and during the regular working hours of the industry); 8943–Vt. R, Vol. 7, No. 11 (second shift; claimant was laid off first shift work which she had done for many years. unemployed one month); 10058–Wash. A, Vol. 8, No. 11 (day work; cashier; most recently on cafeteria night shift).

Benefit Series: Not disqualified: Day work (or first shift): 10603–Ala. A, Vol. 9, No. 7; 10940–Ark. A, Vol. 9, No. 11 (work began 7 A.M., too early to procure child care); 9208–Colo. A, Vol. 8, No. 3 (temporary lay off); 11028–Idaho A, Vol. 9, No. 12; 10099–Ind. A, Vol. 8, No. 12 (mostly night shift work history); 10256–Ind. A, Vol. 9, No. 2; 9223–Ky. A, Vol. 8, No. 3; 11150–Minn. A, Vol. 10, No. 1 (husband would care for children at night; wages offered insufficient to permit paying for day care); 9624–N.Y. R, Vol. 8, No. 7 (no one to care for children mornings); 12316–Pa. R, Vol. 11, No. 2 (no one to care for child during the day).

Benefit Series: Evening work (or second shift): 11117–Hawaii R, Vol. 10, No. 1 (daytime work history); 5755–Ill. R, Vol. 4, No. 5; 10250–Ill. R, Vol. 9, No. 2 (3:30 P.M.–1 A.M.; plus two hours total travel time: claimant's previous experience showed loss of sleep); 11208–Ind. R, Vol. 10, No. 2; 9683–Kans. A, Vol. 8, No. 8; 11329–Nebr. R, Vol. 10, No. 3; 12477–Vt. R, Vol. 11, No. 5 (first shift work history); 9859–Wis. A, Vol. 8, No. 9 (first and third shift work history).

Benefit Series: Night work (or third shift): 9298–Calif. R, Vol. 8, No. 4 (work 14 miles away); 8015–Ga. R, Vol. 6, No. 6 (textile worker; five-month-old baby); 8748–Ga. R, Vol. 7, No. 9 (work 10 miles away; young baby); 10862–Ga. A, Vol. 9, No. 10 (never worked on third shift); 8898–Ind. A, Vol. 7, No. 11; 10255–Ind. A, Vol. 9, No. 2; 10031–N.J. R, Vol. 8, No. 11; 4612–N.Y. A, Vol. 3, No. 10: 6961–N.Y. A, Vol. 5, No. 2 (formerly employed on day shift; four-month-old baby); 7741–N.C. R, Vol. 6, No. 1; 4616–Ohio A, Vol. 3, No. 10; 10916–Okla. R, Vol. 9, No. 10; 6021–Pa. A, Vol. 4, No. 6; 10580–Pa. R, Vol. 9, No. 6; 10399–S.C. R, Vol. 9. No. 3; 5573–Tenn. A, Vol. 4, No. 5 (reasonable opportunity of getting day work); 8454–W.Va. A, Vol. 7, No. 3.

Benefit Series: Rotating shift: 10871–Kans. A, Vol. 9, No. 10; 7892–Va. R, Vol. 6, No. 4 (month-old infant, work 10 miles away; formerly employed in shift work); 10677–Va. A, Vol. 9, No. 7 (never worked rotating shift; day work available).

51. *Benefit Series: Available:* 9296–Ala. R, Vol. 8, No. 4 (18 years on first shift; decision an "exception"); 12724–Calif. R, Vol. 11, No. 9; 2355–Conn. R, Vol. 3, No. 1; 7778–Del. R, Vol. 6, No. 2 (last employment on alternating shifts; daytime "the normal period of work in this community"); 8254–Ga. R, Vol. 6, No. 12 (former second shift worker); 10085–Ga. A, Vol. 8, No. 12 (8 years on day shift); 6661–Ill. A, Vol. 4, No. 11 (affirmed by Board of Review, 41–BRD–175, unp.; general office worker); 8898–Ind. A, Vol. 7, No. 11; 10722–Kans. A, Vol. 9, No. 8 (day work history; day work available); 10871–Kans. A, Vol. 9, No. 10; 4096–Me. A, Vol. 3, No. 8 (hotel housekeeper); 10634–Me. A, Vol. 9, No. 7 (sales clerk experience); 5895–Mass. A, Vol. 4, No. 6 (12 years on day shift); 9234–Mich. R, Vol. 8, No. 3; 9240–Mich. R, Vol. 8, No. 3; 10891–Mich. R, Vol. 9, No. 10 (base period day work history); 12979–Miss. A, Vol. 11, No. 12; 8363–Mo. A, Vol. 7, No. 2; 10367–Mo. A, Vol. 9, No. 3 (recent day shift work history); 11329–Nebr. R, Vol. 10, No. 3 (short unemployment; found work); 6961–N.Y. A, Vol. 5, No. 2 (day work history); 12843–N.Y. R, Vol. 11, No. 10; 13086–N.C. R, Vol. 12, No. 1; 7741–N.C. R, Vol. 6, No. 1; 5460–Ohio A, Vol. 4, No. 3 (accepted first employment offer made); 6591–Okla. A, Vol. 4, No. 10; 6973–S.C. A, Vol. 5, N. 2 (retail sales experience); 8944–Va. R, Vol. 7, No. 11 (day work history); 12477–Vt. R, Vol. 11, No. 5 (daytime work history); 6983–W.Va. A, Vol. 5, No. 2.

Benefit Series: Not available: Dinovellis v. Danaher, 12 Conn. Supp. 122

(1943), 8201–Conn. Ct.D., Vol. 6, No. 11; *Jacobs* v. *Office of Unemployment Compensation,* 179 P.(2d)707 (1947), 11832–Wash. Ct.D., Vol. 10, No. 9; 6090–Calif. R, Vol. 4, No. 7 (waitress, limited to 7 A.M. to 3:30 P.M.); 10255–Ind. A, Vol. 9, No. 2 (seniority rules require new employees to work nights); 9683–Kans. A, Vol. 8, No. 8; 9335–Ky. A, Vol. 8, No. 4; 8307–Mass. R, Vol. 7, No. 1; 9499–Mass. R, Vol. 8, No. 6 (wartime ruling required availability for first and second shifts. claimant, on temporary lay off, had worked first shift for 10 or 12 years); 13071–Mich. R, Vol. 12, No. 1; 8995–N.H. R, Vol. 7, No. 12 (textile worker); 10903–N.H. R, Vol. 9, No. 10; 9825–N.C. R, Vol. 8, No. 9; 9259–Ohio A, Vol. 8, No. 3; 10039–Ohio A, Vol. 8, No. 11; 10916–Okla. R, Vol. 9, No. 10 (power sewing machine operator, limited to 6 A.M. to 6 P.M.); 9021–Pa. R, Vol. 7, No. 12 (Typist-clerk); 9946–Pa. R, Vol. 8, No. 10; 6972–S.C. A, Vol. 5, No. 2 (affirmed by U.C. Commission, S.C. 41–C–18, unp.; three-shift operation); 8939–Tex. A, Vol. 7, No. 11; 8943–Vt. R, Vol. 7, No. 11 (mill-worker, many years on first shift); 7892–Va. R, Vol. 6, No. 4.

52. *Benefit Series: Available:* 9587–Ill. A, Vol. 8, No. 7 (found such work); 9667–Ill. R, Vol. 8, No. 8 (found such work; ample opportunities); 10615–Ill. A, Vol. 9, No. 7 (at least three-week adjustment and exploration period); 13055–Ind. A, Vol. 12, No. 1 (claimant also available for first shift homework); 12283–Miss. A, Vol. 11, No. 3 (arrangement encouraged by employer); 10028–Nebr. R, Vol. 8, No. 11 (wage credits earned on second shift; several firms in locality employing women on that shift; willing to take pay reduction); 11491–N.Y. R, Vol. 10, No. 5 (other employees being recalled); 12316–Pa. R, Vol. 11, No. 2 (found such work).

Benefit Series: Not available: 10860–Conn. R, Vol. 9, No. 10 (most factories reverted to daytime schedule after V–J Day); 9225–Ind. A, Vol. 8, No. 3 (affirmed by U.C. Board, No. 619, unp.; calculating machine operator; employer discontinued second shift); 10256–Ind. A, Vol. 9, No. 2 (claimant insisted on 4 to 12 P.M., refused jobs for 3 to 11 P.M. and 6:30 P.M. to 2:30 A.M.); 12200–Maine A, Vol. 11, No. 2 (multi-shift industry); 12048–N.H. R, Vol. 10, No. 12; 10395–Pa. R, Vol. 9, No. 3; 9841–R.I. A, Vol. 8, No. 9; 9842–R.I. A, Vol. 8, No. 9 (affirmed by U.C. Board, No. 258, unp.; billing machine operator); 9032–W.Va. R, Vol. 7, No. 12.

53. *Vassallo* v. *Administrator,* Superior Court, Fairfield County, Conn., July 19, 1946, 11103–Conn. Ct.D., *Ben. Ser.,* Vol. 10, No. 1.

54. *Ford Motor Co.* v. *Appeal Board* (Koski), 25 N.W.(2d)586 (1947), 11553–Mich. Ct.D., *Ben. Ser.,* Vol. 10, No. 6.

55. *Benefit Series: Available:* 9753–Calif. R, Vol. 8, No. 9 (night work available); 9208–Colo. A, Vol. 8, No. 3 (earned wage credits in night work in a three-shift industry); 4103–N.J. R, Vol. 3, No. 8 (night work commonly available in the community); 5172–N.J. A, Vol. 4, No. 1 (cleaning woman); 10032–N.J. R, Vol. 8, No. 11 (claimant had a car and was willing to drive to other communities for night shift work); 10986–N.J. A, Vol. 9, No. 11 (willing to take any kind of evening work).

Benefit Series: Not available: 10603–Ala. A, Vol. 9, No. 7 (prewar work history in day work); 9126–Calif. A, Vol. 8, No. 2 (night work practically non-existent in claimant's area); 12416–Conn. R, Vol. 11, No. 5 (no independent effort to get work); 8745–Fla. R. Vol. 7, No. 9 (seasonal worker; limited to night work during off-season); 9903–Ill. A, Vol. 8, No. 10 (refused a third-shift job because of one hour travel time); 11779–Ill. R, Vol. 10, No. 9 (also wage and travel time restrictions); 10099–Ind. A, Vol. 8, No. 12 (machine operator; night work history); 8256–Kans. A, Vol. 6, No. 12 (affirmed by U.C. Commissioner, AC–47, unp.); 9223–Ky. A, Vol. 8, No. 3; 9235–Mich. R, Vol. 8, No. 5. 3 (third shift eliminated at former employer's plant; few night jobs available in community); 10651–Nebr. R, Vol. 9, No. 7 (most permits for employing women from 1 A.M. to 6 A.M. were canceled when the war ended) ; 12216–Nev. A, Vol. 11, No. 2; 9248–N.J. A, Vol. 8, No. 3 (employer abolished night shift; law prohibiting night work for women suspended for war emergency only) ; 10058–Wash. A, Vol. 8, No. 11 (no prospects of night work; did not actively seek work).

56. *Judson Mills* v. *U.C. Commission,* 28 S.E.(2d)535 (1944), 8525–S.C. Ct.D., *Ben. Ser.,* Vol. 7, No. 5.

57. *American Viscose Corporation* v. *Board of Review,* Circuit Court, Kanawha County, Apr. 14, 1944, 8725–W.Va. Ct.D., *Ben. Ser.,* Vol. 7, No. 8.

58. *Benefit Series: Available:* 6829–Calif. A, Vol. 5, No. 1 (waitress, dinner shift only; such openings occur occasionally and claimant did find such work) ; 10460–Minn. A, Vol. 9, No. 4–5 (five-hour work day; recent part-time work history) ; 9001–N.J. R, Vol. 7, No. 12; 7093–N.Y. R, Vol. 5, No. 3 (part-time work history) ; 9524–N.Y. R, Vol. 8, No. 6 (short-time work history) ; 13171–Pa. R, Vol. 12, No. 2.

Benefit Series: Not available: Bunyan v. *Administrator,* Superior Court, Fairfield County, Conn., June 24, 1947, 11845–Conn. Ct.D., Vol. 10, No. 10 (1 to 6 P.M., finding of fact that no labor market existed for part-time work suitable to claimant) ; 2851–Conn. R, Vol. 3, No. 3 (laundry workers; Saturdays only or laundry work at home; never did laundry work in the neighborhood) ; 10326–Ill. R, Vol. 9, No. 3 (7 P.M. to 2 A.M. including travel time) ; 10329–Ill. R, Vol. 9, No. 3 (6 P.M. to midnight) ; 10878–Me. A, Vol. 9, No. 10 (full-time work history) ; *Williams* v. *Commonwealth,* Fourth District Court of Berkshire, Mass., Aug. 5, 1948, 12977–Mass. Ct.D., Vol. 11, No. 12; 9067–Mass. A, Vol. 8, No. 1 (1 to 6 P.M.) ; 4998–Mich. A, Vol. 4, No. 1 (10 A.M. to 3 P.M.) ; 9164–Mo. A, Vol. 8, No. 2 (6 to 11:30 P.M.; charwoman) ; 9166–Mo. A, Vol. 8, No. 2 (not after 2 P.M., or over five hours a day) ; 10741–Nebr. R, Vol. 9, No. 8 (9 A.M. — 3 P.M., the hours claimant had worked in a packing house on a "victory" shift; shift now nonexistent) ; 10742–Nebr. R, Vol. 9, No. 8 (8:30 A.M. — 2:30 P.M.; waitress experience, but registered as sales clerk. No attempt to get work as waitress) ; 6113–N.Y. A, Vol. 4, No. 7 (11 A.M. to 2 P.M.; waitress; full-time work history) ; 4532–W.Va. A, Vol. 3; No. 10 (affirmed by W.Va. Board of Review, No. 234, unp.; six hours a day).

59. 9001–N.J. R, *Ben. Ser.,* Vol. 7, No. 12.

60. *Benefit Series: Limited to one employer, held not available for work:* 11516–Miss. A, Vol. 10, No. 1 (affirmed by 34–BR–46, unp.) ; 6974–S.C. A, Vol. 5, No. 2 (had to feed her baby every four hours). See also 3344–Del. A, Vol. 3, No. 5 (claimant had to nurse her infant every three hours during the day; could work only two hours and 25 minutes at a time, 35 minutes being necessary for her to go home, nurse the baby, and return).

Benefit Series: Limited to neighborhood of residence, held not available for work: 9773–Ill. A, Vol. 8, No. 9 (walking distance; no independent effort) ; 11640–N.H. R, Vol. 10, No. 7; 5113–Pa. A, Vol. 4, No. 1 (refused work 11 blocks away) ; 9200–Wis. R, Vol. 8, No. 2 (wanted to get home to make lunch). See also 10488–Pa. R, Vol. 9, Nos. 4–5 (restricted herself to day work where she could get home at noon). *Contra:* 11587–Pa. A, Vol. 10, No. 6; 6609–S.C. A, Vol. 4, No. 11.

61. See Chapter VII for summary of *Smith* v. *Murphy* (46 N.Y. S.(2d)774 (1944), 8643–N.Y. Ct.D., *Ben. Ser.,* Vol. 7, No. 7) and *Salavarria* v. *Murphy,* (43 N.Y. S.(2d)899 (1943), 8426–N.Y. Ct.D., *Ben. Ser.,* Vol. 7, No. 3).

Benefit Series: Available: 9812–N.H. A, Vol. 8, No. 9 (homework history; active search for work) ; 7939–N.J. A, Vol. 6, No. 5 (homeworker 16 years; statute eliminated most homework) ; 6603–N.J. A, Vol. 4, No. 11 (homework history; 13-month-old child) ; 8313–N.Y. Vol. 7, No. 1 (homework history; homework existed in community) ; 4109–N.C. A, Vol. 3, No. 8 (homework history).

Benefit Series: Not available: 12007–Ariz. A, Vol. 10, No. 12 (typist; worked at home for 15 months; 3-month-old baby) ; 9899–Ill. R, Vol. 8, No. 10 (typist, made no independent search) ; Cf. 10180–Ill. R, Vol. 9, No. 1; 8125–Mass. A, Vol. 6, No. 9; 8832–Mo. R, Vol. 7, No. 10 (no showing that work outside home a risk to claimant's health, safety, or morals; homework not ordinarily offered in vicinity; no active search) ; 10818–N.H. R, Vol. 9, No. 9 (homework history) ; 4102–N.J. A, Vol. 3, No. 8; Cf. 8700–N.J. R, Vol. 7, No. 8; 8476–R.I. A, Vol. 7, No. 4 (affirmed by U.C. Board, No. 184, unp.; employer placed on government assignment required by law to be done in the factory) ; 10053–Tenn. R, Vol. 8, No. 11 (employer had removed the machine) ; but see 9458–Tenn. A, Vol. 8, No. 5, where claimant had a longer homework history and a tubercular child in need of mother's care.

Other cases in the *Benefit Series,* not involving care of children, where home workers have been held unavailable for work include : 8613–Ala. A, Vol. 7, No. 7 (typist) ; 9888–Ga. A, Vol. 8, No. 10 (sewing machine operator; last means of obtaining and transporting work) ; 8698–N.J. R, Vol. 7, No. 8 (no homework available in area) ; 12454–N.Y. R, Vol. 11, No. 5 (no special circumstances compelling restriction to homework; no homework available) ; 11421–Pa. A, Vol. 10, No. 4 (refused transfer to factory; did not desire full day work).

The present rule in Pennsylvania is in some doubt. Homeworkers were held unavailable in 9947–Pa. R, Vol. 8, No. 10 (overruling 8788–Pa. R, Vol. 7, No. 9). This, in turn, has been qualified by 10299–Pa. R, Vol. 9, No. 2, holding the home-worker available because heart disease and other ailments made work outside the home unsuitable for her. Another health case is 11268–Utah A, Vol. 10, No. 2.

63. Rhode Island U.C. Board, *Statistical Abstract, Cash Sickness Compensation, Benefit Year 1944–45.* Mar. 12, 1947, p. 11.

For a discussion of pregnancy benefits in a temporary disability insurance system, see *Temporary Disability Insurance Coordinated with Unemployment Insurance,* Social Security Administration, January 1947, pp. 5–6.

64. Limited to husbands with no income other than wages or salary.

65. Some idea of the effect of such a distinction can be obtained from these figures : In the four states which paid dependents' allowances, during the calendar quarter September–December 1946 (Connecticut, District of Columbia, Michigan, and Nevada) such allowances were paid to 43.4 per cent of the male beneficiaries and only 6.2 per cent of the female beneficiaries. By state, the percentage of female beneficiaries receiving dependents' allowances were : Connecticut, 4.5; District of Columbia, 21.4; Michigan, 5.6; Nevada, 8.5. *Employment Security Activities,* Vol. 3, No. 2 (February 1947), p. 25.

NOTES FOR CHAPTER THIRTEEN

1. Oklahoma Employment Security Act, sec. 229 (j).

2. New York is a notable exception. The New York Appeal Board has held that unemployment refers to a lack of employment under a contract of hire and hence cannot be applied to self-employed claimants. Sole reliance in such cases is put upon the availability test. See 7804–N.Y. R, *Ben. Ser.,* Vol. 6, No. 2; 12140–N.Y. R, *Ben. Ser.,* Vol. 11, No. 1.

3. *Benefit Series:* 5297–Ark. A, Vol. 4, No. 2; 5298–Ark. A, *ibid.;* 7769–Calif. R, Vol. 6, No. 1; 7772–Conn. R, Vol. 6, No. 1; 7773–D.C. A, Vol. 6, No. 1; 2855–Ga. A, Vol. 3, No. 3; 4499–Idaho A, Vol. 3, No. 10; 12499–Ill. R, Vol. 11, No. 6; 68051–Kans. A, Vol. 4, No. 12; 11471–Md. A, Vol. 10, No. 5; 6195–Mich. A, Vol. 4, No. 7; 4876–Minn. A, Vol. 3, No. 12; 4795–Mo. A, Vol. 3, No. 11; 2306–N.J. A, Vol. 2, No. 12; 7804–N.Y. R, Vol. 6, No. 2; 7805–N.Y. R, *ibid.;* 10379–N.Y. V, Vol. 9, No. 3; 12220–N. Y. R, Vol. 11, No. 2; 7806–N.C. A,

Vol. 6, No. 2; 3102–Okla. A, Vol. 3, No. 4; 4114–Oreg. A, Vol. 3, No. 8; 12235–Pa. A, Vol. 11, No. 2; 7812–R.I. A, Vol. 6, No. 2; 2392–S.C. A, Vol. 3, No. 1; 12472–Tenn. R, Vol. 11, No. 5; 13260–Tenn. R, Vol. 2, No. 3; 6484–Texas A, Vol. 4, No. 9; 3601–Wash. A, Vol. 3, No. 6; 2575–W.Va. A, Vol. 3, No. 1. Also RAR–U–207.

4. *Jones* v. *Department of Industrial Relations,* Circuit Court, Madison County, July 28, 1944, 8952–Ala. Ct.D., *Ben. Ser.,* Vol. 7, No. 12.

5. *Stevenson* v. *State Labor Commissioner,* District Court, Wyandotte County, July 20, 1946, 11215–Kans. Ct.D., *Ben. Ser.,* Vol. 10, No. 2.

6. *Benefit Series:* 4493–Calif. A, Vol. 3, No. 10 (affirmed by commission, C–209, unp.) ; 6192–Ill. A, Vol. 4, No. 7.

7. *Benefit Series:* 7515–Colo. A, Vol. 5, No. 12; 7774–Ill. R, Vol. 6, No. 1; 12997–Ohio R, Vol. 11, No. 12; 6847–Tenn. A, Vol. 5, No. 1.

8. *Benefit Series:* 12564–Colo. A, Vol. 11, No. 7; 11533–Conn. R, Vol. 10, No. 6; 2975–Iowa A, Vol. 3, No. 3; 7800–Mo. A, Vol. 6, No. 2; 7807–Okla. A, Vol. 6, No. 2; 12149–Pa. R, Vol. 11, No. 1; 12235–Pa. R, Vol. 11, No. 1; 2786–R.I. A, Vol. 3, No. 2.

9. 7807–Okla. A, *Ben. Ser.,* Vol. 6, No. 2.

10. *Benefit Series:* 3825–Ark. A, Vol. 3, No. 7 (affirmed by Industrial Board, 155 I.B., unp.) ; 8737–Calif. R, Vol. 7, No. 9; 3075–Conn. R, Vol. 3, No. 4; 4938–Idaho A, Vol. 3, No. 12; 4841–Ill. A, Vol. 3, No. 12; 707–Ind. A, Vol. 3, No. 6; 2546–Kans. A, Vol. 3, No. 1; 11049–Me. A, Vol. 9, No. 12; 6196–Minn. A, Vol. 4, No. 7; 2982–Mo. A, Vol. 3, No. 3; 12452–N.Y. R, Vol. 11, No. 5; 5901–Ohio A, Vol. 4, No. 6; 8346–Okla. A, Vol. 7, No. 1 (aff. by Board of Review, 64–BR–43, unp.) ; 5422–Pa. A, Vol. 4, No. 3; 9451–S.C. A, Vol. 8, No. 5 (affirmed by U.C. Commission, 44–C–26, unp.) ; 6701–Tenn. A, Vol. 4, No. 12; 5478–Tex. A, Vol. 4; 5479–Tex. A, *ibid.*

11. 8737–Calif. R, *Ben. Ser.,* Vol. 7, No. 9.

12. *Jones* v. *Department, supra,* note 4; *Dellacrose* v. *Industrial Commission,* 138 P.(2d)280 (1942), 8570–Colo. Ct.D., *Ben. Ser.,* Vol. 7, No. 6; *Siegrist* v. *Michigan U.C. Commission,* Circuit Court, Jackson County, Nov. 25, 1942, Docket No. Y429, 7969–Mich. Ct.D., *Ben. Ser.,* Vol. 6, No. 5.

Benefit Series: 10770–Ala. A, Vol. 9, No. 9; 2528–Ark. A, Vol. 3, No. 1; 2529–Ark. A, *ibid.;* 2855–Ga. A, Vol. 3, No. 3; 3966–Idaho A, Vol. 3, No. 7; 2536–Ind. A, Vol. 3, No. 1; 2973–Iowa A, Vol. 3, No. 3; 2224–Kans. A, Vol. 2, No. 12; 2301–Ky. A, Vol. 2, No. 12; 9227–Md. A, Vol. 8, No. 3; 2550–Mich. A, Vol. 3, No. 1; 6196–Minn. A, Vol. 4, No. 7; 1138–Miss. R, Vol. 2, No. 3; 2553–Mo. A, Vol. 3, No. 1; 6197–Nebr. R, Vol. 4, No. 7; 11727–N.Dak. A, Vol. 10, No. 8; 2514–N.Y. A, Vol. 3, No. 1; 2201–N.C. A, Vol. 2, No. 11 (affirmed by U.C. Commission, No. 35, unp.) ; 5901–Ohio A, Vol. 4, No. 6; 11581–Okla. R, Vol. 10, No. 6; 12149–Pa. R, Vol. 11, No. 1; 8599–S.C. A, Vol. 7, No. 6; 1510–Tenn. R, Vol. 10, No. 5; 10998–Tex. A, Vol. 9, No. 1; 5801–Vt. A, Vol. 4, No. 5; 2995–W.Va. A, Vol. 3, No. 3; 13026–Wyo. A, Vol. 11, No. 12.

13. *Benefit Series:* 10938–Ark. A, Vol. 9, No. 11; 6234–Calif. R, Vol. 4, No. 8; 3965–Ga. R, Vol. 3, No. 7; 6034–Idaho A, Vol. 4, No. 6; 1214–Iowa A, Vol. 2, No. 4; 11049–Me. A, Vol. 9, No. 12; 6195–Mich. A, Vol. 4, No. 7; 8697–N.H. R, Vol. 7, No. 8; 12304–N.Y. R, Vol. 11, No. 3; 7806–N.C. A, Vol. 6, No. 2; 3589–N.Dak. A, Vol. 3, No. 10.

14. *Dellacroce* v. *Industrial Commission, supra,* note 12.

15. *Siegrist* v. *Michigan U.C. Commission, supra,* note 12.

16. 8808–Colo. A, *Ben. Ser.,* Vol. 7, No. 10. See also *Benefit Series:* 13278–Fla. A, Vol. 12, No. 4; 4922–Kans. A, Vol. 3, No. 12; 9056–Ky. A, Vol. 8, No. 1; 3256–Miss. R, Vol. 3, No. 4; 7889–Tenn. R, Vol. 6, No. 4 (affirmed on rehearing, 42–BR–57, unp., 8860–Tenn. R, Vol. 7, No. 10).

17. *Benefit Series:* 7790–Fla. A, Vol. 6, No. 2 (hotel) ; 2541–Iowa A, Vol. 3, No. 1 (fish) ; 6601–Minn. A, Vol. 4, No. 11 (affirmed by director, No. 2426–180, unp.) (carnival).

18. 4422–Ala., *Ben. Ser.,* Vol. 3, No. 9; also see 10770–Ala. A, *Ben. Ser.,* Vol. 9, No. 9.

19. *Benefit Series:* 9776–Ill. A, Vol. 8, No. 9; 12359–La. A, Vol. 11, No. 4; 9696–Mich. A, Vol. 8, No. 8; 10326–Wyo. A, Vol. 11, No. 12.

20. 4921–Kans. A, *Ben. Ser.,* Vol. 3, No. 12.

21. *Benefit Series:* 6034–Idaho A, Vol. 4, No. 6 (produce) ; 8697–N.H. R, Vol. 7, No. 8 (paint business) ; 1637–Pa. R, Vol. 2, No. 6 (taxidermist) ; 1909– Pa. R, Vol. 2, No. 8 (swimming pool).

22. *Jones* v. *Department, supra,* note 4; *Dellacroce* v. *Industrial Commission, supra,* note 12; *Maxfield* v. *Administrator,* Superior Court, New Haven County, Conn., Dec. 20, 1948, 13364–Conn. Ct.D., *Ben. Ser.,* Vol. 12, No. 5; *Siegrist* v. *Michigan U.C. Commission, supra,* note 12. *Benefit Series:* 10938–Ark. A, Vol. 9, No. 1; 12564–Colo. A, Vol. 11, No. 7; 7772–Conn. R, Vol. 6, No. 1; 13271– Conn. R, Vol. 12, No. 4; (affirmed, *Stavnitsky* v. *Eagan,* Superior Court, Hartford County, Nov. 3, 1948) ; 6242–Del. A, Vol. 4, No. 8; 3566–Fla, R, Vol. 3, No. 6; 4249–Ga. A, Vol. 3, No. 8; 7792–Ill. A, Vol. 6, No. 2; 2538–Ind. A, Vol. 3, No. 1; 2544–Iowa R, Vol. 3, No. 1; 5300–Kans. A, Vol. 4, No. 2; 11049–Me. A, Vol. 9, No. 12; 9227–Md. A, Vol. 8, No. 3; 2225–Mich. R, Vol. 2, No. 12; 1547–Minn. A, Vol. 2, No. 6; 4428–Miss. A, Vol. 3, No. 9; 7800–Mo. A, Vol. 6, No. 2; 6197–Nebr. R, Vol. 4, No. 7; 7806–N.C. A, Vol. 6, No. 2; 6201–N.Dak. A, Vol. 4, No. 7; 3975–Ohio A, Vol. 3, No. 7; 7807–Okla. A, Vol. 6, No. 2; 12149– Pa. R, Vol. 11, No. 1; 8599–S.C. A, Vol. 7, No. 6; 12794–S.C. R, Vol. 11, No. 9; 8860–Tenn. R, Vol. 7, No. 10; 5800–Tex. A, Vol. 4, No. 5. Note also 13065– Mass. A, Vol. 12, No. 1; 13085–N.C. R, Vol. 12, No. 1.

23. 8599–S.C. A, *Ben. Ser.,* Vol. 7, No. 6.

24. 7889–Tenn. R, *Ben. Ser.,* Vol. 6, No. 4.

25. *Benefit Series:* 13271–Conn. R, Vol. 12, No. 4 (affirmed, *Stavnitsky* v. *Eagan, supra,* note 22) ; 12972–Md., Vol. 11, No. 12; 2225–Mich. R, Vol. 2, No. 12; 7804–N.Y. R, Vol. 6, No. 2.

26. *Benefit Series: Commission salesmen:* 7715–Colo. R, Vol. 5, No. 12; 7774–Ill. R, Vol. 6, No. 1 ; 2977–Ky. A, Vol. 3, No. 3; 2365–Minn. A, Vol. 3, No. 1 ; 2369–N.Y. A, Vol. 3, No. 1; 10379–N.Y. V, Vol. 9, No. 3. *Real Estate brokers:* 7773–D.C. A, Vol. 6, No. 1; 10261–Me. A, Vol. 9, No. 8. *Oil prospector:* 9480–Calif. R, Vol. 8, No. 6. *Milk route operators: Maskovsky* v. *High Brook Farm,* 7 Conn. Supp. 364 (1939), 3243–Conn. Ct.D., Vol. 3, No. 4. Language school: 10663–Pa. A, Vol. 9, No. 7.

Benefit Series: Other businesses: 1127–Conn. R, Vol. 2, No. 3 (grocery store) ; 3248–Iowa A, Vol. 3, No. 4 (farm) ; 950–N.Y. A, Vol. 2, No. 2 (government bond broker) ; 3258–Pa. A, Vol. 3, No. 4 (ice dealer) ; 6801–Tenn. A, Vol. 4, No. 12 (bus and air-line ticket agency).

27. *Benefit Series:* 12564–Colo. Vol. 11, No. 7; 7772–Conn. R, Vol. 6, No. 1; 2225–Mich. R, Vol. 2, No. 12; 2087–R.I. A, Vol. 2, No. 10.

28. *Benefit Series:* 4222–Ala. Vol. 3, No. 9; 2528–Ark. A, Vol. 3, No. 1; 1479– Conn. R, Vol. 2, No. 5; 12491–Conn. R, Vol. 11, No. 6 (not available on other grounds) ; 12190–Idaho A, Vol. 11, No. 2; 2225–Mich. R, Vol. 2, No. 12; 4428– Miss. A, Vol. 3, No. 9; 2392–S.C. A, Vol. 3, No. 1 ; 4919–S.C. A, Vol. 3, No. 12; 2553–Mo. A, Vol. 3, No. 1 ; 4628–N.Dak. A, Vol. 3, No. 10; 5009–N.Dak. R, Vol. 4, No. 1; 5421–N.Dak. A, Vol. 4, No. 3; 6205–Pa. A, Vol. 4, No. 7; 11516– Tex. A, Vol. 10, No. 5.

29. 12278–Mass. R, *Ben. Ser.,* Vol. 11, No. 3 (petition for review dismissed, *Chabot* v. *Board of Review,* District Court, Marlborough, Mass., Oct. 24, 1947).

30. 7797–Mass. A, *Ben. Ser.,* Vol. 6, No. 2.

31. 7599–Ohio A, *Ben. Ser.,* Vol. 5, No. 10. See also 1500–Conn. R, *Ben. Ser.,* Vol. 2, No. 5.

32. *Benefit Series:* 6234–Calif. R, Vol. 4, No. 8 (corporation president-investor); 9331–Ind. A, Vol. 8, No. 4 (beauty-parlor owner); 3095–N.Y. A, Vol. 3, No. 4 (restaurant incorporator).

33. 10803–Me. A, *Ben. Ser.,* Vol. 9, No. 9.

34. 11380–Md. A, *Ben. Ser.,* Vol. 10, No. 4 (affirmed by U.C. Board, Decision No. 1106; affirmed by *Daugherty* v. *U.C. Board,* Superior Court, Baltimore City, Md., Oct. 16, 1946). Also see 13258–R.I. R, Vol. 12, No. 3.

35. Regulations Under Servicemen's Readjustment Act of 1944, Title V, Public Law 346, 78th Congress, Code of Federal Regulations, Title 38, Chapter I, Part 36, Sec. 36.514(a).

36. 10225–Ill. V, *Ben. Ser.,* Vol. 9, No. 1. See also cases cited below in note 46.

37. *Benefit Series: Hospital doctor:* 10164–N.Y. V, Vol. 8, No. 12 (affirmed by State Readjustment Allowance Agent, RA–S–82–45, unp.) *Share Cropper:* 10595–Kans. V, Vol. 9, No. 6; 10227–Miss. V, Vol. 9, No. 1; 10230–N.C. V, Vol. 9, No. 1. (Also RAR–S–31, 36, 37, 44, 71, 107, 109, and 33.) *Corporation officer or owner:* 10846–Oreg. V, Vol. 9, No. 9. (Also RAR–S–80, 123 and 126.)

38. *Benefit Series:* 10302–Colo. V, Vol. 9, No. 2; 10594–Fla. V, Vol. 9, No. 6 (affirmed by Veterans Administrator, RAR–S–74, unp.); 10763–Ga. V, Vol. 9, No. 8; 10157–Ind. V, Vol. 8, No. 12; 10160–Md. V, Vol. 8, No. 12; 10165–Okla. V, Vol. 8, No. 12; also RAR–S–29, 40, 74, 77 and 135.

39. *Code of Federal Regulations* (see *supra,* note 35), Sec. 36.514(b). *Benefit Series:* 10302–Colo. V, Vol. 9, No. 2; 10306–Okla. V, Vol. 9, No. 2. Also RAR–S–109 and 119.

Code of Federal Regulation, Sec. 36.531 provides that labor performed by a self-employed veteran does not preclude an allowance if the labor was casual or incidental to his business and did not conflict with, interrupt, or cause the abandonment, either wholly or partly, of his activities in pursuit of his business.

Veterans who engaged in some employment during the month were considered "fully engaged" in self-employment in these cases: RAR–S–24 (exchanging help with father); RAR–S–105 (10 per cent of time in employment in lieu of rent); 10307–Okla. V, *Ben. Ser.,* Vol. 9, No. 2 (four days' outside work during the month).

40. *Benefit Series:* 10228–Nebr. V, Vol. 9, No. 1; 10163–N.Y. V, Vol. 8, No. 12. Also RAR–S–125.

41. *Benefit Series:* 10157–Ind. V, Vol. 8, No. 12; 10412–Ind. V, Vol. 9, No. 3; 10414–Me. V, Vol. 9, No. 3; 10596–Mass. V, Vol. 9, No. 6; 10228–Nebr. V, Vol. 9, No. 1; 10600–N.Y. V, Vol. 9, No. 6 (affirmed by State Readjustment Allowance Agent, RA–S–86–45, unp.); 10693–N.Dak. V, Vol. 9, No. 7; 10765–Oreg. V, Vol. 9, No. 8; 10696–S.Dak. V, Vol. 9, No. 8. Also RAR–S–76.

42. *Benefit Series:* 10162–N.Y. V, Vol. 8, No. 12 (affirmed, RAR–S–28); 10691–N.C. V, Vol. 9, No. 7. Also RAR–S–28, 54, 64 and 93.

43. RAR–S–52 affirming 10061–Fla. V, *Ben. Ser.,* Vol. 8, No. 11.

44. *Benefit Series:* 10156–Ga. V, Vol. 8, No. 12; 10304–N.Y. V, Vol. 9, No. 2. Also RAR–S–5, 8, 9, 10, 14 and 90.

45. 10155–Ark. V, *Ben. Ser.,* Vol. 8, No. 12 (affirmed by State Readjustment Allowance Agent, RA–5, unp.).

46. *Benefit Series: Family enterprise:* 10842–Colo. V, Vol. 9, No. 9; 10597–Mich. V, Vol. 9, No. 6; 10843–N.Y. V, Vol. 9, No. 9; 10305–N.C. V, Vol. 9, No. 2; 10306–Okla. V, Vol. 9, No. 2; 10308–Okla. V, Vol. 9, No. 2; 10694–S.C. V, Vol. 9, No. 7; 10697–S.Dak. V, Vol. 9, No. 7 (affirmed by State Readjustment Allowance Agent, RAA–S–1, unp.). (Also RAR–S–38, 39, 41, 43, 47, 58, 61, 65, 73, 75, 89, 106, 120 and 128.)

Benefit Series: Salesman or Agent: 10841–Ariz. V, Vol. 9, No. 9; 10228–Nebr. V, Vol. 9, No. 1; 10229–N.Y. V, Vol. 9, No. 1. (Also RAR–S–69, 82, 84, 88, 97 and 131.)

See also farm tenant cases cited above in note 37.

47. *Code of Federal Regulations* (see *supra,* note 35), Secs. 36.514(c) and 36.526–7–8.

48. *Benefit Series:* 10224–Fla. V, Vol. 9, No. 1; 10062–N.Y. V, Vol. 8, No. 11 (affirmed, RAR–S–19). Also RAR–S–17, 19 and 70.

49. RAR–S–6. See also RAR–S–15, 51, 72, 81 and 88. *Benefit Series:* 10155–Ark. V, Vol. 8, No. 12 (affirmed by State Readjustment Allowance Agent, RA–5, unp.); 10598–Nebr. V, Vol. 9, No. 6.

50. Melville J. Ulmer, and Alice Neilson, "Business Turnover and Causes of Failure," *Survey of Current Business,* Vol. 27, No. 4 (April 1947), pp. 10–16.

INDEX

INDEX

Ability to work, 128–129, 139–157
Aging workers, 142–144
Alien controls, 123–126
Amount of work, 105–111
Appeals, volume, 4, 6
Arms or legs, use of, 140–141
Assumptions underlying availability requirement, 84–87
Availability: assumptions, 84–87; criteria, 97–98; dictionary meanings, 3; elements of, 136–137; evidence of, 149–150; principles underlying, 96, 118; subjective and objective approaches, 122

Bargaining process, 28–31
Benefit denials: compared with other issues, 4; variations in, 4–5; volume of, 5–6
Blindness and poor vision, 141–142
Burden of proof, 103–105

Claimant behavior affected by policy, 8–9
Commuting to work, 202–203
Conscientious objectors, 187–190
Contagious diseases, 144–145
Customary or previous work, 167–169

Disability: temporary, 151–155; compensation for, 149–150
Distance to work, 199, 205–206

Employment agencies, private, 60–61
Employment agencies, public, see Employment service
Employment level, and availability policy, 13–14
Employment service, 62–72; job counseling, 71; labor market information, 70–71; labor market penetration, 58–59, 69; unemployment compensation, 66–72

Freedom of association standard, 176–178

Full employment: and availability, 9–10; policy, 10–13

Gate hiring, 59
Governmental restrictions, 122–129, 133–136

Help-wanted advertisements, 61
Home locality, restriction to, 199–204
Homeworkers, 127–129, 233
Hours, restrictions on, 180–185

Involuntary restrictions, 122–136

Jail, or other legal detention, 122–123
Job-finding and hiring methods, 57–66

Labor disputes, 171–172
Labor force, 36–54; composition by age and sex, 36–39; geographic distribution, 39–41; measurement, 9–10, 250–251; size, 36
Labor immobility, 21–24
Labor market, 20–35; collective bargaining effects, 28–31; entrance restrictions, 31–32, 51–53; nonstandardized transactions, 20–22; penetration by public employment service, 58–59, 65
Labor market area, 20, 32–35; job-finding area, 33–35; wage-setting area, 32–33
Labor market process, 20
Labor mobility, 22–24, 44–51; geographic, 45–47; occupational, 47–51
Labor standards provisions, 87–89, 159–163, 176–178
Labor supply, utilization, 51–54
Layoffs, 169–171
Length of unemployment, 111–113
Licenses or permits, 127–129
Living wage, 166–167

Normal industrial conduct and availability policy, 15–16

Objective approach, 122

Part-time work, 183–185, 232, 233
Place limitations, 198–214, 233
Policy, factors affecting, 13–17
Preferred employer, 169–171
Presumption of eligibility, 98–105
Prevailing wage standard, 17–18, 28, 159–163
Previous earnings, 164–165
Principles, 97–138; criteria of, 97–98
"Principles Underlying Availability for Work," 96, 118
Prospects of work, 111–113, 165–166, 169, 200–201
Public concern with policy, 6–8
Public opinion and policy, 14

Registration for work, 81; presumption of availability, 101–103
"Remote area" doctrine, 206–207
"Round-the-clock availability" rule, 181

Sabbath observers, 187–190
Seasonal workers, 190–194
Seeking work, 115–121; statutory provisions, 14, 90, 119
Self-employment, 238–244
Shift employment, 180–183, 230–232
State responsibility for determinations, 75
Statutory provisions, 90–92, Appendix Table A
Students, 194–197
"Substantial amount of work" rule, 105–113; and involuntary restrictions, 131–134
Suitable work, 89–90, 106–107, Appendix Table B

Temporary disability insurance, 152–155
Temporary work, 185–187
Time restrictions, 180–197, 230–233
Transportation, 130–131, 209–212
Travel status, 212

Unemployment: length of, 111–113; statutory meaning of, 239
Unemployment compensation: base period, 77–78, 83–84; benefit amounts and cost of living, 99–101; benefit disqualifications, 81–82; benefit duration, 82–83; benefit year, 77, 83–84; eligibility provisions, 76–81; and employment service, 66–72; interstate benefit plan, 204–205; purposes, and availability policy, 17–19; statutory structure, 74–95
Union status and work conditions, 172–178
United States Employment Service, 62–66. See also Employment service

Veterans' self-employment allowances, 243–246

Wages, and labor supply, 24–26; restrictions, 158–167; variations, 26–28. See also Prevailing wage standard
War manpower policy, 15, 65–66, 126–127
Women workers, 215–237; children, care of, 229–233; as claimants, 215–216; home workers, 127–129, 233; labor force characteristics, 216–227; legal status, 223–225; pregnancy and childbirth, 225–229; place restrictions, 233; time restrictions, 230–233